Eugenio Colorni

THE LEIBNIZ COMPROMISE

Eugenio Colorni

THE LEIBNIZ COMPROMISE

Edited by Luca Meldolesi

Translated by Michael Gilmartin

BORDIGHERA PRESS

Library of Congress Control Number: 2023946265

Copyright © 2023, A Colorni-Hirschman International Institute

All rights reserved. Parts of this book may be reprinted only by written permission from the authors, and may not be reproduced for publication in book, magazine, or electronic media of any kind, except in quotations for purposes of literary reviews by critics.
Printed in the United States.

Published by
BORDIGHERA PRESS
John D. Calandra Italian American Institute
25 W. 43rd Street, 17th Floor
New York, NY 10036

A Colorni-Hirschman International Institute 7
ISBN 978-1-59954-208-9

TABLE OF CONTENTS

Introduction by Luca Meldolesi (1)
Appendix: an evocative letter from Bruno Visentini (28)

Part One
  1. Review of the reprinted edition of *Introduction to Metaphysics* by Piero Martinetti (37)
  2. On Some Relations Between Knowledge and Will (44)
  3. Leibniz and A Recent Interpretation of His Work (66)

Part Two
  4. G. W. Leibniz's *Monadology* (77)
    Preface (77)
    Bio-bibliographical note (78)
    Anthological Exposition of The Leibnizian System (114)
    I. Truths of Reason and of Fact (114)
    II. Individual Substance (140)
    III. Force and Motion (161)
    IV. The Monad (183)
    V. Perfection and Imperfection in The Monad (198)
    VI. Matter, Soul, and Pre-Established Harmony (218)

Part Three
  5. Eternal Truths in Descartes and Leibniz (237)
  6. Leibniz and Mysticism (249)
  7. Leibniz's Aesthetics (283)
  8. Leibniz on Knowledge and Will (302)
  9. Leibniz on Free Will and Grace (324)

Part Four
  10. Letters to Ursula Hirschmann on Leibniz (353)

INDEX OF NAMES (367)

Introduction

Luca Meldolesi

"For years I settled for the Leibniz compromise. With Leibniz I could untangle the knots, I could search for what lies beneath the words without abandoning philosophy, dear old solid soothing philosophy. And I had become more confident, calmer, a good counselor, a valuable friend, a clarifier of problems, a supporter of the uncertain — a good teacher."
Eugenio Colorni to Ursula Hirschmann, Ventotene,
21 February 1939, Lettere. iii, p. 65.

"What remains essential in what we have seen of his thought is the internal structure of the concept of the monad: this synthesis of universal and individual, of matter and spirit, of activity and passivity, which is a point of arrival and a point of departure in the history of philosophy."
Eugenio Colorni, "Anthological exposition of the
Leibnizian system," 1935, p. 125.

Leibniz "applies to the nature of the mind the *continuity, the unbroken transition, the progression from* each law to a *larger law, which* he believes he can discern as the deepest essence of the natural world. That this same *continuity* and expansion is not so much a law of nature as a requirement of the mind in the consideration of nature itself, he does not suspect."
Eugenio Colorni, "Leibniz on free will and grace," 1938.

"We will not understand the history of antifascism," argued Giorgio Amendola,[1] "unless we appreciate the importance of a network of strong friendships able to withstand even the harshest political clashes." Just as in the time of the Risorgimento, these friendship networks, strengthened by acquaintances and by family and social relations (which allowed each anti-fascist to draw up a personal scale of trustworthiness), sometimes played a

---

[1] A cousin of Eugenio Colorni's (cit. in Gerbi 1999, 60).

prevailing role in the Resistance in circulating information and in concrete action — even in wealthy families, even with respect to a specific political affiliation, socio-economic dimension, institutional and territorial location, etc.

I thought[2] that an enlightening (and amusing) example might be in order, to offer a glimpse in a nutshell of the semi-clandestine antifascist milieu in the mid-1930s, in which Eugenio Colorni, seemingly imperturbable, was pursuing important personal and political initiatives while teaching history and philosophy to future female teachers at the Giosuè Carducci Magistero in Trieste and working on his Leibniz project.

The example concerns the clandestine expatriation of Mimmo, a.k.a. Emilio Sereni, Eugenio's beloved cousin,[3] recalled in Bruno Visentini's truly evocative letter to Alberto Boscolo dated April 29, 1963, included here (pointed out and provided to me by two friends, to whom I send thanks[4]). In Rome, having just been released from five years in jail, Emilio had to reach northern Italy and then emigrate to Paris in order to avoid internment. Against the advice of Sereni himself (son of Samuele, gynecologist of the Royal Household, agrarian economist and future bard of the Italian rural scene, but a notoriously militant communist of moralist and dogmatic persuasion), "the Party" decided to entrust the task to Bruno Visentini in Treviso and friends of his with GL and socialist leanings.[5]

---

[2] To come back once again to my resolve to keep Colorni's scientific research in constant contact with his personal and political experience.
[3] Cf., for example, Colorni (2021a, 93 and ff). In addition, Mimmo was long the close friend of Manlio Rossi-Doria.
[4] Elio Franzin and his schoolmate (and now Venetian businessman), Aldo Mariconda, nephew of Bruno Visentini.
[5] It was Antonio Pesenti who put the young Bruno Visentini in contact with the Milanese socialist group led by Rofolfo Morandi, as well as with Eugenio Colorni (whose friend he became). Visentini was the assistant of Tullio Ascarelli (another of Eugenio's cousins), professor of commercial law at the University of Bologna. In 1945, after Eugenio's death, Visentini dedicated his

Visentini organized an adventurous, daring, high-flying expedition. It was quite the scheme. From Milan, the three Serenis (Emilio and his wife and daughter) arrived by train in Trieste the evening of what was a very particular day.[6] On the eve of his wedding to Ursula Hirschmann, Eugenio Colorni had invited his friends to a restaurant that evening for the classic bachelor party dinner (customary at that time) — including, of course, his future brother-in-law, who had come especially from Paris for his sister's wedding, and was then called Otto Albert Hirschmann.[7]

One particular detail he told me personally was that before the evening's libations began to flow, Eugenio asked him to come with him to the train station and to wait outside for half an hour. In case he didn't come back, Albert was to return to the restaurant and inform certain

---

book, *Due anni di politica italiana (1943-45)*, to Eugenio with these words: "To the memory of Eugenio Colorni, with whom I was linked by fraternal friendship and ten years of concurrent anti-fascist action" (Gerbi 1999, 81, 89, 95; and Urettini 2005, 26, 36). Cf. on this theme, Colorni 2019a, 20 n. 31, 92; 2021, 25 n. 33.

[6] Cf. Clara Sereni 1993. "I've just finished reading Clara Sereni [Emilio's daughter]'s book, *Il gioco dei regni*," stated Albert Hirschman(1994, 17), [...]. I found something odd, and I told her so, in Clara's version of events [...] when she says that Mimmo left by car, when I know for certain he left by train. She answered that probably Mimmo had come by car from Rome to Milan and had got on the train at Milan Central station." Obviously the testimony of Bruno Visentini and Albert Boscolo (in the letter below) bear out Clara's version. "Colorni," wrote Sandro Gerbi (1999, 89), "was responsible, according to Lucio Luzzatto, for connections on the Trieste-Milan line. Hence his contacts with groups in Treviso (Antonio Pesenti and Visentini), Venice, Brescia. and apparently also Udine, Padua, Vicenza and Verona)."

[7] "In the summer of '35," Hirschman recalled (1994, 17), "I went to Forte dei Marmi, because Colorni, who in the meantime had become engaged to my sister, had a house there. Then I came back to Italy in December for Ursula and Eugenio's wedding". He finally settled in Trieste at the end of 1936 where, as we know, he took a degree in economics in the 1938 summer session (Hirschman 1994, Chap. 1; Meldolesi 2013, Chap. 2). After that he changed his name on two occasions (when he emigrated to the United States and when, having enlisted in the US armed forces, he became an American citizen) finally acquiring the name he is now universally known by, Albert O. Hirschman.

of his friends that Eugenio had been stopped by the police. Luckily, however, everything went smoothly, and the two future brothers-in-law went back to the restaurant together ... to celebrate.

It is known that at that time Eugenio Colorni was soon to become the leader of the Socialist Party's Internal Center and that he had quite a circle of anti-fascist intellectuals around him. He nevertheless took pains to appear to the outside world as an irreproachable professor, devoted entirely to his teaching and research. It is with this twofold focus (and not through the chilly, scientistic lens of the philological-philosophical tradition) that we must in my opinion observe the point of transition between the first and second phases of Colorni's studies on Leibniz — a piece still missing from the intellectual and political mosaic gradually being pieced together in my editing of this small seven-volume series intended to represent a "complete works" of our author and be accessible to a non-specialist audience.

1 – It is well known that as an alternative to the variously originating "avant-garde" and "futurist" thinking that flanked the regime, Eugenio Colorni, a student of philosophy at the State University of Milan and a budding young anti-fascist,[8] was passionate about "getting to grips" with his discipline. He had dealt with aesthetics under the chair of the same name held by Prof. Giuseppe Antonio Borgese, developing an interest he had cultivated since high school in following Benedetto Croce's work on the subject.[9] And he had begun a close engage-

---

[8] This can already be seen in his article "Roberto Ardigò" (which appeared in *Pietre* III, n. 2 of 10 febbraio 1928 under the pseudonym G. Rosemberg) now in Colorni 2021.

[9] As well as through three reports, two of which, "The Aesthetics of Roberto

ment with theoretical philosophy under Prof. Piero Martinetti (to whom, by way of introduction, the first two texts in this volume refer). In all probability it was Martinetti himself who encouraged Colorni to write his degree thesis,[10] "The Development and Meaning of Leibnizian Individualism." This was the beginning of an intellectual adventure that can be reconstructed only in part — not least because the only copy of Colorni's thesis known to exist is held at a research institute which (hear ye! hear ye!) prohibits the reading and study of it, not to speak of its rightful publication[11] (and also because, unfortunately, Eugenio's subsequent postgraduate thesis on

---

Ardigò and Italian Positivism in the Second Half of the 19th Century" (10 February 1928) and "The Aesthetics of Bergsonism (21 February 1929), were published in Colorni 2022. Unfortunately, the third, an "Essay on the autonomy and disinterestedness of art. Croce's starting points," has been lost (although it is likely that the sense of the paper was taken up by Colorni in the first part of *The Aesthetics of Benedetto Croce. A Critical Study* – 1932). Finally, with Borgese's supervision Colorni also prepared a term paper (which unfortunately has not reached us): "How the contrast can be interpreted between the two phases of Flaubert's aesthetic thinking and its exemplifications in works of art": cf. Riosa 2011, 275.

[10] Which was similar to what he had suggested to Carlo Emilio Gadda (cf. Cerchiai 2009, 47n). Along with the degree thesis and the paper on Flaubert just recalled, Colorni's graduation orals also included discussions — with Lavinia Mazzucchetti and Romolo Caggese, respectively — of two other papers (also, unfortunately, lost): "How justified are the accusations of plagiarism addressed by Goethe to Stendhal about the Italienishe Reise" and "The elements of historical materialism in the doctrine of Filippo Buonarroti" (Riosa, 2011, 275).

[11] I had in fact intended to include in this book Eugenio Colorni's unpublished degree thesis, which Mario Quaranta, before his death, had suggested that I request from the "International center for philosophy, epistemology, cognitive science and history of science and technology," at the Insubria University of Varese. But its Director, Prof. Fabio Minazzi, repeatedly refused to provide me with a copy, despite the fact that I invited him to write the introduction (or an afterword) himself, and despite the obvious national and international public interest in the project I have long pursued, both in Italian and English (and which, it should be pointed out, is at no charge to the state). I thus came to realize that the possibility exists in our country of the private (indeed exclusive) use of a public good (as Eugenio Colorni's thesis certainly is) by a Director of a Cultural Center presumably funded by the public treasury. Unfortunately, I lack the clout of one of my ex-students, the late Dr. Maurizio

Leibniz's early philosophy has been lost).

All that remains then is to pick up the argument beginning with what we already know. Here, we can speak of the interest in Leibniz that then existed in departments of literature and philosophy (Bobbio[12]), of Piero Martinetti's[13] favorable attitude and Colorni's intellectual work within the framework of the Martinettian approach,[14] and of the fact that coming to this point of view allowed Colorni to end his long engagement with Crocian aesthetics. We also know of the pleasure Eugenio found in digging deep into an important part of the past that preceded classical German philosophy (as an "emendatio intellectus," Bobbio wrote,[15] and as the construction of a bridgehead, I would add, from which to observe some "vexata quaestiones" of the discipline with new eyes, as a privileged field of his own philological passion, etc.). We can speak of his engagement in Marburg as lecturer in Italian under Erich Auerbach, and of the Berlin Conference on Hegel,[16] of his time at the Staatbibliothek and of

---

Maturo who, as soon as he was elected mayor of Mugnano di Napoli, unplugged on his own authority the unlawful access to municipal electricity by which the Camorra "ran" the fish market it controlled. I can only alert the Italian Parliament to Prof. Minazzi's scandalous behavior as an indication of an out-of-control situation that should surely be regulated — in the sense that any cultural institute that receives a public or private contribution for any reason should be required (upon request) to provide copies of the documents it keeps in its archives. And finally, I hope that Colorni's dissertation will be published as soon as possible, not least so that it might be included in a possible second edition of this volume...

[12] "Italian idealism," wrote Norberto Bobbio (1975, xxi), "had in its travels never run across Leibniz [...]. But around 1930, in a little less than ten years, in part by Catholics reacting to their ostracism by the idealists, and partly in an attempt on the idealistic side to find precursors everywhere [...] there was a real flowering of Leibnizian studies. It was quite unusual and has not been repeated since."

[13] Cerchiai 2009, 47n; Meldolesi in Colorni 2021a, 30.

[14] As evidenced by Chaps. 1 and 2 of the present collection.

[15] Bobbio 1975, xii.

[16] Second International Congress on Hegel (Berlino, 18-22 Ottobre 1931) marking the centenary of the German philosopher's death.

meeting Ursula and Otto Albert Hirschmann. We know of the commission he received from Giovanni Gentile to edit an edition of Leibniz's *Monadology* for high schools,[17] and finally, we note his condition as an involuntary witness to the beginning of a gigantic impending tragedy.

Now, if we link this knowledge to a simple reading of the texts on Leibniz collected here and to the philosophical and political materials contained in the earlier books in this series (along with news and tidbits useful for our purposes), we begin to get a sharper picture of our author's overall cultural trajectory.

It is true, in fact, that the two papers on the aesthetics of Ardigò and on Bergsonism found by Mario Quaranta[18] convey to us a much more articulate and expansive picture of Colorni's research on aesthetics than what had previously been assumed. Furthermore, the shift from Eugenio's main student interest in science in favor of theoretical philosophy, on one hand, and his post-graduation "German period," on the other (along with the visible maturation of his political awareness), in the end led Colorni to pursue in depth the study of Leibniz's original texts. It is therefore possible that his postgraduate thesis, *The Youthful Philosophy of Leibniz* (1933), contained some foretaste of what would later become a key feature of Colorni's Leibniz studies[19] — "translating" Leibniz's

---

[17] Having won an open competition for teachers of philosophy and pedagogy, Eugenio had taken up service first in Voghera and then in Trieste, where he began his double life, official and unofficial. His excellent treatment of Leibniz's *Monadology* perfectly illustrates the former, while the episode of Emilio Sereni's expatriation recalled above perfectly illustrates the latter. As we will mention later, this double "accommodation" undoubtedly played an important role in his "rencontre" with Ursula Hirschmann.
[18] Cf. above, n. 9
[19] For example, the following passage suggests this: "Leibniz's thesis — to a greater degree than meets the eye — cloaks a naturalistic, Grotian substance in Thomist form. This interpretation can be supported philologically. His youthful legal writings and recently published fragments show that Leibniz

work into modern terms, so as to make it accessible to contemporary philosophers.[20]

In the event, this challenging turnaround was necessarily gradual, since Colorni decided, as mentioned, to accept Giovanni Gentile's proposal that he edit an edition of Leibniz's *Monadology* for secondary schools. It is worthwhile then to begin by "befriending" this well-crafted booklet, which contains the 25 pages of *Monadology*, along with 150 pages put together by Colorni, (a two-page "Preface," a 23-page "Bio-bibliographical Note," and 125 pages containing an "Anthological Exposition of the Leibnizian System," literally stuffed with Leibniz quotations).[21]

---

had studied Grotius's work in depth from a very early age, and that the theory of the validity of eternal truths independent of God had made a great impression on him. The problem obviously had engaged the mind of the young scholar — and the Grotian argument, discussed with some uncertainty in the field of jurisprudence, cast a clearer light in metaphysics." Colorni, mimeo, Trieste, March 1937 (now in Colorni 2009, 90), from the *Traveaux du ix° Congrès International de Philosophie – Congrès Descartes* (Paris 1-6 August 1937, Hermann) which Eugenio was able to attend after having obtained a passport directly from the police chief in Milan (probably through the intercession of Giovanni Gentile). This was the occasion when he met on the sidelines with the socialist leaders in Paris. (Colorni 2019a, 89-94; Meldolesi in Colorni 2019a, 19 n. 27).

[20] "Leibniz and Descartes," Eugenio wrote to Ursula from Ventotene on 1 June 1939 (now in Colorni 2019, 71), "were people who really did have something to say both in the field of science (one invented analytical geometry, the other infinitesimal calculus) and in scientific methodology. Only they preferred, for reasons of convenience, to express these things in the language then in use, a theological-systematic language. Therefore, to understand them it is necessary to "translate" from that systematic language to ours. Once this is done, the theses and demonstrations that appear to be senseless games take on an important meaning, one that is in no way systematic."

[21] "As to the method of this exposition," Colorni wrote (1935, iv), "I have chosen to give the word to Leibniz himself as much as possible, offering on each topic selected passages from his works, and adding on my own only the order and succession of the problems, and brief comments interspersed with the texts." The "Exposition," Bobbio (1975, p.vi) stated, is written "with the clarity and simplicity that can only come from a long familiarity with an author; Leibniz's fragmentary and very scattered thought is taken to pieces in its most basic parts, and then reconstructed and reduced to a system with a brief summary of the main themes, accompanied and illustrated by passages specially chosen

2- "In the biographical note," Eugenio explained, "I have tried to present the personality of the author [Leibniz] in all its multiple aspects, extra-philosophical included, and in the bibliography my aim is to create a small elementary guide through the various editions and commentaries."[22] As for the *Monadology*, "which Leibniz wrote at the end of his life[23] to bring together in one overall vision all his philosophical concepts, [it] can be understood only by someone with a certain familiarity with his thought. For anyone else, it appears to be an undecipherable enigma."

For this reason, Colorni continued, "in order to make this work accessible to the young people of our high schools, I have found it more appropriate [...] to precede it [*The Monadology*] with an orderly exposition of the fundamental principles of the Leibnizian system."[24] This includes, "Truths of reason and of fact," "Individual substance," "Force and motion," "The monad," "Perfection and imperfection in the monad," "Matter, soul, and pre-established harmony," the main titles of the exposition.[25]

---

from the works and letters — a real Leibnizian system in compendium." (The fact that neither the "Exposition," nor the "Note," was included in the selected anthology of Colorni's *Writings* [despite their extraordinary quality], certainly did not promote the reception of Eugenio's Leibnizian studies).

[22] "In the hope, "Colorni adds, "that this book may also be useful to university students who wish to embark on a deeper study of Leibnizian philosophy" (1935, iv).

[23] In 1714, on a commission from Prince Eugene of Savoy, an Italian-Austrian Field Marshal of the Holy Roman Empire, frequent protagonist in the wars against the Turks, and an admirer of Leibniz, whom the latter had met in Vienna.

[24] "Which," he continues (1935, iii) "those who read *The Monadology* can thus refer to, almost as a summary."

[25] Which is to say that if we relate this "exposition" to what Colorni wrote later to his wife from Ventotene (see n. 20 above), it seems to me that we can say that Eugenio was at a halfway point. On the one hand he had "translated" Leibniz into our language in order to make it usable for Italian high school students. On the other, however, given the didactic type of publication, he could not (and perhaps did not intend) to show at this point how Leibniz's theses and

Colorni's preface to this dazzling little book is dated June 1934. It is possible, in my opinion, that in that period Eugenio (mistakenly) felt on top of the situation regarding Leibniz's philosophical work. For if, as he wrote,[26] *The Monadology* appears to be "almost a summary" of the anthological exposition, then despite the current "*mala tempora*," the goal set at the time by Piero Martinetti of emerging within a few years with a convincing presentation of Leibniz's thought may have seemed to Eugenio to be within reach.[27]

This is perhaps why the essay "Leibniz and mysticism," published in the *Rivista di filosofia* in 1938 included the following note: "From a book on the making of the Leibnizian system, forthcoming from the publisher Hermann in Paris" — which however never saw the light of day.[28]

---

demonstrations acquired "an important and not at all systematic significance." This, if I am not mistaken, was an important purpose of the second part of Colorni's Leibnizian studies.

[26] Cf. above, n. 24.

[27] As early as February 1926 Martinetti had written to Emilio Gadda: "if in three or four years you could come out with a fine exposition of Leibniz (no need to fear competitors on this subject!) the way to the university [in history of philosophy] would be open to you". (Gadda 2007, 63; cit. in Vigorelli 2011, 255). Of course for Colorni a university career was now precluded, but that did not mean that he had abandoned the idea of coming to grips with the issue as a whole (in his own way, of course)...

[28] In other words, after submitting the manuscript on the *Monadology* (June 1934) Colorni, by now well entrenched in Trieste, experienced a particularly effervescent (and happy) period. He had achieved a certain intellectual tranquility (as evidenced by the first "epigraph" to this Introduction). He embarked on his project of translating Leibniz's thought for contemporaries (which, with "Eternal Truths in Descarte and Leibniz" later debuted at the Descartes Congress in Paris in August 1937 — see below Ch. 5). He fell in love with and married Ursula Hirschmann in late 1935. He began the systematic study of psychology, mathematics and physics, and at the same time started his association with the socialist press. He became involved in clandestine anti-fascist politics, assembled a group of anti-fascist intellectuals, welcomed his brother-in-law Albert Hirschman etc....

3 – Bobbio writes that in 1937 Colorni "came to an agreement with the publisher Hermann, whom he met in Paris during the philosophical congress on Descartes held on the occasion of the third centenary of the *Discourse on Method*, to publish a book on Leibniz, of which the articles appearing in the *Rivista di Filosofia* should eventually constitute the different chapters."[29]

But things did not go as planned. To clarify this point (and position ourselves *in medias res*) it is useful to take a step back. "Philosophical and scientific research," Colorni wrote in the "Bio-bibliographical Note" introducing *The Monadology*, "represented the private side of Leibniz's activities" (as opposed to the public activities increasingly demanded of him "at court" by the incumbent patron of the German aristocracy).[30]

His philosophical writings thus acquired an "occasional" character. "In his work as a whole, [they] are not predominant, nor are they organic and systematic. They give the impression of having been written without a prearranged plan, almost in his spare time. And it was not only as a philosopher that he was known in his time — his fame as a mathematician and scholar at least equaled his reputation as a metaphysician."[31]

---

[29] Bobbio 1975, viii. (Cf. above, n. 20). The five essays are those in part three of the present collection. Probably, committed on many fronts (cf. previous note), Eugenio was now beginning to realize that the planned monograph on Leibniz would be a more difficult task than anticipated. Not least because its laborious drafting now had to reckon with Ursula's judgment, which (inevitably) favored Eugenio's new studies over his earlier ones. (See in this regard the letters included later in the fourth part of this collection.)

[30] Colorni 1935, xvi. "This explains the fragmentary way his works in this field have come down to us," Colorni continues, "and the scattered manner in which his conceptions were set out — spread through writings of various kinds, mainly letters."

[31] Ibid. v. "If we wanted to define what [Leibniz] regarded as the main purpose of his intellectual life and his specific cultural mission," Colorni went on to write (ibid. xxii), "we would probably have to turn to the attempts at unification, conciliation, and harmony among the sciences that pervaded his entire life from

In Leibniz's philosophy, Eugenio added, "all the threads of his scientific activity and aspects of his personality converge. The universalist ideas, the projects for general and characteristic science, the theological principles that matured in the disputes over religious reconciliation, the mathematical concepts of the differential, of the integral and of continuity, the physical concept of force — all these in their various aspects and determinations contribute to forming the Leibnizian system, which unfolded progressively, one might say, as his ideas on these various subjects became fixed."[32]

"Leibniz," he went on to say, "expresses his opinion on the particular topic the discussion is focused on — he never starts out with the explicit intention of building a system. His philosophical work comes across first and foremost as a vast collection of specific positions he has taken. Yet the system is not absent from these positions; on the contrary it is always present. Individual problems are gradually shown to be connected to each other and interdependent — solutions converge, justify and confirm one another. We realize that what initially seemed to be a technical question in a specific field, one that ought to be answered within that field, instead derives from and leads to principles that are much more general and are

---

his earliest to his final years. His highest ambition was to give mankind a simple and comprehensive means of embracing all aspects of life and solving all its problems. Even as he penetrated every science with great insight into what was peculiar and irreducible in it and knew how to grasp the specific character of every method, he nevertheless set as the ideal of his life a general method that would apply to every discipline — a way of thinking that makes him almost a link between Renaissance universalism and the rationalism of the Enlightenment."

[32] Ibid. xviii. "When I have managed to get my historical tasks off my back," he wrote to a friend, "I would like to focus on setting out the elements of general philosophy and natural theology, including what is most important in that philosophy with regard to theory and practice." But as Colorni commented, "the moment never arrived, and we have to try to reconstruct Leibniz's system ourselves, out of the countless fragments." Ibid. xx.

linked to other problems and solutions apparently quite distant."[33]

Thus it happened, as I have mentioned, that these (and similar) observations, juxtaposed with the "Bio-bibliographical Note," the extensive "Anthological Exposition of the Leibnizian System" that followed it, and the prospect of showing by degrees how Leibniz's theses and demonstrations acquired "an important and by no means systematic significance"[34] which, once translated into contemporary philosophical language, became key elements in one of the happiest periods of Colorni's (personal, scientific and political) life.[35]

"For years I settled for the Leibniz compromise," he in fact wrote to Ursula retrospectively from Ventotene on

---

[33] "In a word, it is part of a system." Ibid. xxiii. It is this formulation that returns (in simplified form) in the letter of 5 June 1939 (now in Colorni 2019a, 121-2) in which Eugenio, trying to succinctly "coach" Ursula, who was due to take a philosophy exam, wrote: "*Leibniz*: The one thing that impresses him most of all is the causal connection of all things with each other. From any occurrence, through a chain of cause-and-effect links, you can go back to any other occurrence. This means that from anything that happens you can go back into the past and come back into the future, so you can start from any occurrence and describe the world. The world, described by taking any fact as a starting point, is the monad. Therefore, there are infinite monads, all different (because each has a different starting point) but all representing the same world. (This is the pre-established harmony among monads)."

[34] Cf. above, n. 20 and 25. "the essential point here," Colorni writes (1935, 50), commenting on a passage in Leibniz's *Discours de la métaphysique*, "is the *universality of individual substance* which, with the infinite connections contained within it, becomes the universe itself as seen from a particular point of view. It encompasses its own past and its own future, and at the same time the past and the future of the whole universe, achieving the ultimate in universality [...]. And at the same time, it retains all its individuality. The starting point is always the single fact, specific, particular, contingent. It does not disappear into the whole; it remains clear and visible as the head of the endless thread, unwinding to infinity, following every causal connection. [...] And meanwhile it admits the possibility of infinite other starting points. Individual substances are as many as there are facts — in other words, infinite. [...] In this union of the particular and the universal in individual substance lies Leibniz's first great discovery, the fundamental core of the concept of the monad."

[35] Cf. above, n. 28.

21 February 1939[36] (in the passage I quote as epigraph to this book). "With Leibniz I could untangle the knots, I could search for what lies beneath the words without abandoning philosophy, dear old solid soothing philosophy. And I had become more confident, calmer, a good counselor, a valuable friend, a clarifier of problems, a supporter of the uncertain — a good teacher. This was what you found when you came to me a little bit knocked around and at loose ends. [...] I gave you a great sense of tranquility — a safe harbor." And not only — at the same time, under the pseudonym of Agostini, Colorni began his collaboration with the Socialist Party press in Paris.[37]

4 – All right, the reader may think — but this still does not explain the outcome of the second phase of Colorni's studies of Leibniz, which, according to the testimony of Enzo Tagliacozzo (another cousin), ended up leaving Eugenio "annoyed."[38] Our thoughts immediately run, of course, to the racial laws, to prison, to Colorni's confinement.[39] But

---

[36] Colorni (1939, 65).

[37] His first article, "Problems of War," was published in Paris in *Politica Socialista* in August 1935a. Cf. above, n. 17: evidently both the official and unofficial aspects of Eugenio's life appealed to Ursula.

[38] According to Enzo Tagliacozzo (1980, 54), reported Geri Cerchiai (2011, 159), "Colorni, who had been steered toward studying Leibniz by 'that need for something individual, something different, to set against Hegelian universalism and panlogism,' ultimately foundered in his 'multi-year research, remaining [...] annoyed. We were left with his individual essays on Leibniz, but the overall monograph never came.'" (But I would be inclined to comment that perhaps the volume awaited by Tagliacozzo could never have "come," since Colorni had long since pursued a course contrary to the "philosophical system" as such. In other words, what remained unfinished was not "a comprehensive monograph" but a book of essays on Leibniz's work. Cf. Bobbio (1975, xxiii). I would only add that, in addition to Leibniz's thought, texts that have come down to us also — inevitably — reflect some of Eugenio's intellectual interests, such as the relationship between mysticism and intellectualism, knowledge and will, aesthetics, etc. They can therefore also be read in reverse — as a key to some peculiarities that Eugenio was looking for in Leibniz).

[39] If only because only the first of the four essays published in the *Rivista di filosofia*, "Leibniz and mysticism" (1938) predates Colorni's incarceration.

it only takes a moment's reflection to realize that this is still not enough....

To appreciate this, I find it useful to refer to the (sometimes somewhat embarrassed) clarifications contained in Eugenio's letters to Ursula. On 28 November 1938 he wrote to her from prison in Varese[40] that "probably the main thing that took me away from systematic and professional philosophy was having married you. Basically, I was always extremely embarrassed in front of you over my interminable Leibniz. In order to do this sort of work, you have to live a little bit separate from the world in a clique of people who, following university convention, give great importance to these things so as to create the illusion for themselves that they are profound etc. There are people who live their whole lives behind fences of this kind: literati, professors, nearly all of them. But then you happen to find yourself with a person from the real world, and you see in their eyes the question: "Well, but what good is it?" And you realize that the answer that you cooked up long ago for this question, which made such a good impression at home, or at school, or in the university environment, doesn't work with the people "in the world" whose esteem you crave — it just sounds false. [...] By this I don't mean to deny the value of scientific professionalism. But some of it is just tail chasing."

And from prison in Trieste on 20 December 1938 Colorni added,[41] "I also know so well and have suffered so much from that condition of being at the mercy of your own thoughts, futile and banal [...] — sitting for hours at a desk in front of something that perhaps is good and that interests you, but that you can't seem to focus your mind on [... Think] of how very very many of these pointless

---

[40] Cf. below, in part four of this collection.
[41] Ibid.

and mediocre daydreams there are in eight years of work on the philosophy of Leibniz. You say to me: okay, but how can you escape from them, where do you get the willpower? [...] The point is to find the psychological mechanism that drives you to want something, that chains you to the desk so that out of the five hours of which four and a half are daydreams, at least half an hour is work."[42]

All right, but what kind of work? Work on what? No longer on Leibniz alone. We know, in fact, that during those years in Trieste, Colorni had also worked extensively in psychology, mathematics, and physics.[43]

In conclusion, this was not so much a waning of interest in the work on Leibniz as such, in my view, but rather a long foretold positive evolution of Eugenio's research interests — and at the same time, the vigorous growth of the "prolegomena" to what would later become his own

---

[42] "I know of two of these mechanisms," the passage continues, "and both are artificial. One is social convention. The whole world expects a graduate in philosophy to study, write, etc. [...] No one, on the other hand, expects a woman to spend five hours at a desk. For her public opinion is a deterrent rather than an incentive. Live in an environment where it's normal for a woman to pursue intellectually productive activity, and the task will be much easier for you. Outside commitments are also useful for this (exams, obligations to present a paper, etc.). 2. The second "mechanism" I know is axiomatic, perhaps even aggressive, self-confidence. [...] In the end, those university and literary circles I spoke badly about in one of my recent letters at least have the one benefit of being institutes created to keep you chained for those famous five hours to your desk."
[43] "Do you really want me to keep at it with my old friend Leibniz?" Eugenio wrote to Ursula from prison in Trieste on 22 December 1938 (cf. Colorni 1937-38, 78). "We can talk about it further, but in any case, it would be too bulky for now to drag along all the necessary volumes and materials. I will finish it one day, I believe. But for now, I'm in more of a hurry to finish my physico-philosophical work and to complete my education in mathematics and physics." (This is a passage that clarifies several points. First of all, that all of Colorni's essays on Leibniz [included in the third part of this collection] were written before Eugenio's imprisonment and confinement. Also, that in the dialogue with Ursula that preceded Colorni's move to Ventotene, the possibility of continuing his work on Libeniz had nevertheless remained *sub judice*. And lastly, it indicates that despite this, Colorni preferred at the time to prioritize cultural education and the continuation of his physico-methematical work).

extraordinary development.⁴⁴

It thus happened — this is my hypothesis — that the work on Leibniz, although it remained incomplete (against Eugenio's will), had by then begun to exhaust its function on the cognitive level, and thus had also begun to transfer its exploratory and interpretative "mantle," so to speak, to Colorni's first autobiographical and philosophical texts — those of 1936-38⁴⁵ — which he was later to develop galore at Ventotene.

It was for this reason that in the letter to Ursula⁴⁶ of 21 February 1939 Eugenio was able to write that "while you were leaning on me I was drawing the strength from you to live without the rails, and to be free of my posthumous gratitude to philosophy. And I was more and more ashamed of my Leibniz."

5 – Let us try to pull the threads together. It is possible, in my view, that Colorni was ultimately "annoyed" by the interminable Leibniz compromise (i.e., by having settled at such length for a research project that did not fully satisfy him⁴⁷) partly because of the accumulation of personal, intellectual and political events that had not allowed him to

---

⁴⁴ Also in his dialogue with Albert Hirschman (Meldolesi 2013, Chap. 2).
⁴⁵ I refer, of course, to "Beginning of an autobiography" (Trieste, October 1936), "Justification" (Trieste, July 1937a) and "Program" (Trieste, 1938a); now in Colorni 2021a.
⁴⁶ Source of the first epigraph to this introduction: cf. Colorni, *Lettere*, iii, 65.
⁴⁷ "You know," Eugenio had written to Ursula on 14 November 1938 (now in Colorni 2019, 55) "that sometimes you have to tie yourself perhaps a bit artificially to a job or study something that doesn't satisfy you a hundred percent. (Like I did for years with my work on Leibniz). But if you don't do this, the moment for something that really does capture your interest will never arrive. You seem always to be waiting for inspiration, for the occupation that will give you unreserved joy. But this will never arrive if you don't prepare for it yourself with a training program that tests you a bit. As you can see, the books you sent have turned me back into the old grouch." It is true, then, that the interminable Leibniz compromise was also, evidently, a somewhat exhausting goal-oriented training program. Because, as Colorni had declared in his "Beginning of an

finish that work as he would have liked. But I also think that, at least retrospectively, he would later recognize that that work had fulfilled much of its purpose.

In fact, proceeding by comparison, opposition, interaction (without ever lapsing into the Hegelian "argument that must return," in the words of an old friend, formerly a high school professor) Colorni had delimited little by little the logical fields where he could go in search of the keys to his problems.

Thus, in opposition to futurist (and present-day) avantgardism, he had studied the work of Roberto Ardigò — the leading exponent of Italian positivism — noting that there was much to be learned from Ardigò's many attempts to overcome the contradictions he had landed himself in.

Thus, in order to patiently "unpack" the systemic logic superimposed on Benedetto Croce's "transcendental empiricism" he had found it useful to tap into Leibniz's objectivist individualism (though staying within the framework of Martinetti's teaching).

And thus, more generally, the later stages of his study of Leibniz's life and work had helped him to finally free himself from the system requirement in philosophy, as he penetrated deeply into a way of thinking — the Leibnizian way — that contrasted in an almost mirror-like manner with the idealistic mindset within which he had originally been trained.

It was this, then, and his psychological, mathematical, and physics research that finally sparked the autobiographical and philosophical formulations that we know so well.[48]

In the sense that while Leibniz, like Descartes and Spinoza, had constructed a "mechanicist" system inspired by

---

Autobiography" (Trieste, October 1936; now in Colorni 2021a, 75), "being able to see clearly in the field of philosophy is the greatest hope of my life."
[48] I refer, of course, to the texts now collected in Colorni 2021a.

the discoveries of Galileo, Kepler, Copernicus, and Newton,[49] Colorni's anti-systemic (philosophical and political) endpoint was part of the contemporary era ushered in by Einstein.

Indeed, it is the theoretical and practical solutions discussed by the Ventotene circle that underpin the thought and action of the later Colorni — from that small southern island, just as later in Melfi and Rome as well. His democratic and socialist federalism wafted from the south (with all due respect to the "school of Milan") — a Mediterranean inspiration that Eugenio would have liked to extend to the whole world.[50]

This is in fact the intention that this bilingual edition (in Italian and English) of Colorni's *opera omnia* aims to capture. "Dear Eugenio, I hope you like it," one is tempted to exclaim, since in spirit — as Albert Hirschman taught me — Colorni is indeed still with us...*

---

[49] "Rather than becoming a mystic himself," Colorni wrote, for example, in "Leibniz and Mysticism" (see below, p. 269), "he makes mysticism Leibnizian and rationalist. The notes on *William Penn's Journal* published by Baruzi are very interesting in this regard. [...] Our century should apply to the idea of God the 'nouvelles lumières' and the wonderful natural discoveries it is replete with. "L'amour est fondé sur la connaissance del la beauté de l'objet aimé," and the more we are able to love God, the more we will understand nature and "les vérites solides des sciences rèelles."

[50] A viewpoint reminiscent of what Albert Camus would later advocate (and which, in turn, would interest Albert Hischman). Cf. primarily Camus 1951.

* For their generous collaboration, I would like to thank Mario Quaranta (posthumously), Geri Cerchiai, Elio Franzin, Aldo Mariconda, Giuseppina Marangio and Eleonora Galante.

Postscript

To read a book such as this one, there are clearly numerous possible paths. It is up to the reader to identify the one that best corresponds to his or her needs. This does not, however, prohibit me from suggesting to the non-specialist reader that there are several possible paths (alternative to the current mode of reading that separates Eugenio Colorni's theoretical and political writings[51]) that I personally would like to pursue again in order to understand more than I have managed to "unearth" so far — and which at the same time seem consistent with my work as editor of the series of works by Eugenio Colorni for the Editori Rubbettino in Soveria Mannelli and Bordighera in New York.

These trajectories might begin with the texts in the first part of the present collection which are of "Martinettian" inspiration, then proceed to an appreciation of Colorni's formative process mainly through his youthful writings (now in *Art, Aesthetics, Politics*, 2022), and finish by examining his fruitful "compromise" with the "interminable Leibniz" (as Colorni put it), in parallel with the development of his politics (now found especially in *The Discovery of the Possible*, 2019a, and *The Final Year, 1943-44*, 2021a). Also, because it certainly cannot be ruled out — I would observe — that if he had not been arrested in the summer of 1938 or had then survived the terrible spring of 1944, Colorni could have forced himself to finally finish his work on Leibniz....[52]

On the other hand, if I am not mistaken, that reading path might then continue (seeing that "good things come to those who wait"). In fact, beginning the line of reason-

---

[51] Such as Bobbio 1975, xxxix.
[52] Cf. above, n. 43.

ing with the second and third parts of the present collection (i.e., the texts relating to editing the *Monadology* and the five unfinished chapters that Eugenio intended to be part of a Parisian volume on the formative process of Leibniz's thought), the reader might wonder *why* this "*compromise*" was comforting and reassuring for Colorni.[53] With regard, for example, to the (very unusual) evaluation he was then constructing of the history of philosophy, or to the maturation of his point of view (with respect to Cartesian rationalism as well as to the whole spectrum of idealism that then surrounded him), or even to the birth of the "Ventotene texts" (now collected in "*The Philosophical Illness and Other Writings,* 2021a).[54] In brief, such "ruminating" might help explain how Colorni's extraordinary theoretical-practical activity, so important even so many years later, ultimately represents an almost miraculous achievement that undoubtedly sprang from his distinctive fusion of "*vita activa*" and "*vita contemplativa*"...

Let me conclude with a word to the non-specialist who would like to learn from Colorni's life and work. Never lose sight of the summarizing letter that follows, written by Eugenio to Ursula from the Varese prison on December 12, 1938 — before he was transferred to confinement at Ventotene.

> My dearest Ursula,
> ....Reading your letter last night I had the idea that I should outline for you the general drift of my phi-

---

[53] Colorni, *Lettere* iii, 65.
[54] In a certain sense it could be said that Eugenio's "interminable Leibniz" represented a long-term challenge to the author's ability to resist being swept away by idealism, and, in the context of adverse circumstances in which he found himself, it also had a propulsive effect in convincing him to break free of his bonds on two levels — autobiographical and expository.

losophy. So here goes (nothing new or ground-breaking, I hasten to say): Humans have made true progress whenever they notice that they are not the center of the universe. The case of Copernicus is the most typical and striking, but throughout the history of civilization there are these "leaps outside ourselves", this awareness that the laws that we had attributed to reality were, in essence, nothing other than an imagined reality created in our image and likeness as a good servant of our needs. Every time a step like this has been taken mankind has gained understanding from it and engaged better with reality, and powerful tools with which to control nature have fallen into our hands. The more man has dominated nature, the less he has felt like its master, its central figure. And here again you might say it took much more "love" and less "pride" to achieve this understanding. You could say that the entire evolution of thought, from primitive people who attributed rain and sunshine to the will of the gods — that is, to men who were bigger and stronger than themselves — down to Plato, who attributed reality and objective truth to our minds, and to Newton, who held that space and time were real entities, made progress every time the world of "essence" was replaced by that of "relations". But to do this requires an immense effort of honesty and, you might say, of asceticism. It requires the courage to look at ourselves as if we were outside ourselves, to become our own objects of observation (and this is the connection with the dialectic), to give up our habits of thinking. In this sense, morals and science are the same thing. And every scientific discovery, I would say even every technical achievement, is like a slap in the face that says: things are not the way my model would like them to be organized. It is precisely for this reason that every discovery is necessarily incomplete, and that it is pointless to construct vast systems in which everything is well organized. Every discovery is like growing from a child into an adult and saying: "How foolish I was! I thought the moon was a toy made just to entertain me". Essentially, it's an exercise in humility. You might reply: okay, but this is a method like any other. But no: I support this method because it is the only one that yields results. Whoever has applied this method has been enriched with knowledge and tools, and entire regions of the natural world have opened up. They have a nice little saying, the philosophers: our research is disinterested; we don't care about concrete results. But concrete results are the only evidence we have that we are on a track that will be productive for everybody. Otherwise, this so-called disinterest on the part of philosophers just turns out to be an interest in satisfying their curiosity or allaying their fears. The point that modern physics has latched onto, with the enormous results it has achieved, is precisely this: Space, time and motion are not "Platonic ideas", nor are they realities in themselves — they are relations. And in this regard, there are two things that strike me: 1. How exhausting it has been to remove these preconceptions from people — a sign that they were deeply rooted not only intellectually but, I would say, almost organically. 2. The incredible breadth of the landscape that has opened up to human eyes with the removal of these concepts.

I will stop here, my darling. They are old ideas, I know, but it does me good to tell you them.
Your
Eugenio

Bibliography

AA. VV. 2011. *Eugenio Colorni e la cultura italiana tra le due guerre,* Geri Cerchiai and Giovanni Rota, eds., Manduria-Bari-Roma, Lacaita.

Bobbio N. 1975. "Introduzione", "Note" and ed., Colorni E., *Scritti,* cit.

Camus A. 1951. *L'homme révolté,* Paris, Gallimard.

Cerchiai G. 2009. "Nota del curatore", "Introduzione," "Note ai testi," "Note a piè di pagina," and ed., Eugenio Colorni *La malattia,* cit.

Cerchiai G. 2011. "Eugenio Colorni lettore di Leibniz," AA.VV. *Eugenio Colorni,* cit.

Cerchiai G. 2018. *La filosofia di Eugenio Colorni,* Milano, Franco Angeli.

Colorni E. 1928. "Roberto Ardigò," *Pietre,* III, 2, 10 February. Published under the pseudonyim G. Rosemberg); now in Colorni 2022, Chap. 2.

Colorni E. 1928a. "L'estetica di Roberto Ardigò e del positivismo italiano nella seconda metà dell'Ottocento," 2 February, Essay, mimeo; now in Colorni 2022, Chap. 3.

Colorni E. 1929. "Estetica del bergsonismo," 21 February, Essay, mimeo; now in Colorni 2022, Chap. 4.

Colorni E. 1930. "Saggio sull'autonomia ed il disinteresse dell'arte. Punti di partenza del Croce," Essay, mimeo.

Colorni E. 1930a. *Sviluppo e significato dell'individualismo leibniziano,* Bachelor's degree thesis.

Colorni E. 1930b. "Come si possa interpretare il contrasto fra le due fasi del pensiero estetico di Flaubert e le sue esemplificazioni sull'opera d'arte." Term paper.

Colorni E. 1930c. "Fin dove sono giustificate le accuse di plagio rivolte da Goethe a Stendhal a proposito delle Italienishe Reise." Term paper.

Colorni E. 1930d. "Gli elementi di materialismo storico nella dottrina di Filippo Buonarroti." Term paper.

Colorni E. 1932. "*L'estetica di Benedetto Croce. Studio critico.*" *La Cultura* xi; now in Colorni 2022, cit.

Colorni E. 1932a. Recensione della ristampa di P. Martinetti *Introduzione alla metafisica* Milano, Società editrice "La Cultura" (cfr. below, Chap. 1).

Colorni E. 1932b. "Di alcune relazioni fra conoscenza e volontà", *Rivista di filosofia*, xxiii. (cfr. below, Chap. 2).

Colorni E. 1933. *La filosofia giovanile di Leibniz*, Post-graduate thesis.

Colorni E. 1935. "Prefazione", "Nota bio-bibliografica" and "Esposizione antologica del sistema leibniziano," to Gotfried Wilhelm Leibnitz, *La Monadologia*, cit.

Colorni E. 1935a. "I problemi della guerra," *Politica Socialista*, August (under the pseudonym Agostini); now in Colorni E. 2019, cit.

Colorni E. 1936. "Inizio di autobiografia," October; now in Colorni 2021b, cit.

Colorni E. 1937. "Le verità eterne in Descartes e in Leibniz," mimeo, March. Traveaux du ix° Congrès International de Philosophie – Congrès Descartes, Paris 1-6 August 1937, Hermann (cfr. below Chap. 5).

Colorni E. 1937a. "Giustificazione," July; now in Colorni 2020, cit.

Colorni E. 1937-38, *Lettere*, Eva Hirschmann Monteforte ed., vol. II, mimeo.

Colorni E. 1938. "Leibniz e il misticismo," *Rivista di filosofia*, xxix (cfr. below Chap. 6).

Colorni E. 1938a. "Programma"; now in Colorni 2021a, cit.

Colorni E. 1939. *Lettere*, Eva Hirschmann Monteforte, ed., vol. III, mimeo.

Colorni E. 1939a. "L'estetica di Leibniz," signed E.C., *Rivista di filosofia*, xxx (cfr. below Chap. 7).

Colorni E. 1943. "Conoscenza e volontà in Leibniz," *Rivista di filosofia*, xxxiv, signed *** (cfr. below Chap. 8).

Colorni E. 1944. "Libero arbitrio e grazia nel pensiero di Leibniz," *Rivista di filosofia*, xxxv, signed *** (cfr. below Chap. 9).

Colorni E. 1975. *Scritti*, N. Bobbio, ed. Firenze, La Nuova Italia.

Colorni E. 1998. *Il coraggio dell'innocenza*, L. Meldolesi, ed., Napoli, La Città del Sole.

Colorni E. 2009. *La malattia della metafisica. Scritti filosofici e autobiografici*, Geri Cerchiai, ed., Torino, Einaudi.

Colorni E. 2016. *Micorfondamenta*, Luca Meldolesi, ed., Soveria Mannelli, Rubbettino.

Colorni E. 2017. *La scoperta del possibile. Scritti politici*, Luca Meldolesi, ed., Soveria Mannelli, Rubbettino.

Colorni E. 2018. *L'ultimo anno, 1943-44. Genesi di una prospettiva*, Luca Meldolesi, ed., Soveria. Mannelli, Rubbettino.

Colorni E. 2019. *Critical Thinking in Action. Excerpts from political writings and correspondence I*, Luca Meldolesi and Nicoletta Stame eds., New York, Bordighera Press.

Colorni E. 2019a. *The Discovery of the Possible. Excerpts from political writings and correspondence II*, Luca Meldolesi and Nicoletta Stame eds., New York, Bordighera Press.

Colorni E. 2020. *'La malattia filosofica' ed altri scritti*, Luca Meldolesi, ed. Soveria Mannelli, Rubbettino.

Colorni E. 2021. *The Final Year: 1943-44. Genesis of a Perspective*, L. Meldolesi ed., New York, Bordighera.

Colorni E. 2021a. *"The Philosophical Illness" and Other Writings*, L. Meldolesi ed., New York, Bordighera.

Colorni E. 2021b. *Arte, estetica, politica*, Luca Meldolesi and Mario Quaranta, eds., Soveria Mannelli, Rubbettino.

Colorni E. 2022. *Art. Aesthetics, Politics*, L. Meldolesi and M. Quaranta eds., New York, Bordighera.

Colorni E. and Spinelli A. 2018. *I dialoghi di Ventotene*, Luca Meldolesi, ed., Soveria Mannelli, Rubbettino.

Colorni E. and Spinelli A. 2020. *Dialogues*, Luca Meldolesi ed., New York, Bordighera Press.

Curiel E. and Colorni E. 2005. *Il sogno di una nuova Italia*, M. Quaranta, ed., Padova, Sapere.

Gadda C.E. 2007. *I quaderni dell'ingegnere. Testi e studi gaddiani*, 5, Torino, Einaudi.

Gerbi S. 1999. *Tempi di malafede. Una storia italiana tra fascismo e dopoguerra. Guido Piovene e Eugenio Colorni*, Torino, Einaudi.

Hirschman A.O. 1938. *Il franco Poincaré e la sua svalutazione*. Trieste, Bachelor's degree thesis, mimeo. Ibid., G. Gilbert, M. de Cecco and R. Finzi, Roma, Edizioni di storia e letteratura, 2004.

Hirschman A.O. 1994. *Passaggi di frontiera*, Roma, Donzelli.

Leibniz G. G. 1935. *La Monadologia*, Eugenio Colorni, ed., Firenze, Sansoni.

Meldolesi L. 2013. "Eugenio Colorni ed Albert Hirschman a Trieste (1937-'38)," in L. Meldolesi, *Imparare ad imparare*, Soveria Mannelli, Rubbettino.

Meldolesi L. 2017. "Attualità politica di Eugenio Colorni," in E. Colorni, *La scoperta* cit.

Pavone C. 2015. *La mia resistenza*, Roma, Donzelli.

Riosa A. 2011. "Giuseppe Antonio Borgese ed Eugenio Colorni tra estetica e politica", AA.VV. *Eugenio Colorni*, cit.

Sereni C. 1993. *Il gioco dei regni*, Firenze, Giunti.

Tagliacozzo E. 1980. "L'uomo Colorni," *Tempo presente*, n. 6.

Urettini L. 2005. *Bruno Visentini*, Verona, Cierre Edizioni.

Vigorelli A. 2011. "Antifascismo tra i giovani: il caso di *Pietre*," AA.VV. *Eugenio Colorni*, cit.

Visentini B. 1945. *Due anni di politica italiana (1943-45)*, Quaderni di cultura politica, Vicenza, partito d'azione; now 2014, S. Gerbi, ed., Milano, Aragno.

Vittorelli P. 1981. *L'età della tempesta*, Milano, Rizzoli.

Appendix
An Evocative Letter from Bruno Visentini

Prof. Bruno Visentini
Counselor at Law
Piazza di Spagna 15 – Tel. 689.780
Roma

                        Roma, 29 April 1963

Alberto Boscolo, Esq.
Treviso

Dear Alberto,
    I was in Treviso a few days ago and found myself submerged, even there, in an avalanche of leaflets and printed materials.
    Among these I found yours as well and I thank you for wanting to remember me among your friends.
    You also recall our adventure together when we transferred Emilio Sereni, now a senator.
    But you speak of 1936... maybe you're getting old and losing your memory, because that adventure we had was in 1935.
    As you will recall, we left Treviso on 26 December, St. Stephen's Day, and having come through the fog of the Po Valley we stopped for a lavish lunch at the "Pappagallo" in Bologna, arriving at around two in the morning in Florence, where we stayed the night at the Hotel Baglioni.
    The following day we did the stretch of road between Florence and Siena, slept in the afternoon at Siena's so-called "Grand Hotel," where we also had dinner, and set off around midnight so as to arrive, which we did, punctually at 8.30 in the morning on 28 December, in front of the church of Christ the King on Mazzini Boulevard.
    We saw a gentleman with a beard come out who had

very little about him that seemed Christian and would certainly have made a good morsel for Hitler or Eichmann. There was a young woman with him who was visibly pregnant and a child carrying a doll. We ushered them into the "limo." I was the driver and, as you will recall — I cannot — I was so excited that I almost ran over a cyclist without even realizing what was going on.

We reached a place that the gentleman had directed us to, a little past Florence. He cut off his beard and produced marvelous Swiss passports for himself, his wife and the child — I don't remember if he got the passports at that place where we stopped, but I think so.

His wife and daughter had vomited continuously, without interruption, from Rome to Florence.

After the rigors of the Futa and the Raticosa — which, in the absence of the IRI and the Autostrada del Sole, we had to put up with at the time — we arrived in Bologna, in a fog that prevented us from seeing more than ten meters and set out on Via Emilia.

You will recall the adventure of the flat tire between Modena and Reggio Emilia and the hour we lost because we couldn't get the wheel off.

When we finally got to Milan, I stayed with the car at Porta Romana, and you took on the task of accompanying the passengers in a taxi on the final leg to their destination.

I had expected to wait a couple of hours and I actually waited around four — in the heavy fog you hadn't realized we were at Porta Romana and thought we were at Porta Sempione. So, to get back to me you had to get a cab to take you to a piazza where there was a gate with a single opening in the middle.

For reasons of prudence (as well as for reasons of your own) — you had a very pretty girl waiting for you in Cortina — we had to leave immediately, even though it was two in the morning, and we had been traveling for 26 hours. We got on the wrong freeway and realized our mistake only when we were approaching Como, not least because the fog was so bad, we couldn't see the guard rails or the signs.

We went back and took the highway towards Brescia — I drove while you slept peacefully up to the point when I too was sleeping just as peacefully and the car was in a gravelly riverbed near Grumello del Monte, 20 kilometers from Brescia.

I woke up feeling like Attilio Regolo in the barrel.

We got back up onto the road and stopped to rest, surrounded by fog and with the temperature not above five degrees below zero. The man from the toll booth came and took us to a tavern in Grumello del Monte, where you couldn't keep water in the room because it would freeze in the basin — with all this we still slept until 10 the next morning.

In the meantime, they had got the car going again and even though it was all dented up and the windows were shattered, we arrived in Treviso late in the evening of the 29th and immediately took the car to the garage, hiding it from our unsuspecting parents, who thought we were who knows where.

In fact, you left the next day for Cortina, and I came to Cortina myself on the 31st, leaving Treviso around nine o'clock in the evening with a Gino Vaccari tuxedo, and I came directly to the Savoia — just in time to see you at midnight quarreling furiously with Tata Zadra, whom you broke up with then and there, and who a few years later married that guy who physically resembled you so much (at least that's what they say) but who is actually nothing like you since he is a perfect imbecile, except for having wound up enjoying the girl's many millions, now reduced to a few hundred.

This is where the story ends, really. There was the unpleasant aftermath of the 4000 lire we had to come up with to pay for the damage to the car and which we didn't have. Among others, we went to Lucio Luzzato, whose only response was that the damage hadn't been verified nor even that we had actually had the accident. As you will recall, we broke off with him, and I'm sorry to see his name on your election poster.

We got something from Colorni, who had pushed us to do the thing and was Sereni's cousin. And we even had 1000 lire from Dr. Fanoli.

It was only some years later that I learned that the person involved was Sereni, who from Switzerland crossed into France where he was captured by the Germans, condemned to death, escaped and was recaptured but miraculously saved.

Anyway, right after the liberation of Rome I ran into Sereni and his wife at Siglienti's house. He didn't say a single word to me about the incident — an occasion when we had given him a not inconsiderable amount of help. Only just when we were leaving, his wife called me aside and told me with some feeling that she knew who the two people were who in 1935 had taken them across Italy to get them out of the country and that she had immediately recognized me. She thanked me from the heart but said that since we were not "comrades" her husband would never speak of it.

And in fact this is what happened — and I haven't seen Sereni in some years.

Just last year I had occasion to meet a woman in her thirties — already married and divorced more than once I think — who asked me if I remembered her. At my surprised negative answer she said that of course I couldn't possibly remember her because she was the four or five year old child who had vomited continuously for 700 kilometers without interruption apart from the short intervals when, thank God, she was asleep.

So you see, dear Alberto, an election poster can bring back a lot of memories — and along with the ones I wanted to share with you, there are all those that go out to Eugenio Colorni.

I hope you are elected to parliament, although I fear that since we're talking about Saragat's party, some fox more skillful with the clientele will beat you at the preference stage.

I wish you all the best and thank you for giving me the opportunity to write to you.

Warm regards,

Eugenio Colorni

The Leibniz Compromise

Part One

1. REVIEW OF THE REPRINT OF *INTRODUCTION TO METAPHYSICS* BY PIERO MARTINETTI[*]

Almost unobtainable after twenty-five years, this volume is being reprinted. This is a most welcome development because, along with *La Libertà*, it makes the thinking of this author, without doubt one of the most outstanding personalities and profound minds in our philosophical world, accessible to the public in a beautiful and manageable edition.

It is interesting to reread the book now, after more than a quarter of a century in which much philosophy has been done in Italy and many experiences and intellectual currents have come into contact with our own environment. And to find it still fresh, vital in all its parts, organic and contemporary, demonstrates the quality of thinking it contains, the soundness and originality of the doctrine. Indeed, I would say that some of its approaches and formulations have now, after the road they have traveled, taken on a new look and feel, and are at present highly topical. Many of his positions have acquired greater importance than perhaps they were given when the book first appeared.

Martinetti has direct and profound ideas on all the classic authors, and on many who are less well-known and were introduced in Italy by Martinetti himself. But he approaches them from a point of view that differs from what we are accustomed to. For him, as for others, there are things in each of them that are alive and things that are dead, but the part of them he takes to be vital is new and

---

[*] *La Cultura* xi. 3 (1932).

original, and his argumentation is so tight that it convinces us to agree, if not on the final results, at least on the essential nature of some of the points. So that even if the book does not offer a new philosophy, it introduces us into a new environment and opens our eyes to many aspects of reality — in a word, it enriches. And this is what is more than anything needed by young people whose training, under the pressure of highly celebrated doctrines, leads them to have difficulty seeing outside the frameworks these provide. They strain to escape this servitude and to find outside such doctrines the tools and sustenance necessary to solve the aporias they know deep down they cannot eliminate.

Martinetti's book is presented as a vast historical exemplification of a certain doctrinal schema. A conception which, if on the one hand it can be compared to Hegel's, is on the other completely detached from it, since it lacks the anti-empirical and panlogistic preconception that caused Hegel to identify empirical succession over time with an ideal succession, and which obliged him to force factual data to conform to a system, and vice versa.

Free of this obligation, Martinetti can build an entirely ideal schema of the history of philosophy in which succession over time is no longer important, in which philosophy and the history of philosophy are identical, since every doctrine is seen as a moment in the ideal dialectic of the mind.

For Martinetti, building a system means making it flow from the clash of the systems that preceded it. And these are organized into the various essential forms in which the human mind manifests itself — eternal modes of thought that always return — so that in taking part in one of them the ancient philosopher is united with the modern, and the constituent elements of history are not different schools but different philosophical attitudes. In Martinetti's epistemological organization history is thus truly reduced to the system, with every thinker appearing as a chess piece with a well determined place in the great game.

Certainly however, this type of schema is forced to overlook a number of historical and I would almost say personal connections that undoubtedly exist in the history of philosophy. Leibniz, for example, is given a place that ideally is quite far from that of Descartes and Malebranche, to whom he is on the contrary attached by close ties of tradition and culture. Hegel, as has been noted, appears to be detached from Fichte and Schelling, though it was they who prepared the ground for his speculative philosophy. But this can be justified by the fact that Martinetti's intention was not to offer a historical overview, but simply to make use of history and tradition as a foundation and premise for his theory.

This implies, however, that each of these attitudes has an eternal and ever-returning value in the life of the mind. There is a certain contradiction between the position of sublation that M. assumes in the face of approaches such as naive and critical realism, and the value he gives to them as fundamental and irrepressible events. If one admits that thinkers of every era have taken part in a mindset and that it has not been eradicated once and for all by later and superior formulations, then it is difficult not to attribute to it its own irrepressible originality.

Martinetti's history is conceived in such a way that it is distinguished from the dialectic by its characteristic of progress, of ascent. Martinettian sublation has a sense that is even more authentic than Hegel's. Here the succeeding philosophical position completely wipes out what came before, so that there is no possibility of a circle that allows the existence and validity of every attitude of thought, and each doctrine will be valued only insofar as it represents an essential conquest — taken in and assimilated without residue by the superior thought in such a way that the ultimate solution entails the activity of all those preceding it.

But this position is strictly linked to the author's metaphysical conception, to what we can call its transcendence. Suffice it to note for the moment that this continual dialogue among philosophers necessarily gives rise to M.'s own position, one that as I have said is of utmost interest to us since, while not rejecting any fact of absolute idealism, it comes to conclusions that differ from it more than a little.

The book is divided into two parts that deal respectively with sensory and rational knowledge. Basic to the first part is the critique of the Kantian dualism between phenomenon and noumenon. This leads to the negation of absolute idealism (Fichte, Schelling) and of the derivation of object from subject. Alongside this traditional line and neglecting somewhat the line running from the French criticism and contingentism of Renouvier and Boutroux to Bergson, Martinetti introduces the approaches in German philosophy in the last half of the 19th century that tried to take account of the data brought by Kant's critics meant to overcome the transcendence of positivism, but which nevertheless did not arrive at the other form of transcendence represented in idealism by the derivation of object from subject.

The solution given by M. is explicitly linked to that of Schuppe and the so-called philosophy of immanence, affirming that "the reality of consciousness is itself the world" and denying any priority of the subject over the object.

But the chapter on "idealistic phenomenalism" in which empirio-critical positions are criticized, especially that of Avenarius, is not very convincing. Martinetti seems closer to Avenarius than he maintains, and the doctrine of the unity and distinction of subject and object that he lays out in the systematic chapters of the first part come close to Avenarius and his *Menschliche Weltbefgriff*.

In the second part as well, concerning rational knowledge, he holds an immanentist point of view which employs a critique of the philosophers of immanence themselves to deny the distinction — just as it was denied between subject and object in the first part — between matter and form, and between a priori and a posteriori. The argument that none of these terms has any value except in relation to another is fully valid here as well, as is the entire critique of what he calls ontological idealism, running from Plato to Descartes to Malebranche and down to Rosmini, and the criticism of panlogism, under which he groups (not unreasonably, in my view) the conceptions of both Spinoza and Hegel.

In his systematic presentation he sketches out his approach to rational knowledge — an idealist approach, as noted, that clings to the given fact, and that sometimes (pp. 453, 468) brings intuitionism to mind. Martinetti explicitly affirms that there is no distinction between representation and object. And with this the ideality of the real is affirmed. Not because the ideal world (absolute mind) by itself generates the sensory world by a process of degradation or opposition of itself to itself, but because the so-called sensory world is itself something ideal, something objective. We can also say that no real sensory world exists, only an "objective" world in which ideal reality is one with true reality.

In formulations as clear and exhaustive as these we do not see how anyone can fail to follow M., whose theorizing takes us back to a certain and well-established starting point before we abandon ourselves to further inferences and constructions. But it is equally clear that this approach cannot yet be organized into a system, and we can immediately point out the dangers (if they can be called dangers) in its pluralism and in the problem of error.

If Martinetti's position can sometimes be reduced to intuitionism, it also shares the dangers of it, which are fragmentism and an absence of organization. Not that Martinetti is unaware of this, but we are not satisfied with the way he tries to get out of this difficulty. He speaks of the levels of increasing unity in these syntheses that constitute experience, and of an increasingly comprehensive progression "towards that ideal endpoint of knowing that appears to us as definitive and immutable knowledge." But here his epistemological vision turns into a religious vision.

This concept of progress appears to be a correction of the idealist dialectic, but its roots are very different and distant. In both, in fact, the error, the evil, is constituted by the past, by the unity of yesterday, which today — having come as we have to a higher synthesis — appears as abstract multiplicity, as material. But in Hegel this process is endless, while in Martinetti's conception it terminates in an ideal that is indefinitely approached. In addition — and this is much more important — the differing epistemological premises distinguish the two doctrines profoundly.

We believe the Hegelian position to be closely linked to Fichte and his idea of multiplicity as Not-I in the face of the absolute I. Now, once this primary position is denied, the form of dialectic that derives from it is also denied implicitly. And reality can no longer be conceived as a progressive estrangement of itself from itself.

Martinettian "progress" must therefore be given a different meaning and it will have to be based on a different criterion. What will this criterion be? What is the principle this process depends upon and is inspired by? If yesterday's unity appears to us as material when compared with today's, on what basis can we infer that this one is superior to that one?

Hegel places the principle of inferiority in the very fact of being posited as material. In Martinetti's doctrine, on the other hand, being posited as material has to be derived from an ascertained and effective inferiority. And this cannot be demonstrated except by starting from a principle of transcendence that one has faith in but no knowledge of. This is the principle that we cannot accept from M. — this religious principle that is even more accentuated in *La Libertà* and is unsatisfactory from an epistemological standpoint.

And so, we repeat, the value of M. must be sought in the theoretical foundations of his philosophy, in his critique of idealism and in the concept of pure and objective experience that he seems to indicate as a way out of the difficulties modern thought is entangled in. This is the direction in which work needs to be done. And in his method of working Martinetti can also and above all be considered the master — for his discipline in not speaking except of things deeply known, and for that spirit of unflagging research whereby one does not immediately embrace a system or a terminology and see everything through the prism of it, but rather tries to become part of every thought and to look at it almost with a virginity of spirit. So that the system, if one has the strength to build it, arises as the result and synthesis of a much broader and surer range of intellectual experience.

2. ON SOME RELATIONS BETWEEN KNOWLEDGE AND WILL*

It is notably difficult to isolate a particular philosophical problem from the connections and the system orientation that it is inevitably related to. This means that anyone who doesn't want to take a known and tested system as a point of departure will be faced with the task of prefacing any individual treatment with an orderly presentation of the general principles it is meant to rest on. Which means, basically, constructing a new system.

Except that sometimes certain directions of thought are in fact suggested by a partial observation — by a single problem which, when seen in a certain light, reveals the possibility of its developing into a more vast and complete organism. In which case it is perhaps permissible to illuminate the problem itself in greater detail and to leave in the background or sketch in outline the structure onto which it will have to be grafted. And since the various parts that constitute a systematic organism are structured in relations that are deeper and more intricate than a simple order of precedence, it is sometimes possible to employ partial observations as starting points on a path whose further development has been glimpsed only vaguely.

The study of the relations in idealist philosophy between knowledge and will seems well suited to this type of purpose. It is with this problem that we propose to start, showing how some criticisms of these positions may have consequences that also concern other problems in philosophy.

It should be made clear first of all that what we mean

---

* *Rivista di filosofia* xxiii (1932).

here by idealism is strictly limited to the line of thinking which, starting with Fichte, developed throughout the early nineteenth century in Germany and took on great importance in contemporary Italy. Despite differences among various thinkers, it represents a core of thought and a philosophical orientation that is clearly identifiable. It is an approach whose goal is to broaden and finalize the Kantian critique and to transform it from what it was — an examination of the conditions necessary for knowledge — into a complete and definitive doctrine of reality through the development of the principle of transcendental apperception, which in Kant constitutes the a priori form of knowledge but does not permit the deduction and development from itself of all experience.

If this idealist current harks back to Kant for acceptance of the results of the transcendental method and for the new shading given to philosophical terms and concepts, it is at the same time similar to Descartes' position in the deduction of the world from a single and immediately certain initial subjective principle. And the diversity in the mode of deduction derives from the different conformations of the two principles: partial in Descartes, such that the perfection of the idea contained in it suggests something that transcends it; and universal in idealism, this very universality keeping it from conceiving of anything exterior, much less anything able to influence it, so that whatever is outside it has to flow from its own depths.

In this assumption of the subjective moment as absolutely primary, idealism detaches itself from the Kantian formulation — which affirms the objective necessity of a priori forms of knowledge, but not the necessity of deducing the a posteriori from them. And Kant always feels the influence of English psychologism which, from Locke to Hume — while explicitly affirming the subjectivity of knowledge and doubt about the external world — never concludes that the only thing that exists is the subject. It instead adheres to another principle to which various currents of the late 19th century would attach importance. This is the idea that since two correlative terms are not separable from each other, much less conceivable in terms of one being inferior to the other, then it is not permissible to conceive of a pure thought, abstracted from its material and devoid of object. If it is true that content does not exist without the form that makes it what it is, it is also true that form is not possible without content, and in short that priority cannot be established for either of the two terms.

Far from being denied, this necessary reciprocal relationship is indeed explicitly affirmed by idealism. But its two terms are introduced in ideally separate moments, so that the necessity of a subject to conceive each object serves first of all, together with the fact of self-awareness, to give to the subject — to the I — its unique validity as an effective constituent of reality. And then the necessity of an object's content determining it imposes the deduction of it from the subject itself. It is in this deduction that we see the detachment between the practical and the theoretical that remains an inescapable presupposition of idealism. Because the passage from the subject, understood as pure and absolute self-awareness, to the object as the self-positioning of the subject outside itself cannot happen except in terms of an action that is no longer apperception or immediate apprehension, but is rather an exit from itself, a creation — a practical activity. Once an original and primitive union of subject and object is precluded, the only recourse for idealism is a form that gives it a way out of self-awareness itself and once again allows the possibility of knowledge as contact between subject and object in a new synthesis that embraces both and brings them together in unity, a unity that in this way cannot be understood as original, since only one of the terms that constitute it is original — the subject.

This process, essential to idealism for the development of its metaphysics, thus posits a practical stance as a precedent and prerequisite for knowledge. And that this is the case is already clear in the Fichtian concept of the creative imagination, whose derivation from Kantian practical reason is significant, albeit illusory, since practical reason in Kant means apprehension, through the moral imperative, of a superior extra-phenomenal world, rather than the creation and positioning of an object outside oneself. This task of creation is instead explicitly entrusted to practical reason in Fichte's *Wissenschaftslehre,* thus establishing the explicit precedence of the practical over the theoretical: "In fact, we would be unable to think of representation in general as possible in any other way than by presupposing that against the activity of the 'I,' which proceeds in the indeterminate and the infinite, an impact (*Anstoss*) is produced. Therefore, the 'I,' as intelligence in general, depends on an indeterminate — and up to now indeterminable — 'non-I,' and it is only by means of this 'non-I' that it is intelligence."[1] Now how does this non-I originate, which determines intelligence or, as we would put it, the cognitive power of I? "Insofar as pure activity relates to a (possible) object... it is... a striving (*Streben*)" (456).

"This infinite striving is to an infinite degree the condition of the possibility of every object. Without striving there is no object" (454).

And further on, even more explicitly: "The requirement that everything must be in agreement with the 'I,' that every reality must be set absolutely by the 'I,' is the requirement of what is called — and rightly so — practical reason" (456).

---

[1] J. G. Fichte, *Werke,* hrsg. Medicus, Leipzig 1911, vol. I, p. 442 (from the It. trans. by Tilgher).

Practical reason is therefore what allows the subject to place itself outside itself and to go outside its own domain. This is therefore no longer a new and more developed and comprehensive form of knowledge, but a function that differs from it in its own inner constitution. Knowledge is a faculty of unification and synthesis, whereby the subject comes into contact with the object and becomes one with it — in which the individual becomes universal, the contingent becomes necessary, and the ephemeral becomes eternal. Practice, on the other hand, understood in this sense, would be a form of splitting and development whereby the pure subject, this false abstract universal, fashions the particular that it refers to and alongside which it achieves cognitive unification. If knowledge, in short, is understood as the unity of two abstract elements that precede it, and practice as the forming of these two abstracts, then the two activities are sharply separated, and practice precedes knowledge.

In all of idealism, this precedence of the practical over the theoretical is always necessary and continually affirmed, appearances notwithstanding, and attempts to eliminate it as a marginal error not affecting the general concepts of the system have not succeeded. This anteriority is the basis and justification both of the exit of self-consciousness (which is not yet knowledge) from its abstract unity, and of the possibility of the thesis contradicting itself in antithesis, from which the Hegelian concept of dialectics is derived. It is in short the foundation of the entire idealist deduction of the world and the idealist conception of nature. Even Gentile, for whom the attempt to eliminate any dualism between the intellect and the will is essential, notes the close connection between that dualism and the dualism of subject and object.[2] But

---

[2] G. Gentile, *Sistema di logica*, Bari 1922, vol. I, pp. 111-12.

only a different account of the relations between subject and object would make it possible to eliminate such a position, which fatally brings an arbitrary irrationalism into the foundations of idealist procedures.

In fact, a will that is anterior to knowledge and almost the foundation of it, the creator of the base on which it has to function, cannot have the universal character that belongs to the full form of the mind. Idealism accentuates the moment of return, in which the partial nature of the object — or rather the partial nature of the subject-object dualism — ceases as such, because in unification it reaches universality. It is true that in this moment knowledge and will are united. But in the moment that necessarily precedes this we find that the pure subject and the pure object are separate, that both are equally unilateral. And in order to justify the object in front of the subject, one is forced to introduce this pure activity of positing, of creating, of self-contradiction and self-alienation, which does not and cannot give rise to the universal, because it starts from a partial datum, arrives at a partial datum, and produces a dualism of abstract terms that are in need of unification. In an improper sense this activity can be called will, since it has the characteristics of striving and impact cited by Fichte. But we repeat that it is not universal and is therefore not true will. In fact, it is useful to clarify that when idealism is accused of putting the will before knowledge, what is alluded to is of course this partial and arbitrary will, and not the true will — i.e. universal (identical to knowledge) — which idealism allows for, but only at the end of the process.

And the will can only be this — universal and identical with knowledge. These two characteristics are indeed strictly linked with each other and mutually implicating. In absolute idealism knowledge presupposes will, and it is easy to infer from this statement that the will thus transcends knowledge, reaching positions that pure knowledge cannot reach. Knowledge sublates it, it is true, and makes what was particular in it universal — but it is precisely in this particularity that its novelty lies with respect to knowledge. Knowledge brings subject and object together and removes all dualism. The will introduces dualism and distinction. Given a duplication of moments in the process of reality, it is also necessary to introduce two activities that represent them. So knowledge sublates the abstract will insofar as it universalizes it. And the will in a certain way sublates knowledge, in that it creates for it the particular, the abstract to be universalized. But the posing of an abstract duality, prior to unity, is unthinkable, and the proof of this will now be the inconceivability of a will that is beyond knowledge in any way.

When we speak of determinations of the mind as constituting reality, we allude — to repeat — to forms that have the character of absolute universality that is reachable only through the method that Kant called transcendental. Anything that is empirical or contingent should be excluded from them, and the mere presence of such characteristics should indicate that we are not seeing the forms we were looking for.

Now, is it possible to conceive of will as a universal activity anterior to or beyond knowledge? It would be nothing more than brute striving, unconscious tendency, pure object. Something, that is, that absolutely cannot be included among the transcendental forms of what can only be conceptualized as complete. So that if an element of awareness and universality is introduced, it cannot help but belong there in common with knowledge. A will that is only will — passion, that is, or feeling, as we usually say — cannot be anything but partial and therefore abstract, inconceivable on its own. The error of absolute idealism always lies in the misconception of putting the abstract ahead of the concrete, as a position of it that is still incomplete. On the contrary, the abstract cannot be justified except as a further development, an elaboration of the concrete, and rather than criticizing it by saying that it has not yet arrived at the full truth, what should be said is that it is no longer the full truth, and that it must return to it.

So this will that idealism places at the beginning of its cosmogony, as a process not yet fully developed, has no basis on which to rest its particularity, no whole before it of which to be a part. The idea that it can stand by itself as an eternal and indestructible (and therefore universal) moment is a proposition that seems to us fully refutable.

It is inconceivable that feeling — except as a purely subjective moment — is also, and mainly, a pure practical form inherent in the exercise of art and will. We rely on it above all to substantiate an autonomous practical activity, with its own original meaning and function, which accomplishes the splitting of the object from the subject,[3] or which justifies the alogical universal nature of art. But as long as feeling is detached from universality, which is a feature of knowledge (intended in the broad sense indicated above, as identical to subject and object), then no universality belongs to it — that is, no true reality.

Feeling and passion, from this point of view, are in fact nothing more than something that the mind undergoes but has no control over and which it cannot conceive of except in opposition to knowledge or universal will. Feeling, tending, *Streben*, *Sehnsucht* — all these forms disappear the moment they are irradiated by the light of consciousness, when they truly return to the unity of subject and object.

---

[3] Cf. Fichte, *Werke*, cit., pp. 481, 486-87, 494-95.

And is it not said that art is a liberation from the passions? That the true rational (universal) will is identified with necessity, with something impersonal that completely transcends every individual tendency, every instinct? Here the psychological observation confirms the logical reasoning according to which universality of feeling is inconceivable.

If the true universal, the first, is the identity and nondistinction of subject and object, then outside this unity, alogical and irrational feeling cannot be anything but the product of a further split, a successive and therefore partial abstraction. Nature, error, that is, in the words of the actualists, and hence a form that appears to be imposed, or an agent from outside — against which the universal believes it is fighting as if against an external enemy, whereas this struggle is nothing more than the suppression of further development and the return to initial completeness. Feeling, pure will, striving — these are thus nothing but abstract positions, experienced and uncontrollable in their immediacy, that become conscious only when they are completed.

And their incompleteness is the incompleteness of the pure subject or the pure object. It is indeed symptomatic the way feeling can at times take on both these characteristics by turns — that is, emotion, the illusion of self-awareness, solipsism, on the one hand, and on the other, tending, creative striving, and the impulse to get outside oneself. And then also there is instinct to be eliminated, felt as an obstacle standing outside procedures of reason and goodness, as turmoil suffered, passion. It may be said that feeling, this form that is so vague and imprecise, passes by a series of stages from subjectivity to objectivity without ever reaching a unity of the two — which, if it ever did reach it, would change its name to universal knowledge, good will. And we might add, somewhat crudely, that in its subjective aspect it shows up generally as an accompaniment to art, and in its objective form to the will. Crudely, we say, because it always forms a sort of elusive aura in the presence of any form of reality, accompanying it almost like an obscure and confused zone from which reality itself springs and stands apart, clear and precise. But we can say in brief that the aura of art is a violent sense of subjectivity, of passion and direct participation in what is expressed — a warmth, pathos, fullness of heart to which art alone will give a complete, well-defined and eternal value.[4] And the aura, the obscure zone from which morality emerges, is a complex of sensations, feelings that come from outside or that lean toward the outside — instincts, passions and desires that are endured, that are felt as external to our true nature but still part of us, and the empirical personality that they act upon and push to act in its turn, to produce and create, so that what arises from this desire for action and from the discontent left by the partial forms that determine it and that no longer belong to it in the truest sense, is the urge to make a correction — to arrive at an action whose determinants and motives have nothing to do with subjection to something, an action that really belongs to us and not to our empirical 'I.' This is moral or universal action, in which object and subject are identified, and to which feeling is only a precedent.

Feeling, in short, cannot in any of its various aspects be considered an autonomous form. It is something that is elusive because it is incomplete, and which tends to join with the forms that truly constitute reality — art and morality that is, and even the most pure and philosophical knowledge. And there is no thinker who, knowing the labor involved in thought that reaches its original form and frees itself from superstructures, does not see error as

---

[4] Cf., for example, B. Croce, "L'intuizione pura e il carattere lirico dell'arte," in *Problemi di estetica*, Bari 1910, pp. 1 ff.; G. A. Borgese, "Figurazione e trafigurazione," in *Fiera Letteraria*, 16 and 23 March 1926.

blindness to the truth, partial blindness due to sloth and a lack of intellectual vigor and a propensity to be misled by other easier or more comfortable solutions — bad faith, in short — and who does not feel remorse as if from a misguided instinct.

Now how is it possible that a form that is by definition incomplete, abstract and partial could be anterior to what it was isolated from? How can the error be prior to the truth? If the error (and, in this case, the feeling) derives from securing for an instant only one aspect — objective or subjective — of reality, it begs the question of what the reality might be that this aspect belongs to. And it will be necessary to admit that this reality existed at that moment when this aspect of it was isolated. First the reality, therefore, and then its partial aspects. First the unity of subject and object, and then pure subjectivity and objectivity. In this way the feeling is revealed, from this point of view, as occurring after what is usually called its sublation. And if in common psychology this relationship appears inverted, this is because ordinary life presents reality no longer in its original form, but in a form that is already developed, processed and organized, and on which countless splits, abstractions, and manipulations have already been performed, so that what appears as anterior and original is actually only posterior and artificial.

Thus, a form of pure will that creates the object for a pure subject is not conceivable except as an abstraction subsequent to unity. Will, when it is a universal form, an expression of the reality of things — moral, that is — is identical to knowledge and has no position of autonomy in relation to it. The pretense of maintaining such autonomy perhaps derives from the Cartesian formulation of a will that produces error when it is not subsumed under the rational activity that moralizes it.

This doctrine, in fact, is perhaps the source of the concept of an activity that has the general characteristics of will — an individual will, that is, independent in itself and indifferent to morality — which it could then reach only by rising above its own individuality to tap into the sphere of the universal.[5]

In this way, however, the universal would be in a certain sense an ulterior development, an addition to pure will, which even in this new form would not lose its individual characteristics, its aspect of impulse, of feeling. It would still amount to a passion, a passion whose object is the good instead of the useful, a feeling that is not aimed at satisfying an individual inclination, but at achieving an absolute purpose. But a feeling, nonetheless. And thus, one might say that economic activity (which is what the purest and most primal form of will would be) though having been sublated by morality, is not detached from it — it is its concomitant. And, that an act cannot really be a moral act unless it also has the emotional urge, the warmth that belongs to practical, individual, economic action.

In effect, this doctrine comes down to locating morality in the adaptation of the will to the principles of reason or, if you prefer, in its subsumption to a form of universality that is not intrinsic to its own constitution. But we have seen by now that a form of will that is not universal is inconceivable except as an ulterior development, an abstraction. Assuming, therefore, that the true will can only be universal — moral, that is — is it possible to conceive of a practical universal, different, and distinct from the theoretical, a universal knowledge that is not at the same time moral will?

There is no act of moral will that is not based on a principle of action, in recognition of the necessity of the

---

[5] Cf. B. Croce, *Filosofia della pratica*, Bari 1923, pp. 104-5.

intended action. Indeed, we would say that the will itself, insofar as it is truly universal, can be reduced to the status of a truth. Acting in a certain way, when it is a moral action, means recognizing implicitly that things are arranged in such a way that it is necessary to draw from them those consequences. The moral will is the will that turns toward the good, and the good is nothing but the universal, which is outside all incompleteness and abstraction — the principle in its most complete form, subjective and objective at the same time, that Kant determined with his transcendental method and Leibniz prefigured with his concept of substance. Now this universal, when put into practice, cannot help but be simultaneously grasped by cognition. If it really is the unity of subject and object, it necessarily must be conscious and aware.

To morally implement a given moral end is not possible without the recognition of it as an end (since — as is well known — if this recognition were missing, the responsibility for the act would be lost, and it would no longer be moral but simply due to chance). Now what is recognition of a moral end if not the awareness that it is universal? And what is this awareness if not the knowledge of that particular thing as universal? Aiming to avoid a certain action because it is immoral — lying, for example — means knowing that a lie (or that particular lie) does not have the universal character required of a moral action. And indeed, it follows from the very definition of every immoral action that it must be avoided. Thus, reciprocally, true (i.e. universal) knowledge is necessarily identical with the morality that follows from it. And in the affirmation of a truth a positive value judgment of it is implicit as is a negative judgment of its opposite.

This identity holds for all cognitive and moral propositions, even those that appear to be the most one-sided. Saying that the earth revolves around the sun implicitly means branding its opposite as false, and establishing that is the duty of anyone who seeks to resist preconceptions and aim straight at the truth — which is the first and most important moral precept — to affirm and advocate this proposition, perhaps even at the risk of their life. To say that a general must not abandon his troops implicitly recognizes that the relations and relationships between generals and armies are structured in such a way that the abandonment would constitute a fact without true universality. Morality and knowledge, in short, in their fullest and most complete meaning, cannot exist independently of one another — they are identified in a reality that we can call what we like, but which includes them both. It is only by means of a subsequent abstraction that they can be isolated and considered separately, and this may have its utility and importance. But the way this separation came about must not be forgotten.

This also explains, in the field of psychology, the imputation of morality so often associated with theoretical errors, and, on the other hand, the expectation of morality always attached to those who seek the intimate truth of things.

Error, in fact, is nothing but a partial and abstract vision that is being offered as full and complete. Given the concept of truth as the absolute completeness and unity of the fact, with all its relationships and connections, error cannot be other than the abstraction of a single partial element being given the value of the whole. Only in this case can we speak of true error because, when the illusion of the whole is absent and the abstraction is recognized as such, this same awareness presupposes knowledge of the whole from which the partial datum was abstracted. Knowing that it was artfully isolated from a previous unity means already knowing its connection with it and thus knowing something about it — if only that it exists — and voluntarily and consciously limiting its scope on a given occasion or for a given purpose. The abstraction that knows it is such is an error that knows itself to be one, and therefore contains its own correction.

But doesn't a real an error, error posing as truth, perhaps already contain within itself a seed of bad faith, of bad conscience? Isn't it almost always a lack of courage or diligence or honesty that causes us not to look for the whole truth of things and to content ourselves with views that are one-sided, partial, and arbitrary? Untrue knowledge leads to, indeed is identical with, action that is not good, and anyone with arbitrary knowledge of a situation will only be able to act in it arbitrarily. Now arbitrary action is condemned as immoral, and this is therefore the same as also condemning the knowledge that gave rise to it as immoral. The lack of clarity that comes with seeing the reality of things, breaking free of the distinctions we are used to making about things and from the models that make them more comfortable and manageable, always calls for a certain amount of goodwill. And the search for truth is the most morally commendable work that can be done.

But anyone whose research fails to arrive at the pure truth, who stops with a framework, or is held back by a preconception or unable to eliminate an abstraction, has not found the courage or patience or strength to carry their research through to the end. And moral judgment is based on these abilities.

The universal or transcendental — the truth, in other words (our truth, powerfully inherent in our very conformation and which constitutes our purest mode of consciousness) is also our truest way of being, from which the empirical and partial data we live in are derived by abstraction. Il n'y a pas d'objections insolubles contre la vérité.[6] Removing the abstractions that we ourselves have created is within our power — indeed, it is our greatest achievement. Not taking this road is blameworthy and sinful. It is in this way that intelligence (real intelligence, which frees more and more snippets of truth from their shell, not the false and apparent version that performs flashy and brilliant changes with empirical data and enjoys combining them and juxtaposing them and continuously making them into something new) — real intelligence, that is, a sharp, scrupulous, tireless investigator — is a form of morality; indeed it is morality itself, and the more deeply humans penetrate the universal, the more morally they need to act. Limiting ourselves to pure knowledge, failing to complete it with action, would mean that we had not fully understood our research objective in all its connections, or at least that we had allowed a large and fatal abstraction to take root in our mind — one that lies between knowledge and will.

We cannot therefore see how it is possible to believe seriously in a far-reaching morality that has no comprehension of worldly things, or in the sublime ignorance of some saints. A saint, a highly moral person — the creator, indeed, of a new and higher morality, is nothing less than the discoverer of a new way of being, of a more complete and profound moral essence that is displayed to the world in the saint's actions. The expression, the mode of demonstration we would almost say, is different. At the same time, just as aesthetic activity, for example, is not necessarily tied to a particular technique, and the arts can find their expression in words, sounds or colors while still belonging to the same kind of mindset, so too it is not necessarily the case that the great and pure man of action

---

[6] G. W. Leibniz, *Phil. Schr.*, hrsg. Gerhardt, vol. III, p. 144

(to be distinguished from the man of action as commonly known, who is a tinkerer and not a clarifier) differs in the essence of his activity from the great investigator of truths. The long and short of it is that the research method is different, or the tools and reagents used to reach the goal. And the truth that is discovered will therefore have a different look to it, but this will not take away its truthful nature.

True intelligence is thus a form of morality, and true morality a form of intelligence. Which does not mean that in ordinary moral judgment those who are in possession of greater clairvoyance should be valued more highly. Common moral judgment is based on greater or lesser growth in one's intelligence or morality. But in an absolute sense it is unquestionable that those who possess a clearer and more limpid and complete view of life should be given higher moral standing.

Another confirmation of this connection between knowledge and will and the impossibility of a position of the will as autonomous and separate from a vision of the reality of things comes from the doctrine of the identity of necessity and liberty. The concept of the impossibility of a *liberum arbitrum indifferentiae* [uninfluenced free will], whose import has recently been deeply analyzed by Martinetti, comes down to a negation of the alleged autonomous will that we have been seeking to refute. And the definition of liberty as "the state in which a being is not prevented from realizing the predispositions and inclinations that constitute its nature,"[7] is also expressed in this same negation. In the field of psychology as well, even in the particular and partial manifestations that have no universal or moral character, this identity is to be found: "In reality, all the

---

[7] P. Martinetti, *La Libertà*, Milano 1928, p. 340.

acts and occasions of consciousness are, since they are activities, acts of will. Consciousness and will are inseparably connected. The will is not a function that sometimes belongs to consciousness and sometimes doesn't, it is an element of it, an integral part of it that enters into all aspects of consciousness. There is therefore no special category of conscious acts that are exclusively performed by will — there are facts that are mainly theoretical, which we call facts of knowledge, and facts or events that are mainly actions, which we call facts of will."[8]

These two citations are closely linked to one another. And freedom cannot be understood as the discretion to proceed along one path rather than another, an autonomous form that acts independently of other facts of knowledge. It must instead necessarily be conducted with respect to a determined end, by recognition of the actual substance of reality. Just as it is not possible for the universal to resolve itself into incompleteness — at least not without ceasing to be itself — it is also inconceivable that free will should resolve itself into something that is not universal and therefore limits it. Liberty cannot be determined by one limit rather than another — it must necessarily be defined by the absence of limits. And in this way, it is identified with the universal, which is by its very nature necessary.

Martinetti thus shows that the sense of spontaneity that accompanies every act of the mind does not derive from the possibility that it could have been different, but simply from the fact of its being a mental act, the quality of activity and energy belonging to it by nature. The sense of freedom is achieved every time a new synthesis is reached and, we would add, every time incompleteness returns to totality.

---

[8] *Ibid.*, p. 358-359.

Spontaneity in this sense should therefore not be confused with the sense in which we spoke of it above, in which its actual nature as a universal form is denied. In that case it was, by definition, partial and therefore outside any true determination of conscious reality. For this reason, it had nothing to do with freedom — it was experienced as an external stimulus, and eliminated, placated and purified when the true form, the full reality, was attained. Here, on the other hand, the sense of spontaneity, and of activity and energy, is characteristic of conscious reality, which is in itself energy, activity and, in short, will. And this sense of energy, this striving, this pleasure in conscious activity is not emotion, but rather — as we have said — liberty. Liberty that is a fundamental feature of any act that excludes limits and, as Martinetti points out, of any act insofar as it represents the achievement of a new synthesis. But if the synthesis is the elimination of antithesis and a return to unity outside and prior to partiality, it can be concluded that every act that arrives, even in a single aspect, at a complete and total form of reality, every stage of this great return from the abstract particular to the concrete universal, is an act of freedom.

The position idealism finds itself in of needing to introduce a pure and self-contained will that justifies the presence of an object in front of the subject, derives from and is thus resolved into an arbitrary precedence of the abstract over the concrete. The impossibility of such a concept of the will in terms of our logical knowledge, and the concrete observations which show the will to be identical with knowledge, affirm the impossibility of placing such a primitive form at the origins of reality as creator of an antithesis from which at an ideally later moment a synthesis is to be reached. And on the other hand, it appeared that was only in this way that the antithesis could possibly be posited, and the object derived from the subject. Thus, the conclusion was to eliminate the primitive antithesis, or rather the pure abstract subject, which was presupposed by it, and to set up as primitive and original the unity whose antithesis is a cleavage — namely, the unity of subject and object, of knowledge and will, etc.

The idealist criticism of the partial nature of any one of these determinations is justified; but while idealism sets it as a point of arrival, it seems to us more logical and coherent to set it as a point of departure. An original starting point from which so-called everyday reality is far removed, and to which one must return, requiring unceasing effort. In this way the procedure to be followed in order to reach it, consisting of the continuous elimination of incompleteness and the attainment of inclusive unity, might resemble that of idealism. But there is a great difference between understanding manifestations, perhaps identical, as belonging to a process of modifying and moving beyond a given reality and considering them to be a return to a purer reality. In both cases we would be dealing with the search for fuller and more absolute unities, but in one case they would be given as absolutely new, produced by the development, the progress of the fact itself, and in the other as derived from a process almost of despoiling what is provided by common knowledge in order to reach the necessary element that underlies it. In one case, in other words, there would be dialectics, and in the other there would not.

It is in fact evident that the concept of the dialectic — in the Hegelian sense, as the becoming and proceeding of reality by continuous contradictions and the attainment of ever-new unities — presupposes on one hand the existence of organs (so to speak) for these contradictions, and on the other the necessity of a critique of them in order to arrive at unity. Now the organ of contradiction, or of the creation of the object, has been shown to be practical activity — which, however, when it is understood as identical to knowledge, cannot perform the role of creating something else from itself. And therefore, as the organ of this contradiction, can only be a practicality that is abstract and contingent. On the other hand, given the contradiction, i.e., the antithesis, how is it possible to carry out the critique of its terms that is indispensable to the attainment of the synthesis if not by presupposing the synthesis itself?

The difficulty that idealism runs into with regard to the problem of knowledge and will, and the position it finds itself in of having to introduce — sometimes almost unconsciously — the distinction between the two terms, proves to be closely connected to the problem of the relation between subject and object, and to the precedence of synthesis over antithesis. Given the task we set ourselves, we have deliberately left this problem in the background, and we will certainly not set out to deal with it now. We may simply mention that the positions of English psychologism, grafted onto the trunk of Kantian criticism, might have offered solutions more suited to eliminating this difficulty. The unity of subject and object implicit in such doctrines as an epistemological starting point does not contradict Kant's criticism, which indeed accentuates the real and not purely subjective quality of experience, but instead replaces the empirical character it had previous to him with its transcendental form.

The possibility that experience takes on a universal quality (and the *Critique of Judgment* is a luminous proof of this) may suggest a way forward to anyone seeking to eliminate the noumenal limit without going through the idealist dialectic. And once the abstraction that separates the subject from the object is excluded, it makes it possible to overcome the other abstraction positing the datum as empirical — that is, limited in its connections and relations — and to arrive at a universal primitive element that is at once both objective and subjective. The monad of Leibniz, for example — when it has acquired a less abstractly material character through epistemological processing — can provide an image of this datum and can complete itself at this point with the doctrine of Kant. Doesn't a reality that is objective and subjective at the same time, and that implicitly contains all its connections, represent the datum that everyday cognitive experience offers? And what is universality if not the implication of the totality of connections?

The universality of the monad, understood as conscious reality, can thus coincide with the transcendentality of knowing, understood as actual knowledge.

3. LEIBNIZ AND A RECENT INTERPRETATION OF IS WORK*

There are various ways of looking at a philosopher. One of these is to interpret his problems through our own, through issues that are present and current, and to leave aside for the moment his place in the flow of ideas that has led down to us and his place in the development of consciousness over the centuries, reading him as a contemporary and indulging the spontaneous reactions that arise from such a reading. Each of his thoughts is considered as a stimulus to new thoughts by those who study him, and his importance is in a sense a function of his productivity in terms of new philosophy. That this method is in itself legitimate is obvious, and it is the reason why anyone with serious theoretical and constructive interests loves the company of the classics — not so much to reconstruct their thinking as to use them as catalysts for one's own thought. But the pedagogical efficacy of this procedure, the extent to which it lends itself to being communicated to others and entrusted to the press is another matter and can only be resolved on a case-by-case basis.

At any rate, this is the method adopted by Barié, who has presented in a large volume[9] the meditations that arose spontaneously from his reading of Leibniz's work. The book is divided into three parts. The first is introductory, concerning pre-Leibnizian thought, followed by a "logic of self-actualization" which the author presents as an "essay of personal doctrine." The second part, that is, ought to be (to use conventional terms) historical, and the

---

* *La Cultura* xiv.1 (1935).
[9] G. E. Barié, *La spiritualità dell'essere e Leibniz*, Padova, Cedam, 1933.

third theoretical. But it cannot be said that there is much difference in intonation between the two. In one of them we find Leibnizian concepts along with continuous references to the thought of Barié; in the second, Barié's thinking is presented with continuous references to Leibniz. And, to come at once to our main point, we would have preferred less Barié in the historical part, and less Leibniz in the theoretical part. Because the way it is designed, the book does not suit either purpose very well. Barié has read Leibniz, and this reading inspired many thoughts in him. He has published them as they arose — and they are interesting, often insightful, and even profound. But they are not very clear and orderly, so that readers who want to know Leibniz do not easily find what they are looking for, and those who want to know about the personal doctrine of Barié find it so complicated with references, discussions, and polemics that they can hardly get a clear idea of it.

These are, in a certain sense, exterior observations. The essence of the book is a use of Leibniz for post-Kantian and idealistic purposes, and an emphasis, in the exposition of that philosophy, on the unitary motive and the conception of being as mind. This deliberately and openly tendentious character of the exposition exempts the author from absolute accuracy and historical completeness and allows him to neglect many aspects of Leibniz's activity and numerous of his writings[10] that are of more

---

[10] Barié has made almost exclusive use of the seven volumes of the philosophical works published by Gerhardt and the previously unpublished works released by Couturat, but he has not used (although he mentions their existence) the five monumental volumes of the new edition from the Prussian Academy, nor the seven of the Mathematical Works (except for some non-essential quotations), nor the eleven of historical-political writings published by Klopp, nor the seven of the Foucher de Careil edition (besides the two of unpublished letters and fragments), nor the six of the Dutens edition, not to mention the countless fragments missing from these comprehensive editions and published separately by various scholars such as Rommell, Mollat, Baruzi, Jagodinski, etc.

than incidental interest to the philosopher. These would have allowed him to construct an image of the author notably different from the one that results from the letters and essays published in the Gerhardt edition and would have revealed various unsuspected cultural and ideological roots of his thinking — considering that the philosophy of Leibniz (like every philosophy, after all) arose not from conceptual alchemy, but from vast cultural experience.

Thus if he had had recourse to Leibniz's entire opus rather than just a section of it, granted a very important one, his rationalism would have revealed relationships far beyond those with Descartes, Spinoza, Malebranche, and Bayle, exposing intriguing affinities with attitudes of late Scholasticism and the late Renaissance, with some lateral currents of reform and natural law — and in short with the entire complicated process of thought concerning political and religious ideology, publicity, and utopias which, alongside and partly outside the most rigorous philosophical tradition, marks an unbroken line from humanism to the Enlightenment.

In the same way, from another angle, the integral calculus (which Barié does not discuss except to recount the well-known controversy with Newton on the priority of the discovery) could have illuminated the way that led Leibniz to the concept of the monad as a constitutive reality of the world and the passage from his immaterial principle to extended and consistent matter. Thus, the studies of the Characteristic (which Barié considers only in passing) might have interested him because of the decisive influence they had on the logical formulation of the concept of individual substance.

Barié gives us, in short, a Leibniz to be used exclusively for his philosophy. And if this use is not always legitimate, it is always interesting. A deep philosophical spirit pervades the book. This is because Barié is one of the few in Italy whose philosophical interest is genuine, and Leibniz is a philosopher whom we cannot read without continually glimpsing indications of new paths to take, and without being tempted to translate his thoughts into our language and continue his experiences in our own way.

Anyone who approaches Leibniz gets an immediate sense of his topicality and fecundity. But what does this topicality consist of? It appears that we can appreciate him, benefit from him and preach a return to him from the most diverse and opposite directions. Hence the interest in even a literal understanding of his doctrine. Rarely is a more enigmatic thinker to be found, and rarely do we get the impression, as we do here, that the solution to the enigma can lead to further developments.

We believe that to arrive at such an understanding it is fundamentally important to study the succession of thoughts in his system — that is, the ideal order in which one concept preceded another. This is an extremely difficult project of study, and chronology can help only in part, given that even in his earliest youth we find all the basic concepts that would later be developed.

And in this regard, it is appropriate (and Barié rightly observes this principle) to keep the ontological basis of the Leibnizian system distinct from the consequences, epistemological or otherwise, that derive from it. The epistemological factor is in no way primary in this philosophy, which exhibits the characteristics of a clear objectivism and ontologism. And the theory of knowledge derives from this (as Barié makes clear) almost as a corollary, in Leibniz's attempt to refute, in the light of his own system, the anti-innatism of Locke. In general, it can be said that in all Leibnizian philosophy there is a part that can be considered as a premise, and various other formulations that are only developments and consequences.

Now what shall we say this systematic-ontological premise consist of? The tone of any Leibnizian interpretation derives from the answer to this question.

In our view, this premise consists of the concept of substance, which then develops into that of monads. From it derive all the best known and most celebrated Leibnizian theses, from the concept of representation to the "petites perceptions," to pre-established harmony, but to fully understand the concept of substance requires considering it in its full extent and scope.

It presupposes the entire theory of the truths of reason and fact, of the relations between the possible and the real, and between rationality and God, a theory that Leibniz develops extensively and that Barié ignores until the penultimate chapter in the exposition of his system, where he uses it only as a prop for his own personal doctrine. The basic logic of Leibnizian substance is also in close relation with the Characteristic. This is presented as the meeting point and coincidence of two thought processes — one ontological, which we can indicate in a word as the application of the logical-analytic procedure to contingent factual truths and the causal relationship, and the other physical-metaphysical, centered on the concept of strength, on the negation of matter as extension, and on representation as a tendency toward new perceptions.

Now Barié takes into account only this last process and is therefore led to emphasize, as the dominant motif of Leibnizianism, the mentalization and dissolution of the concept of matter. At the same time, he thinks that certain doctrines belong to the logical-ontological premise which are only distant consequences of it. He places at the center of his treatment the pre-established harmony between mind and body but does not sufficiently emphasize (although he does hint at it at times) that such a theory is no more than a special case of the relation and harmony of each substance with all other substances, of monads with each other. For him, the mind-body relationship almost comes to coincide with the relation between final and mechanical causes, between the intelligible and the sensory, and this leads him simply to juxtapose three superficially similar concepts that are in reality very different and have places that are quite distinct from one another in the hierarchy of Leibnizian ideas. The first and most essential requirement that pre-established harmony arises from is to justify the coincidence of the content of each individual substance with that of all the others (since each contains in itself virtually the same universe) while excluding any sort of influence (since a monad has no windows). The relationship between body and mind cannot be considered as other than an application of this principle to a problem that was topical at the time. Body and mind are seen here as two substances, two monads that preeminently correspond to one another (and this correspondence will give rise to difficulties and inconsistencies when Leibniz later conceives of each body as itself formed of monads, and the soul as the substantive form of the body). But in any case, it does not appear that the concept of the duality of the real, corporeal, and mental, develops as an essential consequence of pre-established harmony. Such a conception, as Barié intends it, is extraneous to the central core of Leibnizian thought, deriving instead from an external application of his concepts to a problem in Cartesianism and occasionalism. It takes on an entirely different character when presented as a doubling of the two orders, finalistic and mechanistic — or of the truths of reason and fact.

Barièérelies on this conception, however, even in his exposition of Leibnizian epistemology, where he talks about the distinction between the modes of representation of the mind and the body, when the central point of it is the implication of every representation by its object, insofar as it is connected to it by a logical-causal relation. On this logical-causal connection he does not dwell at all, nor on the monad concept derived from it. And yet this is the pivot that the Leibnizian system turns on, and the dissolution of the concept of matter (a dissolution found in Leibniz which is very important) derives from that center rather than from the body-mind relationship in a pre-established harmony.

The character of reality in Leibniz is timely and active, unfolding by means of a causal relation which — considered logically according to a static concept of causality — is already analytically contained in it. Matter, the world, everything concrete, is resolved and merged in this principle.

And if we want to call this principle mind, we can — as long as we remember that mind, for Leibniz, is this and nothing else.

And yet, every time we come across the word 'mind' or an epistemological determination, we are tempted to interpret it idealistically. This is the violence that post-Kantian thought does to our powers of interpretation and development, considering everything that is not matter in the usual sense of the word to be necessarily occurring in the form of subjectivity and thought. Now, the originality of Leibniz consists in his excluding this construction and pointing in directions other than epistemology. Abandoning this motive, or 'moving beyond it' in an epistemologism, would mean losing the best of his originality and reducing him to well-known models for which, I would almost say, his philosophy was not necessary. It is true that 'mind,' for him, means the dissolution — the elimination — of materiality, but this does not mean anything at all about thinking. And the very concept of representation, which he bases his doctrine of knowledge on, is so closely linked to the logical-causal universality of the monad that it has an essentially ontological character. Barié denies the concept of non-communication between substances, judging it incompatible with the power of representation. But Leibniz's originality lies precisely in this new concept of representativeness based on the universality enclosed in itself of each individual substance. If we want to understand representativeness as thought — that is, to correct it in an idealistic sense, what need do we have then to resort to Leibniz?

Leibniz's 'being,' in short, is something absolutely extra-material, indeed so much so that in it materiality dissolves — but in no way is it either self-consciousness or thought. It differs from thought by about as much as the logical subject of a proposition — the subject opposing the predicate — differs from the thinking subject, the 'I,' that opposes the 'non I,' the object. These are two concepts that have very little in common, except for the name.

What there is in Leibniz that has an idealist character (or at least prefigures idealist solutions) is the concept of matter, which is formed little by little as a partial aspect or further elaboration ('aggregatum') from the original substance and is devoid of any reality that is not merely apparent or 'phenomenal.' But this does not imply that the mental entity at its base is idealistic. This entity has its own value precisely because of its extra-subjectivity, because it rises to the universal ontologically, quite apart from any passage through the relationship of subject-object. Exactly what Barié denies — representativeness understood as belonging to the universal substance and closed in itself, not communicating with others — seems to us Leibniz's fundamental contribution and indeed the direction in which, translated into the terms of our own problems, his experience can be continued.

Basing himself almost exclusively on the superseding of materiality, Barié leaves completely in the shade the individualistic aspect of the universality of the Leibnizian substance and provides an interpretation of it that to us seems too close to Spinoza. In other words, it brings the substance too close to God, here again losing a fundamental motif of Leibnizianism, the development, that is, of the universality of substance from an analytical consideration of a posteriori and being forced to devalue and reject a cornerstone of Leibnizian philosophy — the distinction between possibility and reality, therefore between truth of reason and fact.

But the utility of a philosopher can go far beyond interpretation, and any use is legitimate when it is presented as such. Barié wanted to use Leibniz as a stimulus for his own personal thought. This seems perhaps too far from Leibniz for the union to appear truly productive. But leaving Leibniz aside, there are very interesting insights in it. An entire system is sketched out in the last part of the book — an ontologizing idealism that sets out to negate the dialectic and replace it with the law of continuity. There are new theses, daring developments and original polemics, which I cannot give an account of here, but they legitimize our confident expectation for the theoretical and systematic book that we hope Barié will now prepare.

PART TWO

4. G. W. Leibniz's *Monadology**

Preface

The Monadology, which Leibniz wrote at the end of his life to bring together in one overall vision all his philosophical concepts, can be understood only by someone with a certain familiarity with his thought. For anyone else, it appears to be an undecipherable enigma.

In order to make this work accessible to the young people of our high schools, I have found it more appropriate, rather than accompanying each paragraph with long and complicated notes, to precede it with an orderly exposition of the fundamental principles of the Leibnizian system which those who read the Monadology can thus refer to, almost as a summary. And as to the method of this exposition, I have chosen to give the word to Leibniz himself as much as possible, offering on each topic selected passages from his works, and adding on my own only the order and succession of the problems, and brief comments interspersed with the texts.

In the biographical note I have tried to present the personality of the author in all its multiple aspects, extra-philosophical included, and in the bibliography my aim is to create a small elementary guide through the various editions and commentaries in the hope that this book may also be useful to university students who wish to embark on a deeper study of Leibnizian philosophy.

Trieste, June 1934

Eugenio Colorni

---

* "Prefazione," "Nota bio-bibliografica" ed "Esposizione antologica del sistema leibniziano" di G.G. Leibniz, *La Monadologia preceduta da una esposizione antologica del sistema leibniziano*, a cura di Eugenio Colorni, Firenze, G.C. Sansoni Editore, 1935.

BIO-BIBLIOGRAPHICAL NOTE

There are some thinkers, such as Kant or Spinoza, whose biographies are entirely in keeping with their philosophy. Every new turn in their lives is at the same time a turn in their thinking, or their turns in thinking are the only salient facts in their lives.

Leibniz seems at first glance not to be one of them. The pace of his biography goes far beyond the evolution of his concepts, and this evolution never produced essential changes in his way of life. Although his existence was entirely conducted under the banner of intellectual activity, filled with study, research, and scientific endeavors of all kinds, philosophy proper did not play the leading role. In his work, the philosophical writings are not predominant, nor are they organic and systematic. They give the impression of having been written without a prearranged plan, almost in his spare time. And it was not only as a philosopher that he was known in his time — his fame as a mathematician and scholar at least equaled his reputation as a metaphysician.

But it is precisely for this reason that his biography is a necessary element for understanding his philosophy. Through it we may grasp what surrounded the philosophy in its emergence and accompanied it in its development. The system acquires a salience, an outline. It is positioned in an era and emerges from an environment. The very fragmentary nature of it acquires a special flavor from its connection with a vast and heterogeneous world of studies and activities. Before and beyond its links with other philosophical thoughts and formulations, every idea and formulation are connected to a concrete situation, a specific encounter, a set of precise and determined empirical circumstances. It is to these contingencies that it often owes its outward formulation, the way it is presented, and its expository or polemical form. It could be said that every one of Leibniz's philosophical writings is occasional. His biography gives us the set of occasions out of which the various ideas were born and, as a whole, the concrete, historical, and cultural background from which the organism of thought arose.

There is a difference in perspective between our way of considering the Leibnizian work and the way it was formed and conceived by the author himself. The philosophical side is the only interesting part for us, and everything else hangs on that. For him, however, philosophy proper was only one aspect of a larger whole — almost a fragment in the big picture. For us, this fragment has become the center. We draw from it concepts and ideas that are still very much alive, methods which, translated into the terms of current problems, may yield new and very interesting results. But in studying this philosophy we must not forget that it was conceived as a part of a whole that we must take into account, at least as background. And we cannot get a better idea of this harmonious and comprehensive whole that Leibniz envisioned but never succeeded in realizing — of this universal panorama — than by recounting his life.

Early years — Gottfried Wilhelm Leibniz was born in Leipzig on 21 June 1646, son of a high-ranking official and professor of morals at the university there, and the daughter of a well-known professor of law. His father died in 1652, and the boy's education fell to his mother. Leibniz recounts various episodes of his childhood and the enormous precocity that distinguished him even then. He satisfied his longing for knowledge more in his father's library than at school. He learned Latin on his own, guessing the meaning of words through engravings found in a book and the explanation of what they represented at the bottom of the page. He read the Latin and Greek classics, studied logic at school, and quickly arrived at his own points of view. In his last years of high school, he became interested in theology and scholasticism.

In October 1661 he enrolled in the law faculty of the University of Leipzig. Here, among others, he took the philosophy courses of Scherzer and Tomasius, with whom he subsequently remained in touch. Greatly important in his intellectual development was the semester he spent studying at Jena in 1663, where Erhard Weigel introduced him to various problems in philosophy and mathematics. This was the period when the empiricists and rationalists were brought together as representatives of the new philosophy in opposition to the scholastic dogmatism still prevailing in the universities. In this very general sense Leibniz could be called Cartesian in those years, although he gained a thorough knowledge of Descartes only after 1671.

His first writings were theses written to obtain academic degrees: a *Disputatio metaphyisica de principio individui*, on a scholastic subject; various juridical writings, in which he sought to apply philosophical procedures to the science of law; and the *Ars Combinatoria*, which already contained the germ of his future ideas concerning a form of logic organized according to mathematical principles and an 'alphabet of human thoughts.'

For reasons not well specified, it was impossible for him to graduate from Leipzig. He therefore moved to Altdorf, near Nuremberg, where he became doctor *utriusque juris* at the university after a brilliant thesis discussion (1666). The legal faculty offered him a chair, but he turned it down. He then settled at Nuremberg, where he immediately set out to establish contact with the intellectual world of the city. He joined the strange and mysterious alchemist society 'the Rosicrucians,' which gave him the opportunity to initiate himself in the mysteries of naturalist research. Extremely important for his future was his meeting at Nuremburg with the Baron von Boyneburg, former minister of the archbishop-elector of Mainz and one of the sharpest politicians of the time, with an interest in every sort of cultural issue.

Boyneburg immediately recognized the young scholar's outstanding qualities, became his close friend, and appointed him as his secretary. He took him to Frankfurt where he presented him to the elector of Mainz. As a worthy introduction to the prince, Leibniz wrote his *Nova methodus discendae docendaeque jurisprudentiae*, the most important of his legal writings. In this paper, as in those that had preceded it, technical legal problems were approached using logical, mathematical and generically philosophical methods, and grafted into the harmonious and universalistic vision that was already beginning to take shape. Along with another legal consultant, he was entrusted by the elector with the task of reorganizing and reconciling Roman legal principles with those of the law of the time.

He soon moved to Mainz, where he was appointed counselor to the elector and carried out scientific and political tasks of various kinds on behalf of himself and Boyneburg. Of particular interest is a memorial on the occasion of the election of the King of Poland in 1669, following the abdication of John Casimir. In it the candidacy of a German prince, the Palatine Count of Neuburg, is supported with a rigorous demonstration *more geometrico*. Of interest also are his *Thoughts on the security of the German Reich*, in which he advocates a union of German princes against the imminent threat from the France of Louis XIV.

In the field of concrete politics, it cannot be said that Leibniz had any real independence of thought. His political writings were often composed to order, and the theses he advocated at the time followed the current interests of the princes he was serving. There is a personal mark on them, however, which is very strong. It lies in the universalizing tone of the discussion, in the desire to make every specific and concrete solution derive from very general principles, and in looking at every individual problem within a framework of universal harmony. At the same time, he sought as to make each of the various arguments he was called upon to support an instrument for the creation of the universal organization that he envisioned as an attainable end. In attempting to achieve this dream, he tried to make concrete use of the political situations and powerful people he encountered. Louis XIV, Peter the Great, the reunification of the churches, the missions in China were all for him pawns in this immense game.

The philosophical writings from his time in Mainz (1668-1671) are of fundamental importance in the study of Leibnizian philosophy. They represent, even in their youthful insufficiency, the basic lines of his many speculative interests in a pure and original form, still barely troubled by polemical and cultural concerns — precisely the way they took shape in the young scholar's mind. His subsequent career as a thinker would only be a deeper exploration and enrichment of these ideas.

The *Ars Combinatoria* had already been published. The problems that Leibniz now dealt with were theological (*Confessio Naturae contra atheistas, Defensio Trinitatis*, and various fragments only recently published), logical (a preface to a book by Mario Nizolio), and especially to do with physical philosophy. Dating from 1671, in fact, the *Hypothesis physica nova*, divided into a *Theoria motus concreti* and a *Theoria motus abstracti*, presents very important principles on the nature of bodies, motion, continuity, the divisibility of matter, etc...

In these early years Leibniz was already beginning to spin the threads of the prodigious correspondence that would establish personal relationships with all the most important scientists of his time. The letters to his teacher Thomasius are very important for logical and physical philosophy, those to Conring for legal concepts, to Guericke for physical problems, and to Oldenburg for mathematical problems. Some of his letters to the Duke of Hanover contain comprehensive presentations of his ideas in various fields of knowledge. He also prepared a memorandum for the Duke of Hanover on *Divine omnipotence and omniscience and on the free will of man*, in which he dealt with what was to become the problem of *Theodicea*.

In this period, he attempted to contact Hobbes and Spinoza, but Hobbes failed to answer his letters, while Spinoza's response was courteous but cold.

Journey to Paris (1672-1676) — Early in 1672 Leibniz was invited to Paris following a diplomatic mission. Louis XIV was planning an invasion of the Netherlands, which would pose a direct threat to the princes of the Rhineland. The elector of Mainz was anxious to avert the danger while there was still time. Boyneburg and Leibniz devised a way to achieve this goal. They drew up a plan for an expedition to Egypt, to be submitted to the French king, in the hope that in accepting and implementing it, he would be diverted from his immediate designs on Holland. The memoranda for this project are almost entirely the work of Leibniz. They naturally conceal the immediate goal, putting the emphasis on the conquest of Egypt in all its political and moral aspects as an enterprise extremely beneficial to this most Christian king, both in terms of his mission of propagating the faith and fighting against the infidels, and in terms of his aims of dominance over Europe — a dominance that Leibniz would not have liked to see based on war and conquest, but on peace and arbitration. But the project had no luck. Leibniz did not even manage to be received by the king. War was declared against Holland. The memoirs were transferred to the French State Archives, and it was later claimed — probably apocryphally — that Napoleon got the idea for his expedition to Egypt from them.

Leibniz was permitted by his master to remain in Paris without losing his office. At the same time, he was entrusted with the care of Boyneburg's young son, who was staying there. In the cultural capital of Europe his hunger for knowledge was satisfied. He established connections with the most important men of his time, and from his discussions with Arnauld, Malebranche, Huygens, etc., he would derive the formulations of many of his principles and concepts. Having arrived in Paris as a virtually unknown youth, he left after four years as a scientist renowned throughout Europe. From then on, he handled French with the same facility as German and Latin, and his major works and correspondence were written in French.

His most direct knowledge of Cartesian philosophy and his interest in Spinoza belong to this period. Cartesianism was dominant in France at the time, but it cannot be said that Leibniz was ever a Cartesian. He discussed this philosophy at great length and struggled at times to solve the problems it presented. But such problems took on a different meaning for him than they had for Descartes — they were framed in other systemic interests. Leibniz cannot be situated on the line that in modern philosophy begins with Descartes. His thought, while often referring to Cartesian thinking, followed a path that is clearly divergent from it.

In the meantime, he went ahead with the studies and projects that had begun with his youthful *Ars Combinatoria*. These now took shape for him on a broader scale. He contemplated a general science of human thought, by which it would be possible to work out any line of reasoning by a calculation — a universal language based on signs standing for the simplest elements, from which, by means of combinations, more complex ones could be reached. There are innumerable fragments, notes and drafts on this subject that remain from the end of his stay in Paris.

But his main interest during this period was mathematics. In Paris he had met Christian Huygens, the great scientist, and in a brief trip to London (1673) he had the opportunity to contact other scholars in the circle of the Royal Society of science, of which he himself became a member. His explorations of mathematics soon led to original innovations and the formulations and solutions of new problems. His 1676 discovery of integral calculus won him a place among the top-ranking mathematicians of all time. This same discovery, albeit in a different form, was made at almost the same time by Newton, but neither author published his theorems until some years later. This led to the disagreement over the priority of the discovery, which then degenerated into an unpleasant quarrel, with mutual accusations of plagiarism. Modern scholarship has established that the two scientists arrived at the same formulation absolutely independently of one another.

This is not the place to go into detail on the significance of differential calculus. Suffice it to say that it is based essentially on two concepts that are also of great importance in Leibnizian philosophy — continuity and the infinitesimal.

At the Court of Hanover (1676-1716). — Boyneburg having died in 1672 and the elector of Mainz in 1673, Leibniz no longer had anything tying him to the court there. In 1676 he accepted the invitation of John Frederick of Brunswick-Lüneburg, Duke of Hanover, who had repeatedly offered him a position. Traveling from Paris to

Hanover, he spent several days in The Hague (November 1676), where he made the acquaintance of Spinoza, with whom he engaged in long conversations. Spinoza was to die a few months later. At that time he was known mainly as the author of the *Theologico-Political Treatise*, which had provoked a major scandal and earned him his reputation as an atheist. Leibniz took an active interest in his work and read his *Ethics* with close attention as soon as it was published following the philosopher's death.

Leibniz was to remain in the service of the Dukes of Hanover for the remainder of his life. This was the period of the Brunswick-Lüneburg dynasty's greatest ascendancy. With their essentially dynastic politics, the princes succeeded in increasing their power and authority through diplomacy and marriages. Duke Ernest Augustus, who succeeded John Frederick in 1679, is regarded as the second founder of the house. In 1693 he acquired the title of elector. His daughter Sophia Charlotte, a great friend and protector of Leibniz, married the elector of Brandenburg and became Queen of Prussia in 1701. Ultimately, in 1714, the House of Hanover assumed the succession to the throne of Great Britain, and Ernest Augustus's son, George Ludwig, united in himself the titles of King of England and Duke-elector of Hanover.

Leibniz witnessed this rise and took part in it. His assignment, as it were, was to lay out the theory behind the politics. He was entrusted with the genealogical research that would justify the dynastic claims of the Dukes, and with the legal arguments that would demonstrate their rights. And the increase in the power of his masters enlarged his field of knowledge and his range of action. His friendship with the Queen of Prussia allowed him to live for many years in Berlin, where he founded the Academy of Sciences. The marriage of a princess of Brunswick with the son of Peter the Great gave him the opportunity to make contact with that monarch as well.

Leibniz's official position at court was first as librarian and then as historiographer, but he was given a wide variety of assignments. These included attempts to bring about the efficient exploitation of certain mines, the formulation of plans for the unification of the Catholic and Protestant churches, and the foundation of scientific societies and academies, along with philosophical conversation and correspondence with his learned and powerful pupils, the electress Sophia of Hanover and Queen Sophia Charlotte of Prussia. And in the midst of all this, he did not neglect his private scientific interests, his mathematical, physical, theological, and philosophical studies, his projects in general science and universal language, nor his correspondence with the learned men of his time.

Political and historical activity — While his political activity, as indicated above, was now based on the interests of the House of Hanover, he still maintained a certain line of coherence. The hopes placed in Louis XIV had come to nothing. The king of France was pursuing a policy completely opposite to what had been desired by Leibniz, who had envisioned him as an arbitrator among the European states and had tried to turn his arms against the infidels. Instead, he proceeded from conquest to conquest, not least at the expense of the German princes, and used the infidels (following a tradition of French politics) to create difficulties for the Emperor. Leibniz vented his bitterness in a satirical booklet published in 1683, *Mars Christianissimus, or an apologia for the arms of the Christian king directed against Christians*. Many other writings and memoirs were directed against French policy and in line with the interests of the Empire, among which *Reflections on France's Declaration of War on the Empire* (1688), *Status*

Europae incipiente novo saeculo (1700), and *Considerations on the peace being concluded at Rastadt* (1713). This gave him the opportunity to make many trips to Vienna, where he met and gained the high regard of Eugene of Savoy, for whom he wrote the *Monadology* in 1714.

Other writings instead served the interests of the house of Hanover more directly. A long treatise, *De jure suprematus ac legationis principum Germaniae,* published under the pseudonym Caesarinus Furstenerius, was designed to demonstrate the right of the ambassador of the Duke of Hanover (then not yet elector) at Nijmegen to receive the title of Excellency and to be treated with the same honors as the ambassadors of electors. Trivial as this matter was, it gave Leibniz the opportunity to make interesting observations on the concept of sovereignty and other similar topics.

Leibniz's greatest work in this field, designed to reflect the glory of his masters, was the body of historical and genealogical research he did on the origin of the house of Braunschwieg, which he worked on from 1687 until the end of his life. The Braunschwieg, direct descendants of the Guelph Henry the Lion, claimed to trace their origins back to the same Marquis Azzo from whom the Este dynasty derives. In order to prove the accuracy of this genealogy on paper, Leibniz undertook a long journey that lasted three years (1687-1690) and took him to the major cities of Germany and Italy. He stopped in Frankfurt, Munich, and Vienna, where he established important relationships at the imperial court, and then went on to Venice, Ferrara, Modena, Bologna, Rome, and Naples. Wherever he went, he combed through archives and uncovered documents, and the work grew in his hands. In the meantime, he took advantage of the opportunity to pursue his other scientific interests. Among the Italian scholars he met during this journey, were Malpighi, Magliabechi, and Father Grimaldi, a missionary in China, who gave him interesting information about that country.

In opposition to the writers of fairy-tale genealogies, Leibniz favored a historical method based on a rigorous selection and critical analysis of the documents, and he acted as editor of the documents themselves — a conception that brought him closer to our own Muratori, his contemporary, with whom he was in active correspondence. This study and research gave rise to various works, including the *Codex juris gentium diplomaticus* (1693), a collection of documents of public law, for which he wrote a preface that was very important for the concepts on legal philosophy it contained. In addition, a collection of documents emerged concerning the house of Braunschwieg, entitled *Scriptores rerum Brusviciensium illustrationi inservientes* (1707-11). And finally, he embarked on a vast historical work, the *Annales Brunsvicienses,* in which the history of the development of the house of Braunschwieg was meant to illustrate the general history of the Empire. Leibniz never finished this work, and it has come down to us incomplete.

Linked with these studies and with his naturalistic research on mines is the *Protogea*, a geological history of the earth. Here, beginning with the study of the composition of the soil of the Duchy of Hanover, we pass to more general considerations — just as through the history of the Braunschwieg we glimpse the history of the Empire and of Europe.

Reunification of the churches — Closer to his theoretical and spiritual interests was the great enterprise of reuniting the Catholic and Protestant churches, which Leibniz devoted a great deal of effort to, and whose success he longed for with all his heart and mind. The idea of such a union was widespread at the time, and after the initial fury of the struggle had subsided along with the moral and political interests that had aroused it, the differences between the two modes of confession were becoming more dogmatically and theologically refined and, when compared in the tranquil setting of scholarship, did not appear insurmountable. Moreover, political motives impelled the Emperor and the Pope to desire this reconciliation. Leibniz, a Protestant, found himself early in his career in the service of a Catholic prince, the archbishop-elector of Mainz. His first patron, Boyneburg, was a Protestant convert to Catholicism; and the *Demonstrationes Catholicae* (1670-71), written by his order, seeks to demonstrate the dogmatic conciliation of the Augustan Confession with the Council of Trent. And then at Hanover he found himself at the center of the entire movement. Duke John Frederick, himself recently converted to Catholicism, was in the position of having to reign over a Protestant country. It was therefore obvious that he should work toward re-unification. Ernest Augustus, a Protestant, continued his work for political reasons. And Leibniz participated, so to speak, in all the negotiations that took place at different sites and involved numerous intermediaries. His correspondence on this issue with Bossuet, who represented the Catholic point of view, is famous and decisive. The very impossibility for these two thinkers to find a point of agreement was one of the causes of the failure of the undertaking. Each of the courts interested in the project had instructed its scientists and theologians to systematically formulate the principles according to which the union could be achieved. Spinola wrote and acted on behalf of the Emperor, Molanus in the name of the Duke of Hanover. Leibniz himself attempted his own framework for an accommodation, writing the *Systema theologicum*, an essay *On methods of re-unification*. His personal interest in this was very great, as it offered the opportunity to achieve his great dream of universal harmony. He discovered possibilities for reconciliation among the various dogmas. He advocated for a 'catholic' church in the etymological sense of the word, a church universal that would unite and reconcile the various disparate branches, giving each the opportunity to make its case. But it was exactly this way of thinking that stood in the way of his accepting formal Catholicism. Various attempts were made to bring him into the Church of Rome, especially by Ernest, Landgrave of Hesse, his friend and admirer. He always refused, on the grounds that he did not want to submit his scientific studies to any control based on dogma.

All attempts to reconcile Catholicism and Protestantism having failed, Leibniz took on the task of smoothing out the conflict that was tearing apart the very bosom of the Protestant church, between Lutherans and Calvinists. He again collaborated with Molanus, writing a *Tentamen irenicum*. But these attempts, like the others, came to nothing. He saw his dream of harmony slip away. But in the studies, he undertook as a theoretical grounding for the union of the churches, he found himself dealing with arguments that would have great importance in the shaping of his philosophical system. The problem of transubstantiation, for example, led him to fundamental formulations in physical philosophy — on the essence of the body, of matter, etc. The problem of grace, of predestination, would be crucial in the determination of his metaphysical principles.

Organization of the sciences — Thus the idea of harmony and universalism remained with him throughout his life. He left its mark on each of his assignments and his political and diplomatic appointments. And along the way he always tried to make the most of his good relations with the sovereigns of the time, trying to bring them into his plans for organizing the sciences and marshal their resources behind this ideal.

We have already spoken of his plans for a 'Characteristic' — for a general science that would bring together in a well-ordered way all the fundamental elements of human knowledge (simple ideas, primitive and impenetrable concepts, concrete facts, observations, experiments, events handed down by history, etc.) and would be able to derive any concept or idea from them by means of logical and mathematical methods. Through this collection of all possible simple elements and the method of combining them, he hoped to greatly simplify all research, and reduce everything to frameworks and repertoires that would make the knowledge of facts and the discovery of new truths accessible to all and rigidly controllable.

This utopian idea was not utopian to him. He spent his whole life trying to make it a reality, but for this he needed the collaboration of his contemporaries. For this reason, he never grew tired of designing societies, academies, libraries, and archives that would provide the tools for achieving this goal. Plans for a society of the sciences and a bibliographic organization to collect and account for all book production date from his earliest years. In 1688 he met the historian Ludolf in Munich, and together under the auspices of the Emperor, they founded the *Collegium historicum imperiale* in Vienna in 1690, designed for the study of Germanic historical documents. In 1700 Leibniz had the great satisfaction of founding what today is the Prussian Academy of Sciences in Berlin, modeled on the societies in Paris and London of which he was a member, and serving as its first president. This office frequently took him to Berlin for long periods, especially while Queen Sophia Charlotte was alive, that is until 1705.

The Academy published a periodical, *Miscellanea Berolinensia ad incrementum scientiarium*, and Leibniz was the main contributor. His idea was an organization of interconnected scientific societies in all the capitals of Europe — a true republic of letters and sciences through which the work of each scholar would be facilitated by the opportunity to establish relations with other academics throughout the world. He had plans for Dresden and Vienna, where he lived for nearly two years at the end of his life (1712-14), on a diplomatic assignment. But his projects never came to fruition.

Leibniz was always looking for a concrete power in the political world that would be willing to help implement his universalist plans. But caught up in the complications of their own particularist politics, the Western monarchs would not prove able to carry out such a mission. Louis XIV, in whom he had initially placed his trust (recall the plan to conquer Egypt), had not lived up to expectations. Leibniz looked to the East, to this vast virgin and unknown world whose rich civilization was still almost unknown in the West. His interest was in China and Russia. He learned of Chinese matters from the Jesuit missions, particularly from Father Grimaldi, and of the Emperor's great interest in the sciences, rejoicing and marveling at the convergence of his own projects on the Characteristic with those of Chinese scientists. He envisioned cultural and spiritual contacts with the Chinese people and the propagation of the Christian faith among them.

Contact with Russia came through Peter the Great, the enlightened sovereign in whom Leibniz believed to have found what he had long been searching for. He met with him three times (1711, 1712, 1716), becoming his advisor on cultural initiatives, and planned for him an academy, a library, a museum, a 'theater of nature,' a 'theater of the arts,' 'schools of virtue, science, and art,' and a university — in short, all the institutions he deemed necessary to establish his 'general science.' And thereafter Peter the Great in fact often followed the advice of his great friend.

Mathematics, physics — With all this bustle of public, political, and organizational activity, one might have thought there was no room for his theoretical interests. But on the contrary, these were what Leibniz considered to be most intimately his own. He worked on them in his own name, independently of his position at court and it was in fact the effects of this activity that make him great in our eyes today.

Philosophical and scientific research represented the private side of Leibniz's activities. This explains the fragmentary way his works in this field have come down to us, and the scattered manner in which his conceptions were set out, spread through writings of various kinds, mainly letters. It was the custom of the time that the communication of one's ideas to other scientists should take place not only through books and journals, but more often through the direct exchange of letters, and Leibniz offers the most classic example of this. Thousands and thousands of his missives have come down to us on the most wide-ranging topics, and only through a careful study of them can a comprehensive view of his ideas be achieved. At times these letters prefigured the positions he took on various topics and sometimes they followed them as polemics. They were published, mostly in the form of short essays, in journals such as the *Acta Eruditorum* in Leipzig, the *Journal des savants* in Paris, and the *Nouvelles de la république des lettres* in Amsterdam.

He followed this procedure in the fields of both philosophy and mathematics. It was customary for scholars who succeeded in formulating a new theorem or solving a problem to communicate the discovery to their colleagues privately before making it public, so that its accuracy could be checked. Or alternatively, they could pose the question to them without revealing their own solution so that the results could be compared. Here once again we see the great importance of the letters in providing an insight into the development of Leibnizian mathematical formulations. And in this formative process philosophical concepts play a sometimes-notable role, just as such formulations sometimes lead to philosophical conclusions.

We have mentioned the discovery of the integral calculus, made towards the end of his stay in Paris. This was preceded by studies on rectifying the curve and squaring the circle, and publication came only later, in a famous article that appeared in *Acta Eruditorium* in 1684, entitled "Nova Methodus pro maximis et minimis." Leibniz later applied his method countless times to solve previously unsolved problems, and it became one of the cornerstones of mathematical science. By another route and a different formulation, Newton had arrived at the same result. But what particularly marks Leibniz's formulation is the discovery of the algorithm of integral calculus — that is, of the sign indicating a sum of infinitesimals, which allows the quick and easy application of the calculus itself. It is for this reason that the integral calculus in Leibniz's formulation is applied today, rather than in Newton's.

Problems of mathematical language interested Leibniz no less than those of logical language. Along with his project of the universal characteristic, Leibniz left behind numerous outlines for a *geometric characteristic*. With his analytic geometry, Descartes had introduced a new method of calculating geometric problems algebraically. Leibniz thought he discerned in geometry a system of spatial relations calculable by its own methods and not reducible to others. He tried to formulate the rules of this calculus and assign symbols that would make it possible to formulate relationships and operations in a universalist manner.

The system of these symbols and relationships constituted what he called the geometric characteristic, or *calculus situs*. It is a system plainly based on principles similar to those that use signs and operations to collect and represent in synthesis all the processes of logical reasoning. For Leibniz, mathematics was the science whose rules eminently represented the principles of thinking in general. All sciences, whether physical and experimental, or those of thinking and of mathematics proper, can be reduced to very simple rules, to common principles — that is, to a limited number of fundamental characters and the method of their combination. The presentation of these fundamentals of mathematical procedure, and thus of every rational procedure, can be found in various Leibnizian manuscripts concerning the *Mathesis universalis*, the *Initia mathematica*, etc.

In addition to mathematics, Leibniz also viewed physics from an original perspective. His correction of the Cartisian law concerning the conservation of the quantity of motion, first formulated in an article appearing in the *Acta Eruditorum* in 1686, was especially important for the philosophical consequences deriving from it. The concept of substance as force, closely related to this law, is formulated in the 1694 essay *De prima philosophiae emendatione et de notione substantiae*. While traveling in Italy he wrote a wide-ranging book on physics which he decided not to publish but whose manuscript is entitled *Dynamica, de potentia et legibus naturae corporeae*.

Philosophy — Regarding Leibniz's philosophy [...] we shall only note that it is here that all the threads of his scientific activity and aspects of his personality converge. The universalist ideas, the projects for general and characteristic science, the theological principles that matured in the disputes over religious reconciliation, the mathematical concepts of the differential and the integral and of continuity, the physical concept of force — all these in their various aspects and determinations contribute to forming the Leibnizian system, which unfolded progressively, one might say, as his ideas on these various subjects became fixed. Scholastic, Cartesian, Hobbesian, Spinozian and occasionalist influences are recognizable, but all converge around a central idea that is not reducible to any of them, and indeed diverges from them.

The year 1686 may be taken as a central point in the history of Leibnizian thought. On the eve of his great journey to Italy he arrived at an overall vision that unified all the basic concepts that he had been formulating. It was in that year that he wrote the work now known under the name *Discours de Métaphysique*, a brief essay tracing the basic outline of the system and setting out the essential principles of his philosophy. This paper is perhaps the key document for understanding Leibniz's thinking, in which the system appears, one might say, in the rush of its creation — in its most genuine and authentic form. Leibniz did not publish it, and it remained unknown until the middle of the last century. Even today it is little known in comparison with his other works. Leibniz had sent a summary of it to Arnauld, the celebrated Jansenist theologian, which gave rise to a rich correspondence that was fundamental in establishing the concepts of substance, predetermination, force, etc.

From then on Leibniz's studies were entirely given over to an exploration of the concepts set out in the *Discours,* and in using them to solve new problems and comparing them with other theories. And here again his instruments were epistolary and polemical. Overall views and authentic presentations are rarely offered. An example would be the "Système nouveau de la nature et de la communication des substances aussi bien que de l'union qu'il y a entre l'âme et le corps," which appeared in the *Journal des Savants* in 1695 and presented the system of pre-established harmony. This gave rise to an interesting dispute with Bayle, who had criticized this hypothesis in the article "Rorarius," in his *Historical and Critical Dictionary of Philosophy*. Others were the *Principes de la nature et de la grace fondée en raison* (1714), or the *Monadology* (1714), neither published by Leibniz. But every one of the concepts expressed in these short and significant essays shows itself in its true light only when complemented by all the clarifications, further developments and qualifications contained in the other countless writings, fragments and letters. Gerhardt's edition collected a good number of writings arguing against Cartesianism, and Couturat (in addition to Gerhardt) published numerous fragments on the Characteristic, general science, etc. The correspondence with De Volder and Hartsoeker are fundamental for the relations between Leibnizian physics and his philosophy, and the one with the Jesuit De Bosses for metaphysical concepts in general and for the interesting problem of the *vinculum substatiale*. The dispute with Clarke covers pre-established harmony and various theological concepts, and the letters to Lady Masham, electress Sophia, and Queen Sophia Charlotte offer an overall presentation of his system.

Leibniz wrote only two books on philosophical subjects, and only published one of them. His *New Essays on Human Understanding* is a collection of observations, notes, and criticism concerning Locke's essay of 1690. Leibniz, upon whom Locke's book had made a great impression, had begun expressing his position in letters, articles, and conversations, promoted especially by Queen Sophia Charlotte, on the ideas expressed in it, mainly defending innatism against the book's attacks. These observations were gradually expanded, giving him the opportunity to expound his ideas on the problem of knowledge; and out of this Leibniz's book took shape. It clearly retains the imprint of its origins and, rather than a systematic work, appears as an enormous review of Locke's essay. It takes the form of a dialogue in which one of the speakers expounds Locke's theses, and the other Leibniz's objections. The arrangement of the chapters is the same as Locke's. Finished in 1705, the book remained unpublished, however, until the Raspe edition appeared, fifty years after Leibniz's death.

His *Theodicea* also had a fortuitous origin, developing out of the theological discussions and conversations Leibniz held with Queen Sophia Charlotte and taking its cue from the ideas set forth by Bayle in his *Critical Dictionary*. The collection of the notes he was writing at the time gave rise to the book, which came out in 1710 in Amsterdam and was a great success. Again, it is not a systematic work, but rather a set of observations *on the goodness of God, the freedom of man, and the origin of evil* (as the subtitle says), as deduced from the author's principles. The system remains in the background as the premise necessary for such consequences — it is not neatly laid out. This feature of the work was recognized by Leibniz himself, who assigned to it a popular and popularizing function, and always planned to produce a systematic version. "When I have managed to get my historical works off my back," he wrote to a friend, "I would like to focus on setting out the elements of general philosophy and natural theology, including what is most important in that philosophy with regard to theory and practice." But the moment never arrived, and we have to try to reconstruct Leibniz's system ourselves, out of the countless fragments.

Nor can the *Monadology* be recognized as a systematic work. It was written in 1714 for Eugene of Savoy, who had asked the philosopher for a summary of his system. The prince preserved it religiously, treasuring it and showing it only to his most intimate friends. It was first published in Latin translation in the *Acta Eruditorum* of 1721, under the title of *Principia philosofiae seu theses in gratiam principis Eugenii conscriptae*. The title of Monadology was given it by Erdmann, who published it in its original French in his 1840 edition of Leibniz's works. The *Monadology* is a collection of the various doctrines and main points that Leibniz had formulated conclusively. It is a panorama, in short, rather than a systematic construction — usefully gathering everything for those who already know Leibniz's thought, but all but incomprehensible to anyone facing it without previous knowledge.

The last years — It has been noted that the favor of the princesses was of utmost importance to Leibniz's position at court. Electress Sophia, joint progenitor of two monarchs, mother not only of the first king of England from the Hanover dynasty that still occupies the throne today, but of the first queen of Prussia as well, had been his great protector at Hanover, especially after Ernest Augustus died in 1698 and his son George Ludwig became elector, a time when relations with Leibniz had grown increasingly sour. And Sophia's daughter, Queen Sophia Charlotte, had been the driving force behind the founding of the Academy in Berlin and was a great admirer of Leibniz's philosophy. As we have seen, it was from conversations with her that the basic concepts in *Theodicea* and the *New Essays* had emerged. The years from 1700 to 1705, spent in Hanover and Berlin, were perhaps the happiest of Leibniz's life. But in 1705 the queen died, and the philosopher's relations with the court immediately began to deteriorate. The Academy itself, of which he was the president, did not spare him bitterness and disappointment. He was distrusted, maligned, and even subjected to open acts of hostility. And at the same time, the many tasks and duties that kept him from pursuing his responsibilities in Hanover with due zeal and attending to his historical work on the House of Braunschwieg increasingly alienated him in George Ludwig's mind. Only the elector's mother Sophia was somewhat able to mitigate her son's displeasure with him. But in 1714 Sophia died, and when Leibniz returned for the last time from Vienna, George Ludwig had already been crowned Great Britain's king, with the name George I.

At that time Leibniz himself held the following positions: librarian and historiographer in Hanover, librarian in Wolfenbüttel, president of the Berlin Academy and secret adviser to the court of Prussia, secret adviser to Peter the Great, court adviser to the Emperor, and member of the Academies of London and Paris. Almost all these positions brought with them lavish stipends. And it is undeniable that these honorifics had not come to him unwanted or unsolicited. He had actively and persistently worked to win them and enjoyed his success. Such desire, which in a man like him may seem strange and unappealing, can to some extent be justified. We have seen that the focus of his interest was the universal organization of the world of knowledge. This accumulation of offices and tasks was for him almost the tangible symbol of this effort — it gave him the concrete sense that he was the center of an endless enterprise that extended outward in all directions.

But to others this in itself might have looked like vanity, ambition, and greed for money. And in fact the elector himself was inclined to such a view, seeing in Leibniz's frequent, often unlicensed travels and endless occupations only a way of distracting himself from his more specific duties as courtier and historiographer.

His last two years were the unhappiest of his life. By order of the King, he was shackled to his historical work. He was forbidden to leave Hanover and subjected to bitter humiliation. Even his own secretary Eckhardt was disloyal to him, casting him in a bad light with the sovereign. He died, completely forgotten, on 14 November 1716 of an attack of gout. It is not known precisely where his bones are buried. The academies of Berlin and London ignored his death. Only at the Academy of Sciences in Paris was he commemorated, by Fontenelle.

Conclusion — Leibniz was thus not a philosopher by profession. His activities at the courts of Mainz and Hanover involved a wide variety of fields — cultural, political, technical, and organizational. These alone fell properly within his duties. He found himself acting as a philosopher at court only with the intellectual Princesses, who made use of him as a brilliant conversationalist and correspondent, helping them satisfy their craving to further know and explore their own culture. And even in the scholarly activity he carried out in his own name, through his immense correspondence with all the scholars of his time and his relations with scientific societies and journals, it was mathematical and physical, theological and generically cultural problems, projects for the unification of the various sciences, for universal languages and the founding of scientific societies and academies, that were often the essential objects of his studies and the primary focus of his activity.

Leibniz was essentially a man who was curious about all problems and interested in all arguments. Whatever question arose or came under his eye, he attempted to solve it, and most of the time he succeeded brilliantly. Whatever environment he found himself in, he tried to adapt to it quickly. He acquired the tools and techniques of virtually every science with astonishing rapidity, and in this he was often guided by chance or circumstance. He arrived in Paris with little or no knowledge of mathematics, but the environment and the knowledge he gained there led him to study it, and after four years he arrived at the discovery of infinitesimal calculus. It was in this way that his and his masters' ambition to prepare a reconciliation between the Catholic and Protestant churches prompted him to deal with theological problems that would also be of great importance for his philosophy.

If we wanted to define what he regarded as the main purpose of his intellectual life and his specific cultural mission, we would probably have to turn to the attempts at unification, conciliation, and harmony among the sciences that pervaded his entire life from his earliest to his final years. His highest ambition was to give mankind a simple and comprehensive means of embracing all aspects of life and solving all its problems. Even as he penetrated every science with great insight into what was peculiar and irreducible in it, and knew how to grasp the specific character of every method, he nevertheless set as the ideal of his life a general method that would apply to every discipline — a way of thinking that makes him almost a link between Renaissance universalism and the rationalism of the Enlightenment.

One might say that he was led to philosophy by all his intellectual interests. He needed it as a logical basis for his projects for a universal language (and we shall see that his conception of the relationship between subject and predicate was to have crucial importance for the doctrine of the monad). In addition, philosophy supplied a foundation for solving theological problems and provided further development and confirmation of the laws he discovered. And at the same time, even apart from these applications, philosophy as an end in itself was one of his main interests. Taking a position regarding the problems posed by Cartesianism, which then represented the last word in philosophical speculation, discussing the Gassendian atomistic and mechanistic hypothesis, or Malebranche's occasionalism, or Locke's epistemological empiricism — these were all arguments seemingly designed to attract his interest.

His stimulus in dealing with these problems was, as we have seen, almost always the occasion itself. Leibniz expresses his opinion on the particular topic the discussion is focused on — he never starts out with the explicit intention of building a system. His philosophical work comes across first and foremost as a vast collection of specific positions he has taken. Yet the system is not absent from these positions; on the contrary it is always present. Individual problems are gradually shown to be connected to each other and interdependent solutions converge, justify, and confirm one another. We realize that what initially seemed to be a technical question in a specific field, one that ought to be answered within that field, instead derives from and leads to principles that are much more general and are linked to other problems and solutions apparently quite distant. In a word, it is part of a system.

It can be assumed that Leibniz himself became aware of this intimate concordance between the various aspects of his work only during his journey, or that he came to it with difficulty only in the time of his maturity. Everywhere we have echoes of one problem in another, applications of principles found in other fields, coincidences, and unexpected confirmations. The system is not merely external, a supervening arrangement — rather, it is the soul of every observation, through which everything is explained and justified. And the system is also the most interesting, instructive, and 'new' side of Leibniz's philosophy. Its various particular principles give us ingenious observations, keen reflections and useful hints for further development, but only the system, seen as a whole, gives us the true greatness of his thought. He offers a new and original worldview, a particular attitude to things and problems that casts them in a new light. And this attitude flows solely from the whole and shows itself in its completeness through the totality of all its interdependent aspects. Leibniz differs in this from other thinkers who are apparently more coherent and organized, but whose richness must be sought beyond the system, in their various particular formulations.

Grasping this whole is the most difficult thing about Leibnizian thought — and the essential reason why it is worth studying. The system is always implicit and almost never explicit. To bring it out in a constructive and organic way, as an edifice harmonious in all its parts, built according to a plan and unfolding in accordance with a single idea, is almost impossible. We can perceive centers around which it gathers — points of view that present the whole in a particular light. In Leibniz's case, this may be a more worthwhile way to proceed. And it is, after all, a typically Leibnizian way. One such center or point of view from which a view of the whole can be reached, indeed perhaps the most important, is the problem of the monad.

Publications — A complete edition of Leibniz's writings does not yet exist. The very fact that he did not compose a systematic treatment makes a faithful reconstruction of his thought possible only through a complete examination of everything he left in writing, including his countless personal notes, fragments, letters, etc., for the most part preserved in the Hanover library.

The Prussian Academy of Sciences has set about publishing Leibniz's writings in full, but only five of the projected 40-volumes of this monumental edition have thus far been published. These include the general, political and historical epistolary up to 1860 (series I, vols. 1, 2);

the philosophical epistolary up to 1685 (Series II, vol. 1); the political writings up to 1685 (Series IV, vol. 1) and part of the philosophical writings up to 1672 (Series VI, vol. 1). The other series will cover the letters and the mathematical, naturalistic, and technical writings (Series III for the letters, VIII for the writings) as well as the historical writings (Series V). The title of the work is:

> G.W. LEIBNIZ, *Sämtliche Schriften und Briefe* hrsg. von der Preussischen Akademie der Wissenschaften. Darmstadt, 1923 ff.

Clearly, this edition has been useful up to now only for some points of Leibnizian thought. The researcher is therefore obliged to resort to the partial collections, integrating them with each other, to the various papers published in journals and academic proceedings or as appendices to monographs, and if necessary to manuscripts. Rather than providing a history or list of the various editions, which can easily be found in the major books on Leibniz's thought, we prefer to indicate in summary form which works those who wish to embark on an in-depth study of his philosophy should turn to.

First and foremost, the Gerhardt edition should be relied upon as a base:

> *Die philosophischen Schriften* von G. W. LEIBNIZ; hrsg. v. C. J. Gerhardt, Berlin, 1875, in seven volumes, three made up of letters.

This is the most complete collection of the philosophical writings. It should be supplemented with the mathematical works, also edited by Gerhardt:

> LEIBNIZENS *mathematische Schriften* hrsg. v. C. J. Gerhardt, Berlin and Halle, 1848-1863, also in seven volumes, four of which are letters, to which a volume

was later added containing the epistolary with Wolff (Halle, 1860), and *Der Breifwechsel von* G. W. LEIBNIZ *mit Mathematikern* hrsg. v. Gerhardt, Berlin, 1899.

These mathematical works also include very important writings of a philosophical character. Also worth consulting, because it contains writings not included in the Gerhardt edition, is:

G. W. LEIBNIZ, *Opera philosophica quae exstant, latina, gallica, germanica, omnia,* ed. J. E. Erdmann, Berlin, 1839-40.

In addition, it is useful to keep in mind the main collections of Leibniz's writings that also include non-philosophical arguments, especially:

G. G. LEIBNITII, *Opera omnia,* nunc primum collecta, in classes distributa etc., studio of Ludovici Dutens, Geneva, 1768. This is the first major overall edition, in 6 volumes.

The writings included are theological, logical, metaphysical, physical, mathematical, philosophical, philological, and concerning China. It includes various texts not contained in the later special editions.

For political writings, the fundamental text is:

Die Werke von LEIBNIZ. Erste Reihe: *Historisch-politische und staatswissenschaftliche Schriften,* hrsg. v. Onno Klopp, Hannover, 1864-84, 11 vols.

Much inferior as an edition, but containing material not included in Klopp, especially about the project for reuniting the Churches is the Foucher de Careil edition:

Oeuvres de LEIBNIZ, publiées pour la première fois

d'après les manuscrits originaux par A. Foucher de Careil, Paris, 1859-75, 7 vols.

These are the main collections. They must, however, be supplemented with a great many unpublished items taken from the Hanover Library and published separately by various scholars. Of these we mention only the most prominent. Indispensable to anyone concerned with philosophy is:

Opuscules et fragments inédite de LEIBNIZ, extraits des manuscrits de la bibliothèque royale de Hannover par Louis Couturat, Paris, 1903.

This is a large collection of fragments mainly concerning the Characteristic, combinations, general science, etc.

Important texts are also to be found in:

LEIBNIZ's *deutsche Schriften*, hrsg. v. G. E. Guhrauer, Berlin, 1838, 1840, 2 vols.,

and in:

Lettres et opuscules inédits de LEIBNIZ par A. Foucher de Careil, Paris, 1854,

and in:

Nouvelles lettres et opuscules inédits par A. Fouché de Careil, Paris, 1857.

Interesting philosophical-legal writings may be found in:

Mitteilungen aus Leibnizens ungedrückten Schriften von Georg Mollat, Leipzig, 1893.

And key philosophical texts, especially concerning the relationship between Leibniz and Spinoza, are published in the almost unobtainable:

> I. JAGODINSKI, *Leibnitiana. Elementa philosophiae arcanae de summa rerum*, Kasan, 1913.

See also:

> JEAN BARUZI, "Trois dialogues mystiques inédits de Leibniz," in *Revue de métaphysique et de morale*, 1905.

The most complete exchange of letters with Arnauld is found in:

> *Der Briefwechesel zischen Leibniz, Arnauld und den Landgrafen Ernst von Hessen-Rheinfels*, hrsg. v. C. L. Grotefend, Hanover, 1846.

For relations with Ernest of Hesse and his position regarding Catholicism and Protestantism, the basic text is:

> *Leibniz und der Landgraf Ernst von Hessen-Rheinfels. Ein ungedrückter Briefwechsel...* hrsg. v. Chr. von Rommel, Frankfurt am Main, 1847, 2 vols.

For the unification of Protestant doctrines, see the very recent:

> G. W. LEIBNIZ. *Lettres et fragments inédits*, publiés par Paul Schrecker, Paris, 1934.

Other unpublished papers can be found in appendices to some of the monographs mentioned below, for example that of STEIN, of KABITZ to the Essays of TRENDELENBURG, and to BARUZI's "Liebniz" (Paris 1909). Other monographs, such as COUTURAT's, and BARUZI's *Leibniz et l'organization religieuse de la terre* are based on unpublished documents that are either cited in the notes or accurately described in the text.

Anyone wanting to work with manuscripts will need to draw on Bodeman's two outstanding catalogs:

Der Briefwechsel des G. W. Leibniz in der K. Bibliothek zu Hannover, beschrieben von Dr. EDUARD BODEMANN, Hanover, 1889. *Die Leibniz-Handschriften der K. Bibliothek zo Hannover,* beschreiben von Dr. EDUARD BODEMANN, Hanover, 1895.

The Commission of the Prussian Academy of Sciences, which is preparing the overall edition and is headed by Prof. Ritter, has compiled a complete catalog of all extant manuscripts, arranged in chronological order. The first two parts of this catalog have been published: up to 1672, and from 1672 to 1676:

P. RITTER, *Kritischer Katalog der Leibniz-Handschriften.* Erstes Heft (1846-1872), Berlin, 1908 (lithographed handouts).

Catalogue critique des manuscrits de Leibniz, fol. II (1872-1876), Poitiers, 1914-1924.

The following works are translated into Italian:

G.G. Leibniz, *Opere varie,* selected and translated by G. De Ruggiero, Bari, 1912.

G.G. Leibniz, *Monadologia ed altri scritti,* translated by G. Seregni, Milano, 1926.

G.G. Leibniz, *Discorso di metafisica,* translation and introduction by M. Giorgiantonio, Napoli, 1934.

There are also several scholastic editions.

Interpretations — For writings on Leibniz we again give only the essential indications. An excellent comprehensive look at the entire literature on Leibniz is:

D. MAHNKE, *Leibnizens Synthese von Universalmathematik und Individualmetaphysik,* Halle, 1925, valuable not only as an annotated bibliography, but for its independent interpretation of Leibnizian thought.

Still the best biography:

G. E. GUHRAUER, *G. W. Freiherr von Leibniz,* 2nd edit., Breslau, 1846.

Excellent as well and more organic than Guhrauer, though less rich in information, is the biographical part of the volume on Leibniz in K. Fischer's great history of modern philosophy:

K. FISCHER, *Geschichte der neueren Philosophie,* vol. III, *Leibniz,* Heidelberg, 1920 (5th ed. with additions by W. Kavitz).

This work also contains a classic exposition of Leibnizian philosophy.

Other presentations are:

L. FEUERBACH, *Darstellung, Entwicklung und Kritik der Leibnizchen Philosophie,* Leipzig, 1837.

ERDMANN, *Leibniz und die Entwicklung des idealismus vor Kant,* Leipzig, 1842.

F. DILLMANN, *Neue Darstellung der leibnischen Monadenlehre,* Berlin, 1891.

NOURRISSON, *La philosophie de Leibniz,* Paris, 1860.

At the beginning of this century, three seminal works breathed new life into Leibnizian studies, each interpreting Leibniz in an original, if one-sided, way. These are:

B. RUSSELL, *A critical exposition of the philosophy of Leibniz,* Cambridge, 1900.

E. CASSIRER, *Leibniz' System in seinen wissenschaftlichen Grundlagen*, Marburg, 1902.

L. COUTURAT, *La logique de Leibniz*, Paris, 1901.

The last of these, based entirely on unpublished texts, reveals the hitherto little-known logistical aspect of Leibniz's thought.

Other authors moving on more solid ground with more faithful, if less original, interpretations are:

W. KABITZ, *Die Philosophie des jungen Leibniz*, Heidelberg, 1909, a very well-documented work on Leibniz's youth, in which the early origins of his thought are clearly shown.

H. HEIMSOETH, *Die Methode der Erkenntniss bei Descartes und Leibniz*, Giessen, 1912-14.

See also:

H. SCHMALENBACH, *Leibniz*, Munich, 1921.

A. HANNEQUIN, in *Études d'histoire des sciences et d'hisoire de la philosophie*, Paris, 1908.

E. BOUTROUX, *La Philosophie en Allemagne au XVII siècle*, Paris, 1929, in addition to the classic commentary on the *Monadology*, cited below.

A useful reference for supplementing one's knowledge of particular aspects of Leibnizian work and thought are the articles on Leibniz in the collection of:

A. TRENDLENBURG, *Historische Beiträge zur Philosophie* vols. II, III, Berlin, 1855, 1857,

along with:

L. STEIN, *Leibniz und Spinoza*, Berlin 1890, not always reliable.

J. BARUZI, *Leibniz et l'organization religieuse de la terre*, Paris, 1907.

L. DAVILLÉ, *Leibniz historien*, Paris, 1909.

M. GUEROULT, *Dynamique et métaphysique leibniziennes*, Paris, 1934.

Italian works include:

G. CARLOTTI, *Il sistema di Leibniz*, Messina, 1923.

G. OLGIATI, *Il significato storico di Leibniz*, Milano, 1929.

G. E. BARIÉ, *La spiritualità dell'essere e Leibniz*, Padua, 1933.

See also the entry on Leibniz in the *Enciclopedia Italiana*, by G. CARLOTTI and, for the mathematical side, G. VACCA.

For the introductory anthology I made use of Gerhardt's editions of the philosophical writings (cited as G.), and mathematical writings (M.), the unpublished papers collected by Couturat (C.), and only rarely the Academy edition (Ak.). For the *New Essays* and *Theodicea,* I have cited paragraphs rather than pages. For the *Discours de métaphysique* I used the excellent Lestienne edition,[1] the only modern one taken directly from the manuscript, and here I have cited paragraphs. For the *Monadology* I used the Boutroux[2] edition, also from the manuscripts. I have noted the translations of Cecchi, DeRuggiero and Seregni.

---

[1] LEIBNIZ: *Discours de metaphysique*, édition collationnée avec la texte autographe... par HENRI LESTIENNE, Paris 1929.
[2] LEIBNIZ: *La Monadologie* publiée d'apres les manuscrits... par ÉMILE BOUTROUX, 13th edit, Paris 1930.

Anthological Exposition of the Leibnizian System

I. Truths of Reason and of Fact

OBJECTIVISM AND HARMONY — In its early stages Leibniz's philosophy has a clear, objectivist character. By this we mean that there is not at the heart of it any question concerning the greater or lesser validity of our knowledge of the external world, nor in general about relations between knower and known. The relativism that comes to the sophist from the observation that "man is the measure of all things" is foreign to Leibniz — he studies the real in itself, in its divine or human essence, in accordance with its rational or empirical laws. He starts from the given fact of the world in all its aspects, which he wants to scrutinize, understand, and reduce to unity, to simple and easily learned formulas. His purpose is to transport to the philosophical and metaphysical field the approach of his great predecessors or contemporaries, Copernicus, Galileo, Newton, in their investigations of the physical world — an attempt, that is, at an overall, harmonious, coherent view of all the facts under study, a search for hypotheses that explain the whole that is as homogeneous and linear as possible. It is to this sort of approach that he turns, rather than that of Descartes, who wants to deduce the world with its laws from a single principle posited initially as the only valid one. And, while there are many connections with Cartesian philosophy to be found in Leibniz's formulation and development of various problems, he nevertheless sets himself off from it fundamentally in his essential conception of the world as a distinct whole, for which a unifying principle must be sought, and not as something initially problematic, whose existence and laws must be demonstrated and deduced. And if this latter attitude is meant to represent the guiding thread of modern epistemology and modern philosophy in general, it must be said that Leibniz departs from this direction, adhering rather in this respect to the lines of Greek thought, assuming an attitude that we might approximate to that of Aristotle.

But wisdom (*sapientia*) consists essentially in the most perfect knowledge of nature, and what apart from philosophy has ever demonstrated more lucidly not only how it exists and operates, but also the special care it has for all things, and the fact that it has not only created things from nothing, but also creates and resuscitates them all the time? For my part I confess that understanding the power of such reasoning has given me great joy, and I congratulate philosophy, which finally looks as though it will make peace with religion; with which it used to be at odds, not through any fault of its own, but as a result of the opinion of men and their rash judgments, or even their ill-considered expressions. So let pious men, inflamed with zeal for divine glory, stop fearing anything from reason; if only they would pay it attention to it, they would find out what is right... And let philosophers, in their turn, stop referring everything to the imagination and to figures, and stop denouncing as trifles and fraud anything that conflicts with those crass and materialistic notions by which some people think the whole of nature is circumscribed.

(*Pacidius Philalethi* Dialogue, 1676 C., 626)

This objective study of nature through its laws, along with his striving for a unified view of the whole, led Leibniz to complex and harmonious vistas, where faith and reason, the divine nexus and the human world, the natural sciences and the metaphysical sciences, are organized in a homogeneous order. Harmony was what he strove for with all his powers as a scientist and thinker. Beginning in his earliest years, the mirage of universal harmony was at the center of his thoughts.

The physicists of our time, seeking the material causes of things, neglect the rational ones. And instead, the wisdom of the Supreme Author shines forth principally in having so constructed the world's clock that everything should derive from it by necessity, for the supreme harmony of the universe. There is thus a need for natural philosophers who not only introduce geometry into the field of physical sciences (since geometry lacks final causes) but also reveal in the natural sciences an organization, so to speak, of civilization. For the world is like a great republic in which minds correspond to free men (citizens or enemies) and other creatures to slaves.

(Letter to Thomasius, 1670, G. I, 32-33)

In this supreme harmony, all the sciences and all the ways of considering the world are reconciled and unified.

Initially solving the labyrinth of continuity and motion, which shrouds all ingenuity in its complications, is an enterprise of great importance in establishing the foundations of the sciences and rebuking the vainglory of the skeptics. So as to give a solid basis to the geometry of indivisibilities and the arithmetic of infinities, the generators of so many important theorems; to work out a physical hypothesis of universal coherence, and finally — and this is the essential thing — to arrive at absolutely geometrical and hitherto unattained proofs of the intimate essence of thought, the eternity of mind,[3] and the first cause. Out of this flow the sources of goodness and fairness and of rights and laws — so clear and limpid, so small in scope and at the same time profound in content that they may count as great volumes and may suffice for the solution of any problem with a conciseness that is astonishing to those who make use of them, and which the vulgar, I believe, do not even know of.[4]

(*Hypothesis physica nova, Theoria motus abstracti*, 1671 pref., G. IV 225)

---

[3] The Latin word *mens* is translated as "mind."
[4] The meaning of the terms used here (continuity, indivisible, infinite, thought, etc.) will be clarified below.

This idea of the convergence of every form of reality and every method of inquiry in the supreme harmony and coherence of nature is a feature of the projects pursued by Leibniz throughout his career — for a systematic organization of the sciences, for an Encyclopedia providing an overall view of all knowledge, concordant and interlinked in all its parts. Such projects hark back to the *Pansofia* Comeniana[5] and to carry them out Leibniz became a promoter of scientific societies and founder of academies.

This harmony, however, as we have seen, does not in any way derive from seeing all the sciences as a product of the human mind and thus subject to its laws. It is instead the expression of a divine objective reality in its own right, with its own concordant and harmonious laws. Science discovers this world unity through the laws of the mind which, by virtue of the harmony itself, correspond to the laws of the world.

TRUTHS OF REASON AND OF FACT — This objective reality can present itself in two guises: as *truths of reason or truths of fact*. These are the two modes of being of the real, each governed by its own laws, each with its own unmistakable characteristics, which then also correspond to the two different ways of apprehending the real — rational and sensory. What follows are two definitions of these two types of truth, taken from two works that are very far apart in date and subject matter:

Truths of reason are necessary, and those of fact are contingent. The primary truths of reason are the ones to which I give the general name *identities*, because they seem to do nothing but repeat the same thing without telling us anything. They are either affirmative or negative. Examples of *affirmatives* are: *What is, is; Each thing*

---

[5] John Amos Comenius (1592-1670), known primarily in the field of pedagogy for his *Didactica Magna*, conceived of knowing as an organization of all the elements of knowledge according to universal laws (*Pansophy*), transforming the concept of an encyclopedia from that of a simple collection of data, to that of a unitary arrangement of the data itself. Leibniz knew and greatly admired his works.

is what it is, and as many others as you want: A is A; B is B; I shall be what I shall be; I have written what I have written...

Conjunctions, disjunctions, and other propositions can likewise be identities. Furthermore, I take affirmatives to include even Non-A is non-A. Also, these hypotheticals: If A is non-B it follows that A is non-B; If non-A is BC it follows that non-A is BC...

I now turn to *negative* identities, which derive from either the *principle of contradiction*[6] from *'disparities.'* Stated generally, the principle of contradiction is: *a proposition is either true or false.* This contains two assertions: first, that truth and falsity are incompatible in a single proposition, i.e. that *a proposition cannot be both true and false at once*; and second, that the contradictories or negations of the true and the false are not compatible, i.e. that there is nothing intermediate between the true and the false, or better that *it cannot happen that a proposition is neither true nor false.*[7] Now, all of that holds true in application to every proposition one can imagine, such as *What is A cannot be non-A...*

As for *'disparities,'* these are propositions which say that the object of one idea is not the object of another idea; for instance, that *warmth is not the same thing as color,* or that *man and animal are not the same* although every man is an animal. All this can be established independently of any proof — i.e., without *reductio ad absurdum* or to the principle of contradiction — when the ideas are sufficiently obvious not to need analysis. But when this is not the case one is liable to error: someone who said that the *triangle and the trilateral are not the same* would be wrong, since if we consider it carefully, we find

---

[6] Leibniz, like many others, refers to as the 'principle of contradiction' what ought more precisely to be called the 'principle of non-contradiction.'

[7] This is the principle usually called the 'excluded middle.'

that three sides and three angles always go together. And if he said that the *quadrilateral rectangle* and the rectangle are not the same, he would be wrong again, since it turns out that only a four-sided figure can have all its angles right angles. However, one can still say in the abstract that *triangularity is not trilaterality,* or that *the formal causes*[8] of the triangle and of the trilateral are not the same, as the philosophers put it. They are different aspects of one and the same thing.

Anyone who has been listening patiently so far to what I have just been saying will eventually lose patience and say that I am wasting time on frivolities and that all identical truths are useless. But such a judgment would come from not having sufficiently considered these matters. The inferences of logic, for example, are demonstrated by means of identities, and geometers need the principle of contradiction for their demonstrations by reductio ad absurdum. At this point let me merely show how identities can be used in demonstrations of the development of reasoning.

This is followed by the development of these theses and other observations on the application of the principle of contradiction to logical procedures.

This shows that the purest identities, which appear entirely useless, are really of considerable use in abstract and general matters; and can teach us that no truth should be scorned....

As for *primary truths of fact*, these are immediate inner experiences, with an immediacy of feeling.

(*New Essays*, 1701, IV, 2, § 1)

---

[8] The term is Scholastic-Aristotelian, as indeed are all the logical concepts discussed in this passage.

It must be noted that the entire art of combinations[9] is addressed to theorems or propositions of eternal truth, which have validity not because of God's will, but by their own nature. As for singular and so-called *historical* propositions such as "Augustus was emperor of the Romans," or *observations* — propositions that are certainly universal, but whose truth is based not on essence but on existence, and which are true almost by accident, i.e., by the will of God, such as, for example, "all adult men in Europe have cognizance of God" — such propositions are not demonstrated, but induced, except where it is possible to deduce an observation from another observation through a theorem. Such observations include all particular propositions that are not converted from or subordinate to one that is universal.[10] It is clear from this what it means to say that one does not provide a demonstration of a singular proposition, and why the extremely profound Aristotle situated in the *Topics* the places of other arguments whose propositions are contingent and reasons probable, while the place for demonstrations is only one — in the definition.[11] But when what is to be said of a thing is not deduced from its own viscera, e.g. that Christ was born in Bethlehem, no one will be able to arrive at such propositions through definitions. The material will be provided by history, and the texts will aid the memory.

(*Ars Combinatoria*, 1666, G. IV, 69-70)

Truths of reason are thus based on pure logical principles, and those of fact are instead based on experience. The former

---

[9] The art of combinations, which this passage refers to, will be considered later.
[10] The particular propositions of syllogisms, for example, which always have an analytical character, would be the inverse or subordinate of a universal.
[11] In the books of the *Topics* Aristotle deals with the 'places' (τόποι) or aspects under which each thing can be considered. He also considers the criteria of probability and induction, while demonstration and syllogism are discussed in the two *Analytics*.

concern *essence*, what is *necessary*, and the latter *existence*, what is *contingent*.

Truths of reason are *analytic*. They merely develop what is already contained in the viscera of each concept — that is, they add nothing to our knowledge of things. They form the basis of *deductive* reasoning. The sciences that derive from them are the logical and mathematical sciences; the principles on which they are based are those of non-contradiction, of the excluded middle, all of which are then reduced to the principle of *identity*.

Factual truths are *empirical*. In propositions derived from them the predicate is not, as in propositions of reason, already contained in the subject. It is added to it as something new which augments and enriches it but does not necessarily belong to it as part of its own essence. Its presence must instead be concretely ascertained, experienced case by case. *Induction* applies to them, as do the natural sciences, historical sciences, and any investigation that starts from concrete and contingent data. They stand, these truths, on the principle of *causality* or *sufficient reason* (Cf. p. 122 ff.).

TRUTHS OF REASON AS POSSIBILITIES. — Truths of reason therefore have the advantage over those of fact in that they are absolutely certain and necessary, and that the contrary is impossible. They form an unshakable foundation on which all reality rests, an absolute and infallible point of reference. On the other hand, however, they have a static nature that does not permit them any development or variation — they remain immobile in their fixity. Factual truths, on the other hand, are indeed accidental, contingent; they do not depend on any a priori law. But precisely this character of not being deducible from already known principles, and thus of never being demonstrable, but only perceivable via the senses, makes them the carriers of what is new, unforeseen, and changeable. It positions them as the expression of the reality of the world in its concrete unfolding. One might say that truths of reason constitute the necessary order of relationships, the relations within which all things occur — the frame and form, almost, of reality — while truths of fact make up the content, reality itself in all its particulars. And indeed, truths of reason are conceived by Leibniz rather as *relations* than as *things*. He expresses this by saying that truths of reason, being necessary, give us only the *possibility* of things, which does not yet imply their actual reality at all.

In fact, if everything possible, and everything imaginable (even if absolutely reprehensible) were to happen someday — if every fable or fiction became or should become actual history — then there would be nothing other than necessity and there would be neither choice nor providence.

(Polemic published in the *Journal des Savants*, 1697, G. IV, 341)

This world of possibilities given to us by the truths of reason, which can assume an infinity of aspects and shape itself in endless guises representing all the forms in which reality could possibly manifest itself — actually manifests itself in only one of them. What we see and experience is factual reality, which unfolds and manifests itself within the framework provided by the principles of reason (in fact, no concrete fact could ever deviate from the principle of non-contradiction). Such principles, however, could frame countless other forms of reality besides that of this concrete, actually existing world. This is the principle of the *infinity of possible worlds* — the infinity of possibilities, that is, that are contained in the truth of reason, necessary logical patterns within which any and all reality plays out.

When I say that there is an infinity of possible worlds, I mean that they do not entail contradiction, just as one can create novels that will never take place and yet are possible. For something to be possible it is enough for it to be intelligible.

(Letter to Bourguet, 1712, G. III, 558)

Thus, the difference between a *true* and a *false idea* also becomes clear. An idea is true when the concept is possible; it is false when it implies a contradiction. Now we know the *possibility* of a thing either a priori or a posteriori. We know it a priori when we resolve the concept into its necessary elements or into other concepts whose possibility is known, and we know that there is nothing incompatible in them... We know an idea a posteriori when we experience the actual existence of the thing, for what actually exists or has existed is in any case possible.[12] Whenever our knowledge is adequate, we have a priori knowledge of a possibility, for if we have carried out the analysis to the end and no contradiction has appeared, the concept is obviously possible.

(*Meditationes de Cognitione, Veritate et Ideis*, 1684, G. IV, 425)

The truths of reason and fact also correspond to the two modes of knowledge, *rational* and *sensory*. But such truths belong first and foremost to the objective order of reality. This is the sense of Leibniz's opposition to the clear and distinct ideas posited by Descartes as the criterion for truths of reason. For him this criterion does not consist of any sort of cognitive evidence, but of possibility and non-contradiction.

He [Descartes] posited our own clear and distinct perception as the criterion of truth. That is, the truth of the fact that the circle is the figure of maximum area with a given perimeter would not in his view be otherwise recognizable except through our clear and distinct perception of this property of it. And if God had shaped our nature in such a way that we had a clear and distinct perception of the opposite, then the opposite would be true. This is his

---

[12] This means that what exists must fall within the laws of possibility, but that these laws can also go far outside the realm of what currently exists.

opinion, which I do not endorse, period. And his universal metaphysical principle is absolutely not true in stating that there is necessarily the idea in us of all things we think or reason about, for example a thousand-sided polygon or the supremely perfect entity. Armed with this principle as if armed with Achilles's shield, he scorned not without arrogance anyone who doubted his demonstrations of the existence of God. With such an argument, he could certainly have easily put into us the idea of impossible things as well — for example, of supremely fast motion. And among these impossible things, those who oppose his demonstrations will also put the supremely perfect entity. I know, for my part, that the supremely perfect entity is something else, and so is supremely fast movement. I believe, in any case, that Descartes's reasoning is imperfect, and that those who wish to bring it to fruition must add much of their own to it.

(Fragment from 1677,[13] G. IV, 274-5)

GOD AND TRUTHS OF REASON AND FACT — In these statements, Leibniz submits clear and distinct ideas to an objective criterion of logical possibility, or 'non-contradiction.' And to this same criterion he also submits the concept of the supremely perfect entity, the basis of the Cartesian ontological proof of the existence of God.[14] The idea of a supremely perfect entity, he says, could be contradictory, like that of a maximum speed or a highest number (which are contradictory ideas because it will always be possible to conceive of a speed or number greater than any other speed or number chosen at will, so that the maximum can never be reached). It is therefore not enough to have the idea of the most perfect entity. It is also necessary

---

[13] This date was kindly communicated to me by Prof. Ritter, director of the Leibnizian Commission of the Academy of Sciences in Berlin.
[14] The ontological proof, which Descartes took from Anselm of Aosta (1033-1109), asserts that the supremely perfect being must contain existence among its perfections. Therefore, it exists. This proof thus regards existence as an attribute of the essence of the supremely perfect being.

to demonstrate the possibility of it — that is, to show that it belongs not only to the world of our representations, but also to the world of the eternal truths of reason.

Leibniz's objections to the ontological proof generally stop at this declaration of incompleteness, and indeed there is no shortage of claims in his work that the supremely perfect entity is actually possible and implies its own existence. Nevertheless, it is already clear to him that truths of reason and truths of fact belong to two different and, as it were, incommensurable spheres, so that it is not possible to bring one of them into the domain of the other.

But in general, it cannot be said that Leibniz worried too much about proving the existence of God. We have already seen that his problem was not so much to demonstrate and deduce the basic concepts of his system as it was to organize them in harmonic units. God was a premise that Leibniz started out from, not a conclusion to be arrived at.

So, what about the relationship between God and truths of reason and fact? Here again Leilbniz's position stands in contrast to that of Descartes. The latter, having deduced the existence of God a priori, then has the whole world of truths, whether of reason or fact, descend from God by a free act of his will.[15] Leibniz vehemently opposed this dependence of truths of reason on divine will. For him, these truths represent the absolute regulatory relations of the universe — such that even the decrees of the will of God are encompassed within them. We have seen that truths of reason are valid "not because of God's will, but by their own nature" and this opinion runs through

---

[15] See, for example, *Metaphysical Meditations,* Answers to the Sixth Objection, no. 6: "...I say that it is impossible that such an idea [of what is good or true] preceded the determination of God's will ... so that this idea of good led God to choose one thing over the other. For example, it is not because He saw that it was better for the world to be created in time rather than from eternity that he wanted to create it in time; and it was not because he saw that it could not be otherwise that he wanted the three angles of a triangle to be equal to two right angles, etc. Quite the contrary — because of the fact that he wanted to create the world in time, it is better that way than if it had been created in eternity; and precisely because he wanted the three angles of a triangle to be necessarily equal to two right angles, this is now true and cannot be otherwise, and so it is with all other things."

the whole of Leibniz, from his earliest youth.

It is necessary for everything to be grounded in some reason, nor should we stop until we come to the first one.. And what then is the ultimate reason behind the divine will? The divine intellect. What is the reason behind the divine intellect? The harmony of things. What is behind the harmony of things? Nothing. For example, no reason can be given for the proposition $2 : 4 = 4 : 8$, not even through the divine will itself. It is a truth that depends on the very essence or idea of things.

(Fragment from *De resurrectione corpum*, 1671, Ak. II, I, 117)

In short, the divine intellect is determined by the truths of reason, and the divine will cannot act except within the framework they set out. The divine will, then, is expressed in *factual truths*. They and they alone are created by God by a free act of his will.

God is the first reason of things: since things that are bounded — all that that we see and experience — are contingent and have nothing in them to render their existence necessary, it being plain that time, space, and matter, united and uniform in themselves and indifferent to everything, might have received entirely different motions and shapes, and in another order. Therefore, one must seek the *reason for the existence of the world*, which is the whole assemblage of *contingent* things, and seek it in the *substance which carries with it the reason for its existence*,[16] and which in consequence is necessary and

---

[16] That substance is God. Cf. the first definition in Spinoza's *Ethics*: "*Per causam sui intelligo id, cujus essentia involvit existentiam; sive id, cujus natura non potest concipi, nisi existens.*" [By that which is self-caused, I mean that of which the essence involves existence, or that of which the nature is only conceivable as existent]

eternal. Moreover, this cause must be intelligent: because since this existing world is contingent and an infinity of other worlds are equally possible and hold, so to speak, an equal claim to existence with it, the cause of the world must have had regard or reference to all these possible worlds in order to fix upon one of them. This regard or relation of an existing substance to simple possibilities can be nothing other than the *intellect* which has the ideas of them, while to fix upon one of them can be nothing other than the act of the *will* which chooses. It is the *power* of this substance that renders its will efficacious. Power relates to *being*, wisdom or intellect to *truth*, and will to *good*. And this intelligent cause has to be infinite in all ways, and absolutely perfect in *power, wisdom,* and *goodness*, since it relates to everything that is possible. Furthermore, since everything is connected, there is no ground for admitting more than one. Its understanding is the source of *essences*, and its will is the origin of *existences*. There in few words is the proof of one only God with his perfections, and through him of the origin of things.

(*Teodicea*, 1710, §7)

Truths of reason are thus the content of God's intellect, and truths of fact the product of his will. Among the infinite possibilities that could be realized within the framework of the principle of non-contradiction, God chooses one and puts it into action. Here again, Leibniz opposes Descartes, who believes that matter takes on all possible forms. He cites, in rebuttal, this passage from the *Principles of Philosophy* (Part III, Art. 47): "For due to these laws, matter takes on, successively, all the forms of which it is capable. Therefore, if we considered these forms in order, we could eventually arrive at that one which is our present world, so that in this respect no false hypothesis can lead us into error."[17] Leibniz responds:

---

[17] Descartes is bound to the notion that all possible worlds actually exist by his commitment to inferring the world solely from clear and distinct ideas or from

I do not believe that a more dangerous proposition than this could be formulated. For if matter successively takes on all possible forms, it follows that nothing can be imagined that is so absurd, so bizarre, so contrary to what we call justice, that it would not have happened and will not some day happen... In my opinion, this is the πρῶτον ψεῦδος (first falsehood) and the basis of atheistic philosophy, though it always seems to say the most beautiful things about God. The true philosophy, on the contrary, must give us an entirely different concept of God's perfection, one that will be of use in both physics and ethics.

(Letter to Philippi, 1680, G. IV, 283-4)

THE PRINCIPLE OF SUFFICIENT REASON — The contingent reality put in place by God is the tangible world we experience. To justify it the immutable laws of logic are not sufficient. The world — factual reality — exists, but it could also not exist, or be different than it is. It does not derive from any absolute truth. The logical principle that will have to be applied to account for it is not the principle of non-contradiction, but that of *sufficient reason* — that is, that principle by which from a given fact one goes back to its cause and from it, in turn, back to its cause, and so on back to the first cause, which is God.

The universal principle *nihil esse sine ratione*[18] resolves almost all metaphysical arguments. Nothing happens which, once having been produced rather than not

---

reason. Leibniz, with his principle of a clear separation between possibility and existence, is able to avoid this passage through all forms of possibility and solves the problem of the origin of the tangible world by direct recourse to the principle of factual truths.

[18] This is the principle of sufficient reason, which Leibniz sometimes also calls the 'principle of reason,' not to be confused with truths of reason. The *principle of reason* is the general rule governing factual truths. *Truths of reason*, on the other hand, are opposed to the latter, and are based on the principle of non-contradiction. The similarity of two terms with such different and almost opposite meanings is due to a different use of the term 'reason.' In the phrase 'principle of reason' it is equivalent to 'motive or cause.'

produced (*cur factum sit potius quam non sit*), that God, if he wants, cannot account for.

(Fragment of *Scientia Media*, 1677, C. 25)

Now we must rise to *metaphysics* and make use of the great, but not commonly used, principle that *nothing takes place without a sufficient reason*; in other words, that nothing occurs for which it would be impossible for someone who has enough knowledge of things to give a reason that would adequately determine *why the thing is as it is* and not otherwise. This principle having been stated, the first question which we have a right to ask with: *Why is there something rather than nothing?* For nothing is simpler and easier than something. Further, assuming that things must exist, it must be possible to give a reason *why they should exist as they do* and not otherwise.

Now this sufficient reason for the existence of the universe cannot be found in the series of contingent things, that is to say, of bodies and their representations in souls. For since matter is in itself indifferent to motion or rest, and to one motion rather than to another, one cannot find in it a reason for motion and still less for some particular motion. Although the present motion in matter arises from preceding motion, and that in turn from motion which preceded it, we do not get any further however far we may go, for the same question always remains. The sufficient reason, therefore, which needs no further reason, must be outside this series of contingent things and is found in a substance which is the cause of this series, or which is a necessary being bearing the reason for its existence within itself — otherwise we would never have a sufficient reason, where the process stops. This final reason for things is called God.

(*Principes de la nature et de la grace*, 1713-14, G. IV, 602)

FINAL CAUSE AND THE "BEST" — God is thus the cause or sufficient reason of all factual truths — that is, of the perceptible world. But in his creation, what criterion did he use in choosing, from the infinite possibilities offered to him, just this one and not some other? What guided him in his choice?

Nothing happens without a sufficient reason for it, or rather without a determining reason. In accordance with this principle, which takes us beyond our predecessors, God never changes his will and operation without having some valid grounds for doing so. And when the thing in question is of a uniform and simple nature, we are in a position (poor creatures that we are) to judge if there can be a reason or not. When God's will is employed by itself, without there being in the natures of creatures the reason for this will or the way in which it works, then it is a miracle pure and simple, inappropriate in philosophy, as if God willed (for example) that the planets move in curved lines without being pushed by any other bodies.... Every time we know something of God's works, we find order in them.

(Letter to Hartsoeker, 1711, G III, p. 529)

The principle of sufficient reason, then, just as it applies to tracing causes from existing data back to God, must also be applied to God himself, who, in creating this world, did not act arbitrarily, but was guided by a criterion for his action. Not even he acted without a reason for his action — and this reason, which determines his will, is the criterion of the highest good, of the highest perfection.

God was inspired by this principle in creating the world, and this criterion must therefore be appealed to as the ultimate reason for all creation. Goodness and perfection as the reason for the existence of things is called the *final cause*.

For my part, I hold that far from excluding final causes

from physics, as M. Descartes tries to do in Part I, Article 28 of *Principles of Philosophy*, it is rather by means of them that everything must be determined, since the efficient cause of things is intelligent, having a will and therefore striving for the good.

(Letter to Philippi, 1680, G. IV, 284)

Thus, God puts in place only one of the infinite possible worlds, but he is governed by a criterion in this creation. This criterion ensures that the world he chooses is *the best of all possible worlds*.

This supreme wisdom, united to a goodness that is no less infinite, could not help but choose the best. For just as a lesser evil is in a certain sense good, a lesser good is a kind of evil if it stands in the way of a greater good — and there would be something to correct in the actions of God if it were possible to do better. As in mathematics, when there is no maximum nor minimum and in short nothing distinguished, everything is done equally, or when that is not possible nothing at all is done, the same may be said regarding perfect wisdom, which is no less orderly than mathematics — that if there were no best (*optimum*) among all possible worlds, God would not have produced it. I call 'World' the whole succession and the whole agglomeration of all existing things, lest it be said that several worlds could have existed in different times and different places. For they must be reckoned all together as one world or, if you prefer, as one *universe*. And even though all times and places are filled, it still remains true that they might have been filled in innumerable ways, and that there is an infinity of possible worlds among which God must have chosen the best, since he does nothing without acting in accordance with supreme reason.

(*Theodicea*, 1710, § 8)

God thus does not choose arbitrarily. Again, he is inspired by a principle — the principle of the best — that regulates his actions in setting in motion the reality of the world. What does this principle consist of? What is the 'best,' this final cause of factual truths? A criterion of maximum fulfillment, maximum perfection, maximum happiness, goodness, etc. — harmony, in short, which seeks to ensure that within the limits of possibility the fullest possible existence is realized.

It follows from the supreme perfection of God that he has chosen the best possible plan in producing the universe, a plan which combines the greatest variety together with the greatest order; with situation, place, and time arranged in the best way possible; with the greatest effect produced by the simplest means; with the most power, the most knowledge, the greatest happiness and goodness in created things which the universe could allow. For just as all possible things have a claim to existence in God's understanding in proportion to their perfections, the result of all these claims must be the most perfect actual world which is possible. Without this it would be impossible to give a reason why things have gone as they have rather than otherwise.
(*Principes de la nature et de la grace*, 1713-14, G. VI, 603)

It is my principle that everything that can exist and is compatible with other things, does exist. For the *ratio existendi* above all other possible things should not be limited for any reason except that not all things are reconcilable with each other. The only determining reason is therefore *ut existant potiora, quae plurimum involvant realitatis.*
(Fragment from 1676, C. 530)

There is a reason in nature why something exists rather than nothing. This is a consequence of that great principle that nothing happens without a reason, just as there must be a reason why this exists rather than another.

This reason must be in some real being, or cause. For a *cause* is nothing other than a *realis ratio*, and truths about possibilities and *necessities* (i.e., where the possibility of the opposite is denied) would not produce anything unless the possibilities were founded in an actually existing thing.

Now this being must be necessary, otherwise a cause would in turn have to be sought outside it for why it exists rather than not, which is contrary to the hypothesis. Plainly, this being is the ultimate reason for things, and it is usually referred to by the single word "God."

There is, therefore, a cause on account of which existence prevails over non-existence, in other words, *Ens necessarium est existentificans*.

But the cause which brings it about that something exists, that is that possibility demands existence, also brings it about that every possible has a tendency towards existence, since in general a reason for restricting this to certain possibles cannot be found. So, it can be said that *every possible is existence-seeking*,[19] as it is founded on an actually existing necessary being, without which there is no way a possible may attain actuality. However, it does not follow from this that all possibles exist, but it would if all possibles were compossible.

But because some things are incompatible with others, it follows that certain possibles do not attain existence. Some possibles are incompatible with others not only with respect to the same time, but also universally, because future possibles are enfolded in present ones.

Meanwhile, however, from the conflict of all possibles

---

[19] Our translation of the term *existiturire*.

demanding existence this at least follows, that there exists that series of things through which the greatest number of things comes into existence — that is, the maximal series of all possibles. Further, this series alone is determined, just as of lines is the straight line, of angles the right angle, and of shapes those of maximum capacity, namely the circle or sphere. And just as we see liquids naturally collect in spherical drops, so in the nature of the universe the most capacious series exists.

Therefore, what exists is the most perfect, since perfection is nothing other than quantity of reality.

Further, perfection is not to be located in matter alone, in what fills time and space, that is, whose quantity would have been the same in any event, but in form or variety.

From which it follows that matter is not everywhere alike, but rendered dissimilar by forms, otherwise there would not obtain as much variety as possible...

It also follows that the series that prevailed was the one from which the maximum of distinct cogitability was derived.

Further, distinct cogitability gives order to a thing and beauty to the thinker. For *order* is nothing other than *relatio plurium distinctiva*, and confusion is when many things are present but there is no way of distinguishing one from another.

This rules out atoms, and in general any bodies in which there is no reason for distinguishing one part from another.

And it follows in general that the world is a χόσμος, a harmonic organism, i.e., made in such a way that it fully satisfies an intelligent being.

The *pleasure* of an intelligent being (*voluptas intelligentis*) is nothing other than the perception of beauty, order, and perfection. And every pain contains something disordered, albeit relative to the percipient, since absolutely speaking all things are ordered.

Consequently, when something in the series of things displeases us, this arises from a defect of our understanding. For it is not possible that every mind should understand all things distinctly, and the harmony in the whole cannot appear to those who observe only some parts rather than others.

It is a consequence of this that justice is also observed in the universe, since *justice* is nothing other than order or perfection with respect to minds.

(Fragment, G. VII, 289-90)

NECESSITY AND FREEDOM — This criterion of perfection, goodness and harmony is also, like the truths of reason, absolute, objective, stand-alone, independent of God's will, and imposed by the necessity of things. God chooses the best, but he could not have chosen differently. Here we are in the presence of the famous question of the *reconciliation of necessity and freedom*, which our argument is only marginally concerned with, and which instead falls within the problem of *Theodicea*. Here too, Leibniz opposes Descartes.

Against those who claim that there is no goodness in the works of God; or that the rules of goodness and beauty are arbitrary.

Thus, I am far from holding to the opinion of those who maintain that there are no rules of goodness and perfection in the nature of things or in the ideas which God has of them and who say that the works of God are good only for the formal reason that God has made them. For if this were so, God, who knows that he is the author of things, would have had no reason to regard them afterward and find them good, as is reported in the Holy Scriptures,[20] which seem to have used this anthropological conception only to make us understand that the excellence of God's works may be recognized by considering them in themselves, even without reflecting upon this empty designation which relates them to their cause. This is all the truer, since it is through a consideration of his works that we can discover the craftsman. Thus, his works must carry his mark in themselves. I confess that the contrary opinion seems to me extremely dangerous and to come very near to that of the latest innovators,[21] whose opinion it is that the beauty of the universe and the goodness which we ascribe to the works of God are nothing but the chimeras of men who think of him in terms of themselves. Then, too, when we say that things are not good by any rule of excellence but solely by the will of God, we unknowingly destroy, I think, all the love of God and all his glory. For why praise him for what he has done if he would be equally praiseworthy in doing exactly the opposite? Where will his justice and wisdom be found if nothing is left but a certain despotic power, if will takes the place of reason, and if, according to the definition of tyrants, that which is pleasing to the most powerful is for that very reason just? Besides it seems that every act of will implies some reason for willing and that this reason naturally precedes the act of will itself. This is why I find entirely strange, also, the expression of certain other philosophers[22] who say that the eternal truths of metaphysics and geometry, and consequently also the rules of goodness, justice, and perfection, are

---

[20] Leibniz refers here to the narrative in the first chapter of Genesis, in which each act of creation is followed by the phrase: "And God saw that this was good."
[21] He is referring to the Spinozists (cf. the cited edition of LESTIENNE). Leibniz's opinion of the doctrines of Spinoza is in many ways in error and distorted by preconceptions.
[22] Descartes (cf. *ibid.*).

merely the effects of the will of God, while it seems to me that they are rather the consequences of his understanding, which certainly does not depend upon his will any more than does his essence.

Against those who believe that God might have made things better.

Nor am I able to approve the opinion of certain moderns[23] who maintain boldly that what God has done is not supremely perfect but that he could have done much better. For it seems to me that the consequences of this opinion are wholly contrary to the glory of God. *Uti minus malum habet rationem boni, ita minus bonum habet rationem mali.* And acting with less perfection than one is capable of is acting imperfectly. To show that an architect could have done his work better is to find fault with his work...

These moderns also believe that in this way they are safeguarding God's freedom, as though it were not the highest freedom to act in perfection according to sovereign reason. For to think that God acts in any matter without having any reason for his will, even overlooking the fact that this seems impossible, is an opinion which is hardly in accord with God's glory. Let us assume, for example, that God chooses between A and B and that he takes A without having any reason for preferring it to B. I say that such action by God is at least not praiseworthy, for all praise should be based on some reason, and there is none here, *ex hypothesi.* I hold, instead, that God does nothing for which he does not deserve to be praised.

(*Discours de métaphysique*, 1686, §§. II, III)

The criterion of goodness and "best" is therefore not a consequence of the divine will. It is rather the divine will that is

---

[23] The Scholastics of his time (cf. *ibid.*).

inspired by this criterion, which has an objective validity in its own right, just as the truths of reason do. God's action is on the one hand circumscribed by the limits of *possibility*, given to it by the principle of non-contradiction, within which it must take place. On the other hand, it is determined by this finalism, by this principle of the "best," of goodness, that constitutes the necessary object of his choice. On both sides, therefore, it is found to be determined — and this determination constitutes the very law of its perfection.

There is necessity in the truths of reason, therefore, since their principles are inescapable, so that they could not be conceived of as other than what they are. And necessity also in the truths of fact, since their sufficient reason cannot be anything but the principle of supreme perfection and goodness. But these two forms of necessity by which the divine intellect and will and therefore all things in the world are constituted, are not identical to each other. If they were, it may be said, all distinction between truths of reason and fact would cease, and the one would descend from the same principles as the other, they would be based on the same laws. Instead, factual necessity has characteristics of its own. It does not imply the impossibility of the contrary which is an essential characteristic of the necessity of reason.

MORAL NECESSITY — Necessity of reason is a regulatory law of the divine intellect. Factual necessity is the sufficient reason that determines God's will, and this reason is indeed necessitating, but not in such a way that the contrary would be impossible. This second kind of necessity Leibniz sometimes distinguishes from the necessity of reason by calling it *inclining* (as opposed to *necessitating*) *reason*, or *moral necessity*.

We must distinguish between absolute and hypothetical necessity. We must also distinguish between a necessity which takes place because the opposite implies a contradiction (which necessity is called logical, metaphysical, or mathematical) and a necessity which is moral, whereby a wise being chooses the best, and every mind follows the strongest inclination.

Hypothetical necessity is what the supposition or hypothesis of God's foresight and preordination imposes upon future contingents...

...But good, either true or apparent — motive, in a word — inclines without necessitating — that is, without imposing an absolute necessity. For when God, for instance, chooses the best, what he does not choose, and is inferior in perfection, is nevertheless possible. But if what he chooses were absolutely necessary, any other way would be impossible, which is against the hypothesis. For God chooses among possibles, that is, among many ways of which none implies a contradiction.

But to say that God can only choose what is best, and to infer from this that what he does not choose is impossible is to mix up terms — it is blending power and will, metaphysical necessity and moral necessity, essences, and existences. For what is necessary is so by its essence, since the opposite implies a contradiction. But a contingent which exists owes its existence to the principle of what is best, which is a sufficient reason for the existence of things. And therefore, I say that motives incline without necessitating and that there is a certainty and infallibility but not an absolute necessity in contingent things.

And I have sufficiently shown in my *Theodicea* that this moral necessity is a good thing, agreeable to the divine perfection, agreeable to *the great principle of existences*, which is that of the want of a sufficient reason, whereas absolute and metaphysical necessity depends upon the other great principle of our reasoning, viz., that of essences, that is, the principle of identity or contradiction. For what is absolutely necessary is the only possible way, and its contrary implies a contradiction.

(Controversy with Clarke, 1715, G. VII, 389-391)

We must distinguish what is necessary from what is contingent though determined. Not only are contingent truths not necessary, but the links between them are not always absolutely necessary either. For it must be recognized that there is a difference in the manner of determination between the consequences that take place in necessary matters and those that take place in contingent matters. Geometrical and metaphysical consequences necessitate, but physical and moral ones incline without necessitating. There is even a moral and voluntary element in what is physical, through its relation to God, since the laws of motion are necessitated only by what is best. Now God chooses freely, even though he is determined to choose the best. But since bodies do not choose for themselves, God having chosen for them, they have come to be called *necessary agents* in common usage. I have no objection to this, provided that no one confounds the necessary with the determined and goes on to suppose that free beings act in an undetermined way — an error which has prevailed in certain minds, and destroys the most important truths, even the fundamental axiom that *nothing happens without reason*, without which neither the existence of God nor other great truths can be properly demonstrated.

(*New Essays*, 1701 ff., II, 21 § 13)

Multiple problems hinge on this subject of necessity and freedom, and on very many others connected with it (the origin of evil and its justification in the world, free will, responsibility etc.), problems that concern another aspect of Leibnizian thought which we need not examine here — that of *Theodicy*.

II. Individual Substance

Truths of reason and fact are thus what reality is made up

of. The former are absolute, necessary universals, but whose universality is abstract and occurs only in the ideal world of possibilities, of essences. The latter are concrete, tangible, existing, but at the same time contingent and individual, such that their existence cannot be demonstrated a priori, nor derive mathematically from any form inherent in the make-up of reality. Moral necessity, based on the principle of reason or finalism, does not, as we have seen, eliminate contingency. It does not, that is, yield the absolute certainty that belongs to the truths of reason and derives from the impossibility of the opposite.

Leibniz's problem now was the search for universality even in the realm of the contingent — or, in other words, to reduce the principle of sufficient reason to a line just as fixed and unchanging as that of the principle of non-contradiction. *Individual substance* would be the solution to this problem, and it was through it that Leibniz, in his own way and always within the framework of his objectivist conception of reality, would achieve a synthesis of the universal and the individual.

THE CHARACTERISTIC — Leibniz's chimera was to be able achieve mathematical certainty in all known things, so as to eliminate everything based on opinion, and to reduce all reasoning to calculation. This is the foundation of the *General Science, Characteristic, Ars inveniendi*, an idea he yearned for from the time of his first writings on the *Art of Combinations* in 1666 until the end of his life.

I can say without vanity that among my contemporaries I am one of those who have most deeply explored mathematical science, and I have discovered completely new methods and procedures that take this science beyond the limits that had been prescribed for it.

The essays I have offered on the subject have gained success in France and England, and it would be easy for me to offer many more. But I do not take much notice of individual discoveries, and what I most desire is to perfect the art of inventing in general, and to offer methods rather than solutions for problems — since one method includes an infinity of solutions...

And since I have had the good fortune to perfect considerably the mathematicians' art of invention or analysis, I have begun to have certain fresh conceptions that aim to reduce all human reasoning to a kind of calculation that could be used to discover the truth, within the limits of what is possible *ex datis*, i.e., what is given or known to us. And when given knowledge is not enough to answer the posed question, this method, as in mathematics, would bring us as close as possible to a solution and allow us to determine exactly what is most probable.

Such a general calculation would at the same time stand as a sort of universal form of writing that would have the same advantages as that of the Chinese, because everyone would be able understand it in their own language. But it would infinitely surpass Chinese in that it could be learned in a few weeks, having characters neatly connected following the order and connection of things, whereas the Chinese have an infinity of characters in accordance with the variety of things, and it takes a lifetime to learn their writing well.[24]

This script or language (if the characters were made pronounceable) could quickly be accepted in the world, because it could be learned in a few weeks and would provide a general means of communication. This would be of great importance for the spread of the faith and for the education of distant peoples.

But this would be the least of its advantages, since this

---

[24] Chinese characters would come close, according to Leibniz, to those of his Characteristic, in that they represent, as do Egyptian hieroglyphics, not the letters that form each word, but the very object it represents. They differ, however, from hieroglyphics in that "they are perhaps more philosophical, and seem to be founded on more intellectual considerations, such as those which yield numbers, order, relations." (Unpublished letter cited in J. Baruzi, *Leibniz et l'organisation religieuse de la terre*, Paris, 1907, pp. 82-3).

same writing would be a kind of general algebra, and would afford a way of reasoning by calculating, so that instead of arguing, one could say: let us count. And it would be found that errors in reasoning are merely errors in calculation, recognizable through testing, as in arithmetic.

People would thus have a truly infallible adjudicator in disputes. They could always ascertain whether it was possible to decide a matter by means of the knowledge they already possessed, and when it was not possible to be wholly satisfied, they could still determine what was most likely....

To arrive at this script or characteristic, containing such an astonishing calculation, one would have to look for the exact definitions of the concepts. For since our words are in fact quite obscure and often give us only confused notions, we would be obliged to replace them with other characters whose notion is precise and determined. Now definitions are nothing but a distinct expression of the idea of the thing.

And having carefully studied not only history and mathematics, but also natural theology, law and philosophy, I have pursued this project considerably and worked out a number of definitions. For me, for example, the definition of justice is as follows: *Justice* is the charity of the wise, or charity in conformity with wisdom. *Charity* is nothing but general benevolence, *wisdom* is the science of happiness, *happiness* is a lasting state of joy, *joy* is a feeling of perfection, and *perfection* is a degree of reality.

I think I can offer similar definitions of all human passions, virtues, vices, and actions, as needed. And by this means it will be possible to speak and reason accurately. And since the new characters will always include the definitions of things, it follows that they will give us a way to reason by calculating, as I mentioned above.

But in order to bring to term a project of such importance, one that would give humankind a type of tool as suitable for refining the vision of the mind as spectacles are for that of the body, will require much meditation and some amount of assistance.

(Letter to the Duke of Hanover, 1685,[25] G. VII, 25-27)

It was mainly to implement this vast project that throughout his life Leibniz advocated the founding of academies and scientific societies. The project was never realized. But what is interesting is the development in Leibniz's thinking that resulted from the studies he undertook for it. The method of arriving at these simple elements or "characters" from whose composition all the objects of human knowledge derive, is a method that involves breaking down the ideas we find before us already composed, starting from their definitions.[26]

---

[25] Date furnished by prof. Ritter.

[26] Here is the primitive formulation of this method in Leibniz's youthful *Art of Combinations*:

"The analysis occurs in the following way: Any given term is resolved into its formal parts, that is, a definition of it is laid down; these parts are again resolved into parts, that is, a definition of the definition of the terms is laid down, and so on, right down to simple parts, or undefinable terms. For, 'one does not always look for a definition,'* and these last terms are now better understood not by means of a definition, but by means of an analogy.** As soon as one has found all the primitive terms they should be placed in one class and designated by certain symbols. It will be most convenient if they are numbers. Among the primitive terms should be placed not only things, but also modes or relations.*** Since the composite terms vary in their distance from the primitive terms according to the number of primitive terms they are composed of — that is, according to the exponent of the complexion [combination] — one must create as many classes as there are exponents, and terms that are composed of the same number of primitive terms should be included in the same class. Terms that arise through the combination of two cannot be written except by writing the primitive terms of which they are composed; and because the primitive terms are designated by numbers, two numbers must be written to designate two terms. As for terms that arise through combination of three or other complexions of even greater exponent — that is, terms that are in the third and higher classes, they can all be written in as many different ways as there are complexions that make up their exponent (no longer viewed as an exponent but as the number of things)... For example, let the primitive terms be designated by the numbers 3, 6, 7, and 9, and consider a derivative term of the third class, that is, a term composed by a combination of the three simple terms 3, 6, and 9. Also, let the combinations in the second class be: (1) 3. 6; (2) 3. 7; (3) 3. 9; (4) 6. 7; (5) 6. 9; (6) 7. 9. I say that the given term in the

By such a method any demonstration will be possible. Indeed, once the inner constitution of each concept is known, it will always be possible to determine in any proposition whether the predicate falls within the subject — that is, whether it shares its constituent elements with it.

Nothing can be demonstrated to us about anything, not even by an angel, until we know its constitutive (*requisita*) terms. For in every truth all the constitutive terms of the predicate are included among the constitutive terms of the subject, and the terms of the effect sought include the means that were necessary to produce it.

---

third class can be written either as 3. 6. 9, expressing all its simple terms, or expressing one simple term, and in place of the other two simple terms a combination such as: 1/2. 9; 3/2. 6; or 5/2. 3. ... Whenever a term is referred to outside its class, it should be written in the form of a fraction in such a way that its upper number, or numerator, is the number of its place in the class, and its lower number, or denominator, is the number of the class.**** With derivative terms it is more convenient not to write all the primitive terms, but some intermediate terms, on account of the great number of the former, and to choose from them those that occur most readily to someone thinking of the matter in question. But it would be more rigorous to write all the primitive terms. On this basis, all subjects and predicates can be found, negative as well as affirmative, particular as well as universal. The predicates of a given subject are in fact its primitive terms, and all derivative terms nearer than it to the primitive terms, whose own primitive terms are all in the given subject. Accordingly, if the given term considered as a subject is written with primitive terms, it is easy to find those primitive terms that are predicated of it, and we can also find the derivative terms that are predicated of it if we arrange the complexions in order. But if the given term is written with derivative terms, or partly with derivative terms and partly with simple terms, then whatever is predicable of one of its derivative terms is predicable of the given term.***** ...With this analysis, it will now be easy, having recourse to numbers, to investigate all the predicates that can be stated of a given subject." (*Ars Combinatoria*, 1666, G. IV, 64-6).

* In Greek in the text. The citation is from Aristotle.
** By 'analogy' Leibniz means a more immediate and direct mode of apprehension than the logical process of definition; for example, a sensory image. Elsewhere he says that simple terms are apprehended by the senses.
*** This means that simple terms are not only to be understood as concrete, factual, sensory data, but also include abstract data, relations, etc. What the true nature is of these simple terms is very unclear, and Leibniz was always vague and imprecise in this regard.
**** For example, 5/2. 3 means the combination of the simple term 3 with the compound term having the fifth place in the second class — namely, following the list given above, with 6.9. The notation 5/2. 3 thus denotes the compound term 3.6.9.
***** This is, in essence, the outline of the syllogistic procedure, in which what is predicated of the more general term can also be predicated of the particular contained therein.

(Initia et specimina scientiae generalis, G. VII, 62)

THE PREDICATE CONTAINED IN THE SUBJECT — Thus, the criterion of truth is that the predicate falls within the scope of the subject, and this falling within is perfectly calculable. But this criterion is only valid for the truths of reason that are analytical. It is only there that the predicate is already contained in the subject, because it is only there that everything that is affirmed (predicated) about something has already to be in that same thing. If I say that the angles of a triangle are equal to two right angles, I am doing nothing more than throwing light on an aspect of the concept of the triangle, on a quality already implicit in it. The predicate (being equal to two right angles) is a priori part of the subject (the angles of a triangle). But can I affirm that the concept of Julius Caesar, for example, already contains, a priori, the action of crossing the Rubicon? The proposition "Julius Caesar crossed the Rubicon" is not analytical — that is, its predicate is not already included in the subject, but is added to it by direct, contingent experience. This proposition falls within factual truths.

Now, will rigorous proof be possible in this field if every demonstration is, as we have seen, a simple calculation to establish that the component terms of the predicate are part of the set of component terms of the subject? Leibniz sometimes says that demonstration as regards factual propositions only yields probability and not certainty. But he also attempts to ground the logical arrangement of these truths more rigorously, and also bring them under the rule of the predicate contained in the subject. For this purpose, he uses the principle of causality, to which all factual truths are subject. "The terms of the effect sought," as we have seen, "include the means necessary to produce it" — that is, the effect already includes in its own concept all the causes that brought it about. And, reciprocally, we may say that the notion of the cause already implicitly encompasses all the effects to which it will give rise. Now, since every fact belongs to a series of causes and effects, and is both effect and cause, it can be said that every individual concept contains within itself the concepts of the causes that produced it and the effects it will give rise to.

And this cause and these effects in their turn will contain their causes and effects, and so on, back to the first cause of everything and of itself — God, that is — so that every single datum is linked, through such causal effects, with the entire universe.

Knowledge of all these infinite causal nexuses is beyond the powers of human ingenuity, which is therefore content to fall back on the experience of the given fact, forgoing inferring it from its causes, something that would, however, be possible in principle.

Propositions certain in themselves are of two kinds: the first of these find their validity in reason — in the content, that is, of their terms — and I call them "known in themselves" or even "identical." The others are factual, and are revealed to us through indisputable experiences, and are also the immediate testimony of consciousness. But really, even factual propositions have their reasons, and therefore they may be resolved in their own make-up.[27] But we cannot know them a priori through their causes, except by knowing the totality of the universe (*cognita tota serie rerum*), which exceeds the power of the human intellect. Therefore, we learn them a posteriori, through experience. But since we often have to act on things for which we lack sound science, it is preferable that we at least know for sure that a certain proposition is probable.

(*Praeconita ad Encyclopaediam*, G. VII, 44)

Learning by experiment and the method of probability derive from the imperfection of human knowledge. In principle, even any factual truth can be given an analytical, a priori conception, such that it contains in itself, already fully developed, all the predicates — that is, all the effects and causes.

The hallmark of perfect knowledge is when there is

---

[27] That is, they could be considered analytical.

nothing about the thing under consideration that cannot be accounted for, and there is no event whose occurrence cannot be foretold.
(Fragment from *De la Sagesse*, 1676, G. VII, 83)

Now, this a priori knowledge of contingencies, if impossible to the human mind, is not impossible to God who chose them and set them into action.

Thus, any truth whatever can be justified, for the connection of the predicate with the subject is either evident in itself as in identities, or can be explained by an analysis of the terms. This is the only, and the highest, criterion of truth in abstract things — that is, things which do not depend on experience — that it must either be an identity or be reducible to identities (*ut sit vel identica vel ad identicas revocabilis*). From this can be derived the elements of eternal truth in all things insofar as we understand them, provided one knows how to proceed in as demonstrative a manner as in geometry. In this way God understands everything a priori and through eternal truth, since he does not need experience and knows all things adequately, whereas we know hardly anything adequately, few things a priori, and most things through experience. In this last case other principles and other criteria must be applied.
(*De Synthesi et Analysi universali*, G. VII, 295-296)

Any created thing, therefore, when considered a priori, as in the mind of God, contains in itself as predicates all other contingencies that have been or will be in any causal connection with it — in a word, the entirety of its past and future. What were the simple terms in the constitution of the concepts of reason are, in the case of factual truths, this series of causes and effects.

Any factual truth understood in this way — as the subject

of infinite predicates — is what Leibniz calls individual substance. It encompasses within itself, when understood in all its inclusivity and with its infinite connections, the entire universe.

To distinguish the actions of God from those of creatures we must explain what the concept of an individual substance is.

Now since actions and passions pertain distinctively to individual substances (*actiones sunt suppositorum*), it will be necessary to explain what such a substance is.

It is indeed true that when a number of predicates are attributed to a single subject while this subject is not attributed as a predicate to any other, it is called an individual substance. But this is not enough, and such a definition is merely nominal. We must consider, then, what it means to be truly attributed to a certain subject.

Now it is certain that every true predication has some basis in the nature of things, and when a proposition is not an identity, that is to say, when the predicate is not expressly contained in the subject, it must be included in it virtually.[28] This is what the philosophers call *in-esse*, when they say that the predicate is in the subject. So the subject term must always include the predicate term in such a way that anyone who understands perfectly the concept of the subject will also know that the predicate pertains to it.

This being premised, we can say it is the nature of an individual substance or complete being that the concept of it is so complete that it is sufficient to make us understand and deduce from it all the predicates of the subject

---

[28] That is, in identical (analytical) propositions, the predicate is contained in the subject by the conformation of the subject itself (expressly). In factual propositions, on the other hand, the predicate is contained in the subject because it is connected to it by a cause-and-effect relationship (virtually).

to which the concept is attributed. An accident, on the other hand, is a being whose concept does not include everything that can be attributed to the subject to which the concept is attributed. Thus, the quality of king which belonged to Alexander the Great, if we abstract it from its subject, is not determined enough to define an individual, for it does not include the other qualities of the same subject or everything which the concept of this prince includes. God, on the contrary, in seeing the individual notion or *hecceitas* of Alexander, sees in it at the same time the basis and the reason for all the predicates which can truly be affirmed of him — for example, that he will defeat Darius and Porus, even to the point of knowing a priori (and not by experience) whether he died a natural death or by poison, something we can know only through history. Moreover, when we carefully consider the connection of things, it can be said that there are at all times in the soul of Alexander traces of all that has happened to him and marks of all that will happen to him and even traces of all that happens in the universe, though it belongs only to God to know them all.

(*Discours de Métaphysique*, 1686, § VIII)

In this vein, we can say that the act of crossing the Rubicon does not attach itself to the concept of Caesar as something new, contingent and unexpected. Caesar, for those who understand this concept of him with all its connections, already contains in himself a priori the whole development of his personality, including the act of crossing the Rubicon. This, when it takes place, will only be the necessary consequence of the causes that produced it, and thus the development of what was already contained in them.

FREEDOM AND CAUSALITY — Here again, in much the same way as what we have just seen about God's determination to choose the "best," the problem of freedom arises. If every contingent fact is present in God's mind, will it not cease to be contingent? Will it not itself be necessary, predetermined? And will not any freedom in man's action that takes place in the realm of factual truths also thereby disappear? And along with it all human responsibility for good and evil? On this issue, closely related to the one mentioned above, Leibniz also makes a distinction between a connection that is necessary and one that is an inclination.

Since the individual concept of each person includes once and for all everything that can ever happen to him, one sees in it a priori proofs or reasons for the truths of each event and why one has happened rather than another, but these truths, however certain, are nevertheless contingent, being based on the free will of God and of creatures. It is true that their choice always has its reasons, but these incline without necessitating.

We must try and resolve a great difficulty which may grow out of the foundations we have laid above. We have said that the concept of an individual substance definitively includes everything that can ever happen to it, and that in considering that concept, one can see everything that can truly be predicated of it, just as we can see in the essence of the circle all the properties which can be deduced from it. But it seems that this will destroy the distinction between contingent and necessary truths, that it will leave no place for human liberty, and that an absolute fatalism will rule over all our actions as well as over the other events of the world. To this I reply that we must distinguish between what is certain and what is necessary. It is universally agreed that future contingents are certain, since God foresees them, but this does not make us say that they are necessary. But someone may object that if a certain conclusion can be deduced infallibly from a given definition or concept, that conclusion will be necessary. And we are now maintaining that everything that happens to some person is already contained virtually in his nature or concept, just as the properties of the circle are contained in its definition. Thus, the difficulty still subsists. To answer it squarely, I say that there are two kinds of connection or sequence. One is absolutely necessary, for its contrary implies a contradiction, and this deductive connection occurs in eternal truths like those of geometry. The other is necessary only *ex hypothesi*, and by accident, so to speak, and this connection is contingent in itself when its contrary implies no contradiction. A connection of this kind is not based on pure ideas and on the simple understanding of God but also on his free decrees and on the sequence of events in the universe.

Let us take an example. Since Julius Caesar is to become perpetual dictator and master of the republic and will destroy the liberty of the Romans, this action is contained in his concept, for we have assumed that it is the nature of such a perfect concept of a subject to include everything, so that the predicate is included in it — *ut possit inesse subjecto*. One could say that it is not by virtue of this concept or idea that he must commit this act, since the concept fits him only because God knows everything. But, someone will insist, his nature or form corresponds to this concept, and since God imposed this personality upon him, it is henceforth necessary for him to fulfill it. I could reply by pointing out the case of future contingents, which as yet have reality only in the understanding and the will of God, but since God has given them, this form in advance, it is all the same necessary for them to respond to it.

But I prefer to meet difficulties rather than to extenuate them by pointing out certain other similar difficulties, and what I am about to say will serve to clear up the one as well as the other. It is here, then, that we must apply the distinction we have made between the classes of connections, and I say that whatever happens in conformity to these divine anticipations is assured but not necessary and that if anyone were to do the contrary, he would not do anything impossible in itself, though it would be impossible (*ex hypothesi*) for it to happen. For if some man were able to carry out the complete demonstration by virtue of which he could prove this connection between the subject, who is Caesar, and the predicate, which is his successful undertaking, he would actually show that the future dictatorship of Caesar is based in his concept or nature and that there is a reason in that concept why he has resolved to cross the Rubicon rather than stop there, and why he has won rather than lost the day at Pharsalus, and why it was reasonable and consequently assured that this should happen. But this man could not show that these events are necessary in themselves or that their contrary implies a contradiction. In the same way it is reasonable and assured that God will always do what is best, even though what is less perfect implies no contradiction.

For it will be found that this demonstration of the predicate of Caesar is not as absolute as that of numbers or of geometry but that it supposes the sequence of things which God has freely chosen and which is founded on the first free decree of God, which leads him always to do what is most perfect, and on the decree which God has made about human nature (following the primary one), which is that man shall always do, though freely, that which appears to him to be best. But every truth which is based on this kind of a decree is contingent, even though it is certain, for these decrees do not change the possibility of things. And as I have already said, though God assuredly always chooses the best, this does not prevent something less perfect from being and remaining possible in itself, even though it will never happen, for it is not its impossibility but its imperfection which causes God to reject it. Now nothing is necessary whose opposite is possible.

So we are in a position to meet difficulties of this kind, no matter how great they may seem (and in fact they are no less pressing for all the other thinkers who have taken up this matter), provided that we consider carefully that all contingent propositions have reasons for being as they are and not otherwise or (which amounts to the same thing) that they have a priori proofs of their truth which make them certain and which show that the relation between subject and predicate of these propositions has its basis in the nature of both. But we must consider too that these proofs are not demonstrations of necessity, since these reasons are based only on the principle of contingency or of the existence of things — that is to say, on what is or appears to be the best among several equally possible things. Necessary truths, by contrast, are based on the principle of contradiction and on the possibility or impossibility of essences themselves, without considering in this relation the free will of God or of the creatures.

(*Discours di métaphysique*, 1686, § XIII)

On the other hand, Leibniz also uses other arguments to save freedom and responsibility in this universal causal connection. Freedom is not always necessarily an opposite of causal determination.

Regarding free will, I am of the opinion of the Thomists[29] and other philosophers who believe that everything is predetermined, and I do not see any reason to doubt it. Yet that does not stop us from having a freedom exempt not only from constraint, but also from necessity,

---

[29] The principle that the world of the senses is supported by the law of causality belonging to the tradition of Aristotle, absorbed by Leibniz from the Scholastic.

and in that our situation is analogous to that of God himself, who is always determined in his actions too, since he could not fail to choose the best. But if he did not have any choice, and if what he did were the only thing possible, he would be subjected to necessity. The more perfect one is, the more one is determined to the good, and therefore freer at the same time. For we have a power and knowledge all the more extended, and a will all the more bounded within the limits of perfect reason.

(Letter to Bayle, G. III, 58-59)

Even though all the facts of the universe are now certain in relation to God, or (which amounts to the same thing) are determined in themselves and even linked among themselves, it does not follow that their connection is always truly necessary — that is to say that the truth that establishes that one fact is the consequence of another, is necessary. And this must be applied particularly to voluntary actions.

When a choice is proposed, for example to go out or not to go out, it is a question whether, with all the circumstances, internal and external, motives, perceptions, dispositions, impressions, passions, inclinations taken together, I am still in a contingent state, or whether I am required to make the choice, for example, to go out. That is to say, the question is whether this true and in effect determined proposition, "In all these circumstances taken together I shall choose to go out," is contingent or necessary. To this I reply that it is contingent, because neither I nor any other mind more enlightened than I, could demonstrate that the opposite of this truth implies contradiction. And supposing that *liberty of indifference* is understood as a liberty opposed to necessity (as I have just explained it), I acknowledge this liberty for I am really of opinion that our liberty, as well as that of God and of the blessed spirits, is exempt not only from co-action, but, also from absolute necessity, although it cannot be exempt from determination and from certainty.

But I find that there is need of great caution here in order not to fall into a chimera which shocks the principles of good sense, and which would be what I call *absolute indifference or an indifference of equilibrium*; which some introduce into liberty, and which I believe chimerical. It must be observed then that this connection, of which I just spoke, is not necessary in an absolute sense, but that it is nonetheless certainly true, and that in general every time that in all the circumstances taken together the balance of deliberation is heavier on the one side than on the other, it is certain and infallible that that side will carry the day. God or the perfect sage would always choose the best that is known, and if one thing were no better than another, they would choose neither. In other intelligent subjects, passions often take the place of reason, and it can always be said in regard to the will in general that *the choice follows the greatest inclination*, in which I include passions as well as reasons, true or apparent.

Nevertheless, I see that there are people who imagine that a determination sometimes goes for the side, which is the less weighted, that God sometimes chooses the less good, everything considered, and that man chooses sometimes without object and against all his reasons, dispositions, and passions — indeed, that one chooses sometimes without any reason at all that determines the choice. But this I hold to be false and absurd, since it is one of the greatest principles of good sense that nothing ever occurs without cause or determining reason.

Thus, when God chooses, it is by reason of the best; when man chooses, it will be the side which shall have struck him most. If, moreover, he were to choose what he sees as less useful and less agreeable, it will perhaps have become agreeable to him through caprice, through a spirit of contradiction, or through similar reasons of depraved taste, which would nonetheless be determining reasons, even if they should not be conclusive reasons. And never can any example to the contrary be found.

Thus, although we have a liberty of indifference which saves us from necessity, we never have an indifference of equilibrium which exempts us from determining reasons. There is always something which inclines us and makes us choose, but without being able to impose necessity. And just as God is always infallibly led to the best although he is not led necessarily (other than by a moral necessity), in the same way we are always infallibly led to that which strikes us most, but not necessarily. The contrary not implying any contradiction, it was not necessary or essential that God should create, nor that he should create this world in particular, although his wisdom and goodness has led him to do so.

(Letter to Coste, G. III, 1707, 400-402)

PREDICTION AND PREDETERMINATION — Given this, it is possible to think that God's prediction of contingent predicates does not contradict freedom. To foresee does not mean to predetermine. God chooses from among those possible a series which already contains certain actions with the character of freedom. In choosing, he neither creates nor determines them — he merely puts them into action, actualizing their possibility. In doing so, he sees the whole series and foresees its developments. By doing this, however, he has not determined these actions, and they retain, in the actual as well as the possible series, their characteristic of freedom.

God inclines our soul without necessitating it; there is no reason whatever for complaint; we must not ask why Judas sinned, but we must ask only why Judas the sinner is admitted to existence in preference to other possible persons. Original imperfection before sin and degrees of grace.

As for the action of God upon the human will, this involves many rather difficult problems which it would take too long to pursue here. Some rough indications may nevertheless be given. In concurring ordinarily with our actions, God follows only the laws which he has established — that is to say, he continually preserves and produces our being in such a way that our thoughts come to us spontaneously or freely in the order which the concept of our individual substance implies. In this concept they could be foreseen for all eternity. Furthermore, by virtue of the decree which he has made that the will always strive toward the apparent good by expressing or imitating God's will under certain particular conditions (with respect to which this apparent good always is to some extent a true good), God determines our will to choose what seems to be the best, but without constraining it. For in an absolute sense the will is in a state of indifference, since this is the opposite of necessity, and it has the power to act otherwise or also to suspend its action altogether, since both alternatives are and remain possible.

It rests with the soul, therefore, to guard itself against surprises coming from appearances by means of a firm will to reflect, and not to act or judge in certain circumstances until after careful and mature deliberation. It is nonetheless true and, indeed, even assured by all eternity that certain souls will not make use of this power in such circumstances. But whose fault is that? Can the soul complain of anyone but itself? For all such *post factum* complaints are unjust and would have been unjust *ante factum* as well. Could this soul, just before sinning, in good faith complain about God as if he had determined it to sin? Since the determinations of God in such matters cannot be foreseen, how can the soul know that it is determined to sin unless it is already sinning in fact? It is merely a question of not willing, and God could not grant an easier and juster condition. In the same way, all judges consider only the question of how evil a man's will is, without seeking the reasons which have disposed him to have an evil will. But can it perhaps be assured for all eternity that I shall sin? Answer this for yourselves; perhaps it is not. So instead of musing on what you cannot know and what cannot give you any light, act according to the duty which you know.

But someone else may say, "How does it come about that this man will certainly commit this sin?" The reply is easy — it is that otherwise he would not be this man. For God foresees for all time that there will be a certain Judas, whose idea or concept of God's contains this future free act. There remains then only this question: Why does this Judas, a traitor, who is merely possible in the idea of God, actually exist? But to this question no answer can be expected here on earth, except the general one that since God has found it good that he should exist in spite of the sin which God foresaw, this evil must be compensated for with interest in the universe and that God will draw a greater good from it, and that it will turn out in the end that this sequence of events, including the existence of this sinner, is the most perfect among all other possible sequences.[30]

But while we are sojourners in this world, it will be impossible always to explain the admirable economy of this choice — it is enough to know it without understanding it. Here it is time to acknowledge the *altitudinem*

---

[30] This concept of evil as an integral and necessary part of universal harmony would become the basic theme of *Theodicea*.

divitiarm, the depth and the abyss of divine wisdom, without getting into problems of detail which involve infinite considerations.

It is well understood, however, that God is not the cause of evil. For it was not only after man's fall from innocence that original sin took possession of the soul. Even before, there was an original limitation or imperfection natural to all creatures, which made them capable of sin or failure. There is therefore no greater difficulty in Supralapsarianism[31] than in other views. And it is to this, I believe, that the opinion of St. Augustine and other authors should be reduced who hold that the root of evil lies in nothingness — in the privation or limitation of creatures, that is, which God graciously corrects with that degree of perfection which it pleases him to give. This grace of God, whether ordinary or extraordinary, has its degrees and measures. In itself it is always efficacious in producing a definite proportional effect, and furthermore, it is always sufficient not only to protect us from sin but even to accomplish salvation, provided that man meets it to the extent that he can. But it is not always sufficient to surmount the inclinations of man, for otherwise he would have nothing more to strive for, and this is reserved solely for the absolutely efficacious grace which is always victorious, whether through itself or through agreeable circumstances.

(*Discours de mètaphysique*, 1686, § XXX)

But apart from these problems of necessity, freedom, prediction, and predetermination, which fall rather within the scope of *Theodicea,* the essential point here is the *universality of individual substance* which, with the infinite connections contained

---

[31] Unlike the Infralapsarians, the Supralapsarians believed that divine predetermination took place even before original sin (*supra lapsum*, before the Fall), and that Adam's wrongdoing had not been an act of free will. Leibniz, with this reconciliation of predetermination with contingency or freedom, makes the problem moot.

within it, becomes the universe itself as seen from a particular point of view. It encompasses its own past and its own future, and at the same time the past and the future of the whole universe, achieving the ultimate in universality — it is a total, comprehensive vision of everything.

And at the same time, it retains all its individuality. The starting point is always the single fact, specific, particular, contingent. It does not disappear into the whole; it remains clear and visible as the head of the endless thread, unwinding to infinity, following every causal connection. It remains and provides a foothold, a possibility to travel in good order all along the interminable path. And meanwhile it admits the possibility of infinite other starting points. Individual substances are as many as there are facts — in other words, infinite. And each one is the whole universe. But each from a different point of view, with a different starting point. The universe is one, and each particular is an infinitesimal part of it. But from each particular there is the possibility of going back to the totality as a whole. In this union of the particular and the universal in individual substance lies Leibniz's first great discovery, the fundamental core of the concept of the monad.

III. FORCE AND MOTION

Another area of activity in Leibnizian thought is the philosophy of nature, a field quite distinct from what we have seen up to now and involving tools and methods of another type altogether. The problems analyzed here have a particular affinity with those of the physical sciences: the composition of matter, the existence or non-existence of atoms and of the vacuum, the origin and function of motion, energy, etc. For Leibniz the solutions to these problems do not derive from general principles of metaphysical philosophy. He deals with them as themselves, following techniques specific to them, maintaining his practice of getting to the heart of every inquiry while appropriating the particular characteristics of each science for his own use. Then later, having arrived at certain solutions and definitive positions, he relates them to the solutions obtained in the other fields, thus achieving ever richer and more comprehensive syntheses.

CONTINUITY AND MATTER — Leibniz's ideas in physical philosophy underwent a profound transformation between his youthful *Hypothesis physica nova* and his more mature conceptions. During the course of this evolution, he formed his fundamental concepts in the field. He began as an atomist, following Gassendi (1592-1665), who revived the doctrines of Epicurus and Democritus, conceiving of matter in all its aspects as formed by varied combinations of atoms in a vacuum. Leibniz soon abandoned this theory, however, as irreconcilable with his *principle of continuity*.

This is one of the cornerstones of his thinking and is applied not only to the problem of matter, but to many other aspects of his philosophy as well. It says that in the development of things, there are no stops, interruptions, or gaps. It says that *natura non facit saltus*. Applied in considering the world of the senses logically, this principle is the basis of the uninterrupted passage from cause to effect and effect to cause, without admitting — given the initial miracle of creation — new *ex novo* creations, new miracles. According to this principle the whole world is linked together in all its parts, so that it is possible through an unbroken process to pass from any one of them to any other.

> Nothing takes place suddenly, and it is one of my greatest and most widely applied maxims that *nature never makes leaps*. I call this the Law of Continuity... and the use of this law is very considerable in physics. This law declares that any change from small to large, or vice versa, passes through something in between, in respect of degrees as well as of parts, and that no motion ever springs immediately from a state of rest, or occurs except through a lesser motion. In the same way one can never move along a certain line or distance without first covering a shorter one, although those who have set forth the

laws of motion up to now have not observed this law, believing that a body can receive in an instant a motion contrary to the preceding one. All of this supports the judgment that even noticeable perceptions arise by degrees from those which are too minute to be observed. To think otherwise is to have little knowledge of the immeasurable fineness of things, which always and everywhere implies a present infinity.
(*New Essays*, 1701 ff., Preface, G. V 49)

Applied to a consideration of the material world, the principle of continuity establishes that matter is infinitely divisible, and that is not possible to conceive of an end point in this divisibility or to think of an element that is indivisible and could stand as a starting point for the composition of bodies. This is the fall of the doctrine of the *atom*[32] as the simple primary element from which the composition of the various forms of matter is derived. Any material element, no matter how small, is seen as made up of parts.

Since the continuum is infinitely divisible, any atom will be in a certain way like a world of infinite species, and there will be *mundi in mundis in infinitum*.
(*Hypothesis physica nova, Theoria motus concreti*, 1671, G. IV, 201)

All nature is filled with organized bodies — that is, animals and plants and still others, and there is not an atom that does not contain a world of creatures, since everything is actually divided to infinity.
(Letter to Burnett, 1699, G. III, 250)

MOTION — Matter, then, is not made up of atoms. It is infinitely divisible, continuous, and homogeneous such that it will never be possible to get to the smallest element of it. On the

---

[32] *Ατομος* in fact means indivisible.

other hand, it is not reducible to pure extension, as Descartes would have it.[33] Such a conception, which in the case of matter takes into account only geometric elements and considers it only in terms of the space it occupies, is not sufficient for Leibniz. Matter is for him something more — it is first and foremost compactness, motion, inertia. It is what puts up resistance.

That the common nature of corporeal substance consists of extension is something I see asserted by many with great confidence, but never proved. Certainly, neither motion or action nor resistance or passion can be derived from it, and nor can the natural laws which are observed in the motion and collision of bodies arise from the concept of extension alone, as I have shown elsewhere. And indeed, the notion of extension is not a primitive one but is resolvable. Something that is extended is in fact required to be a continuous whole in which various elements exist simultaneously. To speak of this more fully, extension, a relative notion, requires something which is extended or continued, as whiteness is in milk, and that very thing in a body which constitutes its essence. The repetition of this *quid*, whatever it may be, is extension. I fully agree with Huygens[34] (whose opinion in natural and mathematical matters I value highly), that the concept of an empty place and of extension alone is the same. In my judgment mobility or ἀντιτυπία[35] can be explained

---

[33] It will be recalled that Descartes, in deducing the world from God, takes as a starting point the two substances: *res cogitans* (the mental principle) e *res existens* (the material principle).
[34] CHRISTIAN HUYGENS (1629-1695), the great Dutch scientist, the author of the wave theory of light and the first to apply the principle of the pendulum to the construction of clocks, is among those who most influenced the development of Leibniz's scientific ideas. Their friendship and correspondence lasted from the year of their acquaintance in Paris (1672) until Huygens's death. And as early as 1669, Leibniz had drawn from Huygens's laws of collisions the inspiration for some of his ideas on the composition of matter.
[35] *Antitypia* is the term Leibniz uses to indicate the solidity and impenetrability of matter.

by pure extension, but only with a subject of extension that not only determines, but also fills a space.
(*Animadversiones in partem generalem Principiorum cartesianorum*, before 1692, G. IV, 364-5).

Where do these qualities of matter come from? This action, this resistance, etc. that make up its essence? In his early studies, Leibniz has all the qualities of matter derive from motion.

Primary matter is mass itself, in which there is nothing but extension and ἀντιτυπία or impenetrability. The extension comes from the space it fills. The very nature of matter consists in its being something solid (*crassum*) and impenetrable and therefore mobile when something else strikes it (since one must give way to the other). Now this continuous mass, which fills the world while all its parts are at rest, is primary matter, from which all things are produced by motion and into which they are reduced through rest. There would be no diversity in it but only homogeneity, if there were no motion....

Let us now pass from matter to form. Here too everything agrees remarkably if we assume that form is nothing but figure. For since figure is the boundary (*terminus*) of a body, a boundary is needed to form figures out of matter. But a discontinuity of parts is necessary in order to have a variety of boundaries arising in matter. For by the very fact that parts are discontinuous, each one will have separate boundaries (and in fact Aristotle defines continua as things whose limit is one[36]). But discontinuity can be introduced into the formerly continuous mass in two ways: first, in such a way that contiguity is at the same time destroyed, when the parts are separated from each other so that a vacuum is left, or in such a way that contiguity remains, which happens when the parts are

---

[36] In Greek in the text: ὧν τὰ ἔσχατα ἕν.

left together but moved in different directions. For example, two spheres, one included in the other, can be moved in different directions and yet remain contiguous, though they cease to be continuous. This makes it clear that, if mass were created discontinuous or separated by spaces to begin with, certain forms of matter would be created at the same time.. But, if the mass is continuous from the start, forms must necessarily arise through motion... For division comes from motion, the bounding of parts comes from division, their figures come from this bounding, and forms from figures — therefore, forms come from motion. From this it is clear that every arrangement into a form is motion, and the vexatious problem of the origin of forms is solved....

It now remains for us to come to change. Changes are commonly and rightly classed as generation, corruption, increase, decrease, alteration, and change of place or motion. Modern thinkers believe that these can all be explained by change of place alone. And the matter is obvious in the case of increase and decrease, for change of quantity occurs in a whole when a part changes its place and is either added or taken away. We need only to explain generation, corruption, and alteration through motion... In any case, generation and corruption, as well as alteration, can be explained by a subtle motion of parts. For example, since white is what reflects the most light and black is what reflects the least, those things whose surfaces contain many small mirrors will be white. This is why foaming water is white, for it consists of innumerable little bubbles, and each bubble is a mirror... It is clear from this that colors arise from a mere change of figure and position in a surface. If we had space, it would be easy to explain light, heat, and all qualities in the same way. And indeed, if qualities are changed by motion alone, substance will also be changed by that very fact,

for a thing ceases to be if all (or even some) of the qualities requisite to it are changed. For example, if you remove either light or heat, you destroy fire.
(Letter to Thomasius, 1669, G. I, 17-19)

Everything to do with matter thus derives from motion, and without motion, when it is at rest, that is, it loses all its solidity and consistency, its material nature. Leibniz repeatedly affirms that *"nullam esse cohaesionem seu consistentiam quiescentie."*

I have to say that Descartes has an entirely different opinion, as it seems to him that the stability of cohesion in bodies needs no other connecting element (*gluten*) besides stillness. I am of the opposite opinion — this *gluten* is motion... What is at rest is empty space.
(Letter to Oldenburg, 1671, Ak. II, I, 166-7)

We need to explain the cause of greater or lesser connectedness and thus of the heterogeneity in bodies. The question is why bodies have parts that are more or less cohesive. I assert that one should look for no other cause for this than the fact that these parts stand or move together. They move together because amid such a wide variety of general movements throughout the overall mass it was in any case necessary for some parts to move far away from their neighbors, and others relatively much less so. And the same cause that made these parties move away from their neighbors only a little or not at all also makes them tend to remain in the same state, because the cause persists. And that cause is the combination itself of general movements, and general movements are always present. They are therefore disturbed by anyone who suddenly changes any effect produced and established by them and which all nature allows. It clearly follows from this that external pressure is the primary cause of solidity, and that the stillness or concurrent motion of the parts is the proximate cause, but only when it results from a permanent external cause. Thus, just as concomitance — i.e., stillness or concurrent motion, constitutes the *solid body*, similarly the varying motion of the parts constitutes the *liquid*. And this is the principle of the specific diversity in bodies, and the fact that some are denser than others — more solid, that is — or composed of larger solid parts. This thesis is also confirmed by experience.

(Letter to Honoré Fabri, 1677, G. IV, 250)

"CONATUS" — The concept of matter therefore dissolves into that of motion. But how, then, does this creation of materiality take place? What is the starting point of the action of motion? And what, initially, does such action act upon? Leibniz cannot resort to atoms, as primary elements, having already rejected them in the name of the principle of continuity. He modifies his starting point, making it devoid of extension — considering it no longer as the smallest particle of matter (which would still be material, albeit extended), but as a limit or a beginning, something therefore unextended. In this principle, which he calls (borrowing a term from Hobbes) *conatus*, he makes the beginning of materiality and the beginning of movement coincide.

There are indivisibles or unextended beings, for otherwise we could conceive neither of the beginning nor the end of corporeal motion. The proof of this is as follows. What is to be found is a beginning or an end to some given space, body, motion, and time. Let that whose beginning is sought be represented by line *ab*, whose middle point is *c*, and let the middle point of *ac* be *d*, that of *ad* be *e*, and so on. Let the beginning be sought at the left end, at *a*. I say that *ac* is not the beginning, because *cd* can be taken from it without destroying the beginning; nor is it *ad*, because *ed* can be taken away, and so forth. So nothing is a beginning from which something on the right can be removed. But that from which nothing extended can be removed is unextended. Therefore the beginning of body, space, motion, or time (that is, the point, *conatus*, or instant) is either nothing, which is absurd, or is unextended, which was to be demonstrated. *The point* is not something with no parts, nor whose parts are not considered. It is rather *that whose extension is nothing* — that is, whose parts have no distance between them; whose magnitude is inconsiderable; incapable of being designated, less than that which can be expressed by a non-infinite ratio to another discernible magnitude; less than any which can be given. This is the foundation of the method of Cavalieri,[37] and clearly shows the truth of the principle that we must think of certain rudiments, so to speak, or beginnings of lines and figures, as smaller than any given magnitude whatever...

Conatus is to motion as a point is to space, or as one to infinity, for it is the beginning and end of motion. Hence, *whatever moves*, no matter how feebly, and no matter what obstacle it meets, *will propagate its conatus in full against all material obstructions into infinity*, and therefore will impress its *conatus* on all other things. Nor can it be denied that even when a moving body does not proceed in its motion it still has a *conatus*, and therefore strives (*conetur*), or — the same thing — begins to move the obstructing bodies, even though they may exceed it in size. *There can therefore be many contrary conatuses in the same body at the same time...*

At the time of impulsion, impact, or collision, the

---

[37] BONAVENTURA CAVALIERI (1598-1647), author of *Geometria Indivisibilium*, and of the concept of the indivisible, had great influence on Leibniz's mathematical thought. He can perhaps be considered the main precursor of Leibniz and Newton's discovery of infinitesimal calculus.

boundaries or points of two bodies either penetrate each other or *are in the same point of space*. Indeed, when one of two colliding bodies strives to penetrate the position of the other — it begins to be in it, that is — to be united with it. For *conatus* is beginning, penetration, union. The bodies are therefore at the beginning of union, or their boundaries are united. Therefore *bodies which push or impel each other are in a state of cohesion*. In fact, their boundaries that are one, since things whose limits are one,[38] as Aristotle too defines them, are continuous or coherent. And if two things are in one place, one cannot be put in motion without the other.

(*Hypothesis physica nova, Theoria motus abstracti*, 1671, G. IV, 228-30)

BODY AND MIND — The *conatus* is thus the initial point of contact, one might say, between matter and movement, the act in which movement, applying itself to a spatial point, marks the beginning of the body. But what is movement with respect to matter if not a principle of the mind?

Physics deals with matter, and the unique affection resulting from the combination of matter with other causes, i.e., motion. For mind (*mens*) supplies motion to matter in order to achieve a good and pleasing figure and state of things for itself. Matter in itself is devoid of motion. Mind is the principle of all motion.

(Letter to Thomasius, 1669, G. I, 22)

This is Leibniz's as yet immature formulation. Once he had arrived at the *conatus* concept, it was what he established as the essence of mind. The extension and development of *conatus* in space gives rise to matter, and its extension in time (in the form of memory) generates the mind. This way the body is to

---

[38] In Greek in the text. Cf above, n. 36.

the mind as the moment is to time, and the mind is to the body as the point is to space.

No conatus without motion lasts longer than an instant except in minds (in mentibus). In fact, what is *conatus* in an instant is the motion of a body in time. This opens the door to the true distinction between body and mind, which no one has explained heretofore. *Omne enim corpus est mens momentanea, seu carens recordatione,* because it does not retain its own *conatus* and the other contrary one together for longer than an instant. Two things are in fact necessary for sensation and for pleasure or pain, without which there is no feeling at all — action and reaction, confrontation and then *harmony.* Hence body lacks memory: it lacks the perception of its own actions and passions; it lacks thought (*cogitatio*).
(*Hypothesis physica nova, Theoria motus abstracti,* 1671,
G. IV, 230)

Just as the actions of the body consist of movement, the actions of the mind consist of *conatus* or, let us say, of the minimal movement or point. In fact even the mind itself consists properly only of a point in space, while the body takes up space. And this, in common parlance, I will demonstrate by the fact that the mind must be at the meeting place of all the movements imprinted on us by the objects of the senses. Given that, when I want to establish that a given body is gold, I take together its luster, its sound, its weight, and conclude that it is gold, it is therefore necessary for the mind to be at a place where all the lines of sight, hearing and touch meet — that is, at a *point.* If we were to give the mind a space greater than a point, it would then be a body and would be divisible into parts, and would therefore not be always intimately present to itself and so could not also be reflected in all its elements and actions. And yet this is what the essence of the mind consists of. Given then that the mind consists of a point, it is indivisible and indestructible. From this principle and others as well I have demonstrated many wonderful things about the characteristics of the human soul and in general about all intelligent minds — things that no one had thought of up to now, even though the truth of religion, divine providence, the immortality of our souls and the possibility of many sublime mysteries (such as that of divine justice, predestination and presence in the sacrament) flow from them in a hitherto unseen way. And I hope eventually to be able to show all this in the clearest possible way, and thus to acquire for myself some merit with all intelligent men, who hate today's encroaching atheism and are concerned about eternity.

(Letter to the Duke of Hanover, 1671, G. I, 52-53)

From this contact between mental and material substance in *conatus*, Leibniz draws his first conclusions concerning the function of mind in the physical world, and the importance of the mind in relation to any corporeal or material element.

I am able to demonstrate from the nature of motion in the physical field, which I discovered, that motion cannot exist in bodies taken on their own unless the mind is added, ... that the mind is incorporeal; that the mind acts on itself, that no action on itself can be motion, that the action of the body is nothing but motion, and that therefore mind is not body. That the mind consists of a point or center, and that it is therefore indivisible, incorruptible, immortal. As all rays converge in a center, so all the sensory impressions through the nerves converge together in the mind; and therefore, the mind is a small world conceived in a point, which consists of its own ideas just as the center consists of angles, since the angle is a part of the center, despite the fact that the center is indivisible. Thus, the entire nature of the mind can be explained geometrically.

(Letter to the Duke of Hanover, 1671, G. I, 61)

THE CONSERVATION OF FORCE — These are the physical theories of the young Leibniz. But a new discovery led him to abandon his concept of movement as the essence of bodies, and to replace it with the idea of *force*.

Descartes had affirmed the immutability and constancy of the quantity of motion in the universe — that is, however much motion is lost by one body is the amount gained by another, so that the overall amount in the universe is always constant, quantity of motion being the product of mass times velocity. Leibniz showed that this principle is not exact, and that what remains constant is not the quantity of motion, but the quantity of *living force* or *motor action*, which is equal to the product of mass times the square of velocity.

What the significance of this discovery is in the field of physics need not detain us here. To understand Leibniz's use of it in philosophical and metaphysical questions, it must be noted that the impelling action no longer represents, as the quantity of movement does, the simple transfer of a body from one place to another, but rather the possibility of producing a certain effect — for example, lifting a body to a certain height. This motor action of Leibniz's is what today is called *energy*.

Generally *absolute force* must be estimated by the violent effect which it can produce. What consumes the force of the agent I call the *violent effect*, for example giving a certain velocity to a given body to raise it to a certain height, etc. And we can conveniently estimate the force of a heavy body by the product of the mass or of the weight multiplied by the height to which the body might rise by virtue of its motion... When a heavy body has made some progress in descending freely and has acquired some impetus or *living force,* then the height this body might then attain is not proportional to the velocity but to the square of the velocity. And it is for this reason that in case of living force, the forces are not at all like the quantities of motion or the products of masses times velocities...

Now it is found by reason and by experiment, that it is *absolute living force* — determined by the violent effect it can produce — which is preserved, and not at all the quantity of motion. For if this living force could ever be augmented the effect would be more powerful than the cause or there would be perpetual mechanical motion, that is to say which could reproduce its cause and something more, which is absurd. But if the force could be diminished it would in the end perish entirely since, never being able to increase and being able nevertheless to diminish, it would always fall more and more into decay, which is without doubt contrary to the order of things. Experiment confirms this as well...

Now I am very happy to turn the matter around and also to show the conservation of something closer to the quantity of motion, namely *the conservation of motor action.* Here then is the general rule that I establish. Whatever changes may take place between concurrent bodies of whatever number *there must always be in the concurring bodies in a closed system the same quantity of motor action in the same interval of time.* For example, there must be during this hour as much moving action in the universe or in the given bodies acting between themselves in a closed system as there will be during any other hour whatsoever.

To understand this rule it is necessary to explain the estimation of motor action, wholly different from that of the quantity of motion, understood as has been explained above. Now in order that the motor action may be estimated we must first estimate the *formal effect* of motion.

This formal or essential motion effect consists of what is changed by the motion, namely the quantity of the mass which is transferred and the space or length through which this mass is transferred. This is the essential effect of motion or the change it determines, since the body was there, and now it is here; the body is such-and-such and the distance is such-and-such....

It is necessary carefully to distinguish what I call the *formal effect*, essential to motion, from what I called above the *violent effect*. The violent effect consumes the force and is exercised upon something external; but the formal effect consists of the body in motion taken in itself and does not consume the force at all — indeed, it conserves it, since the same transfer of the same mass must always be continued, if nothing external prevents it. It is for this reason that absolute forces are like the violent effects that consume them but not at all like the formal effects.

Now it will be easier to understand what motor action is. It must thus be estimated not only by the formal effect that it produces but also by the vigor or velocity with which it produces it. We wish to transport 100 pounds the distance of a mile; this is the formal effect demanded. One desires to do it in one hour and another in two hours. I say that the action of the first is double that of the second, being doubly quick with an equal effect...

This definition of motor action is justified a priori because it is clear that in a purely formal action taken by itself, in the way a moving body is here considered by itself, there are two points to examine — the formal effect or what changed, and the rapidity of the change, for it is very clear that what produces the same formal effect in less time is more active.

(*Essay du Dynamique sur les loix du mouvement*, M. VI, 218-21)

FORCE AS ACTIVITY — Force, energy, thus takes the place of motion. From the simple and objective transfer of bodies from one place to another, Leibniz moves the center of attention to the cause of this transfer, to what it already contains in itself, so to speak — to the motion in a potential state which produces it. Motion thus loses reality in favor of force. Force comes to be considered absolute and motion relative.

We must realize, above all, that force is something absolutely real in substances, even in created substances, while space, time, and motion are, to a certain extent, beings of reason, and are true or real, not *per se*, but only as divine attributes encompassing the immensity, eternity, action or force of the substances created. From this it immediately follows that there is no empty space and no empty moment in time. Moreover, it follows that motion separated from force — that is, motion insofar as it is taken to contain only geometrical notions (size, shape, and their change) — is really nothing but the change of situation, and furthermore, that *as far as the phenomena are concerned, motion is a pure relation,* something Descartes also recognized when he defined motion as the translation from the neighborhood of one body into the neighborhood of another. But in drawing consequences from this, he forgot his definition and set up the laws of motion as if motion were something real and absolute. Therefore, we must hold that however many bodies might be in motion, one cannot infer from their exterior aspect which of them really has absolute and determinate motion or rest. Rather, any one of them one chooses may be considered to be at rest, and yet the same exterior manifestation will result.

(*Specimen Dynamicum*, part II, M. VI, 247)

Motion is relative; force alone is absolute. And the concept of force has, much more than that of movement, a clear character of *activity*. It seems that in it the *conatus* of the youthful writings has found its completion and fulfillment.

Elsewhere we argued that in corporeal things there is something over and above extension — indeed, prior to extension — namely, that force of nature implanted everywhere by the Creator. This force does not consist of a simple faculty, as the Scholastics seem to have been content to say, but is further endowed with *conatus* or striving, attaining its full effect unless it is impeded by a contrary *conatus*. This effort frequently presents itself to the senses and, in my judgment, is understood by reason to be everywhere in matter, even where it is not obvious to senses. But if this force is not to be attributed to God, acting by miracle, then it is certainly necessary that he produces that force in bodies themselves, so that it constitutes their innermost nature, since to act is the mark of substances, and extension, far from determining substance itself, means nothing but the continuity of diffusion of an already presupposed striving and reacting (that is, resisting) substance. Nor does it matter that every corporeal action derives from motion, and that motion itself comes only from motion, either previously existing in the body or impressed from without. For, strictly speaking, motion (and likewise time) never really exists, since the whole never exists, inasmuch as it lacks coexistent parts. And furthermore, there is nothing real in motion but a momentary *quid* which must consist in a force striving toward change. Whatever there is in corporeal nature over and above the object of geometry or extension reduces to this.

(*Specimen Dynamicum*, M. VI, 235)

The body, matter, thus contains within itself a *vis activa* that transcends materiality and has a spiritual character.

Τὸ δυναμιχόν, power, is twofold in the body: passive and active. The passive force properly constitutes matter or mass, while the active force constitutes *entelechy*[39] or form. Passive force is resistance itself, by which the body resists not only penetration, but also movement, and by which another body cannot take its place without its giving way. On the other hand, it does not give way except by delaying somewhat the movement of the body that pushes it, and so it tends to persevere in its previous state, so that it not only does not spontaneously deviate from it, but also resists anything that tends to change it. Thus, there are two resistances or masses. The first is what they call *antitypia* or impenetrability, and the second is what Kepler calls the natural inertia of bodies, which Descartes recognized somewhere in his epistolary from the fact that due to it, bodies do not accommodate a new movement except by force, and therefore resist the body that presses them, and weaken its force. This would not happen if in the body, in addition to extension, there were not also τὸ δυναμιχόν — that is, the principle of the laws of motion, by which it follows that the quantity of forces cannot be increased, and that a body cannot be pushed by another body except by decreasing the force of the latter.

Active force, which is also known simply as force, should not be thought of merely as the vulgar force learned of in school, i.e. as a capacity for action, but implies a *conatus*, namely a tendency to action, such that if there is no impediment, action ensues. And this is precisely what entelechy, misunderstood in the schools, consists of; for such a power encompasses the actual deed. Nor does it remain a

---

[39] Entelechy, from ἐντελές (complete) or ἔχειν (have) is the term Aristotle uses to indicate fully realized form. Leibniz uses it again to define the active aspect of substance and the monad. This term is also often used by him as a synonym for monad. Cf. *Monadology*, §§ 18, 48.

mere faculty, although it does not always proceed directly to the action it aims at; sometimes it sets up an impediment against it. In the second place, the active force is twofold, primitive and derivative — that is, substantive or accidental. The primitive active force, which Aristotle calls the first entelechy (ἐντελέχεια ἡ πρώτη), commonly known as the form of substance, constitutes corporeal substance. This is in itself a unity, i.e., not a mere aggregate of several substances — in the same way for example that an animal is very different from a herd of animals. And therefore, this entelechy is either a soul or something similar, and always naturally activates some organic body which, taken separately in itself and deprived of or separated from the soul, would not be a single substance, but an aggregate of many — in short, a contrivance of nature...

The derivative force is what some call impetus — *conatus*, that is — or the tendency, so to speak, towards some determined motion, by which the primitive force or principle of action is modified. As for this force, I have shown that it does not always remain the same in the same body, but that however it is distributed across several bodies, its overall quantity remains the same, unlike the motion itself, the quantity of which is not preserved...

Many reasons lead us to establish an active force in bodies, mainly experience itself, which shows that there are movements in matter that must be attributed originally to the universal causality of things, i.e. to God — but immediately and specifically they must be explained through the power placed by God in things. Indeed, saying that God in creation gave bodies a law of action is the same as saying that He gave them something by virtue of which that law is to be observed. Otherwise, he himself would have to continually ensure the observance of that law; whereas it is rather his law itself that is effective, and he has made the bodies active — that is, he has given them a force that

is inherent. It must also be considered that derivative force and action are modal, because they are subject to change. And each *mode* comprises a modification of something that is persistent, or rather absolute. Just as the figure is in a certain way a limitation or modification of the passive force or extended mass, so the derivative force and motor action is in a certain way a modification not of something purely passive (otherwise the modification or limitation would contain more reality than the itself, which is limited), but of something active — that is, of the primitive entelechy. Hence, derivative and accidental or mutable force will be a qualifying modification of the essential primitive *virtus* that endures in any corporeal substance. For this reason the Cartesians, not recognizing any modifiable substantial active principle in the body, were forced to deny it any action and to transfer the action exclusively to God — a *Deus ex machina*, a principle that is anything but philosophical.
(Fragment from 1702, M. VI, 100-103)

METAPHYSICAL VALUE OF FORCE — This entelechy, this force that matter is made of — which indeed constitutes its innermost essence — is something similar to the soul.

Matter has essentially in itself the principle of movement, but in my opinion this should only be understood in the sense that there are souls in matter, which are indivisible and indestructible.
(Letter to Burnett, 1704, G. III, 299)

It is this principle of the animation of matter that pushes Leibniz to a view of the material world as not purely mechanical — that leads him to see in it, through the principle of mind, a finalist element and, through this, the hand of God.

I must state at the outset that, in my opinion, everything in nature happens mechanically, and that the notions of figure and movement are sufficient to give an exact and complete reason for any particular phenomenon (such as weight or elasticity). But the actual principles of mechanics and the laws of motion arise, in my opinion, from something superior, which depends on metaphysics rather than geometry and which cannot be arrived at by the imagination, although the mind can conceive it well enough. So I think that in nature, along with the notion of extension, it is appropriate to invoke the concept of force, which makes matter capable of acting and resisting. And by force or power I do not mean power as the mere faculty, which is no more than a proximate possibility of acting and which, being as if dead, never produces even a single action without being excited from outside. What I mean is something midway between the power and the action that involves an effort, an act, an entelechy, by virtue of which power passes into action as long as nothing stands in its way. This is the reason why I consider it a constitutive element of substance — the principle of action which is the essential characteristic of substance.

In this way I see the efficient cause of physical actions as deriving from metaphysics, an opinion that distances me greatly from those who do not recognize in nature anything that is not material or extended, and who for this reason make themselves rightly suspect to persons of piety. I also believe that the concept of good or of a final cause, insofar as it contains in itself a moral element, can also be usefully employed in the explanation of natural phenomena, since the author of nature acts according to the principle of order and perfection, with a wisdom not susceptible of improvement. And I have shown elsewhere, with regard to the general law of the radiation of light, how

the principle of the final cause is often sufficient to discover the secrets of nature until the efficient proximate cause, which is more difficult to discover, has been found.
(*Système nouveau pour expliquer la nature des substances,* first draft, 1695, G. IV, 472)

True physics should in fact be derived from the source of divine perfections. It is God who is the ultimate reason of things, and the knowledge of God is no less the beginning of science than his essence and his will are the beginning of beings. The more one is versed in the profundities of philosophy, the more one agrees with this, but few up to now have been able to deduce any truths of importance from a consideration of divine attributes. Perhaps these little examples will arouse some of them to go further. Philosophy is thus sanctified by the infusion into it of currents flowing from the sacred springs of natural theology. Far from excluding final causes and the consideration of a wise being who acts for the best (whereby goodness and beauty would become arbitrary or merely relative to us and not attributable to God: one the opinion of Descartes, the other of Spinoza),[40] it is from these that everything in physics must be derived.
(*Principium quoddam generale,* M.VI, 134)

In this divine organization of the world, we see force pervade and permeate all of nature. No more corporeal atoms — this is something equally unitary and indivisible, but devoid of any materiality whatever. These substantive units lie at the boundary between matter and mind, capable of developing in both directions, and they contain within themselves a force that allows them to develop spontaneously towards the universal. In this spontaneity and activity lies the mental character

---

[40] Descartes, according to Leibniz, derives the rules of goodness and harmony from the will of God (cf. above, pp. 124-25). For Spinoza, on the other hand, goodness is a relation of the individual creature to the absolute Substance, i.e. God.

of the elements of corporeal substance, which is what draws them closer to the soul and the self.

Since corporeal nature requires the existence of true units, without which there could be neither multiplicities nor aggregates, it is necessary that what constitutes corporeal substance be something corresponding to what in us is usually called the self, which is indivisible and at the same time has agency. This self, being indivisible and without parts, cannot be a compound being, but being an agent, it will be something substantive.
(*Système nouveau*, first draft, 1695, G. IV, 473)

IV. THE MONAD

CONSTITUTION AND FUNCTION OF THE MONAD. — Two fundamental principles of Leibnizian philosophy were examined in the previous chapters: the universality of individual substance, and the incorporeal principle of force in the material world. The first was derived from the elaboration of logical concepts, and the second from the rigorous consideration of physical theorems. The union and fusion of these two principles gives rise to the *monad*.[41] What they have in common is the fact of enclosing within themselves, in a potential state, an infinite possibility of development. Individual substance is the starting point in a chain of causes and effects that encompasses within its links the past and the future of the entire universe, and the animated unity of the corporeal world is a force capable of developing motion and, despite its incorporeal character, of giving rise to the formation of materiality. Of these two elements, one is universal but abstract, while the other is concrete, real, incorporeal, but still without universality. In their fusion, one of them supplies what the other lacks, and the monad will be a

---

[41] *Monad* is a Greek word meaning unity. The term was also used by Giordano Bruno to indicate the prime elements of things. However, it is not certain that Leibniz derived this designation from him.

principle that is immaterial and universal at the same time, but nevertheless concrete, such that it is what the existing world actually consists of. The monad is "the atom of nature and the element of things." It is given different names by Leibniz: entelechy, soul, substance, etc., in accordance with the various occasions on which he speaks of it.

Epicurus's atom, though endowed with parts, is a thing united in its interior, whereas the soul, though without parts, contains within itself a great number — actually an infinite number — of varieties, due to the multiplicity of representations of external things, or rather the representation of the universe that the Creator has placed within it.
(*Observations on Bayle's Dictionary*, 1702, G. IV, 544)

Monads are the first and simplest principles out of which the world is constituted. They are not material, but all matter derives from them — they are individual, multiple (in that they are always particular points of view on the universe, and points of view can be infinite), and at the same time each one contains within itself a vision of the whole.

Substantial unity calls for a thoroughly indivisible being, naturally indestructible since its concept involves all that must happen to it. This characteristic cannot be found either in forms or in motions, both of which involve something imaginary — as I could demonstrate — but it can be found in a soul or a substantial form, such as the one called the *I*. These latter are the only thoroughly complete beings, as the ancients recognized and, above all, Plato, who showed very clearly that matter alone does not suffice for forming a substance. Now, the above mentioned *I* or whatever corresponds to it, in each individual substance can neither be made nor destroyed by the

bringing together or the separation of the parts. Such juxtapositions are wholly apart from the constitution of a substance. I cannot tell exactly whether there are other true corporeal substances beside those which have life. But souls serve to give us a certain knowledge of others at least by analogy.
(Letter to Arnauld, 1686, G. II, 6-7)

I do not know whether it is possible to explain the constitution of the soul better than to say: 1) that it is a simple substance, or rather what I call a true unity; 2) that this unity nevertheless expresses multiplicity, i.e. bodies, and that it expresses them as best as possible according to its point of view or relationship; 3) that in this way it expresses phenomena according to the metaphysical-mathematical laws of nature — that is, according to the order most in keeping with intelligence and reason. It follows finally, 4), that the soul is an imitation of God, in the highest degree possible for creatures, that like him it is simple and yet also infinite, and envelops everything through confused perceptions; but that, with regard to distinct ones, it is limited. Instead, everything is distinct in the sovereign substance, from which everything emanates, and which is the cause of existence and order and, in a word, the ultimate reason for things. It can also be said that each soul is a separate world, but that all these worlds are attuned, and are representative of the same phenomena, in different ratios; and that this is the most perfect way of multiplying beings as much as possible, and in the best way possible.
(Letter to Bayle, 1702, G. III, 72)

The concept of individual substance was first formulated by Leibniz in *Discours de Métaphysique* in 1686. He introduced the word monad in 1696. Toward the middle of his life, in other words, he came into possession of the fundamental element that for him constituted the world. Having found this, he set himself the problem of explaining, by means of this element, the make-up of the world itself. Just as in the art of combinations the goal was to find, by means of the decomposition of concepts, the simple terms of which human thought consists, and then, through various combination of them, to form again every possible concept, so now an analytical investigation in the logical, physical, metaphysical field led to the notion of the monad as a simple substance, constituting the world. Now the task was to show concretely how the world consisted of monads, how every aspect, every phenomenon of it could be explained through combinations, modifications, and different aspects of monads.

THE BEGINNING AND END OF THE MONAD — Where did the monad come from? What produced it? What is its origin?

It is not possible to conceive of it as derived from any natural entity. Being produced always means being *caused* in some way, and since it already encompasses within itself the whole infinite series of causes and effects, no cause can be attributed to it outside itself: any cause of it would always be included within it. Similarly, the end of the monad is not conceivable within the natural order — such an end would imply an interruption in the series of causes and effects, which is on the contrary continuous and infinite. The origin and end of monads must therefore be sought outside the causal order of the universe, or rather we might say that monads have no origin. They were born with the universe itself — created with it — and their creator is the creator of the universe: God.

As for the beginning and end of these forms, souls, or substantive principles, it must be said that they cannot have an origin except in the creation, and can have no end except by an annulment performed expressly by the supreme power of God... Thus these forms neither begin nor end naturally. And why would they not have the same status as atoms, which, according to Gassendi's followers,

must always remain preserved? This same privilege must be granted to everything that is truly a substance, because true unity is absolutely indissoluble. Given this, one must believe that these substances were initially created together with the world.
(Système nouveau, first draft, 1695, G. IV, 474)

Thus (with the exception of souls that God still expressly wants to create), I was obliged to recognize that the constituent forms of substances were created together with the world and that they subsist in eternity.
(Système nouveau, second draft, 1695, G. IV, 479)

INDIVIDUALITY AND UNIVERSALITY OF THE MONAD — Monads have in themselves a dual nature such that each is a constituent element of the world, and at the same time each in itself embodies the absolute totality of the world's development. The world is made up of monads, but each monad, from a certain point of view, is the world itself. *From a certain point of view.* This is the criterion that allows those two characteristics to be preserved and reconciled. Each monad keeps its individuality and distinction from the others in that it entails and represents the same whole, but from a different point of view. And the points of view are infinite, and monads are infinite as well. The individuality of the monad is thus reconciled with its universality.

Paradoxical as it may seem, it is impossible for us to know individuals or to find any way of precisely *determining* the individuality of any thing except by taking hold of the thing itself. In fact, any set of circumstances could recur, with tiny differences which we would not take in. And place and time, far from being determinants by themselves, must themselves be determined by the things they contain. The most important point in this is that *individuality* involves infinity, and only someone who is capable of grasping the infinite could know the principle of individuation of some given thing. This principle arises from the influence — properly understood — that all the things in the universe have on one another. The case would be otherwise, it is true, if the world were composed of Democritus's atoms, but then there would be no *difference* between two *different* individuals with the same shape and size.

(*New Essays*, 1701 ff, III, 3, § 6)

It is precisely the universality of the monad that guarantees its individuality. Two atoms of equal shape and size, with the same external characteristics, would be indistinguishable from each other. Two monads, on the other hand, cannot be indistinguishable and perfectly identical. The fact that there are two of them implies that they represent the world from two points of view, and each point of view entails links and relationships to infinity that will necessarily be different from those of any other point of view. Two monads perfectly identical in the entire complex of relations involved are inconceivable — they would be one and the same monad. This is the principle that Leibniz calls the *identity of indiscernibles*. Because of it, each monad is guaranteed its individuality and singularity among all the others.

It is a principle of great importance in all philosophy and also in theology that there are no purely extrinsic designations, and this is because of the connection of things to each other. Two things cannot differ only locally or temporally. It is always necessary for some other internal difference to exist between them. Thus it is not possible for there to be two atoms that are similar in shape and equal in size — for example, two equal cubes. These notions are mathematical — i.e. abstract, not real. All things that are different must be distinguished in some way, and position alone is not sufficient to differentiate among real things. The whole of purely atomistic philosophy is disrupted by this principle. Firstly, it is not possible that there are atoms, otherwise there would be two things that did not differ except from the outside. Secondly, if the position taken alone does not in itself constitute a change, it follows that there is no change that is purely a change of place. And in general, place, position, quantity (number, for example), and proportion are nothing other than relations resulting from other things that themselves constitute change. Thus, being in an indeterminate place, abstractly speaking, does not seem to indicate anything other than a position. But actually, what is in a certain place must express in itself that very place, so that distance and the degree of distance also implies a way of expressing in itself the distant thing, of acting upon it, and of being affected by it. In effect, the position implies a degree of expression...

Everything we have set out here stems from the fundamental principle that the predicate is contained in the subject, a principle that struck Arnauld[42] when I once mentioned it to him: — *j'en ay esté frappé* — he wrote to me.

(Fragment, C. 8-10)

REPRESENTATION AND APPETITE — Let us proceed with characterizing the structure of the monad. It contains within itself all its own future development, together with the development of the world. But what determines its distinctiveness and value is that it does not contain this explicitly and extended in time and space, but implicitly, meaningfully, in its potential state.

If we were to imagine the complete unfolding of each monad, we would lose, so to speak, the essential advantage of the monad — we would have before us the world itself in all its immense and elusive multiplicity. The advantage is precisely

---

[42] Antonio Arnauld (1612-1694), French theologian and philosopher of the Cartesian and Jansenist school, engaged in a long and very significant correspondence with Leibniz.

the gathering of the world's multiplicity in individuality — containing in the implicit act what in an explicit state would be superior to any faculty of perception or apprehension.

Now, how does this implication of totality unfold in the monad and what aspect does it concretely assume? On one hand it takes on the aspect of *force* or *appetite,* and on the other, of *representation.* Each monad has a representation of all the future states that it contains within itself, and at the same time it has an impulse, a tendency that impels it to move on to these future states from the present in which it finds itself. In these two forms, the transition to the universal takes place in the individual.

The state of the soul, like that of the atom, is a state of change, a tendency. The atom tends to change location, the soul to change thought — they both change in the simplest and most uniform way that their state allows. Why then (one might ask) is there such simplicity in the change of the atom and such variety in the changes of the soul? The fact is that the atom (as one imagines it, even though it does not really exist in nature), despite its being composed of parts, has nothing that leads to variety in its striving, since it is assumed that the parts do not change their relationships to each other. The soul, on the other hand, though indivisible, contains a compound tendency — that is, a multiplicity of present thoughts each of which tends towards a particular change, depending on what it contains, and these thoughts are all found together in the soul, by virtue of its essential relation to all other things in the world. And indeed it is, among other things, the absence of such a relation that makes Epicurus's atoms impossible in nature. For each thing or part of the universe must represent all the others — so that the soul, in terms of the variety of its modifications, must not compare itself to the material atom, but rather to the universe, which it represents from its point of view, and also in some way to God, whose infinity it represents in a finite way (because of its confused and imperfect perception of the infinite).

The feeling of pleasure, for example, seems simple but it isn't, and anyone desiring to anatomize it would find that it implicates everything that surrounds us and consequently everything surrounding what surrounds us. And the reason for the change of thoughts in the soul is the same as the reason for the change of things in the universe that it represents. For the mechanical relations that are developed in bodies are united and, as it were, concentrated in souls or entelechies, and indeed originate in them. It is true that not all entelechies are, like our souls, images of God, since they are not all made to be members of a society or state of which God is the head; but they are always images of the universe. They are worlds in compendium, in their own way — fruitful simplicities, unities of substances — but virtually infinite, due to the multiplicity of their modifications. They are centers that express an infinite circumference.

(Discussion with Bayle, 1712, G. IV, 562)

Why should God be unable to give to substance in the beginning a nature or internal force which enables it to produce in regular order — as in an *automaton* that is *spiritual* or *formal* but *free* in the case of that substance which has a share of reason — everything which is to happen to it, that is, all the appearances or expressions which it is to have, and this without the help of any created being? Especially since the nature of substance necessarily demands and essentially involves progress or change and would have no force of action without it. And since it is the nature of the soul to represent the universe in a very exact way, though with relative degrees of distinctness, the sequence of representations which the soul produces will correspond naturally to the sequence of changes in the universe itself.

(*Système nouveau*, 1695, G. IV, 485)

One monad by itself and at a single moment cannot be distinguished from another except by its internal qualities and actions, and these can only be its *perceptions* (that is to say, the representations of the compound, or of that which is without, in the simple), and its *appetitions* (that is to say, its tending from one perception to another) which are the principles of change. For the simplicity of a substance does not prevent the plurality of modifications which must necessarily be found together in the same simple substance; and these modifications must consist of the variety of relations of correspondence which the substance has with things outside. In the same way there may be found, in one *center* or point, though it is perfectly simple, an infinity of angles formed by the lines which meet in it.

(*Principes de la nature et de la grace*, 1713-14, G. IV, 598)

In this way, the concept of representation and knowledge in general is also configured, as Leibniz treats it from an epistemological point of view. *Perception* is the expression of multiplicity in unity, and, on the other hand, it is action.

Thought, being the action of a thing upon itself, does not take place in figure and motion, which cannot show the principle of a truly internal action. On the other hand, it is necessary that there be simple beings, otherwise there would be no compound beings or beings by aggregation, which are rather more phenomena than substances, and exist rather νόμῳ than φύσει (i.e., rather morally or rationally than physically) in the words of Democritus. And if there were no change in simple things, neither would there be any in compound things, whose reality

only exists in the reality of the simple things. Now internal changes in simple things are similar to what we conceive in thought, and it can be said that in general perception is the *expression of multiplicity in unity*. You have no need, Sir,[43] of these explanations of the immateriality of thought, which you have spoken of admirably in many places. However, combining these considerations with my particular hypothesis, it seems to me that the one seems to shed light on the other.
(Letter to Bayle, 1702, G. III, 69)

Thoughts are actions, whereas items of knowledge (or truths), in so far as they are within us even when we do not think of them, are tendencies or dispositions; and we know many things which we scarcely think about.
(*New Essays*, 1701 ff. I, 1, § 26, G. V., 79)

I am astonished, Sir, that you insist on twisting my views in a way that is completely different from what I intend. You claim that according to me, we do nothing but notice what is going on within us. I do not know where you get this idea from, but I believe rather that *we do everything that happens within us*.
(Letter to Jacquelot, 1704, G. VI, 567)

Thought as unity of multiplicity and as action — these are two concepts that would be characteristic of post-Kantian idealistic philosophy, which Leibniz already arrived at here with the exploration of the concept of the monad as mind.

---

[43] Pierre Bayle (1647-1706), whom Leibniz addresses here, was the main representative of sceptical philosophy at the time. Founder of the *Nouvelles de la république des lettres*, author of the *Dictionnaire historique et critique*, he engaged in lengthy and very interesting discussions with Leibniz on various topics, such as the hypothesis of pre-established harmony, and the problem of reconciling faith and reason.

PETITES PERCEPTIONS — From this concept, Leibniz also draws arguments to affirm innatism, against the denial of Locke, who, in his *Essay Concerning Human Understanding*, had opposed Cartesian rationalism by asserting that everything comes to the soul exclusively from the senses — from outside, like marks imprinted on a *tabula rasa*. All Leibniz's *New Essays on Human Understanding* are designed to take a stand against Locke's theses. [...] Here we are only interested in noting how the affirmation of innatism in Leibniz is not based solely, as in Descartes, on rationalistic grounds. What is innate to the mind does not for him derive solely from the ideas of reason. Also innate is everything contained in the soul, understood as a monad — that is, the whole series of relations of cause and effect that it has a representation of. All this constitutes the content of the soul and does not come to it from outside, but is already part of it from its creation. The entire universe, in short, is already inherent a priori in the soul.

But the soul has no current knowledge of all this. The field of its knowledge is limited and extends only to what is most immediately in contact with it. How can this be reconciled with its universality and innatism? Leibniz appeals in this regard to *petites perceptions* or unfelt perceptions, which continue to influence the soul, even if they do not reach its consciousness. They belong to the soul's representation, but the soul is not aware of them. In this way, the absolute innatism of all truth, whether necessary or contingent, whether of reason or fact, is brought into agreement with the current limitation of our knowledge. Petites perceptions allow Leibniz to conceive of the monad as both limited and universal.

The question of the origin of our ideas and maxims is not preliminary in philosophy, and we need to have made great progress in order to solve it successfully. I think, however, that I can say that our ideas, even those of sensory things, come from within our own innermost selves... I am not at all in favor of Aristotle's *tabula rasa*; and there is something substantial in what Plato called reminiscence. There is even something more; for we not

only have a reminiscence of all our past thoughts, but also a presentiment of all our future thoughts. It is true that this is confused, and fails to distinguish them, in much the same way as when I hear the noise of the sea I hear that of all the particular waves which make up the noise as a whole, though without discerning one wave from another. Thus, it is true in a certain sense, as I have explained, that not only our ideas, but also our sensations (sentiments) spring from within our own soul, and that the soul is more independent than we think, although it is always true that nothing takes place in it which is not determined, and nothing is found in creatures that God does not continually create.
(*Sur l'Essay de l'entendement humain de Monsieur Locke*, after 1693, G. V, 16)

There is the question whether the soul in itself is completely blank like a writing tablet on which nothing has yet been written — a *tabula rasa* — as Aristotle and the author of the Essay maintain, and whether everything which is inscribed there comes solely from the senses and experience; or whether the soul inherently contains the sources of various notions and doctrines, which external objects merely rouse up on suitable occasions, as I believe and as do Plato and even the Scholastics and all those who understand in this sense the passage in St. Paul (Romans, 2 : 15) where he says that God's law is written in our hearts...

Can we deny that there is a great deal that is innate in our minds and didn't come through the senses, because we are innate to ourselves, so to speak, and within ourselves there are being, unity, substance, duration, change, action, perception, pleasure, and that the same holds for hosts of other intellectual ideas that we have? And since these facts about us are always present to our understanding (even though they cannot always be perceived due to our distractions and needs), is it any wonder that we say that these ideas are innate in us? I have also used the analogy of a veined block of marble as opposed to an entirely homogeneous one, or a blank tablet — what the philosophers call a *tabula rasa*. If the soul were like an empty page, then truths would be in us in the way that the shape of Hercules is in an uncarved piece of marble that is entirely neutral as to whether it takes Hercules's shape or some other. Contrast that piece of marble with one that is veined in a way that marks out the shape of Hercules rather than other shapes. This latter block would be more inclined to take that shape than the former would, and Hercules would be in a way innate in it, even though it would take a lot of work to expose the veins and to polish them into clarity. This is how ideas and truths are innate in us — as inclinations, dispositions, tendencies, or natural potentialities, and not as actions, though these potentialities are always accompanied by certain actions, often insensible ones, which correspond to them... At the same time, there are hundreds of pointers to the conclusion that at every moment there is in us an infinity of *perceptions*, alterations in the soul itself — however devoid of apperception[44] and reflection. We aren't aware of them because these impressions are too tiny and too numerous, or too unvarying, so that they don't stand out enough to be noticed. But when combined with others they do have their effect and make themselves felt, at least confusedly, within the whole. This is how we become so used to the motion of a mill or a waterfall, after living beside it for a while, that we don't attend to it. Its motion does still affect our sense organs, and something corresponding to that occurs in the soul..., but

---

[44] "Apperception" refers to conscious perception (*Apercevoir*: notice) cf. *Monadology*, § 14.

these impressions in the soul and the body, lacking the appeal of novelty, aren't forceful enough to attract our attention and our memory, which are occupied with more interesting things. Many of our own present perceptions slip by unconsidered and even unnoticed, but if someone alerts us to them right after they have occurred, e.g., making us take note of some noise that we've just heard, then we remember it and are aware of having had some sense of it.

Thus, we weren't aware of these perceptions when they occurred, and we became aware of them only because we were alerted to them a little — perhaps a very little — later...

We always have some feeble and confused sensation when we are asleep, however soundly; and the loudest noise in the world would never waken us if we didn't have some perception of its start, which is small, just as the strongest force in the world would never break a rope unless the least force strained it and stretched it slightly, even though the little lengthening that is produced is imperceptible.

(*New Essays*, 1701 ff., Preface, G. V, 42-47)

[...] Here it is interesting to note how the development of the concept of the monad also directly affects all epistemological issues.

V. PERFECTION AND IMPERFECTION IN THE MONAD

The monad increasingly assumes the characteristics of the mind. Universal, devoid of extension, eternal, indestructible, equipped with representation and action, it became the cornerstone on which the edifice of the universe was built. It is mind; but everything, even matter, consists of monads. Both the material world and the mental world must take it as their starting point. From this conception of the monad as the constitutive element of the world, and the commitment to justify everything through it, new developments arise. The question is no longer one of studying this substantive principle in its intimate make-up — but of seeing it act in the world.

The problems that arise in this regard come down to three: the relationship of the monads to the supreme spiritual substance, which is God, the relationship of the various monads to each other, and the problem of justifying a corporeal nature. We shall see how these problems are mutually related.

MONADS AND GOD; AGREEMENT AMONG MONADS — The representation of the entire universe and the tendency towards self-realization that each monad holds within itself are analogous to the tendency and representation that characterize divinity. In this regard the monad is not different from God. At the same time, it is a creature of God, and its aspect as a creature lies precisely in the particular point of view from which it acts and represents the world. In this representation each monad is complete in itself, and it is not possible that anything comes to it from the outside — all its concerns, past, present and future, are already contained in it. Its representation of the world is already closed in itself, and its content corresponds to the content of the other monads, in the same way that two views of a city from different points of view correspond without influencing each other. This completeness of the monad closed within itself is expressed by Leibniz in two famous sayings: first, that monads have no windows; second, that it is sufficient for the existence and universality of the monad that God and it are alone in the world.

God produces diverse substances according to the different views he has of the world, and through the intervention of God the nature proper to each substance involves that what happens to one corresponds to what happens to all the others, without their acting upon one another directly.

Now it is clear, first of all, that the created substances

depend on God, who preserves them and indeed even produces them continually by a kind of emanation, as we produce our thoughts. For as God turns the universal system of phenomena which he has seen fit to produce in order to manifest his glory, on all sides and in all ways, so to speak, and examines every aspect of the world in every possible manner, there is no relation which escapes his omniscience, and there thus results from each perspective of the universe, as it is seen from a certain position, a substance which expresses the universe in conformity to that perspective, if God sees fit to render his thought effective and to produce that substance. And since God's perspective is always true, our perceptions are also always true; it is our judgments, which come from ourselves, which deceive us. But we have already said, and it follows from what we have just said, that each substance is as a world apart, independent of everything outside of itself except God. Thus, all our phenomena, that is to say, all the things that can ever happen to us, are only the results of our own being. And since these phenomena maintain a certain order which conforms to our nature or, so to speak, to the world which is within us, so that we are able to make observations that are useful for controlling our own conduct and justified by the success of future phenomena, with the result that we can often judge the future by the past without deceiving ourselves, this would be sufficient to enable us to say that these phenomena are true, without being put to the task of inquiring whether they are outside of us and whether others perceive them also. Nevertheless, it is true that the perceptions or expressions of all substances intercorrespond, so that each one, following with care the established reasons or laws which it has observed, meets with others who have done this also. When a number of people have agreed to meet together in some place on a previously determined day, they can do this successfully if they wish. But although all express the same phenomena, it does not follow from this that their expressions are exactly alike; it suffices that they are proportional. So, a number of spectators believe that they see the same thing and are in fact in agreement about it, although each one sees and speaks of it according to the measure of his own point of view. It is only God (from whom all individuals emanate continually and who sees the universe not only as they see it but also entirely differently from all of them), who is the cause of this correspondence between their phenomena and who makes public to all that which is peculiar to one; otherwise, there would be no interconnection. We might say, then, in a way, and with good meaning, though not in accordance with common usage, that one particular substance never acts upon another particular substance, nor is it acted upon by it, if we keep in mind that what happens to each is solely the result of its own complete idea or concept, since this idea already includes all the predicates or events and expresses the whole universe. Nothing can in fact happen to us except thoughts and perceptions, and all our future thoughts and perceptions are only the consequences, however contingent they may be, of our preceding ones, so that if I were capable of considering distinctly everything that is happening to me or appearing to me at this hour, I could see in it everything which will ever happen or appear to me. And this would not fail to happen to me, even if all that there is outside of me were to be destroyed, provided there remained only God and myself.

(*Discours de métaphysique*, 1686, § XIV)

The difference between the monad and God thus consists in this — that the monad is a representation of the world from a single point of view, whereas God gathers all points of view together and sums them all up in himself. And this is also the basis for the agreement of monads among themselves, while each maintaining its autonomy and independence.

CONFUSED PERCEPTIONS AND THE RECIPROCAL ACTION OF MONADS — But the monad is also distinguished from God in another respect, and that is the reduced clarity and precision of its representation. With the idea of *confused perceptions* Leibniz once again takes up the concept of petites perceptions. But while the function of the latter was to show the presence in each soul — albeit unconscious and indistinct — of the entire content of the world, confused perceptions point to such unconsciousness and confusion as the cause of each monad's own imperfection.

The representation of monads does indeed contain all the links of cause and effect that constitute the universe, but not as a clear, distinct and perfectly developed perception. As we get further away from the starting point that constitutes the essential individuality of each monad, this perception becomes indistinct and confused. And the deficiency derives from the imperfection that is inherent in creatures. In God, who is the place, as it were, of all monads and gathers within himself the infinite points of view, the representation of the universe in its totality remains perfectly clear and distinct.

Our sense perceptions, even when they are clear, must necessarily contain a certain confused feeling, for, since all the bodies of the universe are in sympathy with each other, ours receives impressions from all the rest, and though our senses are in response to all of them, it is impossible for our soul to pay attention to every particular impression. This is why our confused sensations result from a really infinite variety of perceptions. This is somewhat like the confused murmur heard by those who approach the seashore, which comes from the accumulation of innumerable breaking waves. For if out of several perceptions which do not harmonize so as to make one, there is no single one which surpasses the others, and if these perceptions make impressions that are about equally strong and equally capable of holding the attention of the soul, it can perceive them only confusedly.

(*Discours de métaphysique*, 1686, § XXXIII)

Differentiation in the clarity of perception is thus what constitutes the individuality of each monad, and is what differentiates monads from one another. It also explains, to some extent, how one can speak — however inaccurately — of the *action* of one monad upon another.

Since we do attribute to other things, as causes acting upon ourselves, what we perceive in a certain way, we must consider the basis of this judgment and the element of truth it has in it.

The action of one finite substance upon another consists in nothing but the increase of degree of its expression together with the diminution of the expression of the other, insofar as God has formed them in advance in such a way that they are adapted to each other.

To reconcile the language of metaphysics with that of practice, it will suffice for the present, without entering into a long discussion, to remark that we ascribe to ourselves, primarily and with reason, those phenomena which we express more perfectly and that we attribute to other substances those phenomena which each expresses best. Thus, a substance which has an infinite extension, insofar as it expresses everything, becomes limited through the more or less perfect way in which it expresses each thing. It is in this sense, then, that we can think of substances as impeding and limiting each other, and consequently it is in this sense that we can say that they act upon each other and are obliged, so to speak, to adapt themselves to each other. For it can happen that a single change which increases the expression of one will diminish that of another.

Now it is the virtue of a particular substance to express well the glory of God, and the better it expresses it, the less limited it is. And whenever anything exercises its virtue or power, that is to say when it acts, it improves and enlarges itself in proportion to its action. Therefore, when a change takes place by which a number of substances are affected (as a matter of fact, every change affects them all), I believe it can be said that any substance which thereby passes immediately to a greater degree of perfection or to a more perfect expression exercises its power and acts, while any substance which passes to a lesser degree of perfection shows its weakness and suffers. I hold too that every action of a substance which has perfection involves some pleasure, and every passion some pain, and vice versa. Yet it may well happen that a present advantage may be destroyed by a greater evil in the future, so that one can sin in acting or in exercising his power and in finding pleasure.

(*Discours de métaphysique*, 1686, § XV)

CONFUSED PERCEPTIONS AS CORPOREAL — In the monad, therefore, distinct perception is the active element; confused perception the passive element. Now have we not already seen, regarding the laws of force and motion, that Leibniz defines action as the mental principle, and passion (or passivity) as the material one? Confused perceptions, insofar as they are passive, represent the corporeal principle in the monad.

I have already said that, taking action in a strict metaphysical sense, as what takes place in substance spontaneously and from its own depths, it alone is properly speaking a substance which is active, for all arises for it from itself after God; it being impossible for one created substance to have influence upon another. But taking action as an exercise of perception and passion as its contrary, there is action in true substance only when their perception (for I grant it to all) is developed and becomes more distinct, as there is passion only when it becomes more confused; so that in substances capable of pleasure and of pain, all action is a step towards pleasure and all passion a step towards pain.

(*New Essays*, 1701 ff., II, 21 § 72)

Innate ideas and truths cannot be effaced, but they are obscured in all men (as they are now) by their inclination toward the needs of the body, and oftener still by the occurrence of bad customs. These characteristics of the internal light would always be shining in the understanding and would give fervor to the will, if the confused perceptions of sense did not engross our attention. It is the struggle of which Holy Scripture no less than ancient and modern philosophy speaks.

(*New Essays*, 1701 ff., I, 2, § 20)

It is right to join the ancient philosophers in calling *perturbation* or *passion* that which consists of confused thoughts, in which there is something involuntary and the unknown. This is what in common parlance is not unfairly attributed to the struggle between body and mind, since our confused thoughts represent the body or the flesh and constitute our imperfection.

(Discussion with Bayle, 1702, G. IV, 565)

On the other hand, it is interesting to note that Leibniz, precisely at the same time as defining confused perceptions as coming from corporeal nature, reaffirms that they have nothing essential that distinguishes their nature from that of distinct perceptions, which is like stating that corporeal nature does not essentially differ from the nature of the mind.

Confused thoughts are generally conceived as being of a completely different kind from *distinct* thoughts, and our author[45] judges that the mind is more united to the body through confused thoughts than through distinct ones. This is not without foundation, for muddled thoughts indicate our imperfection, our passions, our dependence on the totality of external things or matter, whereas the perfection, strength, dominion, freedom and action of the soul consist primarily in our distinct thoughts. In any case, it is no less true that at bottom confused thoughts are nothing but a multitude of thoughts which in themselves are like those that are distinct but are so small that each separately does not excite our attention and does not capture our attention enough to distinguish it. Indeed, it can be said that a truly infinite quantity of them is included in our sensations. And this is precisely the great difference between confused and distinct thoughts...

Thus, there is no need to think of confused sensations as something primitive and inexplicable. To do so would almost be putting them on a par with the ancient qualities embraced by some of the Scholastic philosophers,[46] and substituting these sensations would only amount to claiming that the difference was essential — and this would only be shifting the difficulty. And however true it may be that explaining them completely exceeds our powers because of the great multiplicity that they entail, we nevertheless continue to penetrate them more and more, by means of experiences that uncover in them the foun-

---

[45] The Benedictine Francois Lamy, author of *Connoissance de soy même* (Paris, 1699), with whom Leibniz is disagreeing here.

[46] Leibniz refers here to the Scholastic concept according to which all sensations derive from different "perceptible qualities" that move from external bodies to penetrate us. Such a conception made every sensation something primitive original, indissoluble. According to Leibniz, the various sensations derive instead from the differing behavior of a single substance, and the difference between confused and distinct — that is, between soul and body — is a difference of degree, not essence.

dations of distinct thoughts. Light and color offer examples of this. Not even these confused sensations are *arbitrary*, and I do not agree with the opinion widely accepted today and approved by our author that there is no similarity or relationship between our sensations and their bodily traces. Some will perhaps say that the sensation of heat does not resemble movement, and without doubt it does not resemble perceptible movement such as that of a carriage wheel. But it does resemble the sum total of the fire and the organs causing it — or rather, it is nothing but their representation. Thus, whiteness does not resemble a convex spherical mirror, and yet it is nothing more than the set of a number of small convex mirrors that can be seen in foam, looked at closely. And if we could always just as easily discover the causes of our sensations, we would find that they always came down to something of this kind.

(*Addition à l'Explication du système nouveau*
after 1700, G. IV, 574-6)

CORPREALITY IN THE MONAD. IMMORTALITY — So we have arrived at a concept of the body simply as an aspect of the mind — or rather, that body and mind are two different aspects of the original simple substance, or monad. The monad is not in itself corporeal, but it can — indeed it must, as its degree of perfection increases or decreases — develop as mind or as body. In fact, confused perceptions can become distinct, and vice versa.

Besides the perceptions which the soul remembers, there is a mass which is made up of an infinite number of confused perceptions which it does not disentangle. It is through these that it represents outside bodies and comes to have distinct thoughts which are unlike the preceding ones, because the bodies which the soul represents have suddenly changed to something which strongly affects its own. So the soul sometimes passes from white to black or from yes to no, without knowing how, or at least involuntarily, for what its confused thoughts and feelings produce in it we attribute to the body. So, we should not be surprised if a man who is stung by some insect when eating jam should, despite himself, pass immediately from pleasure to pain. For, in approaching the man's body before stinging it, this insect was already affecting it, and the representation of this was, albeit unconsciously, already affecting his soul. However, in the soul as in the body, little by little the insensible becomes the sensible. That is how the soul changes itself even against its will, for it is enslaved by the feelings and confused thoughts which occur according to the states of its body and of other bodies through their relation to it. These, then, are the means through which pleasures are sometimes interrupted and followed by pains, without the soul's always being alerted or prepared for it; as for example when the insect which stings approaches without making a noise, or, if it is a wasp, for example, when some distraction prevents our noticing the approaching wasp's buzz. This we must not say that nothing new happens in the substance of the soul which makes it feel the sting; for what happens is confused presentiments or, better, insensible dispositions of the soul, which represent the dispositions of the body with regard to the sting.[47]

(Observations on Bayle's Dictionary, 1702, G. IV, 546-7)

It necessarily follows from all this that every monad, and therefore every soul, is provided with a body. And since every monad is eternal and indestructible, it is not only the soul that

---

[47] What is stated here contradicts only in part the hypothesis of pre-established harmony, according to which body and spirit are two separate systems, devoid of mutual influence. The confused perceptions of the soul are understood here not as truly corporeal, but as representing in the soul what takes place in the body. It is undeniable, however, that Leibniz does at times attribute to the confused perceptions a distinctly corporeal character (Cf. pp. 186 ff., 203 ff.).

is immortal, but the body as well. Strictly speaking, death cannot be spoken of in nature, but simply the composition and decomposition of various simple elements one into another.

I hold not only that these souls or entelechies all have with them some organic body proportionate to their perceptions, but also that they will always have it and have had it as long as they have existed. Thus, not only the soul, but also the animal itself (or that which is analogous to the soul and the animal, not to put too fine a point on it) persists, and generation and death cannot be anything but developments and involutions of which nature visibly shows us some samples, according to its custom, to help us guess what it conceals. And therefore, neither iron, nor fire, nor all the other types of natural violence, whatever ruin they bring to the body of an animal, cannot prevent the soul from preserving some organic body, since the *organism* — that is, order and artifice — is something essential to matter that is produced and organized by sovereign wisdom, for production must always retain a trace of its author. This also makes me think that there is no mind completely separate from matter, except the primal and sovereign being.[48]

(Letter to Lady Mahsam, 1704, G. III, 340)

In nature, and speaking according to metaphysical rigor, there is neither generation nor death, but only development and envelopment of the same animal. Otherwise there would be too much of a leap, and nature would deviate too much from its character of uniformity through an inexplicable change of essence. Experience confirms these transformations in some animals, where nature herself has shown us a small sample of what she hides

---

[48] That is, God, in whom there are no dark perceptions nor passivity, and in whom everything is fulfilled.

elsewhere. Observations also make the most industrious observers conclude that the generation of animals is nothing other than growth together with transformation, which strongly suggests that death can only be the opposite, the difference being only that in one case the change happens gradually, and in the other it happens suddenly and by some violence. Moreover, experience even shows that too many barely distinguishable little perceptions, such as those that follow a blow to the head, stuns us, and that in a blackout it happens that we remember, and should remember, so few of these perceptions that it is as if we had not had any. Therefore the rule of uniformity should not lead us to make another judgment about death even in animals, according to the natural order, since the matter is easy to explain in this way, which is already known and experienced, and is inexplicable in any other manner. It is impossible to conceive how the existence or the activity of the perceptive principle begins or ends, nor is it any more possible to conceive its separation.

(Letter to Queen Sophie Charlotte of Prussia, 1704, G. III, 345)

HIERARCHY OF MONADS — The concept of distinct and confused perceptions as criteria for perfection and imperfection gives Leibniz a way of establishing a ranking among the various monads. The most elevated and complex perceptions will be distinguishing marks of the most elevated monads. In this way a true hierarchy is set up, whose lower rungs represent the lowest stages of vegetative life, and the highest the loftiest summits of the mind. The human monad is at the pinnacle of this ascent, and what gives it its noble title are its contemplated perceptions, through which it arrives at abstract ideas, self awareness, and memory of itself, which guarantee the preservation of individual personality. And over and above everything, as a supremely distinct and complete perception, and the object also of any singular perception by monads, is God.

Together with a particular body, each monad makes a living substance. Thus, not only is there life everywhere, joined to members or organs, but there are also infinite degrees of it in the monads, some of which dominate more or less over others. But when the monad has organs so adjusted that by means of them the impressions which are received, and consequently also the perceptions which represent these impressions, are heightened and distinguished (as, for example, when rays of light are concentrated by means of the shape of the humors of the eye and act with greater force), then this may amount to *feeling*,[49] that is to say, to a perception accompanied by *memory* — a perception of which there remains a kind of echo for a long time, which makes itself heard on occasion. Such a living being is called an *animal*, as its monad is called a *soul*. When this soul is raised to the level of reason, it is something more sublime and is counted among the spirits, as will be explained presently. It is true that animals are sometimes in the condition of simple living beings, and their souls in the condition of simple monads, namely, when their perceptions are not distinct enough so that they can be remembered. This happens in a deep sleep without dreams or in a swoon. But perceptions which have become completely confused must be developed again in animals... So, it is well to make a distinction between *perception*, which is the inner state of the monad representing external things, and *apperception*, which is *consciousness* or the reflective knowledge of this inner state itself and which is not given to all souls or to any soul all the time...

There is a connection between the perceptions of animals which has some resemblance to reason, but it is grounded only on the memory of *facts* or effects and not on the knowledge of *causes*. Thus, a dog runs away from

---

[49] We have also sometimes translated the French word *sentiment* as 'sensation.'

the stick with which he has been beaten, because his memory represents to him the pain which the stick had caused him. Men too, insofar as they are empiricists, that is to say, in three-fourths of their actions, act only like beasts. For example, we expect day to dawn tomorrow because we have always experienced this to be so, but only the astronomer predicts it with reason, and even his prediction will ultimately fail when the cause of daylight, which is by no means eternal, stops. But *reasoning in the true sense* depends on necessary or eternal truths, as are those of logic, number, and geometry, which make the connection of ideas indubitable and their conclusions infallible. Animals in which such consequences cannot be observed are called *beasts*, but those who know these necessary truths are the ones properly called *rational animals*, and their souls are called *minds*. These souls are capable of performing acts of reflection and of considering what is called 'I,' 'substance,' 'soul,' 'mind' — in a word, things and truths which are immaterial. It is this which makes us capable of the sciences or of demonstrative knowledge.
(*Principes de la nature et de la grace*, 1713-14, G. IV, 599-601)

On the difference between minds and other substances, souls or substantial forms; that the immortality which is required includes memory.

Assuming that the bodies which make up a *unum per se*, for example man, are substances and that they have substantial forms, and assuming that beasts have souls, we must admit that these souls and substantial forms cannot entirely perish any more than can atoms or the ultimate parts of matter in the opinions of other philosophers. For no substance perishes, although it may become entirely different. Those substances, too, express the whole universe, although more imperfectly than do minds. But the chief difference is that they do not know what they are or what they do, and since, consequently, they cannot reflect, they are unable to discover necessary and universal truths. It is also because they lack reflection about themselves that they have no moral quality. Hence, though animals may pass through a thousand transformations like that which we see when a caterpillar changes into a butterfly, yet from the moral or practical[50] point of view the result is just as if they had perished. Indeed, one may even say that they have perished in a physical sense, that is, in the sense in which we say that bodies perish through their corruption. But the intelligent soul, knowing what it is and being able to say this little word 'I' which means so much, not merely remains and subsists metaphysically (which it does in a fuller sense than the others) but also remains the same morally and constitutes the same character. For it is memory or the knowledge of this 'I' which makes it capable of punishment and reward. Likewise, the immortality which is demanded in morals and religion does not consist merely of this perpetual subsistence, which is common to all substances, for without a memory of what one has been, there would be nothing desirable about it. Suppose some private man should suddenly become king of China, but only on condition that he forget what he had been, just as if he were being born anew — would it not be the same thing practically, or as far as discernible effects are concerned, if he were annihilated and a king of China created at the same instant in his place? This particular man has no reason whatever to desire this.

---

[50] For Leibniz and all the philosophers of his time, moral also has the meaning of *practical, contingent, empirical*. We have already seen (p. 139 ff.) how moral necessity applies to factual truths and is opposed to the necessity of reason, which gives absolute certainty. the impossibility of the opposite.

The excellence of minds; that God considers them preferable to other creatures; that minds express God rather than the world, while the other simple substances express the world rather than God.

But in order to support by natural reasons the view that God will preserve for all time not merely our substance but also our person — that is, the memory and knowledge of what we are (though the distinct knowledge is sometimes suspended in sleep and in fainting fits), we must add morals to metaphysics. That is to say, we must consider God not only as the principle and cause of all substances and all beings, but also as the head of all persons or intelligent substances and as the absolute monarch of the most perfect city or state, which is the universe composed of all minds together, God himself being the most perfect of all minds, as well as the greatest of all beings. For minds are surely the most perfect substances and those which best express the divinity. And since the whole nature, end, power, and function of substances is merely to express God and the universe (as we have explained at length) there is no reason to doubt that those substances which express him with a knowledge of what they are doing, and which are capable of knowing the great truths about God and the universe, express him incomparably better than do those natures which are either brutish or incapable of knowing truth or entirely destitute of feeling and knowledge. Moreover, the difference between the intelligent substances and those which have no intelligence at all is just as great as that between a mirror and one who sees.

And since God himself is the greatest and wisest of minds, it is easy to understand that the beings with whom he can enter into conversation, so to speak, and even into society, communicating his opinions and his will to them in a particular manner and in such a way that they can recognize and love their benefactor, must be infinitely nearer to him than all other things which can only be considered the instruments of minds. So we see that all wise persons value man infinitely more highly than any other thing, no matter how precious, and it seems that the greatest satisfaction that a soul can have, which is content in other respects, is to see itself loved by others. However, there is this difference with respect to God — the glory and the worship which we offer cannot add to his satisfaction, since the knowledge of creatures is only a result of his sovereign and perfect happiness, far from contributing to it or being a partial cause of it. However, whatever is good and reasonable in finite minds is found preeminently in him. And just as we would praise a king who prefers to save the life of one man above that of his rarest and most precious animal, so we cannot doubt that the most enlightened and most just of all monarchs is of the same opinion.

God is the monarch of the most perfect Republic consisting of all minds, and the happiness of this City of God is his principal design.

Minds are indeed the most perfectible of substances, and their perfections have the particular advantage of interfering with each other in the least possible degree, or rather of supporting each other, for only the most virtuous can be the most perfect friends. From this it obviously follows that God, who always tends toward the greatest general perfection, will have the greatest concern for minds and will give to them, not only in general but to each one in particular, the greatest degree of perfection which universal harmony can permit.

It can even be said that God, insofar as he is a mind, is the origin of existences, for otherwise, if he had lacked the will to choose the best, there would be no reason why one possible being should exist in preference to others. So this property of God's being himself a mind comes before all other considerations that he might have with regard to creatures. Only minds are made in his image and are, as it were, almost of his blood or like the children of his household, for only they can serve him freely and act with knowledge in imitation of the divine nature. One single mind is worth a whole world, because it not only expresses the world but also knows it and conducts its life there after the manner of God. So it seems that though every substance expresses the whole universe, yet the other substances express the world rather than God, while minds express God rather than the world. This nature of minds, which brings them as close as is possible to divinity for simple creatures, is such that God derives infinitely more glory from them than from all other beings — or rather that the other beings merely provide minds with reasons for glorifying God.

This is why this moral nature of God, which makes him the lord and monarch of minds, is of a quite singular concern to God personally, if we may say so. It is in this relation that he humanizes himself, that he is willing to tolerate human relations, and that he enters into society with us, as a prince with his subjects. So dear is this consideration to him that the happy and flourishing state of his Empire, which consists in the greatest possible felicity of its inhabitants, becomes his highest law. For happiness is to persons what perfection is to beings. And if the highest principle ruling the existence of the physical world is the decree which gives it the greatest perfection possible, the highest purpose in the moral world or city of God, which is the noblest part of the universe, should be to spread in it the greatest possible happiness.

It must not be doubted, therefore, that God has ordered everything in such a way not only that minds can live forever, which is inescapable, but also that they shall forever preserve their moral status, in order that no person may be lost to the city, just as no substance is lost to the world. As a result, they will always be what they are — otherwise they would be incapable of reward and punishment, both of which are essential in a republic and especially in the most perfect one where nothing can be overlooked.

Finally, since God is at the same time the most just and the most benevolent of monarchs and demands only a good will, provided it be sincere and serious, his subjects cannot desire a better state. To make them perfectly happy, he asks only that they love him.

Jesus Christ has revealed to men the mystery and the admirable laws of the Kingdom of Heaven and the grandeur of the supreme happiness which God prepares for those who love him.

The ancient philosophers knew very little about these important truths. Only Jesus Christ has expressed them divinely well and in a manner so clear and simple that the dullest minds have grasped them. His gospel has thus entirely changed the aspect of human affairs, showing us the kingdom of heaven, that perfect republic of minds which deserves the title of the city of God, whose admirable laws he has revealed to us. He alone has made us see how much God loves us and with what exactness he has provided for all that concerns us — how God who cares for the sparrows will not neglect the reasonable creatures who are infinitely more dear to him; how all the hairs on our head are counted; how heaven and earth may pass away, but the word of God and all that pertains to the economy of our

salvation shall endure; how God has more concern for the least of these intelligent souls than for the whole mechanism of the world; how we ought not to fear those who can destroy bodies but cannot do any harm to the souls, since only God can make the souls happy or wretched; and how the souls of the righteous are protected by his hand against all the revolutions of the world, since nothing can act upon them save God alone; how none of our acts is forgotten but everything is placed on account, even idle words and a spoonful of water put to good use; finally, how everything works for the greatest benefit of those who are good, and the righteous shall be as suns, so that neither our senses nor our minds have ever tasted anything approaching the happiness which God has prepared for those who love him.
(*Discours de mètaphysique*, 1686, XXXIV-XXXVII)

Thus ends the *Discours de métaphysique* — in which, from the principle of differing clarity of perception in the various monads, we arrive at a hierarchy of beings, and at the definition of the human soul and personality in itself and in its relations with divine nature. Such a construction affords Leibniz one of those harmonious and comprehensive looks at the whole universe in which physical phenomena, scientific or philosophical concepts, moral principles, and religious dogmas all coincide in supreme harmony.

VI. MATTER, SOUL, AND PRE-ESTABLISHED HARMONY

MATTER AS AGGREGATE — Up to now, the nature of the body has been studied as an essential element of the monad, inseparable from the soul. But for Leibniz there is a way of considering the material world from another point of view. Matter can also be seen not only as a passive force that belongs to each of the fundamental substances that the world consists of, or as what is confused and indistinct in the monad's perception. Matter is, more concretely, everything that surrounds us — everything that in its various aspects falls within the range of our senses. Now this matter, if one were to analyze it in more depth, would also consist of substantial units, of monads, even though it presents itself to us as composed without aspects of activity or mind. Its material nature does not depend on the units that make it up (and we know that purely material units do not exist), but on the fact itself of not being a unit, but rather a group of units — an *aggregate*.

As for substantial forms or primitive entelechies..., I do not endorse them unless they are seen as simple substances, capable of perception and appetite — souls, in other words — or something analogous to the soul that might be called the principle of life. I believe in fact that the whole of nature is filled with living organic bodies. So I do not actually think that a stone is itself an animate corporeal substance or that it is endowed with a principle of unity and life, but I do think there are such principles everywhere in it, and that there is no bit of matter that does not contain an animal or plant or some other living organic body (although we know of no living organic body except plants and animals). Thus, a mass of matter is not properly what I call a *corporeal substance*, but a cluster and resulting (*aggregatum*) of an infinity of such substances, much like a flock of sheep or a heap of worms.
(*Éclaircissement sur les natures plastiques*, G. VI, 550)

I do not say, as I am accused of saying, that there is only one substance in all things and that this substance is the mind. And these monads do not by any means make up an effectively unitary whole. Such a whole, if they did make it up, would not be a mind at all. I also avoid saying that matter is a shadow or is nothingness. These expressions are exaggerated. It is a mass, not *substantia sed substantiatum*, just as an army would be, or a flock, and insofar as it is considered as a component of a single thing, it

is a phenomenon — a very real phenomenon indeed, but whose unity is determined by our conception of it.
(Fragment from 1716, G. VI, 625)

THE AGGREGATE AS PHENOMENON — Matter, understood in this way, ceases to be real. Its essence lies in the fact that it is a gathering of real substances — on its own it is something that is constructed, artificial. When it is observed in depth, it necessarily dissolves into its components. Leibniz expresses this by saying that it has a *phenomenal* nature.[51]

So it seems that strictly speaking the bodies do not in any way deserve the name of substance, a view which seems to have been Plato's, who says that there are transient beings which never subsist longer than a moment. But this point needs fuller discussion, and I have still other important reasons for refusing to give bodies the title and name of substances in a metaphysical sense. It is because, in a word, the body has no real unity at all; it is only an *aggregate*, which the Scholastics call a *pure accident*, a collection — like a herd. Its unity comes from our perception. It is a *being of reason* or rather, of *imagination*, a *phenomenon*.
(*Entretien di Philarète et d'Ariste*, G. VI, 586)

Bodies cannot be substances in the true sense of the word, since they are always merely unions, resulting from simple substances or true monads, which are not extended and therefore are not true bodies. Hence bodies presuppose immaterial substances.
(Letter to Lady Masham, 1705, G. III, 367)

THE CONTINUOUS AND THE DISCRETE — From here, Leibniz derives new arguments to demonstrate the unreality of

---

[51] Phenomenal (from φαίνομαι, appear), is a term used since Plato to indicate something that has an appearance, but no absolute reality.

corporeal nature in general and the need to reach beyond it, to something that is endowed with more robust validity. His denial of the concept of extension also acquires more validity. The monad in itself is not extended — it can only be seen as a "metaphysical point." Extension can only be derived from a multiplicity, from repetition. In this sense it is purely phenomenal, as is the aggregate. The difference lies in the fact that matter as an aggregate is *discrete* — that is, composed of a mass of indivisible units, while extension is on the contrary *continuous* — divisible to infinity. All the more reason why it will not be something real, but a mere order of spatial relations, just as time is an order of successive relations.

It is only *atoms of substance* — that is to say, real unities that are absolutely destitute of parts, which are the sources of action and the absolute first principles out of which things are compounded, and as it were, the ultimate elements in the analysis of substance. One could call them *metaphysical points*. They have something vital, and a kind of *perception*, and *mathematical points* are the *points of view* from which they express the universe. But when a corporeal substance is contracted, all its organs together make only one *physical point* with respect to us. Physical points are thus indivisible in appearance only, while mathematical points are exact but are nothing but modalities. It is only metaphysical points, or points of substance, constituted by forms or souls, which are exact and real, and without them there would be nothing real, since there could be no multiplicity without true unities.
(*Système nouveau*, 1695, G. IV, 482-83)

So even though matter consists in an accumulation of simple substances without number, and even though the duration of creatures, just like actual motion, consists in an accumulation of momentary states, it nevertheless has to be said that space is not composed of points, nor is time composed of instants, nor is mathematical motion composed of moments, nor is intensity composed of extreme degrees. The fact is that matter, the course of things, and ultimately every actual composite is a discrete quantity, but that space, time, mathematical motion, the continuous intensity or increase conceivable in speed and in other qualities, and ultimately everything which involves an estimate which comes down to possibilities, is a quantity which is continuous and indeterminate in itself, or indifferent to the parts which can be taken from it, and which are actually taken from it in nature. The mass of bodies is actually divided in a determined way, and nothing in it is genuinely continuous; but space, or the perfect continuity which exists ideally, only signals an indeterminate possibility of dividing as one sees it. In matter and in actual realities the whole is a result of the parts; but in ideas or in possibles (which includes not only this universe, but also every other universe which can be conceived, and which the divine understanding actually represents in itself), the indeterminate whole is anterior to the divisions, just as the notion of the whole is simpler than that of fractions, and precedes it...

To better conceive the actual division of matter with the exclusion of all exact and indeterminate continuity, we ought to consider that God has already produced as much order and variety as it was possible to introduce in it up to now, and so no indeterminacy has remained in it; whereas indeterminacy is of the essence of continuity. This is what the divine perfection teaches our mind, and what experience itself confirms through our senses. There is no drop of water so pure that one cannot notice some variety in it on a good look. A piece of stone is composed of certain granules, and through the microscope these granules appear like rocks in which there are a thousand tricks of nature. If our power of sight were continually increased, it would

always find something on which to exercise itself. There are actual varieties everywhere and never a perfect uniformity, nor two pieces of matter completely similar to each other, in the great as in the small.
(Letter to Electress Sophie of Hanover, 1705 G. VII, 562-63)

PRIMARY AND SECONDARY MATTER — The *continuous* is thus abstract spatiality (or temporality etc.), while the *discrete* is aggregate, or matter. And Leibniz has two different conceptions of matter. The fist is the one we saw in Chapter III [pp. 161 ff] — a primitive passive power, a substratum of resistance, density, 'antitipia,' to which force is applied, transforming it into activity, entelechy. Secondly, there is this concept of an aggregate, a composition, an artificial construction posterior to the monad, having no real substantial nature itself. Leibniz distinguishes these two different ways of looking at the monad by using the two terms *primary matter* and *secondary matter*.

In bodies I distinguish corporeal substance from matter, and I distinguish primary from secondary matter. Secondary matter is an aggregate or composite of several corporeal substances, as a flock is composed of several animals. But each animal and each plant are also a corporeal substance, having in itself a principle of unity which makes it truly a substance and not an aggregate. And this principle of unity is that which one calls soul, or it is something analogous to soul. But, besides the principle of unity, corporeal substance has its mass or its secondary matter, which is, again, an aggregate of other smaller corporeal substances — and that goes to infinity. However, primitive matter, or matter taken in itself is what we conceive in bodies when we set aside all the principles of unity, that is, it is what is passive, from which arise two qualities: *resistentia et restitantia vel inertia*. That is to say, a body gives way to another rather than allowing itself to be penetrated, but it does not give way without difficulty and without weakening the total motion of the body pushing it. Thus one can say that matter in itself, besides extension, contains a primitive, passive power. But the principle of unity contains the primitive active power, or the primitive force, which can never be destroyed and always persists in the exact order of its internal modifications, which represent those outside it.

(Letter to Burnett, 1699, G. III, 260-261)

THE SOUL AND THE BODY — Through the concept of the aggregate, Leibniz also explains the constitution of organic and animal bodies. Such bodies, he says, are aggregates, with what might be called a dominant and organizing monad, of a superior nature. This monad is the soul and constitutes the permanent element of each individual.

I define the *organism*, or natural machine, as a machine whose parts are also machines,[52] and consequently as one whose subtle structure goes on into infinity, wherein nothing is small enough to be neglected, whereas the parts of our artificial machines are not themselves machines. Herein lies the essential difference between *nature* and *art*, which our moderns have not sufficiently considered.

(Letter to Lady Masham, 1704, G. III, 356)

I distinguish: (1) the primitive entelechy or soul; (2) matter, namely primary matter or primitive passive power; (3) the monad, completed by these two things; (4) the mass or secondary matter, or organic machine for which innumerable subordinate monads come together; and (5) the animal, or corporeal substance, which the monad dominating in the machine makes into one thing.

---

[52] Here as elsewhere, Leibniz intends the word "machine" to mean a composite organism — that is, made up of heterogeneous parts.

(Letter to De Volder, 1703, G. II, 252)

And through the two concepts of primary and secondary matter, two different concepts of soul are established as well. The first is the active principle inherent in the monad, inseparable from its passivity, and the other is the monad of a more strictly mental character that persists in each individual even as the monads forming the mass of the body vary and transform.

Matter without souls and forms or entelechies is nothing but passive, and souls without matter would be nothing but active. A complete corporeal substance, truly one — what the Scholastics call *unum per se* (in contrast to entities by aggregation) — must result from an active principle of unity, and also from a mass of the kind which makes up a multitude, and which would be solely passive if it contained only primary matter. By contrast, secondary matter, or the mass which makes up our body, contains parts throughout, all of which are themselves complete substances because they are other animals, or organic substances, which are individually animated or active. But the collection of these corporeal organized substances which makes up our body is united with our soul only by the relation which arises between the sequences of phenomena which develop from the nature of each separate substance. And all of that shows how one can say on the one hand that the soul and the body are independent of each other, and on the other hand that the one is incomplete without the other, since the one is never naturally without the other.

(*Addition à l'explication du système nouveau*, G. IV, 572-3)

THE LAWS OF THE WORLDS OF MATTER AND MIND — In whichever way it is understood, whether as primary matter or passive power, or as secondary matter or aggregate, corporeal nature thus has something unreal about it. In the first case it is an abstraction — anterior, one might say, to the monad, without whose active force it is still nothing but a simple and initially passive aspect of what will be an active unit. In the other case it is also an abstraction, this time posterior to the monad. It is a gathering, an agglomeration, which nevertheless always refers back to the monad as its essential constituent element.

On the other hand, matter cannot be eliminated from the monad. It always accompanies it, almost as part of its nature. An abstract part, undoubtedly, but nevertheless essential, which must necessarily be passed through on the way to the true concreteness of entelechy. This matter, which when analyzed to the depths of its constitution dissolves and loses all reality, still has a fundamental part in the concrete, natural and human world, as Leibniz represents it. The monad, as we have seen, is immaterial, and yet it retains a material aspect — in this way there is no soul without a body. Having established this Leibniz goes further, almost forgetting his premises making matter something that is only a function of the soul, and seeks laws that are autonomous and proper to the material world, quite distinct from those governing the world of the mind. He almost comes back to the Cartesian conception that he had always opposed — of soul and body as two separate substances. And to justify the distinction he attributes to the body the mechanical law of efficient cause, and to the soul the vital law of purpose. These two laws, which we saw united where the principle of sufficient reason in factual truths pointed directly to God,[53] now apply separately to the soul and the body.

This can also be partly justified by the nature of the monad. As we have seen, it contains within it in the state of causal implication the entire future development of the universe — that is, the effect is already contained in the causes that must necessarily produce it. And this purely mechanical and deterministic causal connection is of a material nature. In this aspect the monad is material. It is a point in the universe that is perfectly and necessarily determined by the causes that it derives from. On the other hand, however, universality is expressed in

---

[53] Cf. above, p. 130-31.

the monad as representation and appetite. The totality of relations is contained in it in the state of pregnant, conscious and active implication. This perception and appetite, which Leibniz imagines as tending towards the good and governed by the final cause of the 'best,' is what he makes the soul consist of. Leibniz also makes this new soul-body distinction coincide with the other in which the body is seen as confused perception and the soul as distinct perception.

Everything in bodies occurs mechanically, through intelligible qualities of bodies such as size, shape and movement, and everything in souls must be explained vitally — that is, through intelligible qualities of the soul such as perception and appetite. And in animate bodies we observe marvelous harmony between vitality and mechanism if what takes place in the body mechanically is represented vitally in the soul, and what is perceived exactly in the soul achieves its complete fulfillment in the body.

It follows that once we know the qualities of the body, we can cure the diseases of the soul and, when we know the qualities of the soul, we can cure the diseases of the body. For it is sometimes easier to know what takes place in the soul than what takes place in the body, and sometimes vice versa. And whenever we use indications from the soul to help the body, we can speak of a vital type of medicine, a method that has a wider scope than is commonly believed. Because the body responds to the soul not only in the movements that we call voluntary, but in all others as well — even though, because of habit, we do not realize that the soul is affected by or allows the movements of the body, or that these latter correspond to the perceptions and appetites of the soul. The fact is, the perceptions of the body are confused, so that the correspondence is not readily apparent. And the soul commands the body insofar as it has distinct perceptions, and the body obeys it insofar as its perceptions are confused. But also, whoever has any perception in the soul can be certain that it will have some effect on the body, and vice versa... And things happen in such a way that sometimes even in natural facts we seek truth through final causes when we cannot easily get there through efficient causes.

(Fragment, C. 12-13)

SEPARATION OF THE TWO WORLDS — Now, having formulated this distinction, Leibniz in a certain sense ceased following the path that, through the conception of the relation of cause and effect as a relation of subject and predicate, had led him to individual substance and had allowed him to resolve the concepts of body and mind into one another. Here he instead accentuated the distinction — body and mind become two separate worlds, two parallel entities without mutual relations. Their situation is now analogous to that of two distinct monads, where the content of each corresponds to the content of the other, but without any implication that one influences the other.[54] So what happens mechanically in the body corresponds to what is in the representation of the mind, but not through the influence of one on the other or through any unification. Their relations must be established through divine intervention.

In our experience, bodies interact with one another according to mechanical laws, and should produce in themselves some kind of internal action. And we see no means of conceiving the soul's action on matter, or of the matter on the soul, or anything that would correspond to it, as there is no mechanism whatsoever that could explain how material variations, that is to say, mechanical laws, can give rise to perception, or how perception can give rise to a change in velocity or direction in animal minds and other bodies, however subtle or brute they may be. Thus, the inconceivability of any other hypothesis, together with the idea of the right order of nature,

---

[54] Cf. above, pp. 198 ff.

which is always uniform in herself (leaving aside any other consideration), have led me to conclude that the soul and the body perfectly follow their laws, each according to its own, without the bodily laws being disturbed by the actions of the soul, or presuming that the body finds windows through which its influence over the souls could enter. One must ask, therefore, where does this accord between the body and the soul come from?
(Letter to Lady Masham, 1704, G. III, 340-41)

PRE-ESTABLISHED HARMONY — The problem that now arises is this correspondence of the physical world with that of the mind. But making such a clear distinction between the two worlds was not necessary for the doctrine of the monad. Leibniz was perhaps induced to accentuate it because of his dispute with Malebranche and the occasionalists[55] and the fact that he had found a more plausible hypothesis that would solve their own identical problem. The desire to correct the occasionalist hypothesis and apply his own perhaps led him to formulate the problem in the same terms as his interlocutors, to a greater extent than the earlier versions of his doctrine required. The hypothesis in question is the famous idea of *pre-established harmony*. A few of Leibniz's many statements of it are offered below.

Imagine two clocks or watches that always tell exactly the same time. This could be done in *three ways*. The first is by mutual influence between them, the second by the care of someone looking after them, the third by their own

---

[55] Nicolas Malebranche (1638-1715) author of the *Recherche de la vérité*, was the leading representative of occasionalism, a doctrine that explained the correspondence between the physical and mental orders through the continuous intervention of God. According to this doctrine, on the *occasion* of each event occurring in the corporeal world, God elicits a corresponding representation in the mind, and vice versa. This problem naturally presupposes a clear separation between the corporeal order and the mental order — a separation of a purely Cartesian stamp.

accuracy. The *first* is the way of influence...

The *second way* of making two clocks (even poor ones) always tell the same time would be to have them constantly looked after by a skilled workman, who adjusts them and keeps them in time from moment to moment. This is what I call the way of assistance.

The *third way* would be to make the two pendulums, from the beginning, with such skill and accuracy that we could be sure that they would always afterwards keep time together.

Put now the soul and the body in the place of these two clocks. Their harmony or sympathy will take place by one of these three methods. The way of influence is that of common philosophy, but as we cannot conceive of material particles or properties, or immaterial qualities, which can pass from one of these substances into the other, we are obliged to abandon this view. The way of assistance is that of the system of incidental causes, but I hold that this is making a *Deus ex machina* intervene in a natural and ordinary matter when, according to reason, he ought not to intervene except in the manner in which he cooperates in all the other affairs of nature. Thus, there remains only my hypothesis — that is, the way of a harmony pre-established by divine preemptive artifice which, from the beginning, formed each of these substances in a manner so perfect, and regulated them with so much accuracy, that merely by following laws of its own, received with its own being, it nevertheless agrees with the other, just as if there were mutual influence, or as if God in addition to his general cooperation constantly applied his hand directly.

(Letter of 1696, G. IV, 500-501)

There is order and connection in ideas, as there is in (bodily) movements, for the one corresponds perfectly to the other, although the determination in the movements be unconscious and free, or with choice in the thinking being whom good and evil only cause to incline without forcing him.[56] For the soul, while representing bodies, preserves its (own) perfections, and although dependent upon the body (in seizing the good) in voluntary acts, it is independent and makes the body depend upon itself in others. But this *dependence* is only metaphysical and consists in the considerations which God has for the one while ruling the other, or rather for both, according to the original perfections of each[57]; whilst physical dependence would consist in an immediate influence, which the one would receive from the other on which it depends.

(*New Essays*, 1701 ff., II, 21 § 12)

The pre-established harmony means that pain comes into a dog's soul when its body is hit. And if the dog were not to be hit now, God would not have endowed its soul at the beginning with a constitution that would now produce pain in it, and the representation or perception that responds to the blow of the stick. But if (which is impossible) God were to repent and, without changing the nature of the soul and the natural course of its modifications, change the course of bodily nature in such a way that the blow did not come, the soul would feel something corresponding to the blow even though its body did not in fact receive it. But, says M. Bayle, I understand the reasons by which the dog's body is hit by the stick, but I don't at all understand how the dog's soul, which experiences pleasure while the dog is avidly eating, can pass so suddenly to a state of pain without the stick being the cause (as the Scholastics would have it), or God causing it specifically (as the *occasionalists* would say). But M. Bayle

---

[56] Cf. above, pp. 138 ff.
[57] We have already seen how by reason of its perceptions being either more distinct or more confused, each monad participates more either in spirit or body--that is, it has greater or lesser perfection. Cf. above, pp. 207 ff.

doesn't even understand how the stick can affect the soul, nor how the miraculous operation can take place by which God continually attunes souls to bodies. I, on the other hand, have attempted to explain how this accord comes about naturally, supposing that each soul is a living mirror representing the universe from its point of view, and above all with respect to its body. Thus the causes that make the stick act (that is to say the man positioned behind the dog, getting ready to hit it while it eats, and everything in the physical realm that contributes to disposing that man to that action) are also represented from the first in the soul of the dog exactly in accordance with the truth, but weakly, by little, confused perceptions, without apperception — that is to say without the dog noticing it, because the dog's body is also only imperceptibly affected. And when in the course of corporeal nature these dispositions finally lead to the blow falling hard on the body of the dog, in the same way the representations of these dispositions in the dog's soul finally produce the representation of the blow of the stick. Since that representation is distinct and strong (as the representations of the predispositions were not, since the predispositions affected the dog's body only weakly) the dog apperceives it very distinctly, and that is what creates its pain. Therefore, it must not be imagined that the soul of the dog, in this case, passes from pleasure to pain with no development and with no internal cause.

(Observations on Bayle's *Dictionary*, 1702, G., IV, 531-32)

Let us say that everything happens mechanically in the body, or in accordance with the laws of motion, and everything happens morally in the soul, or in accordance with perceived good and evil, so that even in our instinctive or involuntary actions where the body alone seems to have a role, there is in the soul an appetite for good or an aversion to evil that drives it, although our reflection is unable to make it out in the confusion. But if soul and body follow their own laws separately in this way, how do they connect up, and how is it that the body obeys the soul and that the soul feels the effects of the body? To explain this natural mystery, we have to have recourse to God, as we do when it is a matter of giving the primordial reason for the order and artifice in things. But this explanation is only valid once and for all, and it is not as if he disturbed the laws of bodies to make them correspond to the soul, and vice versa. Instead, he made bodies in advance so that, following their laws and natural tendencies to movement, they will come to do what the soul will ask at the appropriate time. And he also made souls so that, following the natural tendencies of their appetite, they will also always arrive at the representations of the states of the body. For just as motion leads matter from shape to shape, the appetite leads the soul from image to image. So the soul is made dominant in advance, and is obeyed by the body to the extent that its appetite is accompanied by distinct perceptions, which makes it think of suitable means when it wants something; but it is also subjected to the body from the beginning in the measure of its confused perceptions. For our experience is that all things tend to change, the body by the motive force and the soul by the appetite which leads it to distinct or confused perceptions, depending on whether it is more perfect or less perfect. And we should not marvel at this primordial agreement of souls and bodies, as all bodies have been arranged following the intentions of a universal mind, and all souls are essentially representations or living mirrors of the universe, according to the scope and the point of view of each, and consequently are as enduring as the world itself. It is as if God had varied the universe as many times as there are souls, or as if he had created as many universes in miniature, ultimately agreeing in content and diversified by appearances. There is nothing so rich as this uniform simplicity accompanied by perfect order. And we can conclude that each separate soul must be perfectly well adjusted, since it is a particular expression of the universe — a concentrated universe, as it were — which is again borne out by the fact that each body, and consequently our own as well, is somehow affected by all the others, and consequently the soul takes part in it too. Here, in a few words, is my entire philosophy.

(Letter to Queen Sophie Charlotte of Prussia, 1704, G. III, 346-48)

This is the hypothesis of pre-established harmony that finishes and crowns Leibniz's system, although it cannot be said that it adds much of substance to the doctrine of the monad. The principle introduced here is the same one that underpins the correspondence of the content of each monad with the content of all of them, even with no reciprocal influence. But applying it to the relationship between soul and body forces a distinction and separation between the corporeal order and the spiritual order; whereas it is precisely in overcoming this separation and in the synthesis of the two orders that we see the most distinctive value of the concept of the monad.

But ideally this separation is posterior to the concept. In applying the principles, he had found, in making his monad act as the constituent element of the world, Leibniz sometimes falls back into positions he had previously superseded and misinterprets himself. What remains essential in what we have seen of his thought is the internal structure of the concept of the monad: this synthesis of universal and individual, of matter and spirit, of activity and passivity, which is a point of arrival and a point of departure in the history of philosophy.

Part Three

5. ETERNAL TRUTHS IN DESCARTES AND LEIBNIZ*
OUTLINE OF AN ESSAY

Sommaire — Le problème des vérités éternelles et de la liberté en Dieu est le point essentiel de l'opposition de Leibniz au cartésianisme. Caractère thomiste de la thèse leibnizienne. Le contraste se réduit à une opposition entre intellectualisme et volontarisme: car il faut interpréter l'union carteésienne de l'entendement et de la volonté en Dieu au sujet de la création des vérités éterenelles, comme une manière d'affirmer le primat de la volonté. Volontarisme et intellectualisme sont les traits essentiels de la pensée de Descartes et de Leibniz, dans leur interprétation psychologique de la vie intérieure: ce qui ne saurait rester sans influence sur leur conception des rapports entre volonté et entendement en Dieu. — Rationalisme et mysticisme chez Descartes. "L'adversaire de Descartes" ne serait-il pas Grotius? La contingence des vérités éternelles met une réserve à la base du rationalisme cartésien. — Leibniz et Grotius. La priorité des vérités éternelles sur la volonté de Dieu est chez Leibniz la base de l'autonomie de la loi naturelle. Le problème de l'élargissement de cette loi, et sa solution dans le finalisme leibnizien. La controverse sur les vérités éternelles n'est que l'expression théologique de deux attitudes foncièrement différentes vis-à-vis de la réalité.

Gilson has identified the Scholastic theology of Aquinas and Suarez as the opponent Descartes addresses in asserting that eternal truths were created by God and are not prior to the divine intellect and will. Half a century later, Leibniz would make the reaffirmation of the Thomist position the centerpiece of his critique of Descartes, and his main charge against him. His argument seems almost to echo the Scholastic thesis. The eternal truths impose themselves on God's will and are anterior

---

* Travaux du ix° Congrès International de Philosophie — Congrès Descartes (Paris 1-6 August 1937). The original typescript is dated Trieste, Marzo 1937.

to it. The will of God is not exempt from them, just as it cannot put into effect two realities that are mutually contradictory. God's will, though merged with his intellect, is in a way distinct from it and is set as a consequence of it. So that the laws of justice and truth are not as they are because God wanted them this way, but rather God wanted them as they are because he knew them to be just and good. Finally, God has motives for what he does, and his actions are determined by the representation of a purpose — which must be sought in physics and the natural sciences, and in the study of human nature.

Now, if it is true that the Cartesian theses opposed to the above are marked by the mystical-Platonic-Augustinian mentality of the Oratory, then the Descartes-Leibniz contrast would be an opposition between Augustinian mysticism and Thomistic intellectualism. The fact that Leibniz was familiar with the doctrine of Thomas Aquinas not only in the original and in the Scholastic manuals, but in Suarez's reworking and in-depth study as well, emerges clearly from his biography, the shaping of his education, and repeated quotations from his works. What remains is the most important problem for understanding these two thinkers, accustomed as they were to adopting old theological formulations rich in long tradition in support of their innovative theses. Why did Descartes and Leibniz choose these two different frames to formulate their new vision of reality?

Descartes' works bear witness to his affirmation of the absolute identity, in God, of knowledge and will, eliminating any distinction, however logical or ideal, in his attempt to cut through the controversy regarding the preeminence of one or the other faculty. It remains to be seen however, whether he succeeded in actually — and not only verbally — eliminating this distinction. In other words, whether his is not another of those cases, so often encountered regarding this problem, that affirm the preeminence of one or the other of the two faculties through the affirmation of their identity.

Indeed, throughout the history of philosophy, saying that knowledge and the will are one and the same thing has almost always had a contentious meaning. Against intellectualist theses it has served to reaffirm the autonomy of the will and its independence from reasons or motives that determine it. And against voluntarist theses and uninfluenced free will, it has reasserted the need for the will to have a criterion for its actions. The asserted identity, in short, comes down to a preeminence of one or the other of the two terms. Even Leibniz presents his intellectualist opposition to the Cartesian thesis and the '*stat pro ratione volontas*' as a unification of intellect and will.

But such a unification would only be possible (to limit ourselves to this field of theology) in the case in which the problem of the anteriority or otherwise of the ideas of reason with respect to God were eliminated. The distinction between knowledge and will can only be eliminated in a philosophy that does not recognize the problem of the beginning of things, of before or after — one that has overcome the concept of temporal or ideal anteriority and posteriority.

Laporte, in a recent text (*La Liberté selon Descartes*, R.M.M., 1937, pp. 114 ff.), has attempted to determine on the basis of the texts, primarily the *Entretien avec Burmann*, the features of the Cartesian identity of necessity and freedom — that is, which is the same thing, the unity of knowledge and will, giving it a transcendent and mysterious character. This means, in my view, that Descartes, placed before the problem *ex professo*, was forced to move the unity of will and intellect into a realm inaccessible to our understanding — into a sphere, that is, where it is not even possible to say that truths are a creation of God.

It is clear that in this higher sphere, which can only be determined negatively, Descartes eliminates any anteriority of the will. But here the point is that when he speaks of God — that is, when he wants to explain and determine and describe his essence and action, he conceives of God's will as independent of his intellect. It is not his generic conception of divinity, but his thesis of the eternal truths created by God, with all their consequences, that entails the absolute indifference of God — that the divine will, *as the creator of these truths*, is prior to the intellect. Outside this anteriority the Cartesian theory would have no meaning, because saying that in their relation to the eternal truths will and intellect are the same is like saying that the problem does not exist of whether or not eternal truths preexist. Now in Descartes this problem does exist, and he solves it unequivocally, not by going beyond its terms in a superior synthesis, but rather by taking one of the two opposing theses to the extreme. And the very word 'établir' that, as Gilson notes (Commentary on the *Discours*, p. 372), Descartes habitually uses "pour désigner l'acte par lequel Dieu a imposé au monde, en le créant, les lois stables qui le régissent" indicates the way he accentuates the voluntary character of this act.

The contrast between Descartes and Leibniz is thus the contrast between a voluntarist and an intellectualist conception of reality. These are conceptions that in both thinkers are rooted not so much in the theological influences they suffered as in the conformation of their personalities and their innermost conceptions of mental reality. Historians, relying on the consideration that for them the ontological framework of the system ideally and logically precedes the doctrine of human faculties, have almost always given precedence in their expositions and commentaries to the problem of divine freedom, and have made it almost independent of the question of human freedom. But if it is true that the doctrine of man in Descartes and Leibniz, as in the Scholastic systems, is posterior to the doctrine of God, it is no less true that the concept they formed of the divine nature, and especially of its attributes parallel to human faculties, is closely connected with the set of attitudes, psychological needs, and mental experiences that constitute the core of their humanity. Now this core, which can shed great light on the authors' entire metaphysics, can best be traced to their theory of man, not so much in its systematic aspect or its attitude vis-a-vis the controversies of the time, but in what it can reveal to us of lived experience, of an author's intimate character — understood as anthropology, not deduced from ontological and metaphysical premises, but experienced immediately at the root of one's own being.[1]

Now Descartes, irrespective of his much-discussed position regarding the Molinist-Thomist-Jansenist controversy, has at the basis of all his thinking an immediate and direct intuition of the autonomy of the will as a faculty of choice, of assent, of attention, of suspension of judgement, as the 'puissance positive de se déterminer.' *La IVeme Méditation* and all the writings in which he emphasizes the union of freedom and necessity are attempts to organize this basic and never denied intuition of his mind within a coherent theological system. And even here, as Laporte has clearly demonstrated, the will keeps its autonomy in not being bound beyond the instant of the act, in being able to grant or withhold attention, and with placing "L'indépendance que nous expérimentons e sentons en nous" on a different plane than the "dépendance qui est d'autre nature,

---

[1] Laporte also mentions this, op. cit., p. 142. But he understands human freedom as a reflection of divine freedom, whereas here the emphasis is on the inverse relationship.

selon laquelle toutes choses sont sujettes à Dieu" (to Elisabeth, 3, IX, 1645).

In Leibniz, on the other hand, the will is unambiguously conceived of as a natural consequence of knowledge. From the Characteristic projects to the *Systema theologicum*, from the letters to the Landgrave of Hesse to the *Nouveaux Essais*, from the fragments on the mystics to the *Theodicea*, the Leibnizian will is always a non-autonomous faculty — it exists only as an aspect, a necessary extension of perception. Knowledge is itself conceived as active, tending toward realization, and there is no choice or assent, or suspension of judgment determined by a separate decision-making force, which is not instead the result of a combination of perceptions.

It is obvious that these two antithetical visions of the reality of the mind must have influenced the conception of the relation in God between knowledge and will. And this is not to deny the theological influences; but only to state that this order of affinities and overall mentality led the two thinkers to believe one rather than the other.

So, what we have before us, for Descartes, is a system of truths, necessary for man but contingent for God, that have been set, instituted, and created by a free act of the divine will. For Leibniz we have a system of necessary and eternal truths to which God himself must submit. Here God has a faculty of choice within the scope of these truths, but this is in turn determined by the principle of the best. In Leibniz there are the two orders of mathematical truths and final causes, both imposed by God's intellect on his will, while in Descartes there is only the order of mathematical truths, and these contingent on God's will. What does this mean?

Gouhier (*La pensée religieuse de Descartes*) has highlighted how the Augustinian thesis of the independence of God from eternal truths constitutes in Descartes a requirement of his rationalism and allows him the theological agnosticism that is the basis of his geometric conception of reality. At the same time, he has also noted that in the body of Descartes' thought, it is something much deeper than an expedient allowing him to pursue his studies more calmly. It is an aspect of the overall mentality that causes him to make a very clear distinction between reason and faith, leading him to see in the amplitude of the will as opposed to the intellect, the origin of error. Beyond the limits of reason, Descartes glimpses a vast world without limits, uncontrollable by our mathematical reason — the way of faith, of grace, of the infinite, of divine free will; and, at the lower limit, of the particular, the contingent, the accidental. It is a world in which the will dominates unchallenged. But this typically mystical approach frames a rigidly rationalistic philosophy.

In 1625, Grotius's *De jure belli ac pacis* had been published in Paris, with the bold assertion that natural law would be valid, "etiamsi daremus, quod sine summo scelere dari nequit, non esse Deum" (Prolog., n. II, cf. bk. I, chap. I, § 10; "Even though we had admitted what cannot be conceded without committing a great crime, namely that God is not."). In his 30/5/1630 letter from Amsterdam to Father Mersenne, Descartes rejects this thesis, using almost the same words.[2] But this fact, and his constant opposition to atheism, must not obscure the fact that the path chosen by Descartes leads to another form of naturalism and libertinism, which would have its extreme representative in Bayle. This is the path that had been pursued

---

[2] "Il ne faut donc pas dire que *si Deus non esset, nihilominus istae veritates essent verae*" [*if there were no God, these truths would be no less true*]. I am merely juxtaposing the facts, as I have not yet checked the thesis derived from it, namely that Descartes' 'opponent' on this is not Aquinas, but Grotius and the libertines.

with such tragic results by Bruno and Galilei, the path of distinguishing faith from reason, which was destined to free the field of reason from all dogmatic impediments. Descartes succeeds in giving this conception a systematic arrangement of its own, presenting it as a theological thesis with a right of citizenship alongside the others. He finds reasons to demonstrate and support it in his profound awareness of the autonomy and indifference of the will, and in the Augustinian renaissance he notices around him. It is no longer an expedient for getting rid of troublesome objections. It becomes a pillar of his metaphysics.

But, precisely because of the seriousness of its conception, because of its intimate connection with the system as a whole, the thesis of the dependence of eternal truths on God's will, along with those that are linked to it — the impenetrability of divine ends, the incommensurability between reason and faith, between nature and grace, and between the finite and the infinite — give a distinctive character to the whole of Cartesian rationalism.

If it is true that the whole is greater than the part only because God has willed it and it would not be so if God had willed otherwise, then rational and mathematical law takes on a character of limitation and relativity.

This does not mean that Descartes was a precursor of Kant. He still believes in the absolute reality of eternal ideas, of mathematical laws — indeed, he believes he has found in them and only in them the infallible key to reality. But this absolute certainty, this objectivity, is valid within a system whose laws are necessary to the nature of things and of humans because God, by an act of free will, wanted things and humans made in this way, and could have willed otherwise. And this not only with regard to the criterion for the good and the true, but also the criterion for the necessary. The infinity of possible worlds is a concept that does not exist in Descartes in the

Leibnizian sense of a possibility of choice of the "fact"¹ within the realm of eternal truths. Once these truths are set, the fact derives from them by an infallible chain of deductions. But there is a field of possibility beyond Thomistic and Leibnizian possibility. There is a wider possibility, within which the world of our eternal truths — the principle of non-contradiction, the triangle the sum of whose angles is equal to two right angles — is one of the contingent infinities. It is the awareness of this possibility that leads Descartes to condemn the anthropomorphism and geocentrism of the Scholastics, and to think, even with absolute agnosticism, of the possibility of worlds completely different from our own, whose structure we cannot even imagine (Adam-Tannery, B, 168). This awareness places an initial reservation on the absolute and mathematical certainty with which he establishes his propositions of physics, metaphysics, and morality, which is that all of this is valid and necessary *in a system in which what we know as eternal truths apply.* This reservation frames Descartes' theological agnosticism and perhaps casts a particular light on his grounding the validity of clear and distinct ideas in the argument that God is not a "trompeur."[3] Granted, it is a reservation that always remains in the background and never assumes any particular prominence in Cartesian rationalism. But perhaps it is what gives Descartes the strength and security to 'start afresh,' and the confidence

---

[3] "Si cette croyance est si ferme qu nous ne puissions jamais avoir aucue raison de douter de ce que nous croyons de la sorte, il n'y a rien à recherchez davantage, nous avons touchant cela toute la certitude qui se peut raisonnablement souhaiter. Car que nous importe si peut-être quelqu'un feint que cela même de la vérité duquel nous sommes fortement persuadées paraît faux aux yeux de Dieu ou des anges, et que partant, absolument parlant, il est faux? Qu'avons nous à faire de nous mettre en peine de cette fausseté absolut, puisque nous ne la croyons point du tout, et que nous n'en avons pas même le moindre soupçon?" (Rép. aux. 2eme Objections).

to build from scratch. He never claims to solve problems other than those whose key he has in his grasp, and only to the extent that he has it. But with those, he knows he can proceed without hesitation. He does not aspire to the totality of things — but in his own narrow field, he wants to be the master.

Descartes is a man who, having set limits to reason, has devised within them an infallible and safe way forward. And his emphasis is on the second part of this program. Highlighting the former and pivoting on it would have to wait for Kant.

Leibniz's thesis — to a greater degree than meets the eye — cloaks a naturalistic, Grotian substance in Thomist form. This interpretation can be supported philologically. His youthful legal writings and recently published fragments show that Leibniz had studied Grotius's work in depth from a very early age, and that the theory of the validity of eternal truths independent of God had made a great impression on him. The problem obviously had engaged the mind of the young scholar — and the Grotian argument discussed with some uncertainty in the field of jurisprudence, cast a clearer light in metaphysics.

By 1666, in *L'Ars Combinatoria*, he was already speaking of "propositiones quae sunt aeternae veritatis, seu non arbitrio Dei sed sua natura Constant" (§ 83; "propositions that are eternally true, or rather, exist not by divine will, but by their own nature"), and his letter to the jurist Wedderkopf is even more explicit: "Quae ergo" Leibniz writes, "ultima ratio voluntatis divinae? Intellectus divinus... Quae ergo intellectus divini? Harmonia rerum. Quae harmoniae rerum? Nihil. Per exemplum quod ea ratio est 2 ad 4 quae 4 ad 8, eius reddi ratio nulla potest, ne ex voluntate quidem divina. Pendet hoc ex ipsa Essentia seu Idea rerurn" (Berlin Academy Edition, II, I, 117; "Therefore, what is the ultimate rationale of the divine will? The divine intellect. And what (is the ultimate rationale) of the divine intellect? The harmony of things. And what is (is the ultimate rationale) of the harmony of things? Nothing. For example, since the reason for the ratio 4 to 8 is the same as for the ratio 2 to 4, this reason cannot be changed, even by divine will. It depends on the very essence or idea of things.").

Thomism would sometimes soften the thesis so crudely expounded here, giving it a theological framework and making it presentable in a controversy. But the core of Leibnizian opposition to Descartes remains this; and its significance is the same as that of Grotius's thesis. Leibniz wanted to give natural law the same autonomy that Grotius had given natural justice. The eternal truths are independent of God, who can only act in conformity with them. The mathematism that Descartes had conceived of as a 'system' or 'order' created by God in which everything is perfectly calculable — but which does not exclude, beyond itself, other realities incommensurable with it — here takes on a character of absoluteness, of inflexibility. The law becomes the armor of every reality, human or non-human, and God is merely its executor.

But it is precisely this totalizing quality that constrains natural law to articulate itself in new forms that are broader than deductive mathematism, which proves incapable of embracing all of reality. His agnosticism regarding the realm of the will affords Descartes the modesty and strength to proceed without hesitation in the realm of reason. Leibniz, knowing nothing above reason, must give it the scope to allow it to accommodate everything that transcends pure mathematics. His principle of 'the best,' his sufficient reason, his harmony, all have this meaning. They represent the search for a new law of reality, for a new key to the mysteries of the universe.

His finalism therefore contains something more dynamic than Scholastic finalism — it is not a justification of the real, but rather the need for a justification. It is the sense that this justification cannot be grounded in the pure a priori laws of identity and non-contradiction, nor in anthropomorphic analogies, but in concrete research, bound to reality and animated by the certainty that there is no fact that does not fit into an order, into a law.

Whenever humanity realizes that it has improperly and erroneously used the tools it has in its hands to explain and conquer the world, it is left with two paths. It can turn in on itself, refine its tools, and restrict their use to the terrain they are suited to, thoroughly cultivating this limited field. Or it can turn and face the world in all its variety, examine its hitherto poorly cultivated fields and forge new tools better adapted to working them. These fundamental attitudes are represented, at a certain point in the history of philosophy, by Descartes and Leibniz. And the controversy over eternal truths is merely the theological expression of these two different views of reality.

6. LEIBNIZ AND MYSTICISM*

When one seeks to study a philosophical system in the light of the cultural currents encountered in it and the problems it seeks to solve, one will always be left with a personal factor whose origins neither the sociologist nor the cultural historian, but only the biographer and the psychologist will be in a position to investigate. This factor will explain how these currents and problems came together precisely in this form, with this emphasis, and with this order of precedence. Sometimes the importance of such a component is insignificant and its influence is limited to the exterior order of the system. At other times, however, it is precisely this that leads to developments and discoveries that come to be a permanent part of human thought.

One of the elements that we cannot seem to explain except as the result of each individual's personal psychological processes is the mystical or intellectual character of each personality. Of each personality, that is — not of each philosophy. A philosophy can be full of mystical elements while the personality of the philosopher is intellectualist, and vice versa. What we mean is a particular way of seeing things and reacting to the facts of life — giving precedence to the rational or irrational, to practical or theoretical reason, to will or to knowledge.

Descartes, the rationalist philosopher par excellence, had a typically anti-intellectualist mentality. His constant sense that the sphere of the will is broader than that of

---

* *Rivista di filosofia*, xxix, 1938. "From a book on the formation of the Leibnizian system, forthcoming from the publisher Hermann in Paris."

knowledge, that the world of faith or grace is completely independent of the world of reason, and that divine will itself determines eternal truths beyond all reason — this cannot, it seems to us, be traced back to the intellectual influence of the mystics of the Oratory. It must correspond to something deeper and more ingrained in his character, a system of preferences which the "man" in him could not escape. He did succeed in ensuring that this intimate need of his made itself felt as little as possible in his philosophy. He relegated it to the margins, so that the geometrism of the construction would not be disturbed in any way. But this framing nevertheless sheds a special light on the rationalistic outline of the system.

Leibniz, on the other hand, at the heart of his character, was the purest intellectualist, the anti-mystic par excellence. Even though religious problems were one of his main interests, it is not possible to speak of a Leibnizian religiosity. In him we see the mind of the scientific researcher applied to the object of theology, but he lacks any instinct, sensitivity, or attachment to the irrational. Whenever he speaks of God, especially in the overall presentation of his system, there is always an emphasis on the harmony of the universe, the law inherent in things, and the organization of the cosmos — law, harmony and organization to which the human mind adapts, feeling it to be its own, recognizing in it the presence of that "reason" which enables it to embrace the totality of the world in a logical, causal, finalistic whole.[4] But we are never in the presence of the unconsidered immediacy or intuitive spontaneity that characterizes the experience of the mystic.

Every typically religious attitude necessarily has at its base an irrationalist psychology, founded on the pre-

---

[4] Cf., for example, the closing sections of the *Discours de Métaphysique*, the *Monadologia*, the *Principes de la Nature et de la Grâce*, and the dialogue *Pacidius Philalethi* (C. 62-67).

eminence of non-logical and non-empirical faculties (will, intuition, etc.) over reasoned knowledge.

Leibniz's attitude towards the relationship between knowledge and will, his stance on the psychological problems of the irrational and instinctual, his tendency to deny the autonomy of the various mental faculties in order to bring them back to the fundamental form of cognitive contact with reality show us the deep roots of his non-religiousness. But they also show us the basic psychological tendencies and the *forma mentis* from which the construction of his system arose — they will allow us, that is, to delve into the underlying tone of this rationalism.

Here we will not find (except in the problem of the essence of the will, which has directly metaphysical correlates) definite theories. Leibniz was only occasionally an investigator of the human mind. What he says about it is sporadic in nature and does not correspond to a true conceptual order. More than a set of doctrines, these are generic mental attitudes. They are interesting, however, because we may discern in them the deep motives and origins of various celebrated metaphysical and ontological formulations — if it is indeed true that all objectivism, starting with Plato's, has its basis in a certain conception of the human mind, whose terms are projected into the absolute. Which of course does not give us the right to shift the basis of the ontological approach, but it does not excuse us from studying these epistemological or psychological or anthropological roots as one of the integral elements of the system's formative process. Studying this substratum in Leibniz will give us the key to many fundamental aspects of his ontologism and its difference from other irrationalist systems of his time.

Baruzi, who has the distinction of having discovered and brought to light an entirely overlooked aspect of Leibnizian religious thought and has not neglected any element that might save his author's religiosity, continually refers to it as "mysticism." But he is always forced to add the adjective 'rational,' which completely neutralizes the term. If we want to count as mysticism any burst of enthusiasm for one's subject — a delight in panoramic visions of the kingdom of God understood as the kingdom of order and harmony, with its stable and rational laws, then we might perhaps speak of a mysticism of reason; but the word will have taken on a metaphorical value and no longer mean anything precise. Baruzi shows, based on unpublished documents, that Leibniz often found himself facing problems concerning mysticism. But it was with such remoteness and with such incomprehension, one might say, that these texts are indeed the best documentation of his rational and religious intellectualism. He indeed read many mystical works, but always with the haste and distraction of the scholar who wants to be informed about everything. On St Theresa he pauses to note that he has found an idea in conformity with his philosophy.[5] He forgives her and St Catherine of Genoa for "some credulity that is noticeable in their works," inclined as he is to "attach himself to what is to be praised in things, and paying almost no attention to what is to be blamed."[6] As far back as the *Ars Combinatoria*, he remembers how Valentinus Weigel "nimis entusiastice (too enthusiastically)" maintains that "beatitudinem hominis esse Deificationem" (the bliss of humanity is deification). Of Jacob Böhme and Poiret he says that although he appreciates them, he does not have time to penetrate their hermetic nature; "et j'avance bien mieux par mes propres méditations, qui viennent de cette même divine source de

---

[5] Baruzi, *Leibniz*, 326
[6] *Ibid.*, 338

lumière qui les peut avoir éclairés puisqu'il est sur que Dieu et la lumiere se trouvent en nous."[7]

With a little imagination, can we not detect a hint of irony in these words, and perhaps a hint of annoyance at the intrusiveness of the correspondent, whom we can imagine being too assiduous in recommending mystical readings?

On the other hand, it would be imprudent, faced with such a curious man and formidable reader, to rely on the books he read and the problems he was interested in to pin down the direct influences of authors and doctrines on his thinking. Leibniz's attention to the mental attitudes of others is always very much external. In books he seeks news, information — not spiritual communion. Rarely does he delve into the inner motives, into the inner structure of a system or a mental stance.

When confronted with a philosophical theory, he focuses on the final formulations, comparing them with his own, noting here a concordance, there a distance. His arguments and comments always have this character. They help us to better understand his thinking, but they don't bring us even a step closer to the writer he is debating. For hundreds of pages, he picks apart the thought of Bayle or Locke, and not once does he make an effort to enter the world of these authors, to understand the meaning or position of their theories in a mental system. He simply proceeds chapter by chapter, contrasting thesis with thesis, and intervening where he finds formulations among his own ideas that seem to him better than those of the other author. The reader has the impression of being faced with two men speaking different languages who believe they understand each other, each interpreting the sounds made by the other by analogy with their own way of speaking.

---

[7] Baruzi, *Leibniz*, 344, 345.

This is how he always behaves with everyone, whether faced with official church dogmas or the theories of mystics. He never makes a basic criticism of the point of view from which a book is written, but he does typically remark (when the book satisfies him) on its "plusieurs bonnes choses."[8] And good things for him are ideas he finds that correspond to his own or can be interpreted as such. He always has a great desire to enable, to profit and not to criticize,[9] to prove his counterparts right. And to do this, he cares less about what they really had in mind than about finding an artifice to make their doctrine acceptable. In this way he finds himself at peace with everyone. "Après avoir assez medité sur l'ancien et sur le nouveau j'ay trouvé que la pluspart des doctrines reçues peuvent souffrir un bon sens."[10] Confronted with a mystical doctrine on the love of God, he finds in it "quelque chose de joli," and continues that "on la peut rendre bonne," interpreting the terms of the author in a way that conforms to his own definitions.[11]

I have chosen a couple of examples among many. But with regard to the mystics there are countless such examples. Leibniz cannot be held to share the opinions of all the authors he claims to agree with. His thinking was subject to endless contacts, was expressed and formulated on a thousand different occasions, and it is indispensable to know this in order to understand it. Nevertheless, it cannot be said that it changed as a result of any particular influence. All the fundamental directives were already clear from his early youth. His readings and discussions were only stimuli for the further development of a construction that had already been sketched out.

---

[8] G. III, 133.
[9] G. III, 133, 384.
[10] *Nouv. Ess.*, II, c. 2, §§ 21-22.
[11] G. III, 384-85; cf. *Théod.*, §§ 20, 372

Baruzi refers to what Leibniz wrote about the visions of the young lady of Asseburg as "a psychology of mysticism."[12] But a reading of the texts clearly shows that it is not at all because of any special attention he paid to the content of the visions or their religious value, nor of any interest he had in a new, intuitive, irrational, ecstatic way of reaching an understanding of reality, but simply the normal curiosity of the scientist for a strange and unusual phenomenon outside the known laws of nature.[13] He does not deny its possible miraculous nature a priori, just as he always recognizes the possibility of a deviation by God from natural law for purposes of a higher order, but he tries wherever possible to bring the phenomenon back to the normality of nature.

The affair caused a stir at court, and provoked arguments between those who accused the visionary of heresy and those who worshiped her as a prophetess. To Duchess Sophie of Hanover, who asked him for his opinion, Leibniz replied with a mild tone of playful superiority. The thing must not be taken lightly in the manner of Molanus, he declares. "Quand on rencontre de telles personnes, bien loin de les gourmander et de vouloir les faire changer, il faut plustost les conserver dans cette belle assiette d'esprit, comme on garde une rereté ou une pièce de cabinet."[14] "Le meilleur est de laisser faire ces bonnes gens là, tant qu'il ne se meslent de rien qui puisse etre de consequence"; since sects and heresies gain strength from opposition to them, like a flame that is rekindled by being fanned. "De peur qu'on manque d'hérétiques, Messiurs le Théologiens font quelques fois tout ce qu'ils peuvent pour en trouver et por le immortaliser.... Souvent un homme

---

[12] Leibniz, 326, *L. et l'org.*, 501 ff.
[13] Klopp, VII, 139-68, Rommel, II, 342-43, 357, 369, and a 1692 letter to König, cited in Bodemann, *Briefw.*, n. 490. Baruzi, *Leibniz*, 329-30.
[14] Klopp, VII, 144.

obtient l'honneur d'estre hérésiarque sans le savoir."[15] And as for the phenomenon in question, he is inclined to consider it an example of suggestion.

It is worth lingering for a moment over this bit of physiopathological psychology.[16] Dreams, Leibniz explains to the duchess, differ from true perceptions in two ways: first, in their lack of connection and continuity, "car ceux qui veillent sont dans un monde commun, au lieu que ceux qui songent, ont chacun un monde particulier"; and second, because they are less vivid and distinct. But people with strong imaginations can have visions so vivid that they seem to them to be the truth. "C'est purquoi les jeunes personnes élevées dans les cloistres ou elles entendent de vieilles historiettes de miracles et de spectres, si elles ont la phantaisie fort agissante, son sujettes à avoir de telles visions, parce que leur teste en est remplie."

The proof of this is that such visions "se rapportent d'ordinaire au naturel des personnes," that is, to their inclinations and mentality. This is also the case for the true prophets, "car Dieu s'est accommodé à leur genie." Thus, Ezekiel sees everything in terms of architecture, Hosea and Amos of agriculture, and Daniel of politics. Leibniz has no hesitation in comparing their visions to the visions of the Lady of Assenburg,[17] and this is not to validate the supernatural character of the former, but rather to affirm the naturalness of the latter. By this he does not intend to undermine the holiness of either: "Car pourquoy ne l'appelleray-je pas une grâce? Cela ne luy fait que du bien, elle en est joyeuse, elle conçoit là dessus les plus beaux

---

[15] Klopp, VII, 151-52.
[16] Klopp, VII, 144 ff.
[17] "Cette multitude des prophètes du peuple d'Israel apparemment n'estoit pas d'une autre nature" (Klopp, VII, 147). "Il y a de l'apparence que Ste. Thérèse, Ste. Catharine de Sienne et autres personnes semblables estoient à peu près du meme naturel" (Rommel, II, 343).

sentiments du monde... Il ne faut s'imaginer que toutes les grâces de Dieu doivent estre miraculeuses." Only true prophecies are to be understood as supernatural — prophecies with details, about the specifics of future events, which imply knowledge of all the causal relationships, of a kind that a finite mind cannot have. It would be supernatural if the young lady really did give correct answers, as was reported, about letters presented to her unopened — but Leibniz doubts this and attributes it rather to chance, or to the generic nature of the words she uses.[18]

The girl's mother had consecrated her to Jesus Christ before she was even born. This explains everything. An impression received in childhood can create a lifelong nervous disorder. One person faints at the sight of a pin, another has an idiosyncrasy about grasshoppers. Now, "il est vray que l'amour de Dieu a un objet spirituel et ne sauroit venir des images de la phantaisie, mais l'humanité de Jesus Christ, les phrases de l'Écriture et les manières qui accompagnent ordinairement la devotion, peuvent laisser des traces dans le cerveau."[19] This is how a doctor, or a scientist speaks, not a mystic.[20]

In his youth in Nuremberg, Leibniz had actively participated in the alchemical research of the Rosicrucians. Alchemy would continue to be one of his most important occupations; but he always insisted on treating it as a truly rigorous, experimental science, freeing it from all its magical and mystical trappings. "For years," he wrote to Father Kochanski, "I have kept in touch with these connoisseurs of the arcana of nature, with these 'adepts,' but

---

[18] Rommel, II, 343, Klopp, VII, 146, 156, Bodemann, *Briefw.*, n. 490.
[19] Klopp, VII, 156-57. See also in Klopp, VIII, 22-24 the natural explanation of the phenomenon of the "wood of the True Cross."
[20] All of chap. XIX, 1. IV of *New Essays* speaks of visionaries and mystics, always with reservations and great skepticism and irony. Cf. also his observations on Shaftesbury's *Letter Concerning Enthusiasm* (G. III, 407 ff.).

I have yet to derive a true construct from them. And the deeper I go into these studies, the more skeptical and cautious I become." "Cum certis rationibus, quantum ego intelligo, ad haec magnalia aditus non detur" ("With sound reasoning, as far as I understand it, no access is given to these great things."). But if this sublime art led only to the manufacture of gold it would do more harm than good because of the depreciation of the metal that would follow, which would utterly disrupt commerce. If, on the other hand, it should succeed in discovering a panacea, it would be more precious than anything; but the danger here is that what is reported is not true. "Itaque vereor, ne dum magna et admiranda quaerimus, certiora et magis profutura negligamus" ("Therefore, I am afraid that while we seek great and admirable things, we forget about the surer and more useful ones.") How much better such illustrious men would do in medicine! He does not trust two gentlemen claiming to be Rosicrucian brothers: "nam scire quae remotis locis fiant, invisibilem sese atque invulnerabilem reddere haud dubie nugacia vel potius irrisoria sunt" ("In fact knowing what happens in remote places, making oneself invisible and invulnerable are surely frivolous and rather unimportant things.").[21]

Even the "enthusiastic" alchemist-Kabbalist-astrologer-theosophist Franciscus Mercurius Van Helmont, whom Leibniz held in esteem and affection and from whom, according to Stein, he derived the term 'monad,'

---

[21] Stein, 329-30. Cf. also Baruzi, *Trois dialogues mystiques inédits de Leibniz*, in "Revue de Mét et de Mor." 1905 p. 18: "Si j'avais des panacées et des teintures, que je n'ai point, je ne les compterais pour rien au prix de cette medecine universelle des ames [i.e. regular application of knowledge]... Et moy qui croy que les choses ordinaires comme le feu et l'eau sont les plus efficaces, je m'imagine que ce qu'il y a d'extraordinairement utile ne consiste que dans l'usage et dans l'applicaton. Voyez moy les éléments des géomètres. Y a-t-il rien de plus simple... Cependant leur seul arrangement a produit tant de vérités surprenantes... Vous autres messieurs ne voulez que des nouveautés éclatantes, signa et prodigia."

is sometimes the object of his irony.[22] Leibniz describes his curious way of dressing and speaking,[23] and sometimes recounts his most fanciful theories.[24] Van Helmont wrote about metempsychosis, future life, hell and heaven, and the spiritual substance of all things. Here again, Leibniz patiently sought an opportunity to approve rather than reject. He stresses those points that can somehow be rationally demonstrated or interpreted in conformity with his philosophy. He sympathizes with him in his criticism of Gassendism and Cartesianism, and accepts in his conclusions the concept of indestructible substance.[25] But when Van Helmont ventures into the arbitrary and the irrational; when he gets into the details of other-worldly life, or guesses thoughts; when he wants everything to be made up of water and fire, understood as principles of mind; when he enters into speculations about Adam and Eve and the Messiah and millenarianism, etc., "quant à tout cela," says Leibniz, "je me dispenserai d'y entrer." He is glad to know that everything is so well organized that nothing better can be imagined. "Mais si M. Van Helmont nous en peut apprendre d'avantage, nous en serons ravis."[26] Even when he accepts and agrees, he knows that the agreement is entirely external, and that it concerns the final formulations, to which he tries to "donner un bon sens,"

---

[22] Stein, 208 ff. Cf. some letters from their correspondence, *ibid.*, 331 ff. and a judgment of him in G. III, 427.
[23] Klopp, VIII, 8, Dutens, VI, 170 Rommel, I, 276.
[24] "M. Mercurius van Helmont croyait que l'ame de Jesus Christ étoit celle d'Adam, et que l'Adam nouveau reparant ce que le premier avait gasté c'étoit le même personnage qui satisfaisait à son ancienne dette. Je crois qu'on fait bien de s'épargner la peine de refuter de telles pensées" (to Burnett, 1696, G. III, 306). Cf. Klopp, VII, 155.
[25] Klopp, VII, 303 ff.
[26] To Duchess Sofia, 1694, Klopp, VII, 301 ff. Cf. VIII 13, D. V, 85-86, D. VI, I, 333: "Madame l'électrice avait coutume de dire en parlant de lui qu'il ne s'entendait pas lui même."

but that the method used to reach them and the world they encompass is entirely different from his own.[27] "M. Helmont... convient avec moy, quoyque je ne puisse comprendre ses arguments et ses preuves."[28]

For Leibniz, alchemy need have nothing mystical or irrational about it.[29] His concept of universal animation through infinite monads has (as we shall see more clearly) nothing to do with the animation that alchemists and 'adepts' and mystics posited and sought in the mineral world. It would be worthwhile — he says in *Protogea* — to compare and note the similarity between laboratory products and natural substances, between things that are "known" and things that are "made." The supreme creator of all things loves consistency, and "et magnum est ad res noscendas vel unam producendi rationem obtinuisse: quemadmodum Geometrae ex uno modo describendi figuram omnes ejus proprietates derivant... Neque enim aliud est natura quam ars quaedam magna" ("it is important to have obtained even a single manner of production as a way of knowing things — such as in Geometry, where from a single way of describing a figure, all its properties are derived. Indeed, nature is nothing but a great art"). And while it is doubtful that alchemy can produce simple substances ex novo, it must be recognised that it is equally difficult to see this occurring in nature: "Plerumque enim [nature] dudum alibi conceptos foetus colligit tantum detegitque." ("For the most part, nature collects dense concepts [in other places] and reveals them only once.") One must not believe men's fables about the creation of gold and their fantasies about *homunculi* and *plutonii monaci*

---

[27] Klopp, VII, 300.
[28] Klopp, VIII, 9.
[29] Baruzi says, on the contrary (*L. et l'org.*, 209), in direct reference to alchemy, that "Leibniz devient incompréhensible, si l'on arrache de son être la part irrationnelle." Cf. also *Leibniz*, 84 ff.

and *virgula divina*.[30] Alchemy is reduced to its natural limits in the composition and decomposition of substances, and even in the natural domain it is understood that nature itself does nothing beyond these internal modifications, and that there is nothing miraculous or exceptional in its operations — there is no creation *ex novo* in brute matter, but only the displacement of aggregations. In short, nothing is created, and nothing destroyed.

But the irrational, the mystical, was the order of the day. There were controversies between Jansenists and Jesuits, between Bossuet and Fénelon and M.me Guyon, Quietism, Pietism, Chiliasm. Leibniz found himself continually questioned by his correspondents on these issues. These sects, despite their differences, were nourished by the same spirit that fed the sects of the naturalists, and in one form or another represented the tendency to return to a direct, individualistic, personal religiosity, outside the organization of the Churches. They were bitterly opposed by the orthodoxy, both Catholic and Protestant. Leibniz, from the heights of his official position, ventured to moderate and to plead, among trustworthy friends, for leniency towards these people, who were in fact harming no one.[31]

---

[30] Dutens, II, 2°, 209, See also skeptical expressions on astrology in *Théod.*, § 43.

[31] Three gradations: 1st, with his nephew Löffler, indignation against the zealots of orthodoxy and advocacy for freedom of thought: "Non video quorsum tantae de Pietistis concertationes pertineant; faciat quisque quod suum est et potius mores suos emendet quam alienos carpat. Malim ego quoque hominem pium quam doctum, sed malim tamen pietatem cum doctrina quam zelum scientiae expertem. In censuris nos temperantes esse decet... Quanto quisque prudentior est, eo minus tricas amat, et quanto quisque pietati magis studet eo magis a reprehensionibus non necessariis abhorret" ["I do not understand the purpose of the numerous discussions regarding Pietas. Let each do what pertains to him and correct his own behavior rather than blame the behavior of others. I too would prefer a pious man rather than a wise one, but nevertheless I would rather have piety with learning than a zeal lacking in knowledge. In judgments we must be temperate. The wiser each one is, the less

The controversy over Quietism interested him even before it became famous,[32] and suggested interesting formulations on the essence of religiosity. The problem that was posed touched the very heart of the issue. The stillness, abandonment, and disinterestedness advocated by the Quietists, from Molinos to Fénelon, present the investigator of the nature of the mental faculties with fundamental issues concerning the nature of the will. It is this liberation from the principle of causality, from the motive of interest — this denial of any action linked in any way to utility, that leads, through the Kantian categorical imperative, to the Schopenhauerian annulment of the will in its relation to the *principium individuationis*.[33] The psychology of contemplation and of immediate and direct contact with God, characteristic of all mysticism, is here carried out essentially from the point of view of the negation of the will. "On ne passe insensiblement de la méditation, ou l'on fait les actes méthodiques et discoursifs, à la contemplation dont les actes sont simples et directes,

---

he loves futility, and the more each one pursues piety the more he rejects unnecessary reproach"] (cited in Bodemann, *Briefw.*, n. 571). 2nd, with his friend and protector Duchess Sophie, benevolent intercessor for a persecuted man: "Je souhaiterais que tout le monde fust à son aise, et je ne voudrais pas non plus qu'on tourmentast ceux qu'on appelle Chiliastes... La confession d'Augsbourg semble n'estre que contre les millenaires turbateurs du repos publique. Mais l'horreur de ceux qui attendent en patience le Royoume de Jesus Christ en terre, me parait très innocente" (Klopp, VII, 149, cf. Rommel, II, 459). 3rd, with Bossuet, then in open controversy with Fénelon: "Le soin de réprimer les abus des mustiques a estré digne de vous. La matière est de saison, et la maladie, régnante: une pretendue secte de piétistes donne presque autant d'exercice à nos theologiens que les quietistes en donnent aux vostres. Il est vray qu'il faut prendre garde de ne pas toucher à la véritable dévotion en arrachant l'yvraye. Mais il y a des excès si grands qu'on ne sçauroit les dissimuler. Tel paroist ce qu'n dit de vostre madame Guyon" (F. d. C II, 194). For Pietism and Spener, Leibniz always shows respect and benevolence. Cf. Klopp, VII, 167; Rommel, II, 133-34, 316, 459.

[32] Cf. *Discours de Métaphysique* (1685), § IV, and G VI, 427. The great arguments between Bossuet and Fénelon took place around 1695.

[33] Schopenhauer refers explicitly to the Quietists and to M.me Guyon, Fénelon's friend and protector; cf. *Welt alt W.u.V.*, 1. IV, § 68, e Ergänzungen, chap. 48.

qu'à mesure qu'on passe de l'amour interessé au désinteressé."[34]

Suppression of personality, that is, which in Molinos takes on the character of the absolute annihilation of all individual will — inactivity and passivity.[35] The irrationality of contemplation is by no means described as illumination or intuition or vision, or in other words as some special form of knowledge, different or superior to rational knowledge. Indeed, its mystical superiority consists precisely and exclusively in its rational inferiority. "Know then that the path of the shadows is ... the most perfect and the safest and straightest; for it is there that the Lord sets his throne *et posuit tenebras latibulum suum*. Through the shadows the supernatural light that God infuses into the soul grows and grows. Wisdom is generated in their midst, and great love... Do you see that darkness

---

[34] Fénelon, *Explication des maximes des saints sur la vie intérieure*, avertissement. Cf. art XXI.

[35] Molinos, *Guida spirituale*, Venice 1685 (the first edition is from 1675), Proemio, § 5. "The soul, from which speech has been taken away, must not abuse itself, nor necessarily seek clearer, or more particular information, but rather without the support of consolation, or discernible motive, with poverty of spirit, and stripped of all that is natural appetite demands of it, be quiet, firm, and constant, letting the Lord work, although it finds itself alone, arid, and full of darkness. And if this seems to it to be idleness, it is only in relation to its own sensate and material activity, not to that of God, who is working true knowledge in it." § 17: "When the soul reaches this state, it must withdraw into itself in its pure, deep centre; where the image of God is, there loving attention, silence, forgetfulness of all things, applying the will with perfect resignation, listening to and speaking with God alone, *as if there were nothing else in the world but the two of them*." The italics are ours. This is the phrase that Leibniz also found in St. Teresa that reminded him of his own conceptions (Baruzi, Leibniz, 326, *Discours de Métaphysique*, § 32). But the correspondence is only in the words. Here we are dealing with a psychological process in which the individual soul, alienating itself from the world, places itself in direct and ecstatic contact with God. In Leibniz, it is a matter of the concept of an individual substance that encompasses in itself the whole of the past and future and the entire universe, to which nothing can be considered extraneous. Indeed, it could be said that the two concepts are opposites. In the mystics, the world is denied by the soul approaching God, while in Leibniz it is affirmed and included in itself by substance.

is to be esteemed and embraced? What you must do in its midst is to believe that you stand before the Lord and in his presence, but you must do this with gentle and quiet attention. Do not seek to know anything, nor look for delicacy, tenderness, or sensitive divine devotion, nor long to do anything except the divine good, because otherwise you will not achieve anything in your life but circles, and you will not take a single step towards perfection."[36]

Darkness, obscure and confused knowledge, inactivity. Denial, therefore, of any act or exercise that represents a direct effort towards the attainment of contemplation — even mortification, even the struggle against temptation is blameworthy. "You will not reach this state no matter how hard you try, in the external armies of mortification... and resignation... What you have to do is to prepare your heart like a blank piece of paper, where divine wisdom can form the characters to its liking."[37]

Considering that he had solemnly recanted, the Holy Office sentenced Molinos to life imprisonment instead of burning at the stake.[38] Clearly, the Church was obliged to regard his doctrine as a dangerous heresy, since it eliminated all positive agency on the part of religion and thus

---

[36] Molinos, op. cit., book I, §§ 40-41. Cf. Proemio, § 7: "They will say that the will cannot love but will stand idle if the intellect does not comprehend with distinction and clarity, it being a firm principle that one cannot love except what one knows. The answer to this is that although the intellect does not understand distinctly, by discourse, images and considerations, it understands all the same and is aware through obscure, general and confused faith; the cognition of which, although very indistinct, and general, as in one who is supernatural, has a clearer and more perfect cognition of God than any possible and particular knowledge that can be formed in this life."

[37] *Ibid.*, book I, §§ 43-46.

[38] "Enfin, après être demeuré d'accord des principaux chefs d'accusation portés contre lui, aprés avoir reconnu et détesté ses erreurs, et demandé pardon de ses éxcès, en consideration de sa répentance on l'a seulement condamné à la prison perpètuelle et à des penitances particulières" (Bossuet, *Oeuvres*, Venezia, VIII, 250-51).

threatened it in its essence as a social and political organization, with control and power over individual believers. This attitude of defense of the organization and of positive worship is what Bossuet took up in the controversy. His instructions *Sur les états d'oraison* specify, as elements for recognizing the Molinist heresy,[39] the exclusion of the contemplation of Christ's humanity, the asking of nothing from God, not even the remission of one's sins, the suppression of the Acts, the denial of mortification, the offering of praise only for extraordinary prayers. Bossuet took the field on the side of the regularity, normality, social nature of religious life, fighting any innovation that would tend to make it something exceptional and unattainable through the efforts of the average believer.

Archbishop and court prelate, Fènelon recognized these requirements, oscillating between the mystical principle he was attached to and the ecclesiastical necessity he felt was inevitable. He sought moderation and compromise, tried to leave a place, albeit secondary, for meditation, which Molinos had completely suppressed, and he corrected the doctrine of total passivity.[40] The outcome was the theory of selfless love, in which he achieves great psychological finesse. "On ne veut rien pour soit; mais on veut tout pour Dieu; on ne veut rien pour être parfait ni bienheureux, autant qu'il plait à Dieu de nous faire vouloir ces choses."[41] The will was not denied as such,[42] but only insofar as it was related in any way to our personal well-being. Not

---

[39] Not to be confused with Molina's neo-Scholastic doctrine of free will.
[40] Fénelon, *Explication des maximes des saints*, art. XXI.
[41] *Ibid.*, art. v, *Vrai*.
[42] *Ibid.*, art. v, *Vrai*. "En cet état on ne sent plus le salut comme salut propre, comme délivrance éternelle, comme récompense de nos mérites, comme le plus grand de nos intérêts: mais on le veut d'une volonté pleine, comme la gloire et le bon plaisir de Dieu, comme une chose qu'il veut et qu'il veut que nous voulions pour lui."

even personal salvation should be desired as such, but rather accepted and desired as belonging to the will of God.⁴³ This was the main focus of the fight with Bossuet, according to whom remission of one's sins must be explicitly requested by each believer.

Such, in brief, is the problem of Quietism — and these points perhaps suffice to show how far it is from the interests and the intellectual climate in which Leibniz moved. He addressed it, drawn by the natural curiosity that did not allow him to abandon any problem without trying to solve it. Unlike Bossuet, he didn't need to worry about ecclesiastical discipline, and was able to get to the theoretical and moral bottom of the question of mysticism. His general sense of tolerance for sects did not prevent him from showing his absolute distrust and incomprehension of these doctrines.⁴⁴ "Le moyen d'estre sans

---

⁴³ *Ibid.*, art. v, *Faux:* "Tout désir, même les plus désintéressé, est imparfait. La perfection consiste à ne vouloir plus rien, à ne désirer plus non seulement les dons de Dieu, mais encore Dieu même, et à le laisser faire en nous ce qui lui plait" (It was this doctrine that Fénelon rejected).
⁴⁴ Rommel, II, 136, 194, G. II, 573-74. Indeed, it was perhaps his absolute incompatibility with the mystics that allowed him to take their side more openly when they were threatened with repression. He was certain he could never be accused of any affinity with them, whereas he did not feel as confident about naturalism and Socinianism. Still, he was often annoyed by this fantastical and impassioned way of framing things, even while acknowledging some of its advantages. In the *Discours sur la conformité* (§§ 9, 10) he speaks of Spinoza, understood as a Kabbalist, of Weigel "homme d'esprit" "et qui en avait même trop," of Angelo Silesio, of Gerson, and of Ruysbroeck, "auteur mystique dont l'intention dont l'intention était bonne apparemment, et dont les expressions sont excusable, mais il vaut mieux écrire d'une manière qui n'ait point besoin d'estre excusée. Quoyque j'avoue aussi que souvent les expressions outrées et pour ainsi dire poétiques ont plus de force pour toucher et pour persuader, que ce qui se dit avec regularité." And he does not miss an opportunity at times to mock these attitudes, so contrary to his own temperament, such as when he compliments Duchess Sophie, comparing her spirit with the "vertu farouche et retirée d'une Antoinette de Bourignon, qui en fait des livres, sans peut-être la pratiquer comne il faut. Il est aisé de faire la prude quand on est sur l'âge, et quatre vingt et dix ans sont d'un grand secours contre les plaisirs du monde" (Klopp, VII, 168, cfr. Bodemann, *Handschr.* p. 24). See another case in Rommel, II, 133. He says of M.me Guyon

action, sans pensée et sans volonté?... Il faudrait prendre de l'Opium, ou boire un bon Rausch, pour parvenir à une telle quiétude ou inaction, qui n'est autre chose qu'une stupidité convenable aux brutes... Quoy qu'on dise, il est impossible qu'une substance cesse d'agir." True stillness, found "dans la Sainte Écriture, dans les Pères et dans la raison," is the silence of the senses "afin de mieux écouter la voix de Dieu, c'est à dire la lumière intérieure des vérités éternelles." This is the sense in which Leibniz believed "Gelassenheit" should be interpreted — the resignation or annihilation spoken of by mystical sages such as Tauler, Ruysbroeck, and Weigel.[45] He could not conceive of contemplation, or any activity of apprehension or contact with the absolute, that was not reflective and rational. "Cette contemplation élevée ne sçaurait estre autre chose à mon avis qu'un regard bien claire de l'Estre infiniment parfait. Mais a moins d'une grâce surnaturelle extraordinaire et d'un ravissement semblable à celui de St. Paul — que Dieu ne donne pas à tous les Fidèles et qui n'est pas necessaire à la véritable piété[46] — je crois que cette profonde contemplation est elle même le resultat d'une véritable méditation... Il n'y a que les premiers principes ou axiomes dont on puisse connoistre la Vérité par une simple vue, sans aucune méditation."[47] And after

---

that she is "une devote ignorante" (Bodemann, *Handschr.* p. 26). and "une orgueilleuse visionnaire" (to Nicaise, 1698, G. II, 585).
[45] Rommel, II, 132, cf. 193-94, Baruzi *Leibniz*, 342. Cf. also the 1707 letters to Hansch (D. II, I, 225) and to Nicaise in 1697 (G. II, 578), as well as the preface to the second part of the *Codex Juris Gentium*, from 1700 (Dutens, IV, 3rd, 313), where he accuses mystics such as Weigel, Angelo Silesio, and Molinos of falling into Averroism and Pantheism, denying the immortality of the individual soul and annihilating it in the universal mind. Cf. also *Discours de la conformité*, §§ 7 ff.
[46] This case of extraordinary and supernatural grace is considered by Leibniz in the same way he regards a miracle — as a dispensation made by God in favor of a single person; an absolutely exceptional phenomenon on which no rules of life can be based.
[47] Rommel, II, 134.

all, knowing is always knowing rationally.[48] The question expands and becomes fundamental. Quietism, like all mysticism, presupposes a precedence of the practical over the theoretical. Reason and faith, meditation and contemplation, knowledge and love, 'geometry' and 'finesse,' are resolved in the contrast between these two faculties, and the preponderance of one or the other decides the philosophical — i.e. rational, mediated, discursive — or mystical — i.e. immediate and irrational — character of a thought. The mystic, who always starts out with the denial of rationality, resolves this denial in the affirmation of love and charity, which prepare for and lead to intuition, ecstasy, and direct contact with divinity. The total passivity of Molinos is a state that is attained through a non-rational and pre-rational act (albeit negative) of the will. Any will that arises as a consequence of previous knowledge does not give rise to mysticism, but to the responsible and controlled security of conscious morality.

In Leibniz, on the other hand, the anteriority of knowledge over will is a continuously asserted principle. It is the basis of the relationship between God and truths of reason as well as the essential character of his objectivism, in contrast to that of Descartes which is based on an arbitrary act of divinity. This is both a metaphysical necessity and a psychological conviction, which leaves a fundamental mark on his thought.[49]

---

[48] As far back as the early *Defensio Trinitatis*, ecstasy is theorized as a state in which the soul performs separately from the body those functions that it normally performs through the body by "nempe ratiocinari, cogitare" ("with certainty, by reasoning, thinking") etc. Hence it is usually said that man does not reason, while more properly it should be said that the body does not reason and that the reasoning function is exercised by man "quatenus anima est" ("as long as he has a soul.") (G. IV, 121-22).

[49] "Je ne suis pas dans son [Thomasius'] sentiment lorsqu'il fait l'amour antérieur à la lumière. Nous ne puvouns être unis à Dieu que passivement à son égard; car nous ne saurions agir sur lui et nous devons recevoir son action en nous, pour agir par après conformément à son esprit, tant sur nous que sur

The formulation of the *Discours de Métaphysique* is crucial,[50] and every time Leibniz finds himself faced with mystical theories that speak of love and charity as starting points anterior to reason or of irrational ways of apprehending the divine, he does not so much disapprove as fail to understand or enter into the spirit of the thing. "Pourquoy appeler lumière ce qui ne fait rien voir?"[51] He sometimes interprets these attitudes in such a way that they seem to conform to his philosophy, but in doing so he transforms them, turning their character upside down. To solve the problems involved, he sometimes applies concepts taken from other areas of his thought, which remain abstract and inorganic in their new function. Rather than becoming a mystic himself he makes mysticism Leibnizian and rationalist. The notes on *William Penn's Journal* published by Baruzi[52] are very interesting in this regard. "J'approuve même qu'il y ait des personnes qui prennent des biais extraordinaires pour tirer les autres de leur assoupissement. C'est pour cela qu'il leur faut pardonner certaines pratiques affectées et qui paraissent bizarres. Le monde est adonné à la bagatelle." But these methods should always be united with a theory that is "clear and luminous." "Les idées que Jesus Christ nous donne de Dieu sont grandes, mais en même temps elles sont claires." And when Christ counsels us to love God and our neighbor, "il comprend en même temps et la théorie et la pratique." Our

---

les autres choses. Anisi la lumière est notre passion, l'amour est le plaisir que en resulte, et qui consiste dans une action sur nous mêmes, dont provient un effort d'agir encore sur les autres choses, pour contribuer au bien, autant qu'il dépend de nous" (Baruzi, *Leibniz*, 329).

[50] "Ou sera donc sa [God's] justice et sa sagesse, s'il ne reste qu'un certain pouvoir despotique, si la volonté tient lieu de raison, et se selon la définition des tyrans, ce qui plaist au plus puissant est juste par là même? Outre qu'il semble que toute volonté suppose quelque raison de vouloir et que cette raison est naturellement antérieur à la volonté (*Discours de Métaphysique*, § 2).

[51] *Nouveaux Essais*, 1. IV, c. 19.

[52] Baruzi, *Leibniz*, 342 ff.

century should apply to the idea of God the 'nouvelles lumières' and the wonderful natural discoveries it is replete with. "L'amour est fondé sur la connaissance de la beauté de l'objet aimé," and the more we are able to love God, the more we will understand nature and "les vérites solides des sciences rèelles." Anyone trying to distance humanity from this real science "sous prétexte de certaines lumières dont il se vantent, et qui ne consistent que dans l'imagination émue, font quitter le solide pour des chimères, en flattent notre négligence." If knowledge of God's greatness lies in contemplation of the marvelous order of nature, then love of God will entail participation in these divine perfections, and "tout le véritable bonheur ne consiste uniquement dans un progrès perpétuel de joies provenantes de l'amour céleste ou de la contemplation des véritables beautés de la nature divine." It is this happiness, "qui nait de la connaissance de la divine et éternelle verité," that enables us to detach ourselves from the vanity of the world. Everything said about this asceticism and detachment by "les Weigeliens, Böhmistes, Trembleurs, Quiétistes, Labadistes et autres personnes semblables" is true only insofar as it comes down to preferring "le bien général et les plus grandes expressions des perfections divines à toutes le considerations des choses du monde. S'il y a quelque autre chose, c'est caprice ou chimère."[53]

Rarely did Leibniz express himself with such clarity and passion on these issues. Love is a direct consequence of knowledge — it is intrinsic in it and it extends itself with the extension of it.

---

[53] In my opinion, this is the sense in which we should understand what he writes to Morell about the works of Saint Theresa and Angela of Foligno, "où je trouve des choses admirables, reconnaissant de plus en plus que la véritable théologie et religion doit être dans notre coeur par une pure abnégation de nous-même, en nous abandonnant à la misericorde divine" (Baruzi, *Leibniz*, 337). He even interprets the use of suffering and mortification as a useful exercise for strengthening the body and getting us used to putting up with pain (*ibid.*, 351).

His *Von der wahren theologia mystica*[54] which is almost a translation into mystical terms of the theory of the monad, confirms this idea — participation in non-being is characteristic of creatures; but within each individual lies an infinity, an image of God's omniscience and omnipotence. "God is more intimate to me than the body."[55] And the denial of self, the crucifixion of Old Adam, is the hatred of non-being and the affirmation of being in ourselves, which is the affirmation of God. One who loves God puts the inner light before the image of the senses — one's own being before non-being. A man who merely fears God loves himself and his non-being more than God. But "Faith without light inspires no love... Christ's teaching is spirit and truth; but many make it flesh and shadow. Most men are not serious. They have not tried the truth and abide in sinister unbelief."

Love, dedication to God, religion, and that third stage of natural law that Leibniz calls 'piety' are nothing but the broadening of our view of the harmony of things[56] and our participation in it. Resigning ourselves to evil is the recognition that this harmony has laws wider than we can know — that evil, in short, is merely an appearance due to our partial view.[57] Charity is our contribution to

---

[54] Guhrauer, *Deutsche Schriften*, 411-13.
[55] A sentence similar to the one previously quoted, stating that for each soul there is nothing in the world but God.
[56] "And it is precisely this complacency in the supreme and universal disposition, regardless of what happens once one has done one's part, that is the proper foundation of true religion. And it is based on reasoning; it is also useful for our pleasure" (*Initia Scientiae Novae Generalis*. G. VII, 121).
[57] "Nous devons aimer Dieu sur toutes les choses, puisque nous trouvons tout en lui avec plus de perfection que dans les choses mêmes; et puisque sa bonté nous tient lieu de notre toute puissance.... Et on peut dire que cette résignation de notre volonté à celle de Dieu auquel nous avons tout sujet de nos fier suit du véritable amour divin... Car enfin Dieu ne se néglige dans la nature, rien ne se perd aved Dieu, tout nos cheveux sont comptés, pas le verre d'eau ne sera oublié...; point de bonne action sans recompense, point de mauvaise sans

this harmony, because we are also part of it.⁵⁸ Prayer is nothing more than the "élévation de l'âme à Dieu, c'est à dire une recherche perpétuelle des raisons solides de ce qui nous fait paroistre Dieu grand et aimable."⁵⁹ The best and most blessed in future life are those who are wisest.⁶⁰ Our duty here is to refine our spirit and broaden our knowledge. This general enlightenment is to be achieved by the familiar means that Leibniz never tires of advocating and devising, but which is met with reluctance and incomprehension on all sides⁶¹ — the organization of the sciences, instruments of culture.⁶² Love of God is knowledge

---

quelque châtiment, point de perfection sans une suite d'autres jusqu'à l'infini" (Baruzi, *Trois dialogues mystiques inèdits de Leibniz*, loc. cit., pp. 36-37).

⁵⁸ "Nous devons faire tous les efforts imaginables pour contribuer en quelque chose au bien public; car c'est Dieu que est le Seigneur, c'est à lui que le bien public appartient comme en propre" (Baruzi, *Trois dialogues*, cit., p. 36).

⁵⁹ *Dialogue entre un habile politique et un ecclesiastique d'une pieté reconnue.* F. d. C. II, 335. At other times he understands prayer as an actual request to the deity, at which point his concern is to justify it in the face of the fact that everything is preordained. Cfr. *Théod.*, §§ 54, 310, append. I (G. VI, 433-34, 445), Klopp, X, 43, Gerhardt, *Briefwechsel mit Mathematikern*, 483.

⁶⁰ "Lorsque on connait la nature, on est pour ainsi dire du conseil de Dieu" (Baruzi, *Leibniz*, 352). "Nous devons tâcher de nous perfectionner autant que nous le pouvons, et surtout l'esprit qui est proprement ce qu'on appelle nous; et comme la perfection de l'esprit consiste dans la connaissance des vérités et dans l'exercice des vertues, nous devons être persuadés que ceux qui auront eu dans cette vie plus d'entrées dans les vérités eternelles et des connaissances plus liquides et plus claires de la perfection de Dieu et qui l'auriont par conséquent aimé davantage… seront susceptibles d'un plus grand bonheur dans l'autre vie" (Baruzi, *Trois dialogues*, cit., pp. 36-37). It is notable that this dialogue is earlier than 1679 and thus predates the *Discours de Métaphysique*. And the concept of universal harmony and the *Teodicea* is already present in Leibniz's very early youth. Cf. also Baruzi, *Leibniz*, 342-345.

⁶¹ "J'ai fait mille fois des propositions de cette nature. Mais j'ai trouvé ordinairement que les personnes qui voulaient passer pour les plus pieuses n'était que glace, quand il s'agissait véritablement de bien faire, se contentant de s'évaporer en belles paroles comme si Dieu se gagnait par les cérémonies" (Baruzi, *Leibniz*, 339). Cf. *ibid.*, 150.

⁶² "Sachons enfin une fois pour toutes que la connoissance des grandes vérités, l'exercice de l'amour divin et de la charité, les efforts qu'on peut faire pour le bien général, soulager les maux des hommes, contribuer au bonheur de la vie, avancer les Sciences et les Arts, et tout ce qui sert pour s'acquérir une veritable gloire et pour s'immortaliser par des bienfaits, son acheminements à cette félicité, qui

of God,[63] and the touchstone of loving God was given to us by John: "L'ardeur pour procurer le Bien en general."[64] In short, love of God is for Leibniz "the intellectual love of God."[65] His position is starkly and rigidly intellectualist. But his moral intellectualism differs from Spinoza's in the same way that their two rationalisms differ. In both, perfection consists in the identification of the intellect (and thus of the will) with the reason that is the rule of the universe. But in Leibniz this reason, this rule, is not analytic-mathematical, but synthetic-harmonic — it is not the deduction of principles, but the ordering of facts. The comparison he most readily uses is to the well-constructed building, the well-ordered state. The argument he uses is the one offered to him by contemporary science and the recently invented microscope — the order and homogeneity of the universe in the infinitely small as well as the infinitely large.[66] Pascal as well had had a

---

nous approchera de Dieu autant que nous en sommes capables, et qu'on peut traiter en quelque façon d'apothéose" (Baruzi, *Trois dialogues*, cit., p. 58).

[63] "On ne sauroit aimer Dieu sans en connoistre les perfections" (*Théod*, pref. G. VI, 28)

[64] Baruzi, *Leibniz*, 340-41. The reference is probably to John, Ep. I, IV, 12 (cf. Baruzi, *Leibniz et l'org.*, 458-59). These and similar conceptions are set forth in the fragments on wisdom, justice, happiness, meditation, virtue, etc. published in G. VII, 73 ff. Cf. on prayer also understood as participation in the general welfare, Klopp, X, 43.

[65] "Qui Deum amat, discere conatur eius voluntatem. Qui Deum amat, ejus voluntati oboedit. Qui Deum amat, amat omnes. Quisquis est sapiens, amat omnes. Omnis sapiens multis prodest. Omnis sapiens Deo amicus est." ["Someone who loves God seeks to understand His will. Anyone who loves God obeys His will. Anyone who loves God loves everyone. Whoever is wise loves everyone. Every wise person is helpful to many people. Every wise person is a friend of God."] (G. VII, 75).

[66] "Les machines de la nature sont machines partout, quelque petite partie qu'on y prenne; ou plustôt, la moindre partie est un monde infini à son tour, et qui exprime même à sa façon tout ce qu'il y a dans le reste de l'univers... Et toute cette variété infiniment infinie est animée dans toutes ses parties par une sagesse architectonique plus qu'infinie. On peut dire qu'il y a de l'harmonie, de la géometrie, de la métaphysique, et, pour parler aussi de la morale partout... On peut dire que toute la nature est plein de miracles, mais

similar vision of the harmony of the universe in his thoughts on the *Deux infinis,* which Leibniz copied and enthusiastically endorsed.[67] But Pascal had derived from this the incommensurability of the human mind with the laws of this immense totality — the inferiority of reason, that is, and its need to rely on the transcendent.[68] Liebniz derived the celebration of the human mind understood as the monad, its affinity with God, and its faculty of representing the universe.[69]

The appearance and tone of the morality reflects the theoretical conception that it derives from. Leibniz's is an active morality that operates in the real world. It does not come down to the elimination of the particular and the attainment of an exact and immobile sort of rationality. The vision of the whole is an immense picture that must be put together, starting from the particular. The essential task is organization.[70]

---

de miracles de raison: et qui deviennent miracles à force d'être raisonnables, d'une manière qui nous étonne" (to Bossuet, 18, IV, 1692. F. d. C., I, 277). Cf. *Discours de Métaphysique,* §§ 5, 36-37, F. d. C., II, 528 ff., etc.
[67] Baruzi, *L. et l'org.,* 224 ff.
[68] "Que l'homme, étant revenu à soi, considère ce qu'il est au prix de ce qui est... Qu'est-ce qu'un homme dans la nature? Un néant à l'égard de l'infini; un tout à l'égard du néant, un milieu entre rien et tout... Que fera-t-il donc, sinon d'apercevoir quelque apparence du milieu des choses, dans un desespoir éternel de connaître ni leur principe ni leur fin?" (Pascal, *Les deux infinis*).
[69] "...le seul pourtant qui mérite d'être appelé une substance après Dieu... Et si cette monade est un esprit, c'est à dire une âme capable de réflexion et de science, elle sera en même temps infiniment moins qu'un Dieu et incomparablement plus que le reste de l'univers des créatures... Ce sera une divinité diminutive et un univers de matière éminemment. Dieu en ectype et cet univers en prototype... imitant Dieu et imité par l'univers par rapport à ses pensées distinctes. Sujet à Dieu ent tout et dominateur des créatures autant qu'il est un imitateur de Dieu" (comment on Pascal's *Deux infinis,* Baruzi, *Leibniz,* 300-1). Cf. Cassirer, *Leibniz' System,* 476-77.
[70] Cf. for example, *Grundriss eines Bedenckens von Aufrichtung einer Societät in Deutschland* (AK. IV. I, 530 ff., and Klopp I, III ff.) in which the task of organizing the sciences is made to derive from the knowledge of the divine nature and harmony of the cosmos. "It is only in Amor dei super omnia,

The ideal here, as in Stoicism, is that of the wise person who follows reason and nature. But reason and nature are no longer something that the wise must find within themselves, at the root of their being. They must be sought in the world around the individual, in the great system one is part of and takes part in. A person is no longer self-sufficient by nature, alone with his or her conscience in the midst of the raging of events,[71] but rather a social individual, directed outward by a thousand inclinations, active in the republic of letters and sciences, insufficient alone, and having value only within a collectivity of mutually complementary endeavors[72] tending by an infinity of different paths toward the same cognitive vision, the same moral end. In a dialogue prior to 1679, Leibniz combats skepticism and the intention to retire from a life of scientific research with the consideration "qu'il y a un grand monarque de l'univers, qui prend tout ce qu'on fait pour le pubblic comme fait à luy-même."[73]

The influences of jusnaturalistic doctrines, and especially of Grotius, on the Leibnizian moral conception are

---

Contritio, Beatitudo aeterna that the beauty of God and the universal harmonies are grasped by each according to his own intellectual faculty and reflected back to others. And moreover, also in proportion to the ability of each, their illumination is fostered and enlarged in men and other creatures" (§ 10; and passim. Cf. *Disc. de Mét.*, §4, Baruzi, *Trois dialogues*, cit., 26 ff, G. VII, 92 ff., etc.).

[71] Leibniz accuses Cartesian morality of being Stoic-Epicurean and opposes "cette tranquillité de l'ame ou indolence que les Stoiciens et les Épicurienz cherchaient et recomandait également sous des noms différents... Il me semble que cet Art de la patience dans laquelle il [Decartes] fait consister l'art de vivre, n'est pas encor le tout" (G. IV, 298). Cf. also *Nouv. Ess.*, IV, 8, § 9.

[72] "So we should... remember that no human being can exist alone, and consider ourselves not only as part of everything that is created, but also specifically part of what belongs to this earth — that is, the politics, society and kind to which we are connected through habitation, kinship or other fellowships." (*Initia et Specimina Scientiae Novae Generalis*, G. VII, 93).

[73] Baruzi, *Trois dialogues*, cit., 30. Cf. also the beautiful description of true piety and happiness in the preface to *Theodicea* G. VI, 27-28.

evident. When, in the *New Essays*, he tries to characterize the moral instinct whereby man is led intuitively and without reflection, by confused perception, to those arts which reason will later designate as good and just, he finds in the first place a social instinct, "une affection et douceur pour ceux de leur espèce," also common to animals, which in humans is called philanthropy, and then develops into love between man and woman, between parents and children, "et autres inclinations semblables qui font ce droit naturel ou cette image de droit plustost, que selon les jurisconsultes Romains la Nature e enseigné aux animaux." And in man in particular "il se trouve un certain soin de la dignité, de la convenance," of modesty. A concern for one's reputation, a fear of the future and of a supreme power — virtues, in essence, that are social and expressed in the collective. "Il y a de la réalité en tout cela, mais dans le fond ces impressions naturelles... ne sont que des aides à la raison et des indices du conseil de la nature."[74] The rule of not doing unto others what we don't want done to us is transformed into a method of judging all things from the point of view of others,[75] a method that he recommends elsewhere as best for resolving controversies and winning political and military battles.[76] As noted previously, morality is nothing but the culmination of a scale of social-legal relations, which begin with personal utility.

---

[74] *Nouv. Ess.*, 1. I, c. II, § 9.
[75] "Quant à la règle, qui porte qu'on ne doit faire aux autres que ce qu'on voudrait qu'ils nous fissent, elle a besoin non seulement de preuve; mais encore de déclaration. On voudrait trop, si on est le maitre, est ce donc qu'on doit trop aussi aux autres? On me dira, que cela ne s'entend que d'une volonté juste. Mais ainsi cette règle, bien loin de suffire à servir de mesure, en aurait besoin. Le véritable sens de la règle est que la place d'autruy est le vray point de vue pour juger équitablement lorsqu'on s'y met" (*Nouv. Ess.*, 1. I, c. II, § 4. Cfr. Mollat, 57-58).
[76] Baruzi, *Leibniz*, 363 ff. "La place d'autrui est le vrai point de perspective en politique aussi bien qu'en morale... pour connaître les vues que notre voisin peut avoit contre nous."

Social relations, organization, cooperation. The figure of the inspired mystic or the solitary sage disappears, making way for the worldly scientist, living and working in the midst of social life, at court, in the universities, creating for himself — along with tools to enhance his sensory faculties, increase his physical strength and spread his thoughts — this new human machinery consisting of cultural institutions, academies, societies, and libraries, in which the strength of an individual come to be linked with the strengths of all, in disciplined cooperation and without waste of energy.[77] "Quid ergo cetera moramur?... Tantum virtuti, h.e. intellectus voluntatisque perfectioni, qua licet, studeamus et subinde operam demus, ut bona, quae largitus est nobis Deus — omnibus autem magna largitus est — in ceteros diffundamus!"[78]

This explains the sociable and courteous tone of Leibniz's positive morality, and his frequent advice to show reserve and civility, not to collide with people, especially the powerful, to live in good harmony with everyone, and to care for one's reputation. The sage he envisions is "humanus, affabilis, officiosus" [humane, amiable, caring], "well-disposed and friendly, so that anyone deals willingly with him and wishes to trust him, for he treats everything honestly.... He displays gratitude or amiability to every person he talks to, turning away from all anger, falsehood or other impulses. Not only is he helpful to all who request his presence, he willingly assists them and

---

[77] "He ... performs many acts of charity in a short time, which is like living 1,000 times longer, something that happens to those who can make 1,000 hands cooperate with 1,000 others, so that more good things can happen for the utmost good, and we can thus be blessings that cannot be achieved in many centuries" (G. VII, 89).

[78] ["Why do we linger over other things? Let us concentrate only on virtue — that is, on the perfection of the intellect and will — and let us endeavor at once to spread to others the goodness that is God, which is abundant in us, and is there in great abundance for all!"] Mollat, 16.

is diligent in imparting to others the knowledge they need for their tasks."[79]

In him perhaps more than in any other, the obsequious lifestyle of the century found a profound justification. Society was no longer just an entity to be reckoned with so as to have a peaceful life. It had become the medium of all research, of all intellectual and cultural progress. For a man like Spinoza, separation from it had meant assuring the interior independence necessary for philosophical thought at the price of simply giving up some of the comforts of life. For Leibniz it would have meant giving up thinking itself, along with all his scientific activity — it would have been the end of him as a thinker and scholar.

The objective, naturalistic conception of reason understood as universal harmony shifts the focus of the moral problem from the rational consciousness of the individual to the collective organization of society. Leibniz's moral precepts correspond to this mentality. The Stoic virtues of impassiveness, of imperturbability in the face of misfortune were still part of his moral ideal. Now, however, they were not so much rooted in indifference to the external world and the effort to keep the sphere of his own interests completely independent of it, but rather, in the desire to penetrate ever deeper into the laws of nature.[80] Love for

---

[79] G. VII, 104. Cf. particularly, in the collection *Initia et Specimina* etc., the pieces *Von der Tugend* (G. VII, 92 ff.), *Von der Nützbarkeit der Lebenz Regel* (G VII, 100 ff.) and the one marked with the letter I (G. VII, III ff.).

[80] In this attitude Leibniz also found links with the Stoic doctrine of the harmony and connection of all things. He distances himself, however, from the pantheistic consequences that the Stoics drew from it. The Stoics conceived the law of harmony as identical with the law of necessity — Leibniz draws a clear distinction between the two (*Théod.*, § 217). "Il y a autant de différence entre la véritable morale et la leur [the Stoics and Epicureans], qu'il y en a entre la joye et la patience: car leur tranquillité n'estoit fondée que su la nécessité; la notre le doit être sur la perfection et sur la bonté des choses, sur notre félicité" (*ibid.*, § 254). In the paragraphs that follow he mentions with sympathy impassiveness in the face of physical pain, but he speaks of it as a useful exercise to strengthen the mind, not as the very essence of morality. Cf. the distinction between "fatum

others, as we have seen, is the wellspring of justice, and the love of God is its highest form. But since we cannot be of benefit to God in any real sense, "facimus tamen aliquid simile, cum voluntatem ejus animo praesumptam adimlere conamur."[81] Man must seek, through the means he possesses of acquiring knowledge, to discover the "presumptive or antecedent" will of God; and must act in consequence of it, without complaining if events prove him wrong and that he had erred in his assessment. For events are always right, and what happens cannot fail to happen according to a perfect and insuperable order.[82] "Tout

---

stoicum" and "fatum christianum," in the preface to *Theodicea*: "Faites votre devoir, et soyez contents de ce que en arrivera, non seulement parce que vous ne sauries résister à la providence Divine, ou à la nature des choses (ce qui peut suffire pour estre *tranquille*, et non pas pour estre content) mais encor parceque vous avez à faire à un bon maistre" (G. VI, 31).

[81] "However, we do something similar when we strive to carry out and fulfill his will and that of his soul." Mollat, 37.

[82] "Est autem praesumpta Dei voluntas, ut quisque ea agat quibus videtur se ipsum et, quae sunt circa se ipsum, maxime perficere posse. Itaque debemus pro viribus et modulo nostro in emendandis nostris rebus ac publico bono procurando niti, licet non semper successus faveat. Quo destituente nec tristari nec taedio obrepente desistere lassarive oportet, quoniam Dei solius est tempora nosse et quibus optime exitus reperietur. Itaque ubi nostrum officium fecerimus, contenti simus circa praeterita, in quibus Dei voluntas jam eventis cognita est, quam optima autem reddere conemur futura, de quibus nondum quicquam nobis declaravit Deus et nostre industriae locum reliquit. Et sane pro certo habendum est omnia tam perfecte a Deo fieri in mundo, qui et mala in majus bonum convertit, ut meliora et singulis hoc cognoscentibus atque adeo Deum amantibus et gubernatione ejus contentis utiliora ne optari quidem possent ab intelligente." [God's will is presumed, so that each person performs those actions by which he seems able to perfect himself and the things about him. Therefore, we must rely on correcting our behavior and securing good for all to the extent of our own strength and ability, even though a good outcome is not always useful. Failing this, it is not appropriate to grieve nor, as boredom creeps in, to give up or grow weary, for it is for God alone to know when and above all, how things will end up. Therefore, when we do our duty, we should be happy about past events, in which we learned God's will, and we should try to make the future as good as possible — a future God has not yet let us know anything about and in which he has left room for our own action. And we must consider that God created everything in the world in a perfect way, converting evil into a greater good, so that for those who know this and who primarily love God and are pleased with His government, even wise men cannot choose the

homme sage doit estre content non seulement par necessité et comme ayant patience par force; mais avec plaisir, et par une manière de satisfaction extrême... Car, quand Dieu nous admettra à ses secrets un peu plus que jusqu'ici, alors parmy les autres surprises, il y aura encor celle de voir les inventions meraveilleuses dont il s'est servi pour nous rendre heureux au delà de ce que nous aurions été capables de concevoir."[83]

The peace of mind of the wise man does not come from disinterest or superiority in relation to events, but from the certainty that their perfection is absolute, and that evil is only apparent. The search for good and for moral purpose is carried out by the same procedure as in the physical and natural sciences — grounding itself in known laws and past experience and constructing new laws on the basis of these that enable us to embrace future phenomena as a whole and to assume the universal point of view from which each particular appears framed in the whole.[84] And just as in nature research, a discordance between our law and reality prompts us to change our point of view and correct our notions, but never to complain that nature does not follow the system we have constructed. Similarly, in the moral realm, the occurrence of an event that defies our predictions or practical dispositions must never lead us to rail against fate, but only to recognize the error in the point of view from which

---

most useful things."] (Mollat, 38-39). Cf. *Disc. de Mét.* § 4 *Monad.* § 90, *Syst. Theol.*, 6-8, *Théod.*, § 58.

[83] Baruzi, *Trois dialogues*, cit., 35-36.

[84] "In the end it all depends on these two great rules.... First, that all events that have already passed or already happened should be regarded as well done or good before we can see them from the right point of view. Since we should all try to perform things-yet-to-come to the best of our ability according to what we imagine and, therefore, aim to always come as close as possible to the correct point of view, which already offers us all possible pleasure, this will pave the way in the future to greater bliss and joy" (*Initia et Specimina.* G. VII, 122).

we previously acted.[85]

Not, therefore, an affirmation of reason in ourselves *versus* in nature, but the affirmation of reason *in* nature — and in us, insofar as and as long as we conform to this objective reality.[86] The germs of subjectivism and gnoseologism found in the Stoic-humanistic tradition are absent in Leibniz's objective naturalism. And morality ceases to be adaptation to our deepest and most rational selves and becomes adaptation to ontological rationality.

In addition to the elevation of his mind, man also finds his own self-interest in this adjustment. Consideration of the individual not as the subject of morality, but as an object and a fragment in the overall totality, binds their lot, as it were, to that of the whole. And since the harmony of the universe is the best imaginable, and is derived from a comprehensive expansion of the laws of the individual, in it each individual will be arranged in the way most suited to his or her needs.[87] Leibniz explicitly posits this coincidence as an example of the law of harmony and finalism — not reducible to logical necessity or causal determination — whereby God made the world not only rational, but beautiful and proportionate as well.[88] Evil once again only

---

[85] "Because we are not guilty of the outcome, but only of our personal thoughts" (*ibid.*, G. VII, 92).

[86] "The cardinal rule of our life is that we always do or not do precisely whatever the intellect, not gestures, indicates to us to be the most useful thing or the thing that harms the most respectively. And it is when we have done such a thing and afterwards also let it sprout as it desires, that we consider ourselves blissful and are at peace, without any grievance or sadness, and glad and confident that as long as we are in this state of mind, everything that happens will happen in the best way for us" (*ibid.*, G. VII, 99, cfr. 119).

[87] "Because, since the benefits of the whole are preferable to those of the part, we will derive only pleasure from being useful to all, no one excluded. Moreover, where we want to make the intellect manage everything, we will find that there is a benefit to ourselves as well" (*ibid.*, G. VII, 93).

[88] "Je puis encor nier la conséquence dans l'argument, qui porte que si la volonté n'est mue que par la représentation du bien et du mal, il ne depend pas de nous d'être heureux. La conséquence seroit bonne, s'il n'y avait pas un Dieu,

arises from partial vision, and reveals itself as good, usefulness, pleasure, as soon as the gaze widens to the totality. "Tout bien moral devient physique, ou comme parloient les anciens, tout honneste est utile"[89]. A distinction between utility and morality is conceivable only in a dualistic conception, one that posits a separation between exterior and interior and between rationality and contingency, or at least theorizes two separate, independent faculties of the mind. This is not possible under Leibnizian monism, in which the contingent is the starting point of an unbroken path leading to the universal. The interior acquires value in its absolute adaptation to objective reality — the will is a necessary consequence of knowledge. Good is for Leibniz simply the highest possible overall utility, just as reason is the highest possible degree of proportion and harmony.

---

si tout étoit gouverné par des causes brutes: mais Dieu fait que pour être heureux, il suffit d'être vertueux. Ainsi, si l'Ame suit la raison et les ordres que Dieu lui a donnée, la voilà seure de son bonheur, quoy qu'on ne la puisse point tromper assez dans cett vie" (*Remarques sur le livre de King*, § 18, G. VI, 420).
[89] *Nouv. Ess.*, 1. II, c. 28, § 4.

7. Leibniz's Aesthetics*

"Je tiens que la vertu ferait plus d'effect infiniment, accompagnée comme elle est de tant de solides biens, si quelque heureuse révolution la mettait un jour en vogue et comme à la mode."[90] In laying out the psychological characterization of human adaptation to universal reason along with the contemplation of harmony and the attainment of good, Leibniz discovered a faculty of pleasure and beauty, a "taste" which he could not always reduce to reason, and which seemed to stand on its own, with its own laws and characteristics. God had given man a special instinct "qui lui fait trouver tant de plaisir dans l'exercice de la justice, et tant de laideur dans les actions injustes que les autres plaisirs ou deplaisirs sont obligés de céder."[91] An instinct, that is, for which the rationality of the universe is not only true and just, not only useful and good, but is also sweet and agreeable, inspiring in the soul a sense of elevation not reducible to mere reasoning. It is the sense of proportion, of balance, which represents in man a fundamental feeling whereby the very order of the universe exists within him, as if in microcosm. It is reason understood as harmony and beauty, which then proves to correspond to a logically perfect order, a mode of exact and mathematically calculable balances and counterweights

---

* *Rivista di filosofia*, xxx, 1939, signed E.C.
[90] *Nouv. Ess.*, II, 21, § 37. Cf. G. VII, 97. The initial G. refers to the Gerhardt edition, C. to the unpublished texts released by Couturat, F. d. C. to the Foucher de Careil edition, D. to the Dutens edition, AK. to the Berlin Academy edition.
[91] Mollat, 61

— but which at first appears as pleasing and beautiful. This is the basis of Leibnizian aesthetics, which must be painstakingly reconstructed based on a few fragments, and which in addition do not testify either to a very lively interest or a very keen taste in art. Leibniz does not distance himself from the classical rationalist formalism of his time,[92] and nor does he hesitate at times to attribute to art a position subordinate to natural science.[93]

From his very early years — long before the concept of confused perceptions appeared in his mind — he viewed art not in its psychological aspect, but from an objective point of view; it was identified with *beauty*. He saw beauty as the order of the universe, and of everything that provides an image of this order through its symmetry and proportion. The soul, by its nature, feels drawn toward this harmony and is impelled by it to love.[94] And this is the appetite, the

---

[92] One of his rare critical observations: "Le Père Spee n'avoit aucune idée de la perfection de la poésie Allemande et apparemment n'avoit point oui parler de l'incomparable Opiz, à qui nous la devons. Aussi trouve-t-on qu'encor à present les catholiques Romains nées dans cette religion ne sçavent presque point ce que c'est qu'un bon vers Allemand, de sorte qu'on peut dire qu'ils se sont aussi peu reformés à l'égared de nostre poésie, qu'en matière de culte" (letter to Duchess Sophie, G. VII, 550). Elsewhere (controversy with Clarke, G. VII, 417) he complains of the "chimères" that have crept into poetics: "On s'est lassé des *Romans raisonnables* tels que la Clélie Françoise ou l'Aramène Allemande, et on est revenu depuis quelque temps aux *Contes des Fées*."

[93] "Je ne porte point d'envie à l'excellent Mons. Dryden de ce que son Virgile lui a fait gagner plus de mille livres sterlins, c'est la moindre chose qu'il meritoit. Mais je voudrois que Mons. Halley en gagnât le quadruple pour le moins pour faire son tour du monde, et pour nous decouvrir le secret de la declinasion de l'aimant, et que Mons. Newton en gagnât le decuple et bien d'avantage pour continuer ses méditations profondes sans interruption. Je suis faché de la perte des peintures d'Holbein, bruslées à Witehall; je suis pourtant un peu en celà de l'humeur du Tzar de Moscovie, qu'on me dit avoir plus admiré certaines jolies machines que tous les beaux tableaux qu'on luy a monstrés dans le palais du Roy" (to Burnett, G. III, 222-23).

[94] In *Theodicea*, § 134, Leibniz would take natural objects as finite examples of this representation of universal harmony: "Nous en avons déjà des preuves ed dees essais devant nos yeux, lorsque nous voyons quelque chose d'entier, quelque Tout accompli en soy, et isolé, pour ainsi dire, parmi les ouvages de Dieu. Un tel

pleasure that draws us to works of art, as it does to anything where we find order and perfection. "Est autem voluptas, nihil aliud quam sensus crescentis perfectionis. Dei autem perfectio in nos transfunditur intelligendo atque amando."[95] "C'est ainsi que la contemplation des belles choses est agréable par elle même, et qu'un tableau de Raphäel touche celuy qui le regarde avec des yeux éclairés, quoiqu'il n'en tire aucun profit."[96]

The pleasure a work of art gives us is the pleasure of harmony in itself, or rather of something that carries harmony in its conformation: "Pleasure represents the perception of a perfection or excellence, present in us or in others, since perfection, even of things foreign, is pleasing — such as the special courage and beauty of another man, probably even of an animal, even of an inanimate being, of paintings or works of art. For the image of such unknown perfection, imprinted in us, is such that even a part of it can settle and arouse our compassion, so that there can be no doubt that those who deal much with excellent people and objects also become excellent as a result."[97]

Leibniz tries to account rationally for why this pleasure is conferred by objective beauty, and he finds the reason in mathematical regularity, in the exact proportionality that constitutes it. Music gives him a typical example, an "exercitium arithmeticae occultum nescientis se numerare animia" ("hidden exercise in the arithmetic of

---

Tout formé, pour ainsi dire de la main de Dieu, est une plante, un animal, un homme. Nous ne saurions assez admirer la beauté et l'artifice de sa structure."
[95] "But pleasure is nothing but the sense of increasing perfection, and God's perfection is poured into us through reasoning and loving." Mollat, 17.
[96] To Duchess Sophy, 1693, G. VII, 549. Cf. the identical Latin formulation in the preface to *Codex Juris Gentium Dipolmaticus* (Dutens, IV, 3, 295; and G. III, 387).
[97] *Initia et Specimina Scientiae Novae Generalis* (G. VII, p. 86). Cf. *Théod.*, pref., G. VI, 27: "L'ordre, les proportions, l'harmonie nous enchantent, la peinture et la musique en sont des échantillons; Dieu est tout ordre, il garde tousjours la justesse des proportions, il fait l'harmonie universelle: toute la beautè est un épanchement de ses rayons."

the soul that cannot account for [or possess or consider] itself.") — music, with the proportionality of the vibrations in its chords.[98]

But the enjoyment of the other arts also involves something similar. Verses are in essence nothing but an alternation of long and short syllables, and of matching rhymes, "which, as it were, contain within themselves a quiet music." The rhythms of dances and similar movements "derive their pleasantness from order, because all order is of help to the soul." And the pleasures of touch, taste and smell are of a similar nature.[99] Novels are like an abridged representation of the order of the universe, intricate in appearance, which is ultimately resolved in admirable harmony, so that one should not "prendre le roman par la queue et prétendre d'en déchiffrer l'intrigue dés le premier livre, au lieu que la beauté d'un roman est d'autant plus grande qu'il sort plus d'ordre en fin d'une plus grande confusion apparente. Et ce serait même une faute dans la composition, si le lecteur en puvait deviner trop tôt l'issue. Or ce qui n'est que curiosité et beauté dans les romans qui imitent, pour ainsi dire, la création, est encore utilité et sagesse dans ce grand et vrai poème, c'est à dire mot à mot ouvrage, de l'univers."[100]

Now this perfection by which beauty is generated is

---

[98] *Ibid.*, 86-70. Cf. Baruzi, *Leibniz et l'org.*, 441-443, and *Principes de la Nature et de la Grâce*, G. VI, 605-6: "La musique nous charme, quoique sa beauté ne consiste que dans les convenances des nombres et dans le compte dont nous ne nous apercevons pas, et que l'âme ne laisse pas de faire, des battemens ou vibrations des corps sonnans, qui se rencentrent par certains intervalles. Les plaisirs que la vue trouve dans les proportions, sont de la même nature, et ceux que causent les autres sens, reviendront à quelque chose de senmblable quoyque nous ne puissions pas l'expliquer si distinctement." Cf. *Initia et Specimina*, cit., G. VII, 122. And as almost nothing is as pleasing to the senses of mankind as the harmoniousness of music, so nothing is more pleasing to the intellect than the wonderful harmoniousness of nature of which music is only a foretaste and a tiny sample.
[99] G. VII, 87.
[100] Mollat, 51.

an "elevation of essence" and is manifested in great freedom and strength, "so that all essence is composed of a certain force, and the greater the force, the higher and freer the essence." The greater the strength, the more multiplicity is found in its unity, "in that one individual governs many apart from himself and shapes them into himself. Thus, the consensus in the multitude is nothing but the concordance of opinions, and as something will fit better with one than with another, order therefore flows from it, all beauty derives from order, and beauty arouses love. From this it now emerges, that enlightenment, pleasure, love, perfection, essence, strength, freedom, agreement of opinion and beauty are related to each other."[101]

This is a very important formulation, not only for an understanding of the Leibnizian concept of art, but also for his concept of universal harmony. The determination of perfection as the degree of reality and strength achieved by each thing[102] and the designation of this reality as multiplicity in unity, immediately recalls the concept of monad.[103]

But these theories long predate the period when Leibniz, having understood universal substance as a unity implicitly containing the entire universe and having made this a metaphysical reality, characterized this union of individual and universal as perception and appetite, in this way identifying the monad with the mind. The fragments on general science, in which the concepts set forth are continually repeated, are from around 1676-80 —

---

[101] G. VII, 87. Cf. Mollat, 7.
[102] "La perfection c'est le degré de réalité" (to Duke Ernesto Augusto, 1685, G: VII, 37). "Perfection is a dimension of essence, or what makes essence what it is and more than it otherwise would be, not least by virtue of the fact that in the science of perfection there is, as it were, a metaphysics of the art of measurement" (*Initia et Specimina Sc. Novae Gen.*, G. VII, 112).
[103] Cf. for example *Monadologia*, §§ 13 ff.

they predate the *Discours de Métaphysique*, and are contemporary with the first studies concerning the nature of force.[104] And in 1671, i.e., prior to his trip to Paris, there is the memoir for the establishment of a scientific society in Germany, in which the concept of the reflection of universal harmony in the human mind as a concentration of the multiplicity of unity is very clearly formulated.[105]

God has created creatures so that they may be like a mirror in which the infinite harmony is infinitely multiplied, and "even in his time the felt recognition of the perfection and love of God were measured which must exist in a beatific vision or in transcendental joy, which will bring with it the reflection and, in a given quantity, the concentration of the infinite beauty in a small point of our souls. A burning mirror or burning lenses are a natural model of this."[106] The human mind is a place where the image of universal harmony is captured and concentrated, as if by a lens. And this reflection is always manifested in a sense of pleasure that is characterized as "beauty."

Before giving these concepts a value that is too strictly psychological and interpreting them in light of the development of the notion of the self and the autonomy of the artistic faculty,[107] let us consider their place in the overall Leibnizian world view.

The formulations have an objectivist character. The

---

[104] Cf. Gueroult, *Dynamique et métaphysique leibniziennes*, Paris 1938, p. 21.
[105] Ak. IV, I, 530 ff.
[106] *Grundriss eines Bedenckens von aufrichtung einer Societät in Deutschland* (1669-72), Ak. IV, Klopp, I, 115
[107] Thus Cassirer, *Leibniz System in seinen wisswens. Grundlagen*, Marburg 1902, 464-65: "The point of view of the "I," on whose form the whole of monadism is being shaped, here receives a new meaning in which it is truly fulfilled... Unity, which alone can be held as the truest and most comprehensive expression of the object, is the unity of the "I," which stands before the qualitatively incomparable extensive multiplicity of things."

pleasure of beauty is provided in every case by the perception of order and harmony. This is a perception that the intellect can control, rationally confirm, measure, and count, but it immediately presents itself to our instincts as something intuitive.[108] That is, the perfection of the universe can be learned by us not only rationally, but also in a way that is immediate and comprehensive[109]. And the objects that in their finite beauty awaken in us the idea of the absolute and urge us towards love are virtually images of this perception.[110]

This is the conception of beauty and love found in *Phaedrus* and the *Symposium*. The emphasis is not on the human faculty being exercised here, but on the object, it is

---

[108] "We do not always notice what the perfection of pleasing things is based on or for what single perfection these things are useful to us. In the meantime, we feel them through our exertions, though not through our intellect. It is generally said that it is what I do not know that pleases me about things, this is called sympathy. That which seeks the reason for things, however, finds the foundation of openness, and understands that underneath lies something that, though unseen, is actually useful to us" (*Initia et Specimina*, G. VII, 86).

[109] "Pulchritudo alicuius virginis, exempli gratia, ut cognoscatur, non sufficit contemplari ejus digitum, nec omnes ejus articulos ad poros usque et crines contemplari necesse est sed *ictu quasi oculi* tota obeunda est. Ita Dei opus aliquod contueri non sufficit, nec omnia ejus opera perlustrasse necesse, aut possibile est, sed sufficit ideam quandam in universum sibi de eo solidam formasse" ["For one to know the beauty of a virgin, an example of grace, it is not enough to contemplate her finger, nor is it necessary to contemplate all her limbs down to her nostrils and hair. She must be seen all at once. In the same way it is not enough to look at some work of God, nor is it necessary, or possible, to examine all his deeds, but we are given enough to form in general a solid idea about him"] (Dutens, I, 28-29).

[110] "La marque de l'amour de Dieu est quand on se porte au bien général avec une ardeur suprême et que l'on a un pur mouvement du plaisir qu'on y trouve, sans autre intérest, comme vous vous plairez à un beau visage, à ouïr un concert bien formé, à voir un meschant et insolent rebuté, et un misérable innocent relevé, quoyque vous n'y ayez point d'intérest" (*Dialogue entre un habile politique*, etc. F. d. C., II, 542). In *Theodicea* (§ 73), he compares music and architecture to vindictive justice, which "est tousjours fondée dans un rapport de convenance, qui contente non seulement l'offensé, mais encor les Sages qui la voyent, comme une belle musique ou bien une bonne architecture contente les esprits bien faits."

directed at, and which has these effects on it.[111]

The concept of perfection as beauty serves much more to characterize the tone of Leibnizian harmony than to clarify the background of his epistemology and his conception of the mental faculty.

Mathematical and finalistic harmony here displays a new character, a new root — beauty. We have already seen how mathematics applied to the world of "fact" was no longer deductive logic, but was founded on proportion, order, and balance. Here these concepts show their connection with notions of an aesthetic nature. Beauty, viewed rationally, will always reveal itself in its structure as a mathematical proportion, while mathematical order, viewed as a whole, will always arouse the feeling of beauty. It could be said that these are two different aspects or views of the same reality — one analytical and discursive, the other synthetic, panoramic. The Leibnizian conception of the world, in all its manifestations, is linked to both these aspects.

We have already observed the *a posteriori* character of this rationalism and have related it to the synthetic-rational work accomplished by Newton in the field of physics. These new determinations place it in a special position relative to all the mathematical work of his century. Both Descartes and Spinoza, along with Galileo and Newton, had achieved the hypostasis of logical and mathematical reason, regarding it as the supreme law of reality. Leibniz stands on this ontological foundation as well, also making an attitude of mind an objective law. But mathematics is not enough for him. His vision, ranging beyond the fields of logic and physics, encompassing the

---

[111] "The beauty of nature is so great that its contemplation has such sweetness that even the light and positive emotions derived from it have in themselves excellent uses in this life, since those who savor them have less esteem for all other enjoyable things in comparison." (*Initia et Specimina*, G. VII, 89).

world of nature and the world of man in their most uncontrollable forms, least susceptible to calculation — alchemy, geology, medicine, history, law, linguistics — needs another law, one that is more mobile, more vital, and capable of gathering into unity this infinite and multiform diversity. Finalism as contrasted with mechanism, the legal and architectural character of the universal order, are all efforts in this direction, attempts to formulate such a law. The concept of beauty and the analogy with music and the arts is another aspect of this need.

The mental form whose hypostasis Leibniz carries out in order to make it an objective law of reality is no longer just logical and mathematical reason. It is also the imponderable instinct for proportions of balance and harmony, the vital and ardent sense of the organic nature of the cosmos that was alive in the Renaissance and in the unified vision of a Bruno and a Comenius. This sense, in Leibniz, is not *transformed*, as by the great founders of rationalism, into mathematical reason, but is *reconciled* with it. Logical exactness is the ideal it strives for, the form it resolves into when scrutinized with an analytical eye. Aesthetic perfection matches mathematical perfection just as finalism matches mechanics. The supreme beauty of the cosmos lies in its rationality.

The 18th century would make this synthetic vision its own. Not deriving it from Leibniz, however, whom it had never known in this guise, but by developing it from the same experiences and the same cultural influences — from the union, that is, of the spirit of the Renaissance with that of rationalism. This is in essence Shaftesbury's vision, his conception of the aesthetic experience as entering the intimate order of nature and discovering its "interior numbers." It is Diderot's conception of art and beauty as whatever follows most closely the functions and laws of nature.[112] It is perhaps the Zweckmässigkeit kantian, and the union of aesthetic and theological judgment. It is objective beauty, which for Goethe consists of the free expression of the law in its essential determinations.[113] But the aesthetics of the 1700s, the "Swiss" and Baumgarten, who came to know Leibniz through the systematics of cognitive forms given by Wolff, looked to him primarily for hints of an autonomous artistic faculty. And they found it in the sensory representation, clear but confused,[114] which Leibniz speaks of in *De cognitione veritate et ideis* of 1684, in which, while one cannot "notas ad rem ab aliis discernendam sufficientes separatim enumerare, licet res illa tales notas atque requisita revera habeat, in quae notio eius resolvi possit" ("enumerate one by one the marks which are sufficient to distinguish the thing from others, the thing may in truth have certain marks and constituents by which its concept can be clarified."). This happens

---

[112] Cf. Cassirer, *Filosofia dell'illuminismo*, It. trans. Florence, 1935, 423 ff.
[113] Cassirer, *Leibniz' System* cit., 471-72. Cf., for the entire argument, Cassirer, *Freiheit und Form*, Berlin 1922, especially ch. II; Croce, *Estetica*, part II, ch. IV.
[114] Cf. Baumgarten, *Meditationes philosophicae de nonnullis ad poema pertinentibus*, § 5 XIII "... Poema, cuius repraesentationes clarae, perfectius quam cuius obscurae, et clarae repraesentationes magis poeticae, quam obscurae. Hic eorum refutatur error, qui quo obscurius et intricatius effutire possunt, hoc se loqui somniant ποητιχώτερος." ("The poem whose representtations are clear is more complete than that whose representations are obscure, and clear representations are more poetic than obscure ones. We reject this error on the part of those who can chatter somewhat obscurely and intricately: let them dream of saying this more poetically ποητιχώτερος") § XIV: "Repraesentationes distinctae completae adaequatae profundae per omnes gradus non sunt sensitive, ergo nec poeticae... Haec autem est praecipua ratio cur philosophia et poësis vix unquam in una sede morari posse putentur..." ("The distinct, complete, adequate, and profound representations for each type are not all sensory, and therefore neither are they poetic. This is the main reason why philosophy and poetry can never dwell in the same place.") § XV: "quum clarae repraesentationes sint poeticae, § 13, aut erunt distinctae aut confusae, iam distinctae non sunt, § 14, ergo confusae" ("when clear representations are poetic, § 13, they will be either distinct or confused, or not distinct, § 14, and therefore confused.")

in the recognition of flavors, odors and colors, "sed simplici sensuum testimonio, non vero notis enuntiabilibus" ("but from the simple evidence of the senses, not from marks that can be expressed"), or when "videmus pictores aliosque artifices probe cognoscere, quid recte, quid vitiose factum sit, at judicii sui rationem reddere saepe non posse, et quaerenti dicere, se in re quae displicet desiderare *nescio quid.*"[115] This "I don't know what" returns often in Leibniz's writings to indicate the aesthetic sense of perfection prior to actual knowledge, and in general anything intuitive, immediate, and unconsidered in apprehending the real.[116]

In the *New Essays* he would make use of it as a proof of the existence of "petites perceptions," a confused sphere at the periphery of our awareness that encompasses everything, and which we become conscious of to the degree that it becomes distinct — that is, rational.[117]

Petites perceptions are commonly considered to be the introduction of the subconscious into the field of awareness. And certainly, the Leibnizian principle of continuity and its "natura non facit saltus" is much better suited to this lower form passing unconsciously from the confused

---

[115] ["We see that painters or craftsmen know perfectly well what is done correctly and what isn't, but they are often unable to account for their own judgment and tell the inquirer that a work they don't like lacks something, *I don't know what.*"] G. IV, 422-23; cf. G. III, 247-48.

[116] "Even benevolent nature, or, rather, the benevolent and foundational God, has placed in us, no less than in other animals, a certain hidden force or instinct, so instead of being reasonable in sensory things, we also make use to a certain extent of experience as a conducting principle. This instinct, however, must be governed by the intellect and must preserve a special moderation" (*Initia et Specimina Scientiae Novae Generalis*, G. VII, 113). Cf. *Disc. de Mét.*, § 24.

[117] "Ces petites perceptionnes sont donc de plus grande efficace par leur suites qu'on ne le pense. Ce sont elles qui forment ce je ne sais quoi, ces goûts, ces images des qualités des sens, claires dans l'assemblage, mais confuses dans les parties, ces impressions que les corps environnants font sur nous, et qui enveloppent l'infini, cette liaison que chaque être a avec tout le reste de l'univers" (*Nouv. Ess.*, Pref.).

to the distinct, than the theorization of an autonomous intuitive faculty, proper to a particular mental attitude, with its own specific irreducible characteristics. Confused perceptions are not exclusive to art;[118] they also apply to other phenomena such as dreams and memory, as well as moral and cognitive facts.[119] Art is only one of many examples used to explain their creation. In Leibniz, therefore, artistic intuition is considered an inferior form of awareness (as it would also be in Baumgarten). But unlike the latter, Leibniz is not especially concerned to find a particular form of knowledge that is specific and proper to art. There is between the two of them something like an inversion of the interest and purpose of theorizing. For Baumgarten, confused perceptions serve to explain the artistic fact, while for Leibniz the artistic fact explains the formation of confused perceptions.

Even so, we sometimes find Leibniz in the presence of this "I don't know what," which is not theorizable precisely because by definition it is confused, and any investigation of its content would dissolve it into distinct perception, into rational knowledge. He cannot help but value it precisely because it is confusing and non-rational.

The problem began to gain currency in the science and

---

[118] In the chapter in *Nouveaux Essais* on "Idées claires et obsciures, distinctes et confuses" (1. II, ch. 29), where he offers various examples of confused perceptions, art is not even mentioned. He only advocates a reform of language, abolishing metaphors, and elegant sayings, removing indeterminacy from language, and giving each word a precise meaning.

[119] Cf. *Nouv. Ess.*, 1. I, ch. 2, where, concerning the moral precept "qu'il faut suivre la joye et éviter la tristesse" he says "que ce n'est pas une verité, qui soit connue purement de raison, puisqu'elle est fondé sur l'experience interne, ou sur des connoissances confuses; car on ne sait pas ce que c'est que la joye et la tristesse... Elle n'est pas connue par la raison, mais pour ainsi dire par un instinct." Further on he speaks of an "instinct qui porte l'homme à aimer l'homme" and also extends the notion of instinct to the "vérités de théorie, et tels sont les principes internes des sciences et du raisonnement, lorsque sans en connaitre la raison, nous les emplyons par un instinct naturel."

literature of the time. In a letter to Queen Sophie Charlotte of Prussia, Leibniz criticized Bouhours's book — one of the first to investigate taste as an independent faculty of mind — for its overly minute criticism of works of art: "à mon avis, quand il ne s'agit que de plaire, c'est assez qu'on soit frappé et même trompé agréablement, je pardonne à ce qui me charme du premier coup quelque faute mediocre que j'y pourrois découvrir à force de réflexions. Ceux qui ont l'esprit si pénétrant qu'ils remarquent d'abord les defauts cachés, ont le malheur de perdre les agréments des choses."[120] And in the *New Essays* he repeats, again against Bouhour, the suggestion that reason is almost the enemy of beauty and that intuitive genius is something that eludes rational consideration.[121] In *Préceptes pour avancer les sciences*, 1686,[122] speaking of the sciences subordinate to geometry and arithmetic, in which it is sufficient to apply certain mathematical laws "pour inventer de soy même les règles principales de ces sciences," he cites music as among these, a science entirely founded on "quelques experiences fondamentales des consonances et dissonances" and in which "tout le reste des préceptes généraux dépend des nombres." "On peiut monstrer à un homme qui ne sçait point de musique le moyen de composer sans fautes..." But then immediately, almost struck by the obvious one-sidedness of his statement, he finds himself compelled by the argument itself to correct

---

[120] G. VI, 523. In this letter, while disapproving of Bouhours's "purism" and critical zeal, which is in him more than "le plaisir innocent de se laisser toucher," he follows him on his own ground, and argues against his judgments on Voiture, Balzac, Tasso, Tacitus, Lucan, etc., showing a vast knowledge of classical and modern literature, but critical criteria based on external motives of verisimilitude or stylistics.
[121] "Il faut que des pensées spirituelles ayent quelque fondement au moins apparent dans la raison; mai il ne faut point les éplucher avec trop de scrupule, comme il ne faut point regarder un tableau de trop près" (*Nouv. Ess.*, 1. II, ch. II).
[122] The dating comes from the manuscript catalog of the Leibnizian Commission. The essay is published in G. VII, 157 ff. and the part given here is on pp. 170 ff.

and limit it. Rules and numbers are not enough; something else is needed: "Comme pour faire un bel Epigramme, il ne suffit pas de sçavoir la Grammaire et la Prosodie... de même en musique il faut un exercice et même un genie et une imagination vive d'oreilles à un homme qui veut reussir en composition."

Here we seem to be at the heart of the problem of intuitive and irrational genius, and its autonomy. Leibniz himself gets a little confused, as if bemused by his own argument.[123] He interprets this immediate and unconsidered element, which he cannot help but perceive in music and other arts, as a habit derived from a *forma mentis* created little by little through reading poetry, or by observing "dans les compositions des habiles gens mille et mille belles cadences et pour ainsi dire phrases de musique." Even in people who are "naturellement musiciens" or poets, and "qu'un peu aide et de lecture fait faire des merveilles," everything comes down to imitation, practice: "Car il y a des choses, sur tout celles qui dépendent des sens, ou on reussira plustost et mieux en se laissant aller machinalement à l'imitation et à la practique, qu'en demeurant dans la sécheresse des préceptes... Il faut que notre imagination même ait prise une habitude, apres quoy on luy peut donner la liberté de prendre son vol sans consulter la raison, par une manière d'Enthousiasme. Elle ne manque pas de reussir à mesure du genie et de l'expérience de la personne, et nous expérimentons même quelquesfois dans les songes que nous formons des images qu'on aurait eu de la peine à trouver en veillant."

Even genius, then, is called into play, and there is talk

---

[123] "Comme icy nous ne nous proposons que la connoissance digne d'un honneste homme, qui n'est pas du mestier, nous n'avons dit tout cela que pour prevenir en passant les faux jugemens de ceux qui pourroient abuser de ce que nous venons de dire du moyen aisé d'apprendre les sciences par quelque peu de préceptes ou principes d'invention" (G. VII, 171).

of work that is almost subterranean, subconscious.[124] "Mais il faut que la raison examine par après et qu'elle corrige et polisse l'ouvrage de l'imagination." Leibniz now feels compelled to give explanations of this experience, this genius, this imagination that threatens to disrupt his entire "art of invention," based on a few fundamental data and the mathematical laws of combination. So there are things that depend "plustost d'un jeu de l'imagination et d'une impression machinale que de la raison." But there are also others in which "l'on peut reussir par la seule raison aidée de quelques expériences ou observations." In the case of the former, how should one act? If a resolution must be reached immediately, "les préceptes joints à la méthode ne suffiront pas, au moins dans l'estat oú l'art d'inventer se trouve présentement, car j'avoue que si elle estoit perfectionnée comme il faut e comme elle le purroit estre, qu'on pourroit souvent pénétrer d'une veue d'esprit aisée ce qui a besoin maintenant de beaucoup de temps et d'application." And it will therefore be necessary "qu'on aye une force de genie extraordinaire oú qu'on aye une longue practique qui nous fait venir dans l'esprit machinalement et par habitude, ce qu'il faudroit chercher par la raison."

Here, then, is what could possibly replace reason: either habit and practice, or "genius" — a faculty not clearly determined, but which seems to be understood as an eminently developed rationality capable of rapid synthesis.[125]

---

[124] Cf. Shaftesbury's observations on *Characteristics*: "Les goust distingué de l'entendement consiste dans les perceptions confuses dont on ne sauroit assez rendre raison. C'est quelque chose d'approchant de l'instinct. Et pour l'avoir bon, il faut s'exercer à goûter les bonnes choses que la raison et l'expérience ont déjà autorisées. En quoy les jeunes gens ont besoin de guide" (G. III, 430, I).

[125] "On voit d'excellents génies qui réussissent au primier coup d'essay dans la profession, oú il se mettent et qui font honte aux vieux practiciens par la force de leur jugement naturel. Mais cela n'est pas ordinaire" (G. VII, 171). "Tout sentiment est la perception d'une vérité, et... le sentiment naturel l'est d'une vérité innée, mais bien souvent confuse, comme le sont les expériences des sens

But reason is always the safest tool, and the one everything ultimately comes down to. Its apparent inferiority in the face of "practice" stems only from the fact that it is often neither well utilized nor well organized.[126]

This is what Leibniz's scant contact with artistic irrationality boils down to — to this and to attempts to frame it, reduce it, reconcile it with the rational. There is no effort to give it its own dignity and autonomy as such, much less to attribute to it a cognitive character of its own, a function different from or superior to reason in the apprehension of reality.[127]

What he does observe and emphasizes regarding these mental patterns is the pleasure, the joy to which they give rise, and the enthusiasm with which they are expressed. They possess an aura of feeling that cold reason sometimes

---

externes: ainsi on peut distinguer les *vérités innées* d'avec la *lumiére naturelle* (qui ne contient que de distinctement connoissable) comme le gentre doit estre distingué de son espèce, puisque les *vérités innées* comprennent tant les *instincts* que *la lumière naturelle*" (*Nouv. Ess.*, 1. I, ch. 2, § 9). In the *Addition à l'explication du Système Nouveau*, Leibniz places instinct, passion and habit on the same plane (i.e., that of confused perceptions): "*L'instinct* estant pour ainsi dire une passion durable et née avec nous, et *la passion* estant comme un instinct passager et survenu; à quoy un pourroit joindre l'accostumance qui tient le milieu entre ces deux sortes d'inclinations, estant plus durable que la passion, mais non pas née avec nous comme l'instinct" (G IV, 576-77). Also, in his letter to the Landgrave of Hesse of 8-3-1685 he explains the irrationality of some of our religious or aesthetic judgments as resulting from our confused knowledge and weak memory (Rommel. II, 76-77) and in the *Disc. de Mét.*, p. 24 he considers, again as clear but confused knowledge, the "I know not what" of art.

[126] "Et même la théorie sans practique passera incomparablement une practique aveugle et sans théorie, lorsqu'on obligera le practicien de venir à quelque rencontre fort différent de celles qu'il y a practiquées" (G. VII, 172).

[127] "Je tiens que nous nous appercevons souvent sans raisonnement de ce qui est juste et injuste, comme nous nous apperçevons sans raison de quelques théorèmes de Géométrie; mais il est toujours bon de venir à la démonstration" (to Burnett, G. III, 307). In the face of Shaftesbury's irony towards those who seek proofs everywhere, he adds, almost shyly: "Cependant le plus seur est de satisfaire encor ces gens-là, s'il est possible" (G. III, 431).

lacks, making its realization more difficult and less pleasant. Always present in Leibniz is the concern to make rationality and morality palatable, to reconcile them, rather than contrasting them, with pleasure, happiness, and utility. The aesthetic character of his universal harmony offers him a means to this end, so much so that he sometimes conceives of art almost as the handmaiden of morality.[128] But this is not so much his premise as an attempt to show more clearly the beauty and harmony of reason — that is, to make people as enthusiastic and passionate about it as they are about art. "Sapientis erit semel in universum sibi imprimere pulchritudinem futurae vitae, id est, Dei, in quo consistit et amor Dei, seu harmoniae rerum" ("It will be the task of the wise man to imprint on the universe just once the beauty of the future life — that is, of God — in which the love of God or the harmony of things is also unwavering.").[129] "Ciceron dit bien quelque part, que si nos jeux pouvoient voir la beauté de la vertu, nous l'aimerions avec ardeur."[130] And the thought of this beauty can help people withstand pain and even martyrdom. To which end it will not harm even the wise man to use "pöematibus et allegoriis, et fabulis et adumbrationibus et variegationibus uti. Quia ad rem per se optimam omnia media recta sunt" ("poems and allegories, tales, fictions and ornaments. In this way all common things move directly toward excellence in and of themselves.").[131]

This is not, as it might appear, a push for good action through the representation of future rewards — that is, of

---

[128] "Le but principal de l'histoire, aussi bien que de la poésie doit être d'enseigner la prudence et la vertu par des exemples, et puis démontrer le vice d'une manière qui en donne de l'aversion, et qui porte ou serve à l'éviter" (*Théod.*, § 148). Cf. G. III, 249 (to Burnett): "Le théatre pourrait estre d'un excellent usage pour instruire les gens, s'il estoit bien menagé."
[129] *Otium hanoveranum*, D. VI, I, 306.
[130] *Nouv. Ess.*, 1. II, ch. 21 §§ 31-35. Cf. Mollat, 62.
[131] *Otium hanoveranum*, D. VI, I, 306.

making morality utilitarian. Instead, the idea is to make it pleasant, exciting, impassioned. "Haec porro imaginatio cum assensu conjuncta, quod in fide divus. Thomas piam affectionem vocat, amorem Dei super omnia, et contritionem et proinde certam salutem continet. Fit autem fortis imaginatio aut picturis, aut sonis... Nec dubito posse hominem cantibus in furorem agi, sopiri, excitari, irritari ad risum, ad fletum, ad omne affectuum genus commoveri" ("This vision, combined with assent, which in faith St. Thomas calls pious passion [or disposition], has in it the love of God above all things, contrition and assured salvation. But the imagination becomes strong with paintings or sounds. I do not doubt that a man can be made angry by songs, fall asleep, wake up, laugh, cry, and experience all kinds of feelings."). Hence poets should take moral themes as the subject matter of their works, rather than human vices and love affairs, and should paint "vitae aeternae pulchritudinem" ["the beauty of eternal life"] and "horribiles scelerum poenas" ["horrible punishments for crimes"]. The person will be a boon to the Christian republic "qui effecerit, ut summa sit jucunditas in pietate" ("who makes sure that there is maximum joy in piety.").[132] The purpose of education in general is "qu'on doit être porté à trouver du plaisir dans l'exercice de la vertu et du dégoût et de la répugnance dans l'exercice du vice"[133].

Art, in other words, expresses the beauty and harmony of creation in an intuitive, obscure, as yet indistinct and irrational form, but it expresses it with warmth and feeling, and with a stirring of the emotions that makes the vision not only true, but pleasing, and prompts us to act — that is, to participate and cooperate in this harmony.[134]

---

[132] *Ibid.*, 306-7
[133] Shaftesbury's observations on *Characteristics* (G. III, 424).
[134] Leibniz on a few rare occasions makes personal judgments about the

The pleasure afforded by a work of art is for Leibniz of absolutely the same nature as the pleasure of friendship or of love — in the one we rejoice in the perfection or happiness of animate beings, in the other in the perfection of inanimate things.[135] And the pleasure of art is also of the same kind as the pleasure aroused by perfect and proper knowledge, and by any enhancement, refinement or elevation of being.[136] It is, in essence, the enthusiasm and satisfaction of the mind in action, in all its forms — adapting, that is, to the objective perfection of the world, and thus acquiring perfection itself.

---

emotional (or practical, as he calls it) value of pieces of music: "Il y a quelques phrases pour ainsi dire, qui nous enlevent partout oú elles se trouvent. Parmy 100 airs à peine puis j'en rencontrer un ou deux, que je trouve forts et nobles, et j'ay remarqué souvent, qu ce que les gens du métier estimolent le plus, n'avoit rien qui touchât. La simplicité fait souvent plus d'effect que les ornaments empruntés. Quy-a-t-il de plus simplex que le chant de ce texte: Ecce quomodo moritur justus! Cependant toutes les fois que je l'entends... j'en suis enlevé" (to Henfling, cit. in Bodemann, *Briefw.*, n. 390). Cf. also the letter to Kortholt, 2-VII-1705, D. V, 330.

[135] "Cet amour a proprement pour objet des substances susceptibles de la félicité; mais on en trouve quelque image à l'égard des objets qui ont des perfections sans les sentir, comme serait par exemple un beau tableau" (to Nicaise, 1698, G. II, 581). Cf. Mollat, 37: "Ita dicitur amare statuam, domum, equum, villam, oppidum, patriam, quando gaudemus harum rerum egregio statu atque pulchritudine et ipsa earum contemplatione ac sensu delectamur." ["Thus we are said to love a statue, a house, a horse, a mansion, a city, a country, the moment we enjoy the perfect state of these things and delight in the beauty and the very contemplation of them."] Cf. C. 492, *Nouv. Ess.*, 1. II, ch. 20, §§ 4-5.

[136] "Now is the time to establish that all new knowledge is an accretion of the new perfection, and, for this reason, sharp perceptions and the teaching of new things are related to pleasure; pleasure is also such that surely we can always calculate independently how useful it is for us to pursue it. Through the exercise of a clear point of view, the strength of effort is multiplied in a sure way when we proceed neatly and without hardships and vain pursuits, so this pleasure is the surest of all" (*Initia et Spec. Sc. N. Gen.*, G. VII, 113).

8. LEIBNIZ ON KNOWLEDGE AND WILL*

The anthropology and study of the emotions, which are notably entangled with the Stoic tradition of the Renaissance, reached its fullest development in the 17th century. Descartes presents it as an investigation centered around whatever is positive and real in human nature. The emotions stand before reason as if before something they must submit to, but not at the expense of their own reality and economy. In Descartes, the dualism of body and mind is combined with a dualism of reason and will. The will is intended as something independent, which can grant or deny assent and submit or not submit to reason, and the body as a substance apart from the mind. This permits the construction of a theory separated from affect, which is considered non-rational and is set against reason as a reality that must be fought or absorbed.[137]

In Spinoza, what endures is the reality, the positivity of the affections as something that the mind must beware of ignoring and neglecting, but on the contrary ought to seek to understand with open eyes.[138] But passion is itself

---

* *Rivista di filosofia*, XXXIV, 1943.
[137] Cf. *Les passions, de l'âme*, parte III, art. 211: "On peut corriger les défauts de son naturel, en s'exerçant à séparer en soi les mouvements du sang et des esprits d'avec les pensées auxquelles ils ont coutume d'être jojnts... On doit être averti et se souvenir que tout ce qui se présente à l'imagination tend à tromper l'âme et à lui faire paraître les raisons qui servent à persuader l'objet de sa passion beaucoup plus fortes qu'elles ne sont... Et lorsque la passion ne persuade que des choses dont l'exécution souffre quelque délai, il faut s'abstenir d'en porter sur l'heure aucun jugement... Et enfin, lorsqu'elle incite à des actions touchant lesquelles il est nécessaire qu'on prenne résolution sur le-champ, il faut que la volonté se porte principalement à considérer et à suivre les raisons qui sont contraires à celles que la passion représente, encore qu'elles paroissent moins fortes."
[138] "Affectus itaque odii, irae, invidiae ecc., in se considerati ex eadem naturae

seen as based on a tendency toward perfection, and reason as something that has in itself the faculty of arousing passions. Nevertheless, it always remains self-contained, operating on the passions and regulating them, not connatural with them. Leibniz seeks unification. He has no theory of the emotions as independent and derived from a principle of their own, whether it be a preservation instinct or something else. He does not acknowledge a will that stands on its own before the intellect. The body as something opposed to the mind is a principle that he undermines, dismantling the very concept of materiality and reducing matter to the same substance as the mind. He then reintroduces it as a development of the concept of the monad, while accepting the problem of occasionalism.[139] But in his original conception there were no dualisms of body and spirit, knowledge and will, or reason and passions. Even here, his primary interest was straightforwardly

---

necessitate et virtute consequuntur, ac reliqua singularia; ac proinde certas causas agnoscunt, per quas intelliguntur, certasque proprietates habent, cognitione nostra acque dignas ac proprietates cujuscumque alterius rei cujus sola contemplatione delectamur." ("Feelings of hatred, wrath, or envy, considered in themselves, derive from the same necessity and virtue as nature, like other individual things; and therefore, they acknowledge the certain causes by which they are understood, and have certain properties as worthy of our knowledge as anything else in whose contemplation we delight" [Ethica, pars III, introd.]).

[139] A clear expression of his dual position regarding the concept of the body is offered in Nouv. Ess., I. II, c. 21 §§ 41-41: "On a raison de dire que géneralement toutes ces inclinations, ces passions, ces plaisirs et ces douleurs n'appartiennent qu'à l'esprit, ou à l'âme; j'adjouterai même, que leur origine est dans l'âme même en prenant les choses dans une certaine rigoeur metaphysique, mais que néammoins on a raison de dire, que les pensées confuses viennent du corps parceque là dessus la considération du corps et non pas seul de l'âme fournit quelque chose de distinct et d'explicable" Cf. § 12: "Cette dependance n'est que métaphysique et consiste dans les egards que Dieu a pour l'un en reglant l'autre... au lieu que la dependance physique consisteroit dans une influence immediate que l'un recevroit de l'autre dont il dépend." Cf. Théod., § 65.

ontological, not epistemological nor psychological. All existence, including man and his activities, must organize itself within the system of rational and harmonic law. Knowledge is reasoning along with the organization of experience in a system, and morality is essentially the same thing as knowledge — it amounts to acting within the field of this organization, striving for the advancement of knowledge and the "general good."

The struggle of reason against emotion does also turn up in Leibniz. But the passions are no longer the animal side of man that rational man must stand up to — they are instead the limitation of reason itself, a limitation that presents itself as passivity. They are essentially an imperfection of knowledge,[140] and are, we might say, part of knowledge itself and attributable to its defectiveness.[141] Even viewed as animal phenomena, as movements of the blood, their essence is characterized by how far they limit and deceive the mind.[142] And it is no longer

---

[140] "Il reste encore quelque imperfection dans la constitution de l'ame... car il y a en elle... encore une suite de perceptions confuses ou de passions qui fait son esclavage." Cf. *Théod.*, § 65.

[141] Cf. these two definitions, the first probably youthful and clearly influenced by Spinoza, the second more mature: "Plus on agit suivant la raison, plus on est libre, et il y a d'autant plus de servitude qu'on agit par les passions. Car plus nous agissons suivant la raison, plus nous agissons selon les perfections de nostre propre nature, et à mesure que nous nous laissons emporter par les passions, nous sommes esclaves des choses externes qui nous font patir" (*Initia et Spec. Sc. N. Gen.*, G. VII, 110). Cf. *Nouv. Ess.*, 1. II, ch. 20, §§9-10: "Les passions ne sont ny des contentemens ou des plaisirs, ny des opinions, mais des tendances ou plustost des modifications de la tendance, qui viennent de l'opinion ou du sentiment, et qui sont accompagnées de plaisir ou de deplaisir." Some psychological characterizations of the passions are given in response to Locke at the end of Chapter XX, 1. II, of the *Nouv. Ess.* and in the observations on the works of Shaftesbury (G. III, 407 ff., 423 ff.) there is a list of definitions of various emotions, for the purpose of constituting their general character, in C 492-93.

[142] "Meanwhile, we should not believe those who deceive us often, when they act towards us in a friendly manner. And regarding this, moreover, the remedy against the passions does not seem to be sound either — in which we order ourselves to follow these agitations of the blood, we admonish ourselves and remind ourselves again that this is represented in the imagination, it is there

the body that generates imperfect representations in the mind, it is rather the imperfect representations themselves that, because of their imperfection, are defined as "body."[143] The struggle between mind and body, between reason and emotion, in this way resolves itself into a struggle between distinct perceptions and confused perceptions.[144] And it is not a struggle that is fought by a simple act of will, but through a deepening of knowledge: "En travaillant aussi sur soy, il faut faire comme en travaillant sur autre chose: il faut connoistre la constitution et les qualités de son objet et y accommoder ces operations. Ce n'est donc pas en un moment, et par un simple acte de la volonté, qu'on se corrige et pu'on acquiert une meilleure volonté"[145].

Here again, then, as in Spinoza, adequate knowledge

---

that its purpose is to make the object of passion seem greater and to remove the reasons, so that it can once again be obfuscated" (*Initia et Spec. Sc. N. Gen.*, G. VII, 92-93. Cf. 94).

[143] "On a raison d'appeler perturbations avec les anciens, ou passions ce qui consiste dans les pensées confuses, ou il y a de l'involuntaire et de l'inconnu; et c'est ce que dans le langage commun, on n'attribue pas mal au combat du corps et de l'esprit, puisque nos pensées confuses representent le corps ou la chair et font nostre imperfection»" (argument with Bayle, G IV, 565). Cf. Letter to Coste, 1707, G. III, 403: "Nous sommes toujours dans une parfaite spontanéité, et ce qu'on attribue aux impressions des choses externes ne vient que des perceptions confuses en nous qui y repondent"; *Nouv. Ess.*, 1. II, ch. 21, §72: "Il n y a de l'Action dans les veritables Substances que lorsque leur perception (car j'en donne à toutes) se developpe et devient plus distincte, comme il n'y a de passion que lorsqu'elle devient plus confuse; en sort que dans les Substances, capables de plaisir et de douleur, toute action est un acheminement au plaisir, et toute passions à la douleur." Cf. *Théod.*, §66.

[144] "Les idées et veritées innées ne sauroient estre effacées, mais elles sont obscurcies dans tous les hommes... par leur pendant vers les besoins du corps, et souvent encor plus par les mauvaises coustumes survenues. Ces caracteres de lumiere interne seroient toujours éclatants dans rentendement et donneroient de la chaleur dans la volonté, si les perceptions confuses des sens ne s'emparoient de nostre attention. C'est le combat dont la Sainte Ecriture ne parle pas moins que la Philosophie ancienne et moderne" (*Nouv. Ess.*, 1. I, c. II, § 20). Cf. *Théod.*, §§ 289, 310.

[145] *Théod.*, § 328.

is free from passions. But the tone differs in the two conceptions because of the general approaches of the two systems. In Leibniz, the concrete nature of knowledge is always alive. It starts out from the particular and its adequacy lies in the extent of the network of connections it is able to establish around it. The end point is not simple mathematical rationality, but a more complex harmony and coherence, to be sought and pursued with shrewdness and patience. Between confused and distinct knowledge, and therefore between passion and reason, there is continuity instead of a sharp dividing line. If the pleasure of passion is afforded by the perception of a certain perfection, reason pursues a wider perfection that will give much greater pleasure. The same relationship runs between passion and reason as between partiality and totality.[146] For if passion is the pleasure resulting from inadequate knowledge, even adequate knowledge is not without emotion — indeed it is accompanied by a joy corresponding to its perfection. Hobbes and Spinoza attempted to forge unity in the moral world under the principle that a passion can be overcome by means of another passion with the joy it brings to the mind that contemplates itself and its power.[147] This is brought to fruition by Leibniz. For him what conquers the passions is the passionate nature of reason itself. Emotion is not an exclusive feature of the irrational, but something reason also takes part in. Feelings do not dissolve in the light of

---

[146] "La volonté tend au bien en general; elle doit aller vers la perfection qui nous convient, et la supreme perfection est en Dieu. Tous les plaisirs ont en eux mêmes quelque sentiment de perfection; mais lorsqu'on se borne aux plaisirs des sens ou à d'autres au prejudice de plus grand biens, comme de la santé, de la vertu, de l'union avec Dieu, de la félicité, c'est dans cette privation d'une tendance ulterieure que le defaut consiste. En general la perfection est positive, c'est une realité absolue, le defaut est privatif, il vient de la limitation et tend à des privations nouvelles»" (*Théod.*, § 33).

[147] *Ethica*, pars III, prop. LIII.

knowledge but are empowered and lifted with it. Reason is not cold, impassive and imperturbable. Victory over the passions is the victory of a feeling that is broader and more universal against a one that, because of its limitation and partiality, will inevitably lead to unhappiness.[148] One of the signs by which true reason can be recognized is the greater, more secure and longer lasting joy that it brings the person who reaches it.[149] And there is great pleasure in overcoming emotions — and it increases with the strength of the passions to be fought against.[150]

The contact with Stoicism is therefore only external here.[151] Leibniz's reason and nature are something quite different from reason and nature in the historical tradition of the Renaissance and rationalism.

But neither should his morality be interpreted as a form of hedonism. Pleasure and happiness are not something to be sought after for their own sake — they are a

---

[148] "When the pleasure of the body wears out because of illness and reputation because of misfortune, self-deception ends and one finds oneself unhappy" (*Initia et Spec. C. N. Gen.*, G. VI, 88).

[149] "For this is one of the eternal rules of nature, that we shall enjoy the perfection of things and, from this, the desire that arises in proportion to our knowledge, our good will, and the contribution we make" (*Initia et Spec. C. N. Gen.*, G. VII, 89).

[150] "The more difficult it is to overcome our impulses, the greater the pleasure ... because his toil is replenished ... even with more work, John is greater. Because being confident in one's strength brings great pleasure to those who toil and, consequently, the joy that comes with it." (*ibid,*. G. VII, 98). Cfr. 95 e *Théod.*, § 329. For the precepts of morality and psychology regarding the passions and virtues, see generally all the fragments collected under the title *Initia et Specimina Scientiae Novae Generalis*.

[151] See the invective against the Stoics in the juvenile fragment *Juris et acqui elementa* (AK VI, I e Mollat, 28, 9): "Interroga stoicos illos, illos aërios, nubivolos, μετεωρολόγυς, voluptatis simulatos hostes rationis veros. Circumspice, rimare actus eorum motusve! Senties nec digitum ciere posse, quin mendacium impingant inani suae philosophiae. Honestas ipsa nil nisi jucunditas animi est" ["Question those stoics, elevated, on clouds, prattling on about vanity, feigning pleasure, true enemies of reason. Pay attention, scrutinize their actions and movements. You will feel that they cannot move a finger without imposing the falsehood of their vain philosophy. There is no honesty if there is no pleasure in the soul."]

natural consequence, inherent in the very essence of reason, and always conjoined in what it achieves. Reason is not an instrument for achieving happiness, nor on the other hand is happiness merely a means of making reason palatable. Pleasure is, as we know, the sense of perfection. And the perfection of thought means "ut repraesentatio sit exacta vel, quod item est, ut cogitatio sit distincta, ut sit valide activa, i.e. ut voluntas recta ratione quesita sit firma, denique ut repraesentatio sit ample diffusa h. e. ut multa simul uno mentis ictu comprehendamus" ("that the representation should be exact, which is to say that the thought should be distinct and intensely active — that is, that a righteous will should be gained through righteous reasoning. Therefore, the representation should be extensive so that we understand many things through one single effort of the mind.").[152]

Pleasure and truth and good, utility and reason and morality are now united in a single mental act, so that those who strive for the one cannot help but also strive for the other. This tendency toward good, toward perfection, harmony, and wholeness is nothing other than the tendency toward something that, by expanding our mind, leads it to the most perfect happiness. Each person's perfection — happiness, that is — fits with universal harmony. And a good will is merely the active, passionate and operational awareness of this harmony, as it strives for the implementation of what it learns.

Leibniz at times tries to theorize about what is specifically active in the reality of the mind: the striving, effort, and desire that serve as an immediate trigger for action, the sense of absence that sets us in motion and is only satisfied by a completed action, the element that is something like a pattern for any action as such, regardless of

---

[152] Mollat, 5.

its content and purpose. "La Volition est l'effort où la tendances (conatus) vers ce qu'on trouve bon et contre ce qu'on trouve mauvais, en sorte que cette tendance risulte immediatement de la perception qu'on en a. Et le corollaire de cette definition est cet Axiome celebre: que du vouloir et pouvoir joints ensemble, suit l'action, puisque de toute tendance suit l'action lorsqu'elle n'est point empechée."[153]

To act is to actualize knowledge, but all knowledge, insofar as it leads to consequences and "is acted upon," is expressed as feeling. A person who acts always takes some kind of pleasure in doing so, and there is no action that, as such, does not satisfy a desire. Between Cartesian rationalism, which places reason as the master and regulator of the passions, and the Sensism of the 1700s, which makes the passions the first and only factor in volition, lies this Leibnizian theory of knowledge that is indeed rational, but precisely because of this it is active and passionate as well.[154]

The insightful remarks in the *New Essays* are crucial in this regard. Here, the theory of petites perceptions (dependent directly on the concept of the monad) sparked new developments in the fundamental Leibnizian conception of the relations between knowledge and will found throughout his thought and enabled him to establish on a firm foundation the unbroken continuity and gradual transition from passion to morality which was the trend

---

[153] *Nouv. Ess.*, 1. II, ch. 21. Cf. Mollat, 4: "Cogitatio est active quaedam repraesentatio... Activam volo. Nam ex omni cogitatione sua natura statim sequitur conatus agendi seu voluntas quaedam." ["Thought is an active representation. Let me emphasize — active. In fact, every thought by its very nature is immediately followed by an attempt to accomplish something, or the will."]
[154] Cf. in *Disc. de Mét.*, §15, the metaphysical justification of the identity of the notions of perfection, knowledge, action, pleasure, based on the concept of individual substance.

of the whole century.[155] Perception is regarded in itself as active, as having its own influence on feeling, as prolonging itself into action. The case proposed by Locke in which "video meliora proboque, deteriora sequor" ("I see and approve of better things but follow worse ones."), i.e., where the will does not follow what it recognizes as true good, but only the nearest desire, is resolved by the demonstration that in such a case the notion of good is not true knowledge, but is only nominal, abstract knowledge, devoid of true and proper content — that true and full knowledge also contains within itself the determination of the will.[156] Confused perceptions make it possible to explain, as in the case of art, the fact of instinct and innate moral knowledge in a non-rational form without having to resort to some autonomous practical faculty other than reason. It is still knowledge, but not distinct knowledge, and only through its development can it be added to the proof and definition.[157]

Confused perceptions also explain the state of "restlessness" which is the springboard and the "aiguillon du

---

[155] Cf. Dilthey, *Analisi dell'uomo*, II, 284 ff.

[156] "La pluspart de nos pensées sont sourdes pour ansi dire... c'est à dire vuides de perception et de sentiment... On raisonne souvent en paroles, sans avoir presque l'objet même dans l'esprit. Or cette connoissance ne sauroit toucher, il faut quelque chose de vif pour qu'on soit emû... Ainsi si nous préférons le pire, c'est que nous sentons le bien qu'il renferme, sans sentir ny le mal qu'il y a, ni le bien qui est dans le parti contraire" (*Nouv. Ess.*, 1. II, ch. 21, § 35). Cfr. 1. II, ch. 28, § 19, and *Théod.*, § 154: "Le bien honnete est surmonté par le bien agreable qui fait plus d'impression sur les ames. quand elles se trouent agitées par les passions."

[157] "Il y a des conclusions de la lumiere naturelle qui sont des principes par rapport à l'instinct. C'est ainsi que nous sommes portés aux actes d'humanité, par instinct parce que sela nous plist et par raison parce que cela est juste. Il y a donc en nous de verités d'instinct, qui sont la preuve, qu'on obtient pourant lorsqu'on rend raison de cet instinct. C'est ainsi qu'on se sert des loix des consequences suivant une connoissance confuse, et comme par instinct, mais les Logiciens en démonstrent la raison, comme les Mathematiciens aussi rendent raison de ce qu'on fait sans y penser en marchant et en sautant" (*Nouv. Ess.*, 1. I, ch. 2, §4).

desir,"¹⁵⁸ and in general they offer Leibniz a way of probing all the intermediate states of pre-rationality and the preconscious will. They allow him, that is, to avoid any break or duality in the world of the psyche, to regard every mental act as an overall and inseparable whole, theoretical and practical at the same time, and represented on the scale of values by its degree of clarity and distinction.

What people incline toward initially, instinctively, is their own good and pleasure: "Suivre la joye et eviter la tristesse."¹⁵⁹ But pleasure is nothing other than the perception of order, harmony and perfection in a certain field.¹⁶⁰ The will is the inclination toward the achievement of this order. Every action, therefore, always tends toward the good. Error, evil, and sin lie in offering partial perfection instead of greater perfection,¹⁶¹ or in other words, a present and momentary pleasure instead of more stable and lasting future pleasure.¹⁶² They mean, that is, "qu'on n'a pas bien lu ces caracteres de la nature gravés dans nos ames, mais quel-ques fois assez enveloppés par nos desordres."¹⁶³

Here we see a new aspect of the difference Leibniz

---

¹⁵⁸ *Nouv. Ess.*, 1. II, ch. 20, § 6.
¹⁵⁹ *Nouv. Ess.*, 1. I, ch. 20, § I.
¹⁶⁰ "Je crois que dans le tonds le plaisir est un sentiment de perfection et la douleur un sentiment d'imperfection... Le bien est ce qui sert ou contribue au plaisir, comme le mal ce qui contribue à la douleur" (*Nouv. Ess.*, 1. II, ch. 21, § 42). Cf. G. VII, 290: "Voluptas... intelligentis nihil aliud est quam perceptio pulchriudinis, ordinis, perfectionis. Et omnis dolor continet aliquid inordinati sed respective ad percipientem, cum absolute omnia sint ordinata." ["The pleasure of the wise man is nothing but the perception of beauty, order and its perfection. And every sorrow contains in it something disordered in the eyes of the perceiver, when all things are perfectly ordered."] and C. 475: "Jocundum quod continet perceptionem perfectionis. Molestum quod imperfectionis" ["And this entails that the good is the one who has the knowledge of perfection, wicked that of imperfection."]; etc. ...
¹⁶¹ *Nouv. Ess.*, 1. II, ch. 28, § 10.
¹⁶² *Nouv. Ess.*, 1. II, ch. 21, § 58 and ff.
¹⁶³ *Nouv. Ess.*, 1. I, ch. 2, § 12.

draws between the two Cartesian attributes of clarity and distinction. Distinction indicates rational evidence, definability, demonstrability. Clarity indicates practical and sensory evidence, its vivid and violent presentation to the mind, the arousing of desires and passions. One represents the cognitive moment and the other the volitional moment in the practical theoretical whole that is perception.

Clear but confused ideas are those instinctive tendencies which, due to lack of awareness and rationality and a vision of only partial perfections, lead to momentary pleasures devoid of controlled knowledge. Distinct but obscure ideas, on the other hand, are ones which, though fully demonstrated and exact, remain stillborn due to lack of emotional participation and the mental fullness that immediately turns them into action.[164] And precisely for this reason it is good "qu'on rendre les vrais biens et les vrais maux autant sensibles qu'il se peut"[165]. Here the concept of the monad as perception and appetite finds its psychological explanation and comes to coincide with the union of knowledge and will.[166] Every volition is the result of the concurrence and conflict of various perceptions.[167] This is something more complex and comprehensive than may appear from simply the direction taken. It

---

[164] "Ce combat [entre la chair et l'esprit] n'est autre chose que l'opposition des différentes tendences, qui naissent des pensées confuses et des distinctes. Les pensées confuses souvent se font sentir clairement, mais nos pensées distinctes ne sont claires ordinairement qu'en puissance: elles pourroient l'estre, si nous voulions nous donner l'application de penetrer le sens des mots ou caracteres, mais ne le faisant point, ou par negligence, ou à cause de la brieveté du temps, on opposes des parole; nues ou du moins des images trop foibles à des sentiments vifs" (*Nouv. Ess.*, 1. II, ch. 21, § 34). Cf. *Théod.*, § 120.
[165] *Nouv. Ess.*, 1. II, ch. 21, § 34
[166] "Subjectum seu substantiae simplicis natura, ubi de perceptione et appetitu, et (ubi distincta sunt) ratione et voluntate, consideratur hic aliquid in mutatione permanere." ["The subject or nature of simple substance, with regard to perception and appetite, and reason and will (where they are distinct), is the persistence of something during change"] (C. 528).
[167] "Plusieurs perceptions et inclinations concourent à la volition parfaite, qui

includes the whole set of perceptions that constitute the personality of each individual, and it will be all the more moral, the larger this whole is — that is, the more it reflects the harmony of the universe.[168] Immorality is an error in the calculation of the counterweights that constitute the balance of this harmony, an error that can be corrected by more rigorous criteria and a more exact knowledge of the elements that come into play.[169]

This is an aspect of the most mature form of the Leibnizian doctrine of the will, developed and expanded through the formulations made possible by the notions of the monad, of petites perceptions, and of the subconscious in mental life. But these ideas frame within the whole of the completed system a notion that had been present since Leibniz's early youth, even outside the particular theories that made up his specific philosophical system.[170] It is in essence a general tendency and requirement of his personality. The legal writings in which he

---

est le resultat de leur conflit" (*Nouv. Ess.* 1. II, ch. 21, § 39). Cfr. *Théod.*, §§ 51, 324, 325, *Remarques sur le livre de King*, § 13.

[168] "Il faut bien de choses pour se prendre comme il faut, lorsqu'il s'agit de la balance des raisons; et c'est à peu pres comme dans les livres de compte des marchands. Car il n'y faut negliger aucune somme, il faut bien estimer chaque somme à part, il faut les bien arranger, et il faut enfin en faire une collection exacte" (*Nouv. Ess.* 1. II, ch. 21, § 67).

[169] "Mais on y neglige plusieurs chefs, soit en ne s'avisant pas d'y penser, soit en passant legerment là dessus; et on ne donne point à chacun sa juste valeur, semblable à ce teneur de livres de compte qui avoit soin de bien calculer les colonnes de chaque page, mais qui calculoit très mal les sommes particulieres de chaque ligne ou poste avant que de les mettre dans la colonne... Ainsi il nous faudroit encore l'art de s'aviser et celuy d'estimer les probabilités et de plus la connoissance de la valeur des biens et des maux, pour bien employer l'art des consequences... Enfin il faut une ferme et constante resolution pour executer ce qui a esté conclu, et des adresses, des methodes, des loix particulieres et des habitudes toutes formées pour la maintenir dans la suite" (*Nouv. Ess.* 1. II, ch. 21, § 67).

[170] "La verité est, que l'Ame, ou la Substance qui pense, entend les raisons, et sent les inclinations, et se determine selon la prevalence des representation qui modifient sa force active, pour specifier l'action. Je n'ay point besoin d'employer icy mon systeme de l'Harmonie préetablie.. Car ce que je viens de dire suffit pour resoudre l'objection" (*Remarques sur le livre de King*, § 16, G. VI, 416).

sought to reconcile utilitarianism with morality had led him to his definition of love as one's own pleasure in the perfection of others, which he would not forget throughout the course of his thinking and would always be pleased to be able to recall and apply.[171] The definition seems at first nothing more than a clever contrivance, foreign to the organism of Leibnizian thought, which arose as part of a particular inquiry, concerning a specific problem[172] — but it acquires a broader meaning and a precise function when linked to the above concepts concerning the nature of the will.

The union of utility with morality is expanded. It becomes one of the typical examples of concept definitions, which Leibniz uses in the construction of his Characteristic. It is used both to theorize about the pleasantness and sentimentality that he always strives to attribute to morality, and to solve the problems that had arisen in this regard in the discussion of the mystics. "Justitia est charitas sapientis. Charitas est benevolentia generalis. Benevolentia est habitus amoris. Amare aliquem est eius felicitate delectari. Sapientia est scientia felicitatis. Felicitas est laetitia durabilis. Laetitia est status voluptatum, in

---

[171] The definition was probably suggested by *Guldenes Tugendbuch* by the Jesuit Spee, whose preface Leibniz translated and commented on (Klopp, VIII, 56-84).

[172] The most precise formulation of it in its legal terms is found in the first preface to the *Codex Juris Gentium Diplomaticus* of 1693. "Ut vero universali demonstrationi conficiatur, omne honestum esse utile, et omne turpe damnosum, assumenda est immortalitas animae et rector universi Deus. Ita fit, ut omnes in Civitate perfettissima vivere intelligamur, sub monarcha, qui nec ob sapientiam falli, nec ob potentiam vitari potest. Idemque tam amabilis est, ut felicitas sit tali Domino servire. Huic igitur qui animam impendit, Christo docente, eam lucratur." ["To conclude with a universal demonstration that everything honest is useful and everything foul is harmful, we must assume the immortality of the soul and God, the guide of all things. Thus, it happens that we all understand that we live in the perfect City, under a monarch whose wisdom does not permit error and whose power prevents him from shirking. Likewise, he is so lovable that it is a joy to serve the Lord. He who consecrates his soul to him will earn it following the teaching of Christ."] (D. IV, III, 296).

quo sensus voluptatis tantus est, ut sensus doloris prae eo non sit notabilis. Voluptas seu Delectatio est sensus perfectionis, id est sensus cujusdam rei quae juvat seu quae potentiam aliquam adjuvat. Perficitur cujus potentia augetur seu juvatur" ("Justice is the charity of the wise man. Charity is general benevolence. Benevolence is the clothing of love. To love someone is to rejoice in their happiness. Wisdom is the science of happiness. Happiness is lasting gladness. Gladness is the condition of pleasures, in which the sense of pleasure is so great that the sense of pain is unworthy of notice before it. Pleasure or delight is the sense of perfection — that is, the sense of everything that is beneficial or helpful in some way.").[173] This chain of definitions, constructed by breaking down concepts to arrive at their simple elements, has at its base the idea of perfection as an elevated degree of being, and the idea of pleasure as the sense of perfection.[174] Supreme love is the love directed towards the perfect being, which is God, and the supreme perfection, which is the harmony of things, and it consists precisely of locating one's own happiness in divine happiness.[175] Its essence is the essence of virtue itself,[176] which is identified with pleasure intended not as pleasure of the senses — which may lead to unhappiness, "just as a dish that tastes good can be harmful to the health" — but rather as "the desire that the soul feels for itself from the

---

[173] *Initia et Spec. C. N. Gen.*, G. VII, 73. The passage cited is from around 1678, according to the catalogue of the Leibnizian commission.

[174] Cf. also the German text, slightly modified, and other almost identical formulations, in G. II, 136, 577, G. III, 386-87, G. VII, 27, 549, C. 331, 516.

[175] "Quisquis felicitatem suam collocat in relatione Divinae felicitatis ad se, is... Deum amat" ["Whoever places his own happiness in relation to divine happiness in itself is someone who loves God"] (*Initia et Spec. C. N. Gen.*, G. VII, 75).

[176] "When... the soul senses in itself a great harmony, order, freedom, strength or perfection, and therefore feels a desire for it, this event creates joy... This joy is constant ... when it originates from knowledge and is accompanied by light, and from this arises in the will a predisposition to do good, which is its virtue" (*Initia et Spec. C. N. Gen.*, G. VII, 88).

intellect." It follows that "nothing is more useful to happiness than the illumination of the intellect and the exercise of the will for the purpose of always experiencing the intellect." Such happiness consists of "perceiving a desire in oneself and in one's strength of mind when one perceives within oneself a strong inclination and capability for acts of charity and truth"[177]

This association of happiness, wisdom and virtue[178] is for Leibniz, the basis of natural law, and of the morality that is inherent in man even independently of any consideration of divinity.[179] It also gives him a way of resolving the problem of disinterested mysticism that Bossuet and Fénelon in France and Sherlock and Norris in England were going on about in the controversy over quietism. Can there be a will that wants nothing for itself, whose very principle is anti-utilitarian, which disavows as sin any reference to its own person, and which does not operate on the basis of any contingent motive referring to the acting subject?

Leibniz insisted that this discussion had taken place without sufficient care in the definition of its terms. If love is the pleasure taken from the happiness of others,[180]

---

[177] *Ibid.*, G. VII, 88.
[178] "L'Honneste n'est autre chose que l'Agreable de la Raison" (to Coste 1706, G. VIII, 384).
[179] "Nos affections naturelles font notre contentement: et plus on est dans le naturel, plus on est porté à trouver son plaisir dans le bien d'autrui, ce qui est le fondement de la bienveuillance universelle, de la charité, de la justice... On peut dire qu'il y a un certain dergré de bonne morale independamment de la divinité, mais que la considération de la providence de Dieu et de l'immortalité de l'ame, porte la morale à son comble, et fait que chez le sage les qualités morales sont tout à fait realisées, et l'honnete identifié avec l'utile, sans qu'il y ait exception ny echappatoire" (Observations on Shaftesbury, G. III, 428-29).
[180] A comparison of this definition of love with that of Descartes and Spinoza shows how in Leibniz the process of welding the passions to reason is enclosed within the continuity of mental activity: "L'amour est une émotion de l'âme causée par le mouvement des esprits, qui l'incite à se joindre de volonté aux objets qui paroissent lui être convenables (*Les passions de l'âme*, parte II, art.

it is perfectly permissible to have a love that is absolutely pure — that is, directed exclusively at the good of others — and which is also nothing but a pursuit of the well-being or pleasure of the person one loves.[181] One of the two opposing views sought to nullify individual personality and any will directed toward one's own good, while the other wanted to base social-religious morality on each individual's consciousness of his or her own self-interest in the realization of God's kingdom. With Leibniz's thesis,

---

70). "Amor nihil aliud est, quam laetitia concomitante dea causae externae" [Love is nothing other than internal joy united with the idea of an external cause"] (*Ethica*, pars III, prop. XIII, Scholium).

[181] "Lorsqu'on aime sincerement une personne, on n'y cherche, pas son propre profit ny un plaisir detaché de celuy de la personne aimée, mais on cherche son plaisir dans le contentement et dans la félicité de cette personne. Et si cette felicité ne plaisoit pas en elle même, mais seulement à cause d'un avantage qui en resulte pour nous, ce ne seroit plus un amour sincere et pur. Il faut donc qu'on trouve immediatement du plaisir dans cette felicité et qu'on trouve de la douleur dans le malheur de la personne aimée. Car tout ce qui fait du plaisir immediatement par lui même, est aussi desiré pour luy même, comme faisant (au moins en partie) le but de nos vues, et comme une chose qui entre dans nostre propre felicité et nous donne de la satisfaction. Cela sert à concilier deux verités qui paroissent incompatibles; car nous faisons tout pour nostre bien, et il est impossible que nous ayons d'autres sentiments, quoyque nous en puissions dire. Cependant nous n'aimons point encor tout à fait purement, quand nous ne cherchons pas le bien de l'objet aimé pour luy même, mais à cause d'un avantage qui nous en provient. Mais il est visible par la notion de l'amour que nous venons de donner, comment nous cherchons en même temps nostre bien pour nous et le bien de l'objet aimé pour luy mème; lorsque le bien de cet objet est immediatement, dernierement (ultimato) et par luy même nostre but, nostre plaisir et nostre bien, comme il arrive à l'egard de toutes les choses qu'on souhaite parcequ'elles nous plaisent par elles mêmes, et sont par consequene bonnes de soy, quand on n'auroit aucun egard aux conséquences; ce sont des fins et non pas des moyens. Or l'amour divin est infiniment au dessus des amours des creatures... Ces considérations font voir en quoy consiste le veritable desinteressement du pur amour qui ne sçauroit estre detaché de nostre propre contentement et felicité... puisque nostre felicité renferme essentiellement la connnoissance de la félicité de Dieu et des perfections divine; c'est à dire l'amour de Dieu" (to Nicaise, 1697, G. II, 577-78). cf. also G. I, 357-58, G. III, 207, 382 ff., 425. G. VI, 416, 605-6, F. d. C. I, 143, II, 195, Mollat, 36 ff., Baruzi, *Leibniz*, 340-41, 345, D. II, I, 224-25, *Syst*. *Theol*. 66. On this entire argument, cf. Couturat note X.

disinterested love has, by its very nature, its own desirability — and it leads, simply by being satisfied, to pleasure on the part of the person who loves: "Licet non praemiis poenisque moveantur, felicitate tamen velut necessario virtutis corollario fruuntur, immo virtus sapientis cum summam animi voluptatem pariat, ipsa praemium sibi est ("It is possible that they are moved not by rewards or punishments, but enjoy happiness from the necessary corollary of virtue, or rather that the virtue of the wise man is its own reward, generating great pleasure in the soul.").[182]

Leibniz reintroduces here, with Spee[183] and against Descartes,[184] the distinction between love that aims only at the pleasure derived from the perfection of others, called "benevolent love," and love grounded "dans l'esperance de quelques autres plaisirs que Dieu ou quelque ami nous peut donner," called "concupiscient love."[185] Thus he clearly sets his theory apart from any sort of utilitarianism, however disguised and sophisticated.[186] But what is characteristic of him here is the accompanying usefulness that he wants to see in every action, the most disinterested as well as the most interested, the best and the worst. This accompaniment is different from the coincidence of utility with honesty in universal order and harmony.[187] Here the character of the coincidence is psychological. It is verified in the internal process of volition.

---

[182] Mollat, 89
[183] Klopp, VIII, 76 ff., *Théod.*, § 96.
[184] Cf. *Les Passions de l'âme*, part II, art. 81.
[185] To Coste, 1706, G. III, 385, and to Duchess Sophy, G. VII, 546 ff.; *Nouv. Ess.*, 1. II, ch. 20, §§ 4-5.
[186] "Lors memes qu'on fonde l'amour de Dieu sur ses bienfaits, considérés d'une maniere qui ne marque pas en même temps ses perfections, c'est un amour d'un degré inferieur, utile sans doute et louable, mais qui ne laisse pas d'estre interessé, et n'a pas toutes les conditions du pur amour divine" (to Nicaise, G. II, 579). Cf. 587.
[187] Cf. above.

The very fact of volition brings about satisfaction from the fulfilled will, from the action performed, whatever that action may be. In addition to its content, its specific end, every volition — be it utilitarian or moral, particular (that is, Leibnizianly partial), or universal — has what might be called a form, inherent in its very essence as volition, which is the very fact of its having evolved, which implies a propensity, an effort towards fulfillment. The arrival of an action at its objective, even possibly against the individual interests of the person who acts, in itself brings joy and pleasure. This is what Leibniz means when he says that every action inclines toward pleasure, toward some kind of perfection: "Conatus agendi oritur tendendo ad perfectionem, cujus sensus delectatio est; neque aliter actio vel voluntas constat. Et ad male consulta etiam quadam boni seu perfectionis specie percepta movemur, etsi scopo excidamus, aut exiguum bonum male petitum jactura majoris luamus; neque impulsui a bono suo nisi cum natura sua renuntiare quisquam ultra verba potest" ("The effort to act arises through a striving for perfection, the meaning of which is pleasure, otherwise neither action nor will is worthwhile. Indeed, we are moved to make wrong decisions even by the idea of good or perfection, despite the fact that we fail in a purpose or pay with greater harm for that little bit of good mistakenly pursued. And neither under the impulse of one's own good nor one's own nature can anyone speak of more.").[188]

---

[188] Preface to part II of the *Codex Juris Gentium Diplomaticus* (1700), D. IV. III, 313. Cf. *Nouv. Ess.*, 1. II, ch. 20, § 2: "Le bien est agreable ou utile, et l'honneur luy même consiste dans um plaisir d'esprit"; Mollat, 24: "Nemo est, qui quicquam consulto faciat nisi sui boni causa." ["No one does anything voluntarily except for their own good"]; *Théod.*, § 154: "Le franc arbitre va au bien, et s'il rencontre le mal, c'est par accident, c'est que ce mal est caché sous le bien, et comme masqué"; G. III, 30: " Etiam in malis aliquid est perfectionis" ["Even in evil there is something of perfection."]

Such phrases recall *Gorgias, Meno,* the *Republic*.[189] The theoretical nature of practical error is affirmed, and virtue is reduced to a fact of knowledge. Every person, in every action, tends toward their own good, perfection, and happiness.[190] The person sins who errs in the notion of perfection and happiness and mistakes the true — the universal — for something partial and false. In the *New Essays*, Leibniz distinguishes partial "pleasures" from "happiness," which represents an enduring pleasure that can grow indefinitely "car nous ne savons pas jusqu'ou nos connoissances et nos organes peuvent estre portés dans toute cette eternité qui nous attend... Le bonheur est donc pour ainsi dire un chemin par des plaisirs; et le plaisir n'est qu'un pas et un avancement vers le bonheur... On peut manquer le vray chemin, en voulant suivre le plus court, comme la pierre allant droit, peut rencontrer trop tôt des obstacles, qui l'empechent d'avancer assés, vers le centre de la terre. Ce qui fait connoistre, que c'est la raison et la volonté qui nous menent vers le bonheur, mais que le sentiment et l'appetit ne nous portent que vers le plaisir."[191] This is the basis for the negation of sensory pleasure and the battle against the passions.

---

[189] Cf. Mollat, 35-36, and the letter to Hansch (D. II, I, 224-55) in which he defends ancient philosophy on this point against Augustine, who "philosophos omnia ad se retulisse objicit, creaturamque adeo praetulisse creatori" ["reproaches the philosophers for tracing each thing back to itself, and for preferring the creature to the creator."] Leibniz responds: "Neque enim per naturam rerum fieri potest, ut quisquam suae felicitatis rationem non habeat" ["Nor indeed by the nature of things can it happen that someone does not have knowledge of their own happiness."]

[190] "Voluntatis objectum esse bonum apparens, et nihil a nobis appeti nisi sub ratione boni apparentis, dogma est vetustissimum communissimumque" ["We cannot desire anything except under manifest good will, and as a most ancient and general dogma reveals, it is the good that is the object of the will"] (C. 25).

[191] *Nouv. Ess.*, 1. II, ch. 21, § 42.

With these concepts the doctrine of the utilitarian accompaniment of all moral action is brought to its decisive consequences. The essence of action itself is made to consist in the inclination towards pleasure, but it does not resemble Epicureanism in this respect. Moral differentiation is shifted to the field of knowledge, and it is made to depend on what each individual regards as pleasure. Action — volition as such — has lost all autonomy, becoming in a certain sense mechanical. The will necessarily inclines automatically wherever the representation of pleasure and harmony leads it.[192] It cannot turn elsewhere because of its own essence — otherwise it wouldn't be true will, which by definition tends toward perfection. Thus will and pleasure are not separable because they are the same thing, and it is not possible to attribute to the simple will a negation or even a surpassing of itself inasmuch as it tends toward pleasure.

But this surpassing that is impossible for the will can be accomplished by the intellect. It is the intellect that perceives perfection in a broader or narrower sense and can either limit itself to understanding it as a momentary sensory pleasure of or broaden it to the whole universe. The intellect reaches an overall and objective vision of reality in which the single person is no more than a detail in the whole, an object among objects. Acting on the basis of this vision of the intellect is to surpass one's own personal self and to be pure and disinterested. But this action is always tied to the acting subject since it satisfies his inclination, brings about his perfection, and achieves his happiness.

In this synthesis of the universal and the individual,

---

[192] "The will is nothing but a sensory impulse." (*Initia et Sp. Sc. N.Gen.*, G. VII, 112). Cf. C. 331, § 34, etc.

the intellect represents the universal and the will the individual. And it is precisely these formulations, belonging more to Leibniz's overall mentality than to the technical organism of his system, which show this synthesis not only as the ultimate result of his philosophical construction, but also as a basic and ever-recurring first requirement of his thought. Morality, along with the implementation of and cooperation with the absolute and objective order of the universe. Here the individual disappears, is annihilated. A person's particular nature, good and evil, lose prominence in the totality of supreme balances. But the pleasure provided is personal — linked to and inseparable from the individual. It shows that this universal harmony in the human world is always desired and realized individually, just as in morality reality is perceived from a single point of view.

Here the basis of moral evaluation is completely different from that of Fénelon and the mystics. For them the will was autonomous, independent, and free, facing a known and objective divine reality. And the criterion for morality rested on freely chosen action — how the will behaves with respect to this reality, behavior that can even go so far as to annihilate the will itself. In Leibniz the will, having lost all prominence, no longer has a place in moral evaluation. By its own nature it always leads to what the intellect represents as perfection — that is, as pleasure. It is not my will, then, that will lead me to salvation or damnation, but the makeup, the conformation of my intellect. Not my actions, but the nature itself of my personality, from which my behavior naturally derives.[193] Goodness and justice are

---

[193] "Je pense qu'on est plus louable quand on doit l'action à ses bonnes qualités, et plus coupable à mesure qu'on y a été disposé par ses qualités mauvaises. Vouloir estimer les actions sans peser les qualités dont elles naissent, c'est parler en l'air, et mettre un je ne say quoy imaginaire à la place des causes. Aussi, si ce hasard ou ce je ne say quoy etoit la cause de nos actions, à l'exclusion de nos

not an ideal to which a good man must conform as if to a model, they are his very nature, from which he cannot detach himself without ceasing to be what he is.[194] And given that actions always and necessarily lead to the fulfillment of a desire, people are more or less respected according to whether their desires tend towards the universal good or towards their own particular benefit.[195]

---

qualités naturelles ou acquises, de nos inclinations, de nos habitudes, il n'y auroit point moyen de se promettre quelque chose de la resolution d'autruy, puisqu'il n'y auroit pas moyen de fixer un indefini, et de juger à quelle rade sera jetté le vaisseau de la volonté par la tempête incertaine d'une extravagante indifference" (*Remarques sur le livre de King*, § 19, G. VI, 221). Cf. *Théod.*, §§ 371, 410.

[194] "Ex sola definitione viri boni omnes ejus [Juris prudentiae] proposiciones demonstrari possunt" ["From the definition of a good man alone all its (jurisprudence's) propositions can be demonstrated"] (Mollat, I). Cf. p. 8: "Manifestum est, quod viro bono possibile, impossibile, necessarium est, si nomen suum tueri velit, id justum sive licitum, injustum ac denique debitum esse" ["It is evident what is possible, impossible, and necessary for the good man; (the possible) is what is just and lawful, (the impossible) is what is unjust, and finally (the necessary) is what is obligatory"; and in *Théod.*, § 191, the same concept, with reference to the divinity: "Ce pretendu fatum, qui oblige même la Divinité, n'est autre chose que la propre nature de Dieu, son propre entendement, qui fournit les regles à sa sagesse et à sa bonté."

[195] Cf. on this entire question, S. Del Boca, *Finalismo e necessità in Leibniz*, Firenze 1936, ch. X. The author takes issue with Leibniz, supporting the thesis of the independence of the will from knowledge and stating that Leibniz considers rational actions to be voluntary and those arising from passions to be involuntary. It seems to me, however, that the character of the Leibnizian dependence of the will on knowledge is the same in the realms of both rationality and passion, and that the freedom attributed to rationality is the freedom of the will guided by the intellect (*spontaneitas rationalis*) and not uninfluenced free will. Leibniz sometimes uses the term "voluntary" in the sense of free; but this is of course always the freedom-necessity of reason.

9. LEIBNIZ ON FREE WILL AND GRACE*

There is no will for Leibniz other the will inherent in the intellect itself, inseparable from it, a direct consequence and necessary extension of every individual perception.[196] It is clear that on this basis he must decisively deny any uninfluenced free will. But his identification of freedom and necessity differs from Spinoza's, which is based on the attribution of reality solely to mathematical deductive reason. Spinozian freedom consists of conforming to the necessary law of reason, whose very essence is goodness and whose negation is slavery. Leibniz recognizes a contingent mode, in which reason constitutes the framework, but not the innermost law and cause. Knowledge is also and primarily factual knowledge, the apprehension of data, contact with empirical realities. The necessity attributed to the act of volition is no longer the necessity of adaptation to the unfailing order of things but is psychologically determined in its specifics. If in Spinoza necessity-freedom is a constituent datum of metaphysical

---

* *Rivista di filosofia* XXXV, 1944.
[196] See the striking argument against those who assert the autonomy of the will, in *Remarques sur le livre de King*, § 16, G. VI, 416: "On veut que la Volonté soit seule active et souveraine, et on a coûtume de la concevoir comme une Reine assise sur son trône, dont l'Entendement est le Ministre d'estat, et dont les passions sont les courtisans, ou les demoiselles favorites; qui par leur influence prevalent souvent sur le conseil du Ministre. On veut que l'Entendement ne parle que par ordre de la Reine, quelle peut balancer entre les raisons du Ministre et les suggestions des favoris, et même rebuter les unes et les autres, enfin qu'elle les fait taire ou parler, et leur donne audience ou non, comme bon luy semble. Mais c'est une prosopopée ou fiction un peu mal entendue. Si la Volonté doit juger, ou prendre connaissance des raisons et des inclinations que l'entendement ou les sens luy presentent, il luy faudra un autre entendement dans elle même, pour entendre ce qu'on luy presente."

reality, for Leibniz it is first and foremost an element of human mental conformation, and its metaphysical aspect will derive directly from this initial psychological aspect. Necessity, then, no longer arises from the logical rigor that constitutes the concept of good, identifying itself with the rationality of the real and excluding evil from itself as its negation or limitation, but rather from the non-autonomy of the volitional fact taken on its own, and its identification with knowledge. Leibniz always opposed what he called the blind and brute necessity of the Stoics and of Spinoza and Hobbes,[197] and precisely to distinguish himself from them he introduced the distinction between metaphysical and moral certainty — or necessitating and inclining reason — whose significance we shall see more fully later, and which is the direct correlate of the distinction between truth of reason and fact, between the law of non-contradiction and the law of the "best," and between mathematics and finalism. His denial of uninfluenced free will always refers to the sphere of the factual, to contingent choice within the realm of the possible. This choice never occurs by an arbitrary act independent of motives. The will always chooses based on a reason;[198] and this reason can only be provided by knowledge, which may be obscure or imperceptible.

And if this is the case it is no longer possible to speak of uninfluenced free will, even in the field of contingency.[199] The will is not free because it is not autonomous.

---

[197] *Théod.*, §§ 72, 172 ff., 372; *Remarques sur le livre de King*, § 13; *Causa Dei*, § 22; fragment on *Deux secles des naturalistes*, G. VII, 333 ff., etc.

[198] "Il y a tousjours une raison (mais inclinante et non-necessitante) de la volonté, et la volonté pure et seule ne tient jamais lieu de raison" (to Jaquelot, G. VI, 571). "Omnino statuo potentiam se determinandi sine ulla causa, seu sine ulla radice determinationis implicare contradictionem uti implicat relatio sine fundamento" ["In general I judge that its strength is determined without any cause, and that without any basis it leads to the ability to contradict or implies an argument without any foundation"] (to Des Bosses, 1711, G. II, p. 420).

[199] A statement of this concept in the legal field: "Quae contra bonos mores sunt,

The determination of it, similar to causal determination in the physical world,[200] differs from the latter in that the causes acting in it are motives dictated by knowledge.[201] It is thus always linked to these motives.

Leibniz flatly denies Descartes view that the cause of our errors is the intrusion of the will (an autonomous faculty capable of assenting and denying without reason) into the field of knowledge.[202] It is not the will that errs,

---

ea nec facere nos posse credendum est, atque eo sensu dici potest jus, quod habemus, agendi aut non agendi potentiam quandam sive libertatem moralem esse, obligationem vero necessitatem" ["We must not believe that we can do what is customarily done against good people, and in this sense it can be said that the right we have to act or not act is a kind of possibility or moral freedom, but that obligation is instead a necessity"] (Mollat, VIII). In the original Latin, *Jus agendi* represents uninfluenced free will, *obligatio*, moral necessity.

[200] "Comme les philosophes modernes ont reformé les sentimens de l'Ecole en montrant... qu'un corps ne sauroit être mis en mouvement que par le mouvement d'un autre qui le pousse: de même il faut juger que nos Ames... ne sauroient être mues que par quelque raison du bien ou du mal; lors même que la connaissance distincte n'en sauroit être demelée, à cause d'un concours d'une infinité de petites perceptions qui nous rendent quelques fois joyeux, chagrins, et differemment disposés, et nous font plus gouter une chose que l'autre sans qu'on puisse dire pourquoy." Cf. *Remarques sur le livre de King,* § 3, G. VI, 401-2; *Controversy with Clarke,* G. VII, 389: "Les Raisons font dans l'esprit du sage, et les Motifs dans quelque esprit que ce soit, ce qui répond à l'effect que les poids font dans une balance."

[201] "A proprement parler, les motifs n'agissent point sur l'esprit comme les poids sur la balance; mais c'est plustost l'esprit qui agit en vertu des motifs, qui sont ses dispositions à agir. Ainsi vouloir... que l'esprit prefere quelques fois les motifs foibles aux plus forts, et même l'indifferent aux motifs, c'est separer l'esprit des motifs comme s'ils etoient hors de luy, comme le poids est distingué de la balance; et comme si dans l'esprit il y avoit d'autres dispositions pour agir que les motifs, en vertu desquels l'esprit rejetteroit ou accepteroit les motifs. Au lieu que dans la vérité les motifs comprennent toutes les dispositions que l'esprit peut avoir pour agir volontairement, car ils ne comprennent pas seulement les raisons, mais encore les inclinations qui viennent des passions ou d'autres impressions precedentes" (cf. *Controversy with Clarke,* G. VII, 392).

[202] "Errores pendere magis a voluntate quam ab intellectu, non admitto. Credere vera vel falsa, quorum illud cognoscere, hoc errare est, nihil aliud quam conscientia aut memoria est quaedam perceptionum aut rationum, itaque non pendet a voluntate, nisi quatenus obliqua arte tandem efficitur etiam aliquando nobis ignaris, ut quae volumus, nobis videre videamur... Judicamus igitur non quia volumus, sed quia apparet. Et quod dicitur, voluntatem esse latiorem intellectu, argutum est magis quam verum... Nihil volumus quin intellectui

it is knowledge — with its limitations and imperfections, because of defective attention and memory, as well as its confused perceptions or passions[203] — and the remedy is the deliberation and circumspection in the cognitive process, taking all data into account, repeating experiments, breaking down reasoning, etc.[204] The criterion of freedom cannot therefore be applied to the will as such, but only to the knowledge that it is derived from, meaning that the freer the knowledge, the more perfect it is.

Leibniz sometimes refers *tout court* to the tendency toward goodness or perfection in general[205] as "will," while at other times it is action determined by conscious motive, contrasted with appetition, or tendency, or instinct, which is also a property of confused perceptions.[206]

---

obversetur. Errorum omnium origo eadem est, suo quodam modo, quae errorum calculi ratio apud Arithmeticos observatur" ["I do not accept that errors depend more on the will than on the intellect. Believing something true that is false or something false that is true when this may be known by investigating, this is to err. So also, through knowledge or memory, perceptions or reasons arise. They therefore do not depend on the will, except when, for an unclear reason, we seem to ourselves, in our ignorance, to see what we want to see. We judge it not because we want to, but because it appears to us. And as for the saying that the will is broader than the intellect — it is more clever than true. We do not will anything that cannot be observed with the intellect. The origin of all errors is the same — it is what is observed as the reason for computational errors among the arithmeticians"] (*Animadversiones in partem generalem Principiorum Cartesianorum*, Pars I ad artc. 31-35, G. IV, 361).

[203] "Le choix suit la plus grande inclination; sous laquelle je comprends tant passions que raisons vrayes ou appartentes" (to Coste, 1707, G. III, 401-2). Cf. *Théod*. § 314: "Aussi tost que l'on dit: Je meprise les jugements de ma raison par le seul motif de mon bon plaisir, il me plait d'en user ainsi, c'est autant que si l'on disoit: Je prefere mon inclination à mon interest, mon plaisir à mon utilité."
[204] *Animadversiones in p. g. Princ. Cart.*, I, art. 3-35.
[205] «La volonté consiste dans l'inclination à faire quelque chose à proportion du bien qu'elle renferme» (*Théod.*, § 22, cfr. 33). Cf. *Causa Dei*, § 18, G. VI, 441: "Omnis quidem Voluntas bonum habet pro objecto, saltem apparens, at divina Voluntas non nisi bonum simul et verum" ["Every will therefore has as its object the good, which is sometimes apparent, but the will of God does not (exist) apart from the good and also the truth."]
[206] "Il y a encore des efforts qui resultent des perceptions insensibles, dont on ne s'apperçoit pas, que j'aime mieux appeler appetitions que volitions

By thus defining will as the spontaneity of reason, in which the impulse inherent in all spontaneous perception is applied to rational knowledge, he is able to identify will with freedom — intending will, however, not as a simple and autonomous capacity to act without motive, but the totality of *rational motives* and the action resulting from them. "Quaerere, utrum in nostra voluntate sit libertas, idem est ac quaerere utrum in nostra voluntate sit voluntas. Liberum et voluntarium idem significant. Est enim liberum idem quod spontaneum cum ratione, et velle est ob rationem intellectu perceptam ad agendum ferri; quanto autem purior ratio est minusque impetus bruti et confusae perceptionis admistum habet, eo liberior actio est" ("Looking for whether there is freedom in the will also means looking for whether there is will in our will. Free and willing mean the same thing. For free is that which is spontaneous using reason, and to will is to be impelled to act because of reason received from the intellect. But the clearer the reason and the less it is mixed with irrational impetus and misperception, the more free the action is.").[207] "Summa hominis perfectio non magis est quod libere, quam quod cum ratione agit; aut potius idem est utrumque" ("The highest perfection of man is not acting freely any more than it is acting with reason — or rather both are the same thing.").[208]

There are four ways of understanding freedom: First,

(quoyqu'il y ait aussi des appetitions apperceptibles), car on n'appelle actions volontaires que celles dont on peut s'apercevoir et sur lesquelles nostre reflexion peut tomber lorsqu'elles suivent de la consideration du bien et du mal" (*Nouv. Ess.*, 1. II, ch. 21, § 5).

[207] *Animadversiones in p. g. Princ. Cart.*, I, art. 39.

[208] *Ibid.*, I, art. 37, G. IV, 362-63. Cf. *Initia et Spec. Sc. N. Gen.*, G. VII, 109: "La liberté est une spontaneité jointe à l'intelligence. Ainsi ce qu'on appelle spontaneité dans les bestes et dans les autres substances privées d'intelligence, est elevé dans l'homme à un plus haut degré de perfection, et s'appelle liberté."

as contingency, opposed to necessity; and in this sense anything contingent is free (whose opposite, that is, does not impy contradiction). Second, as spontaneity, as opposed to compulsion. An act of will is free or spontaneous when it results directly from a representation, without the influence of external causes modifying it.[209] Third, as perfection, opposed to slavery, limitation, incompleteness; in this sense one is freer the more perfect one is — that is, determined toward the good (the Augustinian anti-Molinist thesis).[210] Fourth, uninfluenced freedom, the capacity to bring something about without any motive whatever — and this form of freedom does not exist.[211] "On peut mêmes dire, que les substances sont d'autant plus libres qu'elles sont

---

[209] "La spontaneité est une contingence sans coaction, ou bien on appelle spontané ce qui est ny necessaire, ny contraint. On appelle Contingence, ce qui n'est point necessaire, ou (ce qui est la même chose) dont l'opposé et possible, n'impliquant aucune contradiction. Contraint est ce dont le principe vient de dehors»" (*Initia et Spec. Sc. N. Gen.*, G. VII, 110). He then asserts that, strictly speaking, there is no exception to this spontaneity, inasmuch as every external impression is part of the world of our representations, and inasmuch as in a metaphysical sense there is no "outside us." Cf. C. III, 403, *Théod.*, §§ 34, 290-91, 301, C. 25.

[210] "Plus on est parfait, plus on est determiné au bien, et aussi plus libre en même temps. Car on a une faculté et connoissance d'autant plus étendues, et une volonté d'autant plus reserée dans les bornes de la parfaite raison" (to Bayle, G. III, 59).

[211] "Le mot de libre est equivoque. Si on l'oppose au necessaire, il n'est autre chose que qui est contingent, pourveu qu'il se fosse en suite de la deliberation. Si on l'oppose à la contrainte, libre est ce qui est une suite de la nature de la chose, autant qu'elle enferme une puissance, et en ce sens on est d'autant plus libre qu'on est plus determiné de soy même, à bien faire. Je tiens que Dieu et nous sommes libres suo quisque modo, de toutes ces deux façons; entierement suivant la premiere, et à mesure de nostre perfection suivant la seconde; mais nous ne saurions estre libres ny aucune autre substance, de la maniere que quelques Philosophes s'imaginent, comme s'il estoit possible de se determiner lorsque tout est egal" (Cf. to Burnett, 1695, G. III, 168). Cf. to Coste, 1707, G. III, 400 ff., *Théod.*, § 288, G. VI, 441, and *Nouv. Ess.*, 1. II. c. 21, § 8, in which there are other forms of freedom as well: the freedom of having (legal) rights and the freedom to act (i.e., being or not being prevented outwardly from performing one's own actions), etc. Here, however, he eliminates these and other mechanical notions of freedom, specifying that the problem does not concern "des actions extérieures, mais l'acte même de vouloir" (§ 11, cf. § 21 and *passim*).

eloignées de l'indifference et determinées par elles mêmes. Et qu'elles approchent d'autant plus de la perfection divine qu'elles ont moins besoin d'estre determinées par dehors. Car Dieu estant la substance la plus libre et la plus parfaite, est aussi le plus determiné par luy même à faire le plus parfait. Mais plus on est ignorant et impuissant, plus on est indifferent. De sorte que le Rien qui est le plus imparfait et le plus eloigné de Dieu, est aussi le plus indifferent et le moins determiné. Or autant que nous avons des lumières et agissons suivant la raison, autant serons nous determinés par les perfections de nostre propre nature, et par consequent nous serons d'autant plus libres que nous serons moins embarrassées du choix... Contentons nous donc d'une liberté souhaittable et approchante de celle de Dieu qui nous rend les plus disposés à bien choisir et à bien faire, et ne pretendons pas la liberté dommageable, pour ne dire chimerique d'estre dans l'incertitude et dans une embarras perpetuel, comme cet Ane de Buridan fameux dans les écoles."[212]

Here as in Spinoza, then, freedom is found in the nature of humans as reasonable and responsive to the absolute reason that constitutes their deepest and truest being. It is not found in the will as a capacity for choice. The will cannot will anything other than what is represented by the intellect: "Et si nous ne remarquons pas tousjours la raison qui nous determine ou plustost par la quelle nous nous determinons, c'est que nous sommes aussi peu capables de nous appercevoir de tout le jeu de nostre esprit et de ses pensées, le plus souvent imperceptibles et confuses, que nous sommes de demêler toutes les machines que la nature fait jouer dans le corps."[213]

---

[212] *Initia et Spec. Sc. N. Gen.*, G. VII, 110-11. Cf. *Nouv Ess.*, 1. II, ch. 21, § 15, *Théod.*, §§ 191,327, *Remarques sur le livre de King*, § 26, Rommel, I, 286-87.
[213] *Nouv. Ess.*, 1. II, ch. 21 § 13.

Leibniz sometimes seems to re-introduce the disconnect between knowledge and will, and an uninfluenced will, when he examines the psychological fact of suspension of the will — that is, of an interruption whereby knowledge is not immediately prolonged into the action that should result from it. But this phenomenon always comes down to the absurdity and shallowness of perception, to an imperfection in it, that is, such that the resulting impetus for action is too weak. Or to the intrusion of new thoughts and new perceptions into a process of deliberation that has already begun.[214] And therefore, strictly speaking, the long and interrupted journey of the mind to the heart is only the difficult path reason (or distinct perception) must take in making its way through confused perceptions (or passions), which fight it for space and at times overwhelm it with their greater violence and "clarity," just as it is about to reach its goal. The thing that opposes the completion of a deliberation is not the will pushing back, but the intrusion of a new thought: "Ils disent qu'après avoir tout connu et tout consideré, il est encor dans leur pouvoir de vouloir, non pas seulement ce qui plaisit le plus, mais encor tout le contraire, seulement pour monstrer leur liberté. Mais il faut considerer qu'encor ce caprice ou entêtement ou du moins cette raison qui les empeche de suivre les autres raisons, entre dans la balance, et leur fait plaire ce que ne leur plairoit pas sans cela, de sorte que le choix est tousjours determiné par la

---

[214] "Quelque perception qu'on ait du bien, l'effort d'agir apres le jugement, qui fait à mon avis l'essence de la volonté, en est distingué: ainsi... il peut être suspendu, et même changé par une nouvelle perception ou inclination qui vient à la traverse, qui en détourné l'esprit, et qui luy fait même faire quelques fois un jugement contraire. C'est ce qui fait que nostre ame a tant de moyens de resister à la verité qu'elle connoit, et qui'il y a un si grand trajet de l'esprit au coeur: sur tout lorsque l'entendement ne procede en bonne partie que par des pensées sourdes, peu capables de toucher... Ainsi la liaison entre le jugement et la volonté n'est pas si necessaire qu'on pourroit penser." Cf. *Théod.*, § 311; *Controversy with Clarke*, G. VII, 391.

perception."²¹⁵

The suspension of choice thus has nothing to do with free will. It arises from the imperfection of the human mind, from the disorder of its perceptions. In a perfect mind it does not occur. "Car de pouvoir se tromper et s'egarer, est un desavantage; et d'avoir un empire sur les passions, est un avantage à la verité, mais qui presuppose une imperfection, savoir la passion même, don Dieu est incapable."²¹⁶ God, or the perfect sage, has no confused perceptions, no passions, no fluctuations that make him indeterminate: "Il ne sauroit ignorer, il ne sauroit douter, il ne sauroit suspendre son jugement; sa volonté est tousjours arrestée, et elle ne le sauroit être que pour le meilleur... le sage agit toujours par principes; il agit tousjours par regles, et jamais par exceptions."²¹⁷ In him there are no intrusions of partial, individual considerations. "Et l'on preferera tousjours le naturel de Caton, dont Vellejus distoit qu'il luy etoit impossible de faire une action malhonnête, à celuy d'un homme qui sera capable de balancer."²¹⁸

This necessity is thus not the necessity of willing, but the necessity of the intellect from which willing flows by its very nature. To influence the will considered in itself, "to will to will," — that is, to determine one's volitions, is not possible, except in the sense that a present deliberation of ours should determine our future perceptions by directing our attention to certain representations rather than to certain others.²¹⁹ And in this way one's own character can be

---

²¹⁵ *Nouv. Ess.*, 1. II, c. 21, § 25. Cf. §§ 27, 47, *Théod.* 326, *Remarques sur le livre de King*, § 25.
²¹⁶ *Théod.*, §337. Cf. §§ 289, 319.
²¹⁷ *Théod.*, §337.
²¹⁸ *Théod.*, § 318. Cf. 228, *Controversy with Clarke*, G. VII, 390, G. VI, 385, etc.
²¹⁹ "Nous ne voulons point vouloir, mais nous voulons faire... cependant... par des actions volontaires nous contribuons souvent indirectement à d'autres actions volontaires et... on peut pourtant faire ensorte par avance, qu'on juge ou veuille avec le temps ce qu'on souhaiteroit de pouvoir vouloir ou juger aujourd huy. On s'attache aux personnes, aux lectures..." (*Nouv. Ess.*, 1. II, ch.

changed, habits created.[220] But here it is clearly always a question of an influence on perceptions, and not on volition,[221] and it also seems clear to me that these influenced perceptions cannot be considered true autonomous forms of knowledge but simply extensions of the mental act that brought them about.

Our volition does not depend on the will, but on the intellect. And Leibniz denies, against Descartes and with Bayle, that internal experience guarantees us the autonomy of the will, and freedom.[222]

The intellect itself depends on the perceptions it has, and cannot supply itself with the ones it wants.[223] It is tied to the causal order of the universe no less than the body is, and it only acts based on reasons. To speak of an action without motive would be at the same level of absurdity as to introduce, as Epicurus did, a *clinamen* that breaks the determinacy of atoms.[224] The process of deliberation that gives rise to action is comparable to the play of a scale "ou les raisons et les inclinations tiennent lieu

---

21, §23). Cfr. § 25, 1. VI, c. 720, § 16, *Théod.*, §§ 51, 64, 301, 327, 404, *Remarques sur le livre de King.* § 24.

[220] *Nouv. Ess.*, 1. II, c. 21, §§ 47, 48, 49, *Théod.*, § 327.

[221] "Les hommes choisissent les obiects par la volonté, mais ils ne choisissent point leur volontés presentes: elles viennent des raisons et des dispositions. Il est vray cependant qu'on se peut chercher de nouvelles raisons et se donner avec le temps de nouvelles dispositions" (*Remarques sur l'ouvrage de Hobbes*, G. VI, 391-92).

[222] *Théod.*, §§ 50, 293, 295, 299, *Disc. de la conf.*, §69, *Remarques sur le livre de King*, § 23.

[223] "Nous ne formons pas nos idées, parce que nous le voulons; elles se forment en nous, elles se forment par nous, non pas en consequence de nostre volonté, mais suivant nostre nature et celle des choses" (*Théod.*, § 403). "on ne peut pas même juger ce qu'on veut" (*Nouv. Ess.*, 1. III, c. 21, § 23).

[224] *Théod.*, §§ 303, 320, 321. Carneades denied this introduction of uninfluenced freedom in bodies but allowed it for the soul. Leibniz fights it: "Comme si l'ame, qui est la siege de la raison, etoit plus capable que le corps d'agir sans etre determinée par quelque raison ou cause, interne ou externe; ou comme si le grand principe, qui porte que rien ne se fait sans cause, ne regardoit que le corps" (*Théod.*, § 322).

de poids."[225] And the case in which the intellect is in an indifferent equilibrium without a reason leading it to choose one side over another is explicitly excluded. Given that each perception is the result of an infinity of causes that extend to the whole universe, in order for knowledge to oscillate between two perfectly balancing sides, it would have to be possible to divide the universe into two absolutely identical parts, which would contradict its infinite nature.[226] This is the basis of the principle of the identity of indiscernables.

The application of these theories to the theological problem of grace is a confirmation of the intellectualist character of Leibnizian morality and its remoteness from any irrationalist position. Here again he does not penetrate the interior of the problem. In his desire to reconcile Catholics and Protestants, Jesuits and Jansenists, and in his repeated statement that it is only a matter of words, Leibniz remained a stranger to the deeper meaning of the controversy.

We shall continue to limit ourselves to the psychological aspect of the question. The distinction of various types of grace (sufficient, irresistible, internal, external) represents an attempt to reconcile reason with revelation and with various dogmas. But it always refers to the objective world, not the subjective — that is, it indicates to what extent God, in order to bring about universal harmony, has provided for the salvation of men, and how he can allow evil, reconcile foreknowledge with freedom, etc. That is, it

---

[225] *Théod.*, § 324.
[226] "Le cas d'un parfait equilibre est chimerique, et n'arrive jamais, l'univers ne pouvant point estre miparti ny coupé en deux parties egales et semblables... L'univers n'a point de centre, et ses parties sont infiniment variées; ainsi jamais le cas arrivera, oú tout sera parfaitement egal et frappera egalement de part et d'autre" (to Coste, 1707, G. III, 402-403). Cf. *Théod.*, §§ 35, 46, 49, 303-7.

falls within the realm of organization in the best of all possible worlds, of theodicy.²²⁷ But what grace means for humanity, how it acts on the soul, how it affects the will; the transformation, the reversal, the inversion of values such that Paul and Augustine made it the centerpiece of religious life to the exclusion of every other more rational and more human element — of all this there is no trace in Leibniz. He is completely deaf to this line of thinking. For him grace is the disposition of the human intellect to know and appreciate God's goodness (that is, the harmony of things) and to act accordingly, without allowing justice to be disturbed by the passions or by confused and partial visions.²²⁸ There is nothing supernatural and supra-rational

---

²²⁷ "Nostrae etiam bonae qualitates (sive fidem cum nostris, sive opera cum Pontificiis intelligas) non sunt meritoriae, sed conditiones quibus alligare salutem Deo gratiose placuit. Verumenimvero videtur aliqua superesse difficultas circa arcanam dispensationem mediorum salutis, qua fit ut alii per varias vitae occasiones disponantur ac suaviter seu salva libertate perducantur ad conditionem obtinendam, alii secus. Hic ergo redeundum est haud dubie ad βάθος Pauli, altitudinem scilicet divitiarum et sapientiae divinae, non quasi Deus alios ad fidem poenitentiamque finalem perducere statuat, alios secus, decreto ita absoluto ut omni causa impulsiva careat, quale in sapientem non cadit; sed quod rationes sint, nobis occultae, Deo tamen dignissimae et cum justitia ejus ac bonitate maxime convenientes" ["Even our good qualities (think of faith among our own people or good works among the 'Catholics') are not meritorious, but conditions by which it pleased God to 'graciously' grant salvation. In truth, some difficulty seems to remain about the arcane dispensation of the means of salvation, whereby it happens that some through the various moments of life are willing and gentle or by redeemed freedom are led to attain this condition, while others are not. Here we must undoubtedly return to the 'bathos' (depth) of Paul — that is, the height of divine riches and wisdom, not as if God decides to bring some to faith and final penance, but not others, with a deliberation so absolute that it lacks all 'impulsive' cause — which does not happen to the wise — but because there are reasons, hidden to us, that are very worthy of God and befitting of his justice and especially of his goodness"] (Cf. to Fabricius, 1698, F. d. C., II, 196). Cf. Schrecker, 70, 95, 97-98, 107-8, *Théod.*, pref. (G. VI, 38) *passim*.
²²⁸ "Plato voluptatem dicebat escam malorum" ["Plato said that pleasure is the lure of evil."] La Grace y oppose un plaisirs plus grand... l'on aime un objet à mesure qu'on en sent les perfections; rien ne surpasse les perfections Divines: d'oú il suit que la charité et l'amour de Dieu donnent le plus grand plaisir qui se puisse concevoir, à mesure qu'on est penetré de ces sentiments, qui ne sont

about it; it is reason itself in its purity and harmoniousness, as granted or not granted by God according to the inscrutable order of supreme balances. It is not a force that sweeps beyond all intellectual thought or conviction, but rather it is intellectual thought and conviction itself, and the effort to know reality.[229] Sufficient grace (the consequence of the "antecedent will" of God) is the possibility everyone has of being saved. Irresistible grace (God's "consequent will") is what actually ensures that some are saved and others are not.[230] And for the person touched by grace, "ad agnitionem suae miseriae attentionemque animi et firmum propositum scrutandae ac sequendae veritatis salutaris excitatus, et missis aut posthabitis aliis cogitationibus et affectibus, ac mundi carnisque documentis, totus in salutis curam incumbens, ex naturali lumine animadvertit quae sit lex voluntasque Dei" ("Because of the knowledge of his misery and the attentiveness of his soul and the resolute purpose to seek

---

pas ordinaires aux hommes, parce qu'ils son occupés et remplis des objets qui se rapportent à leur passions" (*Théod.*, § 279).

[229] "Il ne s'attribuait rien qui fût au-dessus du vulgaire, que la seule application: Car, dit-il, les hommes ne different que par là: c'est en quoy consiste principalement la grace qui les distingue, puisqu'on peut dire que la nature les a tous également favorisés. Car Dieu donne l'attention à ceux qu'il veut retirer de la corruption publique: il ne leur faut ny des révélations ny des miracles: il n'est pas nécessaire même qu'ils ayent des connaissances plus relevées que le commun, ny de la nature, ny de Dieu; car les semences des plus importantes vérités sont dans l'ame du moindre paysan: qu'il faut seulement les ramasser et les cultiver avec soin." Baruzi, *Trois dialogues*, 17.

[230] "Dieu, et tour autre Sage bienfaisant, est incliné à tout bien qui est faisable, et... cette inclination est proportionnée à l'excellence de ce bien; et cela... par une Volonté Antecedente, comme on l'appelle, mais qui n'a pas tousjours son entier effect: parceque ce Sage doit avoir encor beaucoup d'autres inclinations. Ainsi c'est le resultat de toutes les inclinations ensemble, qui fait sa volonté pleine et decretoire... On peut donc fort bien dire avec les anciens, que Dieu veut sauver tous les hommes suivant sa volonté antecedente, et non pas suivant sa volonté consequente, qui ne manque jamais d'avoir son effect." Cf. *Théod.*, § 80. See the translation of these concepts into the theological terms sufficient grace and irresistible grace in *Syst. Theol.*, 42 ff., *Théod.*, §§ 134, 282. Cf. also Schrecker, 9, 70 ff.

and follow the truth of salvation, driven by other duties and projects and affections and by the testimonies of the world and the flesh, all being focused toward healing salvation, he understands through natural law what God's law and will is.").[231] In other words, such a person behaves wisely and acts based on motives that grace allows him to see. "La grace ne fait que donner des impressions qui contribuent à faire vouloir par des motifs convenables, tel que seroit une attention, un dic cur hic, un plaisir prevenant. Et l'on voit clairement que cela ne donne aucune atteinte à la liberté, non plus que pourroit faire un ami, qui conseille et qui fournit des motifs."[232] Even when grace is understood as something superior to mere natural intellect, as extraordinary knowledge,[233] it always has a cognitive character, it is a "light" that is offered to the mind to guide one's actions.

Grace is an opening of the intellect — it is being placed in certain conditions that lead one to act in a good way. This dual character appears in the distinction between internal and external grace. The former consists of "mentis illuminatione et voluntatis directione; utraque perficitur attentione animi ad sua officia, quae maximum est divinae gratiae donum" ("the enlightenment of the mind and the direction of the will; both are achieved by

---

[231] *Syst. Theol.* 50.
[232] *Théod.*, 298. Cf. Baruzi, *Trois dialogues*, 19. "Pianese: Dieu donne sa grace à qui il veut. Eremite: Ouy sans doute, et à eux qui la veuillent. P: Le vouloir même est une grace de Dieu. E: mais le vouloir ne consistant que dans une forte résolution de s'appliquer à ce qui regarde son salut, il est inutile de chercher la source de la volonté. Car que peut-on souhaiter d'avantage de Dieu et de la nature? Ne suffit-il pas de n'avoir besoin que de volonté ou d'attention pour etre ou heureux ou inexcusable?"
[233] "Gratia haec sufficiens est vel ordinaria, per verbum et sacramenta, vel extraordinaria, Deo relinquenda, quali erga Paulum est usus" ["Such grace is sufficient or ordinary, through the Word and the sacraments, or extraordinary, in which case it must be granted by God, as he did with Paul"] (*Causa Dei*, §110, G. VI, 455).

the attention of the soul to its duties, which is the greatest gift of divine grace."). The second is composed of the "circumstantiae, quae... consistunt... in sorte nascendi, educatione, conversatione, casibus vitae, quibus fit ut alii aliis agant, feliciores reddantur, non tantum in rebus humanis, sed etiam in spiritualibus atque divinis" ("circumstances such as the fortunes of birth and upbringing, comparisons and instances in life by which it happens that some people relate to others and make them happier, not only in human affairs, but also in spiritual and divine affairs.").[234]

Development of the mind, direction of the will, favorable circumstances — these are the instruments, this is the phenomenology of grace for Leibniz. It is grace that therefore does not impose itself in any way as a supernatural necessity, but rather as a natural order, in which, as in all natural things, determination does not exclude contingency and freedom.[235]

Essentially, grace that saves is nothing other than the sum total of the internal and external arrangements that

---

[234] G. III, 37. Cf. also *Théod.*, § 283: "Il ne paroit point necessaire... que tous ceux qui sont sauvés, le souent tousjours par une grace efficace par elle même, independamment des circonstances." Cf. §§ 99, 105, 286, G. VI, 385, and the letter to Schmidt, 1698: "Opus est tum gratia interna, tum gratia, ut sic dicam, externa, id est, occasionibus et circumstantiis, quibus mentes hominum ad bona vel mala, salvo licet arbitrio, plurimum inclinantur." ["It is necessary that inward grace and outward grace, as it is spoken of, should happen in such a way that in occasions and circumstances men's minds very much lean toward good or evil as is said of free will."] F. d. C. II, 203.

[235] "Itaque nec peccatum originale, nec aliae nostrae pravae dispositiones faciunt, ut necessarius sit peccandi actus, etsi tanta sit nostra ad peccandum inclinato... Vicissim nec gratia Dei quantacumque libertatem nostram tollit; aut nobis bonae actionis necessitatem imponit" ["Therefore, neither original sin nor our evil dispositions make the act of sinning at all necessary, even though our inclination to sin is very great. On the other hand, not even divine grace, however great it may be, takes away our freedom or imposes on us the necessity of doing good"] Cf. G. III, 37. Cf. Schrecker, 87.

carry a human being to salvation. It is the fact of salvation itself, seen in the totality of its relationships, through its premises, means, and instruments.[236] The concept of salvation not derived from anybody's free will but from the inscrutable will of God might suggest a Leibnizian Augustinianism, and his contact with Jansenism. But the two conceptions are very different.[237] The dependence and non-autonomy of the will has an intellectualist rather than mystical character in Leibniz and is more akin to the doctrine of Thomas Aquinas. He is flatly opposed to the uninfluenced free will of the Molinists,[238] but this does not place him anywhere near Jansen or Arnauld. Grace for him does not affect the will irresistibly, independently of knowledge. On the contrary, it affects it precisely because the will depends on knowledge. And not irresistibly, but rather with a form of indeterminacy that characterizes causality in the realm of the contingent —

---

[236] "In negotio Electionis non jam videtur primaria difficultas in eo esse, an Deus decernat salvare quos fidem vivam finalem praescit habituros, sed praeterea in ipso decreto conferendae gratiae ex qua nascitur talis fides" ["In the activity of Election there does not seem to be a 'primacy' problem — that is, whether God decides beforehand to save those he knows will have a final living faith, but 'later' in the making the decision to grant the grace from which such faith arises."] Cf. to Schmidt, 1698, F. d. C. II, 203. Cf. *Théod*, Pref., G VI, 45-46: "La conversion est le pur ouvrage de la grace de Dieu... Les circonstances aussi contribuent plus ou moins à nostre attention, et aux mouvements que naissent dans l'ame, et le concours de toutes ces choses jointes à la mesure de l'impression, et à l'etat de la volonté, determine l'effect de la grace, mais sans le rendre necessaire."
[237] Sainte-Beuve called Leibniz "le moins Janséniste de tous les esprits" (Port-Royal, I. III, c. 18).
[238] "A l'egard du Jansenisme je trouve que quelques uns de leurs Antagonistes poussent l'affaire trop loin, non seulement en persecutant et décriant ceux qu'ils font passer pour Jansenistes, mais encor en tirant des conséquences sur des points de dottrine ou plustost de philosophie, qui sont absolument fausses et mêmes contraires au bon sens, par exemple, il nous veuillent faire accroire qu'il y a une certaine liberté qui consiste dans une telle indifference que la volonté se peut determiner sur l'un ou l'autre des contradictoires sans aucun motif veritable... c'est à dire qu'il y a quelque effect sans cause" (to the Landgrave of Hesse, Rommel, I, 286-87).

it inclines, that is, but does not necessitate. It is certain but does not exclude the possibility of being otherwise.[239]

Leibniz often spoke sympathetically of the Jansenists, and he admired and respected the austere lives and depth of knowledge of religious concepts of Arnauld and his followers, with whom he openly sided against the Jesuits — as he always sided with victims of religious intolerance when circumstances allowed him to do so without danger. He sometimes saw Jansenism as one of the internal reform movements that would favor unification of the Church with the protestants.[240]

But on the question of grace he differs sharply from them. Whether between Jesuits and Jansenists or Catholics and Protestants, he wants to take a conciliatory, intermediate position — which he explicitly calls Thomist[241] — that aims to reduce the importance of the dispute. And while in the former he reproaches the autonomy of the will and uninfluenced free will, in the latter he does not accept the arbitrariness of God's action, his saving or damning without reasons. The theory of inclination

---

[239] Cf. Schrecker, 97: "Il n'est point besoin que la grace nous necessite; ny qu'elle soit irresistible. Car quoyque toute bonne impulsion vienne de la grace de Dieu, neantmoins les resistence, et empechemens peuvent venir de nous; lors même qu'ils ne viennent point actuellement."

[240] "L'Eglise a deux grandes obligations à Monsieur Arnauld et a ses amis, l'une d'avoir establi excellement ce grand principe de la necessité de l'amour de Dieu sur toutes choses, l'autre d'avoir travaillé avec succés contre les corrupteurs de la Morale Chretienne; j'espere que d'autres suivront ses traces et qu'on arrivera un jour à la Reforme de tant d'abus assez publiés, que le Concile de Trente même semble desapprouver" (to the Landgrave of Hesse, Rommel, I, 365). Cf. also *Ibid.*, I, 373, *passim*; F. d. C., I, 260 ff.; Stein, 318. Against Jesuit morality, and the practice of mental reservation, see the cautious remarks in Rommel, I, 280 ff. 306-7, II, 110, 141-42, 177 ff., 224. Cf. also G. III, 211, and, against the casuistry of the Jesuits, *Trois dialogues*, 26. He does, however, appreciate the Jesuits' dogmatic tolerance as opposed to the Jansenists' strictness.

[241] "Pour moy je tiens qu'on ne sçauroit donner tort en tout, ny à St. Augustin, ny à Molina, et qu'il y a quelques fois un milieu à prendre. Ce sentiment des Thomistes me paroist assez raisonnable" (Rommel, II, 411). Cf. G. III, 58.

without necessity seems to him to resolve the controversy,[242] and it enables him to envision a possibility of resistance on the part of humanity to the lights and circumstances offered by grace — a possibility that preserves human responsibility in salvation and damnation. This purpose is served by the distinction between *conversio* and *perseveratio*. The latter, which admits of a certain human cooperation with grace, may be absent, and it is its presence or absence decides the question of election or non-election.[243] In this way Leibniz is able to speak of a

---

[242] "J'avoue qu les disputes sur la Grace ne sont pas de cette importance et que peu de gens y entrent, et peut estre qu'il y a quelque chose à dire de part et d'autre; les uns [the Jesuits] rendent l'homme trop independant, et les autres [the Jansenists] donnent de Dieu une idée, qui n'est pas assez conforme à sa bonté; mais comme ils desavouent ces consequences, on peut pardonner aux uns et aux autres les erreurs de pure speculation" (to the Landgrave of Hesse, Rommel, I, 305). Cf. II, 317. He instead regards as extremely important the dispute between the Jansenists and Jesuits over the love of God, which concerns "the essence of morality and piety," while he holds the other to be a question of pure speculation (*ibid.*, II, 367). Cf. Schrecker, 95, 40, 66, *Théod.*, pref (G VI, 46). Cf. also Pellison's letter of 27 VII 1692 (F. d. C., I, 306-7): "J'avoue qu'il y a certaines choses dans la théologie de M. Arnauld que jen ne sçaurois gouster. Il est vray que je suis du sentiment de saint Augustin, de saint Thomas et de leurs sectateurs à l'egard de la predetermination. Cependant... j'ay été longtemps en doute s'il y avait moyen de sauver la contingence et d'éviter la necessité... mais enfin... j'ay vu comment ces raisons inclinent sans necessité... Mais, à l'egard de la grace et de quelques autres matières, M. Arnauld et ses amis ont quelques sentimens un peu durs dont je ne voy pas assez de preuves, et les opinions des jésuites ne sont pas toujours si blasmables que ces Messieurs le disent." Cf. also the clear statement of the question *Théod.*, §§ 39 ff., 76 ff., 280-81, 366; F. d. C. II, XLIV, 203, etc.

[243] "Gratia rursus distingui potest in gratiam conversionis, et gratiam peseveretionis, et haec in perseverationem qualemcumque et finalem, quae novissima coincidit cum gratia Electionis. Gratia conservationis tam necessaria est, ut ne ullos quidem bonos motus spirituales habere possimus, nisi Deo excitante, cum mortuorum instar in spiritualibus nos habeamus. At in conversis gratia perseveretionis, quae in exercitio fidei, spei, charitatisque consistit, non omnia peragit, sed cooperationem nostram, postquam semel nova vita donati sumus, admittit."
["Grace can be divided into the grace of conversion and the grace of perseverance, and this can be distinguished in turn into common perseverance and perseverance to the end, which, more peculiarly, coincides with the grace of election. The grace of preservation is so necessary that we cannot even experience good spiritual inspirations except by divine initiative, since we have the greatness of

grace offered by God and refused by man,[244] and can affirm that no one can be absolutely assured of election, since each person must doubt to the last his own continued existence.[245] From this point of view, grace becomes nothing more than one of the determining elements of the human personality, an element that might even be limited or superseded by others.

The indissoluble union of knowledge and will makes it impossible for Leibniz to conceive of a faith independent of deeds, just as it is impossible for him to conceive of a love of God that is not at the same time knowledge of God. Love, knowledge, charity are the same thing, different aspects of an indistinguishable spiritual act. As between Catholics and Protestants, here too he sees no irremediable disagreement. And, just as he does not accept an "atonement" in which faith is purely an intellectual act without practical consequences, neither can he admit that the outward act is sufficient on its own, unaccompanied by a profound

---

the dead in spiritual things. But in converted men the grace of perseverance, which consists in the exercise of faith, hope and charity, does not accomplish everything; it admits our cooperation, after we have once and for all received new life."] Cf. G. III, 38, Cf. Schrecker, 119.

[244] "[Dieu] donne des secours à tous pour se convertir et pou perseverer, et ces secours sont suffisans [grace sufficient] dans ceux qui ont bonne volonté, mais ils ne sont pas tousjours suffisans pour la donner. Les hommes obtiennent cette bonne volonté, soit par des secours particuliers, soit par des circostances qui font reussir les secours generaux [irresistible grace]. Il [Dieu] ne peut s'empecher d'offrir encor des remedes qu'il sait qu'on refusera, et qu'on en sera plus coupable" (*Théod.*, § 134). "Comme nostre corruption n'est point absolument invincible... il faut dire de même que nous ne sommes pas aidés invinciblement; et quelque efficace que soit la Grace Divine, il y a lieu de dire qu'on y peut resister. Mais lorsqu'elle se trouvera victorieuse en effect, il est certain et infallible par avance qu'on cedera à ses attraits... Ainsi il faut tousjours distinguer entre l'infallible et le necessaire" (*Théod.*, § 279). Cf. *Syst. Theol*, 48, *Théod.*, § 269.

[245] "Etsi enim nemo pius electionem suam in dubium revocare debeat, non datur tamen absoluta perseverandae finalis futurae certitudo, tanta scilicet quanta datur praesentis nostrae conversionis." ["For although no 'pious' person has to retract his or her election, nevertheless the absolute certainty of final future persistence is not given in the way the certainty of our present conversion is given"] (G. III, 38). Cf. *Syst. Theol.*, 62 ff., Schreker, 119.

internal transformation.[246] His positive mind cannot allow miraculous salvation that shows no sign of human will — indeed that is not determined by it.[247] A faith is inconceivable to him that saves independently of deeds, that calls to heaven the dissolute and intemperate and damns to hell the wise and the pious.[248] And this is not because deeds are

---

[246] "A cet égard [concerning atonement] des sentiments de quelques Catholiques me paroissent plus raisonnables que ceux de quelques Protestants. Car la charité met plustost un homme en estat de grace que la foy, excepté ce qui est necessaire au salut, necessitate medii; un erreur de foy, ou heresie ne damne peutestre que parcequ'elle blesse la charité et l'union. En effet ceux qui demandent la foy non seulement dans la creance, qui est un acte d'entendement, mais encor in fiducia, qui est un acte de volonté, font à mon avis un melange de la foy et de la charité car cette confiance bien prise est le veritable amour de Dieu. C'est pourquoy je ne m'étonne pas, s'ils disent qu'une telle foy est justifiante. J'ay tousjours extremement approuvé le sentiment de ceux qui doutent fort qu'on puisse estre justifié par la seule Attrition avec le Sacrement, sans faire jamais un acte du souverain amour de Dieu" (Rommel, I, 277-78). It should be kept in mind that this letter is directed to the Catholic Landgrave of Hesse. With Bossuet, in the heat of the discussion, he would instead stress that it was the Catholic Church that modified and purified its doctrine, in view of the justness of the Protestant thesis (F. d. C., I, 267, 299, 303, 377). Cf. also F. d. C., I, 8, II, 173-74, 184 ff., *Trois dialogues*, 24, Klopp, VIII, 64, 65, 67 ff.
[247] "Dans ceux qui ont la vraye Religion sans en avoir des preuves, la grace interieure suppléera au defaut des motifs de la credibilité... On a des histoires applaudies dans l'Eglise Romaine de personnes, qui ont esté resuscitées exprès pour ne point manquer des secours salutaires. Mais Dieu peut secourir les ames par l'operation interne du S. Esprit, san avoir besoin d'un si grand miracle; et ce qu'il y a de bon et de consolant pour le genre humain, c'est que pour se mettre dans l'estat de la grace de Dieu, il ne faut que la bonne volonté, mais sincere et serieuse. Je reconnois qu'on n'a pas même cette bonne volonté sans la grace de Dieu, d'autant que tout bien naturel ou surnaturel vient de luy: mais c'est tousjours assés qu'il ne faut qu'avoir la volonté et qu'il est impossible que Dieu puisse demander une condition plus facile et plus raisonnable" (*Nouv. Ess.*, 1. IV, c. 20, § 1).
[248] "Errant multo gravius, qui solis electis tribuunt gratiam, fidem, justificationem, regenerationem, tanquam (repugnante experientia)... nullus electus semelque vere justificatus in crimen seu in peccatum proaereticum relabi posset; vel, ut alii malunt, tanquam in mediis sceleribus gratiam regenerationis electus non amitteret" ["They are very wrong who attribute grace, faith, atonement, and rebirth to the elect alone as if, perish the thought, no elect who had truly atoned once and for all, could relapse into crime and heretical sin; or, as others prefer, as if the elect did not accept the grace of rebirth out of guilt"] (*Causa Dei*, § 130, G. VI, 458).

decisive, but because faith determines a psychological situation in which corresponding deeds cannot help but follow. The discussion revolving around atonement is pointless for him. It is absurd, he says, to want to establish a dispute of privilege between faith and charity. "Quemadmodum enim certum est fidem sine caritate esse mortuam, ita quoque constat caritatem sine fide (dilectionem sine cognitione) esse nullam: et proinde fides est caritatis requisitum, caritas fidei complementum."[249] Charity is simply the practical consequence of what has been learned through faith. Faith is a determinate act of knowledge; charity is the resulting action. The controversy arises from viewing the two things as separate. And when we say that faith justifies, we mean faith with its consequences, faith "vive ou formé," made into will — which is then nothing other than charity.[250]

Sometimes, however, Leibniz cannot help but recognize that his reduction of typical forms of religious irrationality (grace, faith) to phenomena of pure intellectual or empirical knowledge constitutes a misunderstanding of religious problems themselves. He recognizes that faith, as commonly understood, is something different from normal knowledge, and that if it is not pure will, it comes close to will in its immediate intuitive and indemonstrable character.[251] He is compelled to admit, after

---

[249] ["For just as it is certain that faith is dead without charity, so also it is clear that charity without faith (love without knowledge) is nothing, and therefore faith is the requirement of charity, and charity is the fulfillment of faith."] *Syst theol.* 56, 58. Cfr. *Trois Dialogues*, 22: "Celui qui aime Dieu veritablement sur toutes choses ne manquera pas d'exécuter ce qu'il sçait estre conforme à ses ordres. C'est pouquoy il faut commecer par cet amour puisque la charité et la justice en son des suites inmanquables."
[250] *Syst. Theol.*, 56, Klopp, VIII, 82, 72: "Les protestans mettent encor la foy dans la volonté, et par consequent ils luy attribuent des effects que l'auteur [Father Spee] icy n'attribue qu'à la dilection."
[251] "Equidem fatendum est secundum receptas quoque notiones fidem sive assensum, de voluntate aliqua ratione participare... et videmus saepe homines

lengthy discussion on the need for "credible grounds" to justify the authority of Scripture before the court of reason, and that in any case, "la Foy Divine elle même, quand elle est allumée dans l'ame, est quelque chose de plus qu'une opinion, et ne depend pas des occasions ou des motifs qui l'ont fait naitre; elle va au delà de l'entendement, et s'empare de la volonté et du coeur, pour nous faire agir avec chaleur et avec plaisir, comme la loy de Dieu le commande, sans qu'on ait plus besoin de penser aux raisons."[252] And elsewhere he opposes faith based on grounds of credibility, the "grace interne du S. Esprit" that "y supplée immediatement d'une maniere surnaturelle, et c'est ce qui fait ce que les Theologiens appellent proprement une foy divine. Il est vray que Dieu ne la donne jamais que lorsque ce qu'il fait croire est fondé en raison; autrement il detruiroit le moyens de connoistre la verité, et ouvriroit la porte à l'Enthousiasme," and he explains this internal grace and divine faith as an immediate and instinctive form of knowledge.[253]

These are concessions that he occasionally offers up, hardly ever stopping to give an explanation for them.[254] He

---

aliquid pro vero habere, etiam si rationem sententiae suae reddere non possint, imo nullam unquam habuerint... ita ut revera assensus rationibus destitutus consistat in eo mentis statu quo fit ut qui eum habent, perinde affecti, atque ad agendum patiendumque compositi sunt, ac illi qui rationum sibi sunt conscii, imo aliquando efficacius." ["Certainly it must be said that in the second place, the notions learned concerning the will participate in some way in the concept of faith or spiritual accord, and we see people who regard something as true, despite the fact that they cannot justify their thinking, indeed they have none, so that in reality spiritual accord, deluded by reason, consists in that state of mind whereby those who have it, who have been provided with it, are led to act and endure like those who are conscious of reason, indeed even more effectively."] *Syst. Theol.*, 58, 60.
[252] *Disc. sur la conf.*, § 29.
[253] *Nouv Ess.*, 1. IV, c. 18 (G. V, 480, cf. 492).
[254] Thus, for example, in a letter to the Landgrave of Hesse (G. II, 83) in which he seeks to explain the use of the natural and rational sciences in order to know God, he adds, incidentally, that all this is referred to as "la lumiere de la grace mise à part," and continues: "J'avoue que tout cela ne sert de rien sans la grace,

approximates these phenomena to those of taste and art (i.e. of confused perceptions),[255] and explains these facts based on the greater clarity and force of acquiescence with which certain uncontrolled impressions impose themselves, as compared to the deafness of reason.[256] These are arguments we are already familiar with which are, however, better suited to phenomena that Leibniz can easily regard as pre-rational and inferior to reason than they are to the justification of supra-rational activities.

These concepts also allow him to admit, in a subordinate way, the possibility of salvation of ordinary people without intelligence.[257] But he strongly repudiates any

---

et que Dieu donne la grace à des gens qui n'ont jamais songé à ces meditations; mais Dieu veut aussi que nous n'omettions rien du nostre, et que nous employons selon les occasions chacun selon la vocation les perfections qu'il a données à la nature humaine."

[255] "Par exemple, on ne sçauroit tousjours dire aux autres ce qu'on trouve d'agréable ou de dégoûtant dans une personne, dans un tableau, dans un sonnet, dans un ragoust: c'est pour cela qu'on dit qu'il ne faut pas disputer des gousts; c'est par la mesme raison qu'on ne sçauroit faire comprendrà un aveugle né ce que c'est que la couleur" (*Controversy with Pellisson*, F. d. C., I, 58).

[256] *Syst. Theol.*, 60, compares these phenomena with the fear of ghosts, which cannot be overcome through rational arguments. "Itaque in illis theoretica quaedam opinio, in his assensus practicus magis esse videtur, quem potissimum in fide desiderari constat" ["So in those a theoretical opinion, in these instead there seems to me to be more of a practical approval which largely consists of being desired in the faith."]

[257] "Il est vray, que, graces à Dieu, dans ce qui importe le plus et qui regarde summam rerum, le bonheur et la misere, on n'a pas besoin de tant de connoissances, d'aides et d'adresses... mais en recompense, il faut plus de fermeté et d'habitude dans ce qui regarde ce grand point de la felicité et de la vertu, pour prendre tousjours de bonnes resolutions et pour les suivre. En un mot, pour le vray bonheur moins ce connoissance suffit avec plus de bonne volonté: de sorte que le plus grand idiot y peut parvenir aussi aisement que le plus docte et les plus habile." Cf. *Nouv. Ess.*, 2. II, c. 21, § 68; cf. 1. VI, c. 18, § 1, c. 20, §1. This is not, as it might appear, a matter of a disconnect between knowledge and will. It is still a question of differentiation within the actual cognitive-active act itself, in which one moment or another may from time to time be accentuated. Cf. *Syst. Theol.*, 62, where after defining irrational faith as "assensus practicus," he nevertheless insists on distinguishing it from practice proper: "omnino a spe et caritate ac fiducia filiali distingui potest

preeminence or primacy of intuitive and irrational faith,[258] and even in the rare cases in which he admits it, he accommodates it and subordinates it to positive faith, as verified by facts and documents.[259] In conclusion, grace — this fact which Leibniz considers as belonging to the reality of the world and framing itself in laws that, while inscrutable to us, are nonetheless real and absolute — does not produce in the human soul anything that differs, except in degree, from normal cognitive-volitional activity. Here, too, Leibniz accepts the introduction of God's supernatural agency, provided that this is reduced to an indefinite extension of natural

---

quibus generalia nobis singulatim applicamus" ["it can be entirely distinguished from the hope, charity, and filial trust by which we individually achieve things in general."] In the fragment *De Justitia* (Mollat, 35 ff.) he also considers people to be just who, though without being knowledgeable, are "promptus obtemerare sapienti" ["ready to obey the wise"]. And elsewhere he posits religion as a substitute for wisdom, which "aliquid honestati (i.e., to the second degree of justice] superaddit" ["adds something to honesty"] (Mollat, 89); cf. *Disc. de la conf.*, § 40.

[258] Speaking of Tertulliano's "certum quia impossibile" ["certain because impossible,"] and of the saying that in matters of faith one must pluck out one's eyes to see clearly he says: "Ces saillies font tort à la religion, qui doit estre raisonnable et fondée en raison" (to Queen Sofie Charlotte, G. VI, 524). Cf. also *Disc. de la conf.* § 50.

[259] "Ceux qui se fondent sur cette lumière, ne peuvent demander d'autre examen à ceux qui se fondent sur une lumière contraire, que celuy de la propre coscience d'un chacun; sçavoir s'il dit vray et s'il sent effectivement la lumière dont il se vante. Mais, comme cette lumière intérieure prétendue est sujette à caution, et que l'examen de conscience sur ce sujet est assez difficile, je voudrois que M. Pellisson eust traité exactement ce point important, en nous expliquant les marques interieures del la lumière divine qui la distiguent de l'illusion... En attendant cet éclaircissement, venons aux raisons explicables" (*Controversy with Pellissson*, F. d. C. I, 59). And later, p. 102: "Je confesse que les motifs inexplicables sont suspect naturellement, et qu'on doit s'en défier." Cfr. Baruzi, *Trois dialogues*, p. 24: "J'avoue que toute action agréable à Dieu ne se fait que par sa grace, mais on est tousjours plus seur de l'obtenir, en la cherchant par les voies convenables, et par choix, qu'en attendant des recontres. Ce cui est même contre le devoir; c'est pourquoy celuy qui est averti de cecy peche gravement quand il détourne ses pensées du soin de rechercher les moyens de parvenir à cet amour qui est la voye du salut."

law. His sporadic contacts with the irrational only enhance the unity of human spiritual reality as he conceives it — as a joint intellectual and moral act of participation, an adaptation to reality. An act whose fundamental explications are to be found in its tendency toward perfection and harmony, in the pleasure that accompanies it, and in the effort of accomplishment that concludes it. It is an act which, through its intimate complexity and infinite gradations, unites in itself and allows us to justify any psychic phenomenon, so that nothing escapes it, and nothing can be opposed to it in a dualism of terms.

Instinct, passion, utility (or *pleasure*), *taste* (or *art*), *will* (or *arbitrariness*), *grace and faith* represent *the scale of activities, from lowest to highest, that from time to time present themselves as contrary to reason.* Either they are inferior to it and to be removed as obstacles to its progress, parallel to it and claiming a right to life alongside it, or superior and transcending its limits, revealing a world it is cut off from. And this opposition comes to Leibniz, often as a polemic against the doctrines and schools of the time: Quietism, Cartesianism, Molinism, Jansenism, mysticism.

But Leibniz is able to eliminate all these contrasts among mental faculties, all these "transcendences" with respect to reason, precisely because for him reason is more mobile, more complex than the mathematical reason of Cartesianism. He applies to the nature of the mind *the continuity, the unbroken transition, the progression from each law to a larger law, which he believes he can discern as the deepest essence of the natural world.* That this same *continuity* and expansion is not so much a law of nature as a requirement of the mind in the consideration of nature itself, he does not suspect. Or rather he makes no distinction between the one and the other and considers mind and nature as homogeneous parts of objective reality. Thus, one conclusion of this chapter on the faculties of the *mind* is that *there is no real epistemology in Leibniz.* An act of the mind is neither an elaboration and modification of the real, nor an apprehension and mirroring of it. It is an *integral element of reality itself.* The *representation* ascribed to the monad, as we shall see better further on, is merely an *index of the totality of the universe* contained in it.

And this reality that is the action of the mind proceeds, like the laws of nature, in ever-widening syntheses and ever more universal harmonies. The *continuous passage between the passions and reason* is made possible by this indefinite procedure whereby previously achieved perfection is rejected as partial. In this way passion is given a positive character — that of tending toward unilateral perfection, even as its autonomy is denied. On the other hand, the unitary complexity of the mental act, the organic quality whereby it encompasses all aspects and functions of the mind, makes it possible to consider all the forms that had been tentatively constituted as autonomous as instances of it. With this Leibniz strikes a decisive blow against the psychology of "faculties" of the mind, intended as entities in their own right that act independently.[260] The harmony and beauty that make up the character of perfection offer him a way of viewing pleasure as a necessary accompaniment of any mental act, and of firmly binding to any form of rationality or morality the utility that had seemed irreconcilably opposed to it.

---

[260] "Quand elles [les facultés de l'âme] seroint des Estres réels et distincts, elles ne sauroient passer pour des Agens réels, qu'en parlant abusivement. Ce ne sont pas les facultés ou qualités, qui agissent, mais les Substances par les facultés" (*Nouv. Ess.,* 1. II, c. 21, § 6).

The respective interplay and the greater or lesser accentuation of the characters of clarity and distinction vs obscurity and confusion, serve to explain all apparent detachment between knowledge and will, and to eliminate any autonomy of the will. Similarly, together with the concept of habit, they account for all intuitive, immediate, irrational forms of contact with reality; from instinct to sensory or artistic taste, from inspiration to faith.

Humanism, along with reform and the Renaissance, had worked toward establishing "autonomies" in the world of the mind: autonomies of art, politics (that is, economics), and religious experience, sufficient in themselves and independent of other aspects of the mind.

The 17th century, with its rationalism and its constructive and unitary spirit, turned the problem on its head. Leibniz had every right to replace the word autonomy with the word Organism. His anthropology, over and above his metaphysics, led him to conceive of a unitary person, composed of a single mental substance, with a will linked to knowledge, and with knowledge consisting of perceptions tending toward ever greater totality — a single mental act, with all the infinite gradations between the two ideal terms of an absolute rationality identified with God. An active, passionate rationality, full of the pleasure of perfection achieved and tending toward new perfection, and a moral criterion based on the essence of each individual in the determination of his or her personality.

PART FOUR

10. SOME LETTERS TO URSULA ON LEIBNIZ

Varese, 14 Nov 1938

My own Ursula,

You can imagine how I flung myself on the books you sent me, which came yesterday. They are everything to me and now that I have them, I am better able to pass the time. Thanks also for your choices. You did very well; they just suit my tastes: a little physics, some classics, a little culture. When I was told that some books had arrived, I thought, I hope there's something by Goethe, and Perucca's physics: and sure enough, there they were. It was also a great idea sending me some books on modern biology, a subject that I don't know at all and that I've wanted to read something about for a long time. In fact, yesterday I immediately started "The Problem of Life" by Enriques, which seems very well done. The way the methods from the various sciences differ and yet always have starting points in common. What interests me more and more is to find reasons deriving from their physical and psychological makeup to explain why people have focused their attention on certain facts rather than others and considered some to be essential and others secondary. It's not so much "natural law" that interests me, but rather how people have come to formulate the regularity of nature precisely in the form of this law rather than some other. And I believe the meaning of this research is more than just philosophical; it is also and mainly scientific because this "genetic" knowledge of natural law allows deeper penetration of its meaning and limitations, so that more appropriate use can be made of it. "Natural law" is not a reality, it is a tool. (Do you like this formulation?)

Since about a week ago I have been allowed a notebook and a pencil for a few hours each day, and I'm writing a physics-mathematics essay in which I think I've worked out some problems that I had been struggling with for some time. Yesterday evening I also started reading Don Quixote and I'll write more to you about it later.

Now, my dearest, I would like to offer you a little sermon; because it seems to me that you are letting yourself fall into a state of apathy and drowsiness that I don't like at all. You know that for the two of us boredom is not an option. And I think you need to busy yourself with something and lead a more active life. Why not think about your thesis? Or if not that, read, or write, or do sports, or anything really: but keep busy. You know that sometimes you have to tie yourself perhaps a bit artificially to a job or study something that doesn't satisfy you a hundred percent. (Like I did for years with my work on Leibniz). But if you don't do this, the moment for something that really does capture your interest will never arrive. You seem always to be waiting for inspiration, for the occupation that will give you unreserved joy. But this will never arrive if you don't prepare for it yourself with a training program that tests you a bit.

As you can see, the books you sent have turned me back into the old grouch.

Your Eugenio

Varese, 28 Nov 1938

My dearest,

    I've started the Simmel book and so far, I'm a bit disappointed. Always the same stories of the spirit as a continuous surpassing of oneself, a setting and overcoming of limits, etc. Variations on a theme that has by now been worked to death. It's strange how hard it is to find an observation, even a tiny one, that's fresh and honest, and that opens up a new point of view to you! I think the problem is in the approach: that philosophers are basically not very interested in "understanding" but are overly concerned with "explaining." And often these two things are contradictory. Explaining in fact means finding such and such a theory or system or organization of reality in which everything has its place and in which there is a place for everything. Understanding means facing things, you might say, in a state of passivity, ready to grasp them in the way that presents itself as most appropriate. This is why I like Goethe. "Systems" for him were not really serious things. In fact, he must have changed them many times in his life. A "system" for him was nothing but an amusing game. The important thing, the serious thing was "understanding," in any way and with whatever method. I would like to read Nietzsche.

    As you see, I am always circling around the same ideas. But I don't believe they are useless to me or to my scientific research.

    Keep sending me your observations on people in the family, which amuse me no end. You show me a complete picture of attitudes that I had always only been half aware of, because these are people I have known from birth, and I have no detachment from. But these scenes you set out are so true!

Getting back to the discussions on philosophy in our last letters, I can tell you that probably the main thing that took me away from systematic and professional philosophy was having married you. Basically, I was always extremely embarrassed in front of you over my interminable Leibniz. In order to do this sort of work, you have to live a little bit separate from the world in a clique of people who, following university convention, give great importance to these things so as to create the illusion for themselves that they are profound etc. There are people who live their whole lives behind fences of this kind: literati, professors, nearly all of them. But then you happen to find yourself with a person from the real world, and you see in their eyes the question: "Well, but what good is it?" And you realize that the answer that you cooked up long ago for this question, which made such a good impression at home, or at school, or in the university environment, doesn't work with the people "in the world" whose esteem you crave — it just sounds false. This is basically what happened with you. I realized that the whole circle of issues that my Leibniz revolved around was valid in that artificial and professional environment but sounded empty in the world outside. By this I don't mean to deny the value of scientific professionalism. But some of it is just tail chasing.

The example you give is really good, about "not being able to live with two gauches." In these times I too always think about mystical conceptions and philosophical systems, as if a child who wants the moon were given a paper-mâché moon by his over-indulgent parents, and he goes around boasting and saying: "I have the moon." And to anyone who notes that there are good reasons to believe that this is not in fact the moon, he replies: "But I can't live without the moon, so this is the moon." This "not being able to live without" is exactly the point where the arbitrariness of these conceptions shows up.

(...)

Your Eugenio

Trieste, 20 Dec 1938

Ursula my dearest,

I also know so well and have suffered so much from that condition of being at the mercy of your own thoughts, futile and banal, which you are ashamed of for their mediocrity — of sitting for hours at a desk in front of something that perhaps is good and that interests you, but that you can't seem to focus your mind on. And everybody thinks you are studying and working hard, and perhaps even admires you for it; and you ... out of the five hours at the desk, you've spent four and a half of them daydreaming about the color of a dress, or singing a little tune to yourself to the rhythm of some noise outside, or imagining in detail a scene where you invent such and such a person and tell him this and that, and he answers such and such, etc. Not to go on about myself, but just to give you the feeling of this "common ailment" — of how very many of these pointless and mediocre daydreams there are in eight years of work on the philosophy of Leibniz. You say to me: okay, but how can you escape from them, where do you get the willpower? I don't know much either, but I want to say two things:

1. Willpower is one of those words that don't mean anything, or at least not much. The doctor tells the patient, "Exercise your will." And the patient answers, "But my illness is precisely that, I don't know how to exercise my will." The point is to find the psychological mechanism that drives you to want something, that chains you to the desk so that out of the five hours of which four and a half are daydreams, at least half an hour is work. I know of two of these mechanisms and both are artificial. One is

social convention. The whole world expects a graduate in philosophy to study, write, etc. The official world of science prepares an environment for him so that what he does, even though devoid of any intrinsic motive, will be valued. But if he can't show that he has spent those five hours at his desk, whatever it was he was doing, no one will take notice of him. No one, on the other hand, expects a woman to spend five hours at a desk. For her public opinion is a deterrent rather than an incentive. Live in an environment where it's normal for a woman to pursue intellectually productive activity, and the task will be much easier for you. Outside commitments are also useful for this (exams, obligations to present a paper, etc.).

2. The second "mechanism" I know is axiomatic, perhaps even aggressive, self-confidence. That confidence that leads you to latch onto any excuse to believe that what you're doing is important. In the end, those university and literary circles I spoke badly about in one of my recent letters at least have the one benefit of being institutes created to keep you chained for those famous five hours to your desk.

O sheet of paper, why can't you be longer?

Your Eugenio

Naples, 4 Jan 1939

My Ursula,

My study plan for the next months is to continue studying physics from the books of De Broglio etc., to complete my study of mathematics to the extent that I need it to understand physics; and in the meantime, to pursue and complete my work on relativity. On this subject, I must say I would have thought there was a way of expressing imaginary and complex numbers in geometric form, for example in analytic geometry. I think such a method could help me understand certain formulas that concern relativity. There is no mention of this in the analytic geometry books, but I know there is a method like this, created by Standt (who lived in the last century) and in any case I would like to know his method. I wonder if you might be able to get me some information on this, either by consulting a large general treatise on analytic geometry or asking someone who knows the subject. I don't know if I've explained it well enough. Treatises on common analytic geometry teach that algebraic magnitudes are to be expressed geometrically, in the form of equations. Now these geometric figures generally express the real solutions to these equations. For imaginary and complex solutions (the elementary treatises say), there are no geometric expressions. Now I have read that there are methods (the work of Standt and perhaps others) for expanding the field of analytic geometry so that these imaginary and complex solutions can also be expressed geometrically. And I would be interested to know these methods. The second volume of Bersolari doesn't have them as I had hoped. Who knows if my cultural guide might also become my scientific secretary and set about skimming through library books, the way she did in Berlin for my Leibniz?

  Your husband,

Eugenio

Ventotene, 1 June 1939

My Urselchen,

If you knew what pleasure and consolation I get from what you write, that the only philosopher you understand is Kant, because I think I also wrote the same thing to you a few days ago. And I also feel shock and anger against Fichte and Schelling and Hegel, who really did ruin the achievement of his thinking, which they cut down to nothing. What is infuriating is the thought that basically these are people who are sick with the philosophical disease, this need to close the circles and this fear of being caught in the open, etc. And instead of recognizing that they are ill and trying to get better, or creating little personal shelters where they can live peacefully, suffer less and not be so afraid, they puff their little shelters up, wave them to the four winds and use them to make careers and become celebrities. What you write about the 30 dice and about the noumenon as a tender spot that they stupidly rage against is perfect. The noumenon is the final tribute Kant pays to the philosophical need to close circles. And they jump all over it: "no, that's not how you close the circle, you do it in a different way." I don't know if I ever told you this fable that comes to mind: A father leaves his children in the house, saying "Here you'll find everything you need, but you'll be in real trouble if you try to go outside. You'll be naked and helpless in the street, with nobody to come to your aid." The children split up. There's one who uses the house, but who every so often looks wistfully out the window overlooking the forbidden street (positivist scientists like Spencer, Comte, Poincaré, and regret the "unknowable"). Another (the mystic) breaks the lock and runs out into the street where, without seeing or understanding anything, he claims to have found the solution to all the problems that existed in the house, presenting the street as a bigger and more beautiful house. Another (the modern scientist) tries to fit wheels onto the house and modify it so that it is possible to move along the streets without ever leaving the house. And what do you think the last one does? He bars the doors, closes the shutters, and declares: the street doesn't exist: the whole world begins and ends inside the house. And this last one — the stupidest of all, the one with the least imagination, the sickest — this is the idealist philosopher, like Hegel and Fichte. Leibniz and Descartes, as a type, are a bit different. They really did have something to say both in the field of science (one invented analytical geometry, the other infinitesimal calculus) and in scientific methodology. Only they preferred, for reasons of convenience, to express these things in the language then in use, a theological-systematic language. Therefore, to understand them it is necessary to "translate" from that systematic language to ours. Once this is done, the theses and demonstrations that appear to be senseless games take on an important meaning, one that is in no way systematic. The introduction to my book is a simple biography and won't help you understand Leibniz; what you need is the first part (the anthology) of the book itself, but it's a little long. Maybe in one of my next letters, if you like, I can write you a brief summary of his philosophy. Some ideas to make you shine at the exam, for the moment I'm not sure. At this point I believe in it so little that I just can't seem to focus my mind on it. But send me a list of subjects you'd like me to ramble on about, and I will do so at once.

For Leibniz and Descartes, perhaps what you need,

more than my book, is that communication on the Eternal Ideas in Descartes and Leibniz that, if I'm not mistaken, you typed a copy of for me. It's an attempt at that "translation" that I was telling you about. But the one who really took Descartes at his word and tried to pursue the ultimate consequences of his thought and close the circle, with a level of diligence and commitment that I don't know whether to call ingenuous, ridiculous, or monstrous, is Spinoza. And with this I proclaim: a) that it's almost nine, the hour when they now sound the retreat; b) that the chocolates, alas, are gone; c) that I'm in a good mood thanks to your letter.

Eugenio

Ventotene, 5 June 1939

Pini my dearest,

Just now you must be on your way to Venice, and I can't wait to hear that you have arrived. Yesterday I had nothing from you. I'm hoping for tomorrow, so please send me a wire as soon as you've done the exam. I would like to write you something helpful for the exam, but I don't know what, because I'm also so far removed from that way of thinking right now. About Fichte, Schelling and Hegel, it seems to me the most important thing is the concept of the dialectic, which represents a real discovery and a liberation from preconceived frameworks. It means, basically, that what we consider to be "reality," to be an "object," is not that in and of itself, but only because we consider it to be, only because we stand before it as before something external to us, acting on us. The concept of the dialectic basically means that the ideas of subject and object, of "me" and "outside of me," are not absolute, but are only relational tools we need to get our bearings. In this sense, the concept of the dialectic has carried forward the inversion of values that began with Kant, saying that all categories — space, time, substance, causality, etc. are not reality in themselves, but our ways of seeing things. The harm Hegel did was to make these discoveries into a myth and, instead of interpreting them as a useful tool for the development of science and knowledge, to devise a sort of world history for which this dialectic would be the mainspring. This type of philosophy is a typical example of the process by which an "instrumental" idea becomes "substantial." Such "substantializing" characterizes all western philosophy, starting with Plato.

About Descartes, to understand him you have to remember this — that he was infatuated with the geometric method of Galileo's that had worked such wonders in physics; and that he realized that in order to introduce this method in the schools, replacing scholastic-Thomistic physics, you would have to be able to use the method to prove all the axioms of metaphysics and the dogmas of religion, beginning with the existence of God and the immortality of the soul. So to do this he brings in a geometric metaphysics, based on math-style syllogistic reasoning and drawing on the vast field of scholasticism itself. (Ontological proof of the existence of God, etc.).

Leibniz: The one thing that impresses him most of all is the causal connection of all things with each other. From any occurrence, through a chain of cause-and-effect links, you can go back to any other occurrence. This means that from anything that happens you can go back into the past and come back into the future, so you can start from any occurrence and describe the world. The world, described taking any fact as a starting point, is the monad. Therefore, there are infinite monads, all different (because each has a different starting point) but all representing the same world. (This is the pre-established harmony among the monads).

Remember that your professor leans toward positivism. Therefore, you will please him if you tell him this original idea of mine: That the idealist proof that nothing exists beyond the spirit has the same logical structure as the ontological proof of the existence of God. In both cases a deduction about reality is drawn from a logical contradiction. Both are based on the tacit presumption that logic is real.

I have to run and set up. A big hug.

Your Eugenio

INDEX OF NAMES

Adam 160, 259, 271
Adam-Tannery, B. 245
Alexander the Great 150
Angela da Foligno 278
Anselm of Aosta 124
Ariste 219
Aristotle 114, 120, 145, 154, 165, 170, 178-9, 194-5
Arnauld, A. 84, 97, 109, 185, 189, 339-41
Asseburg, Lady 255
Augustin, st. 160, 335, 340-1
Augustus 120
Azzo II, A. d'Este 88

Balzac, J-L. G. de 295
Barié, G. E. 66-71, 73-4, 113
Baruzi, J. 142, 251-3, 255, 258, 260, 263, 267, 269-70, 272-6, 280, 286, 317, 336-7, 349
Baumgarten, A.G. 292, 294
Bayle, P. 68, 98-9, 155, 184-5, 191, 193, 204, 207, 231-2, 243, 253, 305, 329, 333
Bobbio, N. 6, 8, 11, 14, 20
Bodemann, E. 110, 255, 257, 262, 266-7, 301
Böhme, J. 252

Bossuet, J.B. 90, 261-2, 264-6, 274, 316, 343
Bouhours, D. 295
Bourguet, L. 122
Bourignon, A. de 266
Boutroux, E. 40
Boyneburg, baron von 81, 83-5, 90
Bruno, G. 183, 244, 291
Brunswick- Lunebùrg, Henry the Lion 88
Brunswick-Lunebùrg, Ernest Augustus 86, 90, 100, 287
Brunswick-Lunebùrg, Georg Ludvig 86
Brunswick-Lunebùrg, John Frederik 85
Brunswick-Lunebùrg, Sophie 87, 98, 100-1
Brunswick-Lunebùrg, Sophie Charlotte 86-7, 92, 98-100
Burnett, T. 163, 180, 223, 259, 284, 298-9, 329

Caesar 146, 152-3
Carlotti, G. 113
Casimir, G. 81
Cassirer E.
Catherine of Siena, St. 256

Catherine of Genoa, St. 252
Caton, M.P. 332
Cavalieri, B. 169
Cecchi, E. 113
Cerchiai, G. 5-6, 14, 19
Christ, J. 28-9, 83, 120, 216, 257, 259, 262, 265, 269, 272, 314
Ciceron 299
Clarke, S. 98, 139, 284, 326, 331-2
Comenius, I.A. (J.A. Komensky) 117, 291
Comte, A. 362
Conring, H. 83
Copernicus, N. 19, 22, 114
Coste, P. 157, 305, 316, 318, 327, 329, 334
Couturat, L. 67, 98, 108-9, 112-3, 283, 317

Darius 150
Davillé, L. 113
Del Boca, S. 323
Democritus 162, 188, 192
De Ruggiero, G. 110
Des Bosses, B. 325
Descartes, R. 8, 10-1, 16, 39, 41, 45, 68, 80, 84, 114, 123-5, 127, 130, 136, 164, 167, 173, 176, 178, 182, 194, 237-47, 249, 268, 290, 302, 316, 318, 326, 333, 363-4, 366
De Volder, B. 98, 224
Diderot, D. 291
Dilmann, F. 111
Dilthey, W. 310
Dryden, J. 281
Dutens, L. 67, 107, 259, 261, 267, 283, 285, 289

Eckhardt, J. 101
Epicurus 162, 184, 190, 333
Erdmann, G.E. 100, 107, 111
Eve 259

Fabri, H. 168
Fabricius 335
Fénelon, F. 261-3, 265-6, 316, 322
Feuerbach, L. 111
Fischer, K. 111
Foucher de Careil, L.A. 283

Galilei, G. 244
Gassendi, P. 162, 186
Gerhardt, C.I. 59, 67-8, 98, 106-7, 113, 272, 283
Gilson, E. 240
Giorgiantonio, M. 110
Goethe, J.W. von 5, 292, 353, 355
Gouhier, H. 242

Grimaldi, F.M. 93
Grotefend, C.L. 109
Grotius, H. 237, 243, 246-7, 275
Guericke, O. von 83
Gueroult, M. 113, 288
Guhrauer, G.E. 271
Guyon, Madame de 261-2, 266

Halley, E. 284
Hannequin, A. 112
Hansch, M.G. 267
Hartsoeker, N. 98, 130
Henfling, C. 301
Hercules 196
Hesse, E. langrave of 91, 109, 242, 298, 339-41, 343, 345
Hobbes, T. 83, 168, 306, 325, 333
Holbein, H. 284
Huygens, C. 84-5, 164

Jagordinski, I. 67, 109
Jansen, C. 339
Jaquelot, I. 193
Judas 157, 159

Kant, I. 40, 45, 47, 50, 56, 64-5, 78, 244, 246, 262, 362, 365,
Kabitz, W. 109, 112

Kepler, J. 19, 178
Klopp, O. 255-7, 259-60, 262, 266, 272-4, 288, 314, 318, 343-4
Kochanski, A. 257
Kortholt, C. 301

Laporte, J. 239, 241
Lestienne, H. 113, 136
Locke, J. 45, 69, 98-9, 104, 194-5, 253, 304, 310
Löffler, F.S. 261
Lucan 295
Ludolf, G. 92
Louis xiv 81-3, 87, 93

Magliabechi, A. 88
Mahnke, D. 111
Malebranche, N. 39, 41, 68, 84, 104, 228
Malpighi, M. 88
Masham, Lady 98, 219, 223, 228
Molanus, G.W. 90-1, 255
Molina, L. de 265, 340,
Molinos, M. de 262-5, 267-8
Mollat, G. 67, 108, 276-7, 279-80, 283, 285-7, 299, 301, 307-9, 317,20, 323, 326, 347
Morell, A. 270
Muratori, L.A. 89

Nicaise, C. 267, 301, 317-8
Newton, I. 19, 22, 68, 85, 95,
    114, 169, 284, 290
Nizolio, M. 82
Norris, J. 316
Nourisson, J.F. 111

Oldenberg, H. 83, 167
Olgiati, G. 113
Opiz, G.E. 284

Pellisson-Fountanier, P.
    346-7
Philarète 219
Philippi 128, 131
Paul, st. 195, 267, 335, 337
Pascal, B. 273-4
Peter the Great 82, 86, 93,
    101
Plato 22-3, 41, 184, 194-5,
    219, 251, 335, 365
Poincaré, H. 362
Poiret, P. 252
Porus 150
Quaranta, M. 5

Raphael 285
Raspe, R.E. 99
Reihe, E. 107
Ritter, P. 110, 124, 144
Rommel, C. 67, 109, 255-7,
    259, 262, 266-7, 298,
    330, 339-41, 343

Russell, B. 111
Ruysbroeck, J. van 266-7

Sainte-Beuve, C.A. de 339
Savoia, E. 30
Scherzer, P. 80
Schmalenbach, M. 112
Schmidt, J.A. 338-9
Schopenhauer, A. 262
Seregni G. 110
Shaftesbury, A.A.C. 257,
    291, 297-8, 300, 304,
    316
Sherlock, W. 316
Silesio, A. 266-7
Spee von Langenfeld, F.
    284, 314, 318, 344
Spencer, H. 362
Spinoza, B. 18, 41, 68, 74,
    78, 83-4, 86, 108, 126,
    136, 182, 266, 273, 278,
    290, 302, 304-6, 316,
    324-5, 330, 364
Stein, L. 109, 112, 258-9,
    340

Tacitus 295
Tasso, T. 295
Tauler, J. 267
Teresa, St. 263
Tertulliano 347
Thomas Aquinas, st. 237-8,
    243, 300, 339, 341

Thomasius, J. 83, 116, 167, 170, 208
Trendelenburg, A. 109

Vacca, G. 113
Van Helmont, F.M. 258-260
Vellejus, P. 332
Vergil 348
Voiture, V. 295

Wedderkopf, M. 246
Weigel, V. 80, 252, 266-7
Wolff, C. 107, 292